SPAIN

TOP SIGHTS, AUTHENTIC EXPERIENCES

Anth   rwood,
Cathe   Noble,

Contents

Bay of Biscay

FRANCE

BASQUE COUNTRY
p205

bao

Irún
San Sebastián

itoria-
Gasteiz

Pamplona

Val
d'Aran

ANDORRA
LA VELLA

ANDORRA

THE PYRENEES p259

Parc Nacional
d'Aigüestortes i
Estany de Sant Maurici

COSTA BRAVA
p109

Logroño

LA RIOJA WINE
REGION p249

Girona

gos

Huesca

Soria

Zaragoza

Lleida

Riu Segre

BARCELONA p69

uero

Río Ebro

Tarragona

Guadalajara

Golfo de
Valencia

SPAIN

Teruel

Cuenca

Castellón de la Plana
(Castelló de la Plana)

Valencia

Palma de
Mallorca

Albacete

MEDITERRANEAN
SEA

arque Natural
rras de Cazorla,
gura y las Villas

Murcia

Torrevieja

ADA p123

acional
Nevada

Almería

ALGERIA

N
0
0
200 km
100 miles

Welcome to Spain

Passionate, sophisticated and devoted to living the good life, Spain is both a stereotype come to life and a country more diverse than you ever imagined.

Spain is a natural wonder. The Pyrenees and Picos de Europa are as beautiful as any mountain range on the continent, while the snow-capped Sierra Nevada rises from the sun-baked plains of Andalucía; these are hiking destinations of the highest order. Elsewhere, the wildly beautiful cliffs of Spain's Atlantic northwest offset the Mediterranean's charming coves.

Spain's man-made environment is just as stunning. Poignantly windswept Roman ruins, cathedrals of rare power and incomparable jewels of Islamic architecture speak of a country where the great civilisations of history have all left their indelible mark. And what other country could produce such rebellious and relentlessly creative spirits as Salvador Dalí, Pablo Picasso and Antoni Gaudí?

But this is a country that lives very much in the present and really knows how to live. Perhaps you'll sense it along a crowded street after midnight when all the world has come out to play. Or maybe the moment will come when a flamenco performer touches something deep in your soul.

Food and wine are national obsessions in Spain. The touchstones of Spanish cooking are deceptively simple: variety, generations-old traditional recipes and a willingness to experiment and see what comes out of the kitchen laboratory.

...this is a country that lives very much in the present and really knows how to live

Plaza de España (p177), Seville
LEOKS/SHUTTERSTOCK©

Cabo Ortegal

Costa da Morte

A Coruña

Santiago de Compostela

NORTHWEST COAST p233

Lugo

Ourense

Avilés **Gijón**

Oviedo

Parque Nacional de los Picos de Europa

Parque Natural Saja-Besaya

Santander

Bil

V

León

Bur

Palencia

Valladolid

Río D

Zamora

SALAMANCA p193

Segovia

Ávila

MADRID p35 ✪

Parque Natural do Douro Internacional

Río Douro

Porto

Parque Natural da Serra da Estrela

Río Tajo

Toledo

Cáceres

PORTUGAL

✪ **LISBON**

Badajoz

Mérida

Ciudad Real

Parque Natural Sierra de Aracena y Picos de Aroche

Parque Natural Sierra Norte de Sevilla

CÓRDOBA p183

Parque Natural Sierra de Andújar

Si Se

Jaén

SEVILLE p163

Río Genil

Golfo de Cádiz

Parque Nacional de Doñana

Arcos de la Frontera

GRA

Parque Sierra

ANDALUCÍAN HILL TOWNS p139

Málaga

Costa del Sol

ATLANTIC OCEAN

Cádiz

Parque Natural Los Alcornocales

Marbella

Gibraltar

Strait of Gibraltar

COVID-19

We have rechecked every business in this book before publication to ensure that it is still open after 2020's COVID-19 outbreak. However, the economic and social impacts of COVID-19 will continue to be felt long after the outbreak has been contained, and many businesses, services and events referenced in this guide may experience ongoing restrictions. Some businesses may be temporarily closed, have changed their opening hours and services, or require bookings; some, unfortunately, could have closed permanently. We suggest you check with venues before visiting for the latest information.

Spain's Top 12

Madrid

Fine arts and irresistible street life

Madrid (p35) is one of the fine-arts capitals of the world, with an extraordinary collection of galleries. The showpiece is the Museo del Prado, but nearby are the Centro de Arte Reina Sofía and the Museo Thyssen-Bornemisza. Few European cities can match the intensity and street clamour of Madrid's nightlife. As Ernest Hemingway said, 'Nobody goes to bed in Madrid until they have killed the night'. Above: Museo del Prado (p38); Right: Why Not? bar (p64)

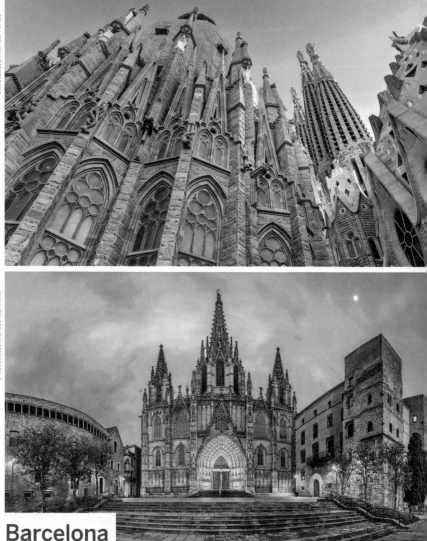

Barcelona

One of Europe's coolest cities

Home to cutting-edge architecture, world-class dining and pulsating nightlife, Barcelona (p69) has long been one of Europe's most alluring destinations. Wander the cobblestone lanes of the Gothic quarter, bask on Mediterranean beaches or marvel at Gaudí masterpieces. By night, Barcelona is a whirl of vintage cocktail bars, gilded music halls, innovative eateries and clubs.

Top: La Sagrada Família (p72); Bottom: La Catedral (p87)

PAWEL KAZMIERCZAK/SHUTTERSTOCK ©

Costa Brava

Beautiful beaches with echoes of Salvador Dalí

Easily accessible from the rest of Europe, and filled with villages and beaches of the kind that spawned northern Europe's obsession with the Spanish coast, the Costa Brava (p109) in Catalonia is one of our favourite corners of the Mediterranean. The spirit of Salvador Dalí lends so much personality and eccentricity to the Costa Brava experience, from his one-time home in Port Lligat near Cadaqués to sites in Figueres and Castell de Púbol. Cadaqués (p115)

Granada

The exotic jewel in Andalucía's crown

Granada's Alhambra is close to architectural perfection and is perhaps the most refined example of Islamic art anywhere in the world. Magnificent from afar and exquisite in its detail up close, the Alhambra is a singular treasure that's worth crossing the country to see. But Granada (p123) promises so much more, from the Middle Eastern touches of the whitewashed Albayzín to its gilded monuments to Christian rule, as well as a wonderfully dynamic and accessible tapas scene. Alhambra (p126)

Andalucian Hill Towns

The whitewashed essence of Spain's rural south

The splendid cities of Andalucía (p139) find their luminous counterpoint in the *pueblos blancos* (white towns) of Spain's south. In Andalucía's east, in the Sierra Nevada, the villages of Las Alpujarras rank among the region's finest, resembling charming outposts of North Africa, oasis-like and set amid woodlands and the deep ravines for which the region is renowned. Other towns, such as Arcos de la Frontera and Vejer de la Frontera, rank among Andalucía's most engaging hamlets. Ronda (p146)

Seville

Spain's Andalucian city par excellence

Nowhere is as quintessentially Spanish as Seville (p163), a city of capricious moods and soulful secrets, which has played a pivotal role in the evolution of so many peculiarly Spanish obsessions, including flamenco, bullfighting, baroque art and Mudéjar architecture. Blessed with year-round sunshine and fuelled culturally by a never-ending schedule of ebullient festivals, everything seems more amorous here. Head south and join in. Seville cathedral (p166)

PACK SHOT/SHUTTERSTOCK ©

Córdoba

Architectural treasures and vibrant, life-filled streets

The sublime Mezquita at the heart of Córdoba (p183) is both a high point of Moorish architecture in Europe and a symbol of Andalucía's fascinating history. Its features include perfectly proportioned horseshoe arches, an intricate *mihrab* and a veritable forest of 856 columns. Elsewhere, there's a storied Jewish quarter, fabulous food and 10th-century landmarks from when the city was the height of sophistication and power. Mezquita (p186)

Salamanca

Stunning architecture, storied history and constant clamour

Luminous when floodlit, the elegant central square of Salamanca (p193), the Plaza Mayor, is possibly the most attractive in all of Spain. It's just one of many highlights in a city whose architectural splendour has few peers in the country. Salamanca is home to one of Europe's oldest and most prestigious universities, so student revelry lights up the nights. It's this combination of grandeur and energy that makes so many people call Salamanca their favourite city in Spain. Right: Catedral Nueva (p196)

LUMICREATIVESTUDIO/GETTY IMAGES©

Basque Country

Fine food and cultural excellence

The Basque Country (p205) has its own unique flavour. Chefs here have turned bar snacks into an art form. Sometimes called 'high cuisine in miniature', *pintxos* (Basque tapas) are piles of flavour and the choice lined up along the counter in any San Sebastián bar will leave first-time visitors gasping: this is Spain's most memorable eating experience. But this is also a relentlessly dynamic cultural region, with visitors drawn to Bilbao's Museo Guggenheim, riverside promenades and quality museums. Far left: Museo Guggenheim Bilbao (p208); Left: *Pintxos*

Northwest Coast

Dramatic coastal scenery and the Camino

Spain's northern shore (p233) is an endless succession of stunning beaches, postcard-pretty villages and wild Atlantic cliffs. The hinterland is a rugged spine of glorious mountains (the Picos de Europa) and one of the world's most popular sacred walks, the Camino de Santiago into Santiago de Compostela. Top: Palacio de Sobrellano (p243); Bottom left: Andara Massif, Picos de Europa (p236); Right: Town along the Camino de Santiago (p238)

JUSTIN FOLKES/LONELY PLANET©

La Rioja Wine Region

Spain's premier wine region bar none

La Rioja (p249) is the sort of place where you could spend weeks meandering along quiet roads in search of the finest drop. Bodegas offering wine tastings and picturesque villages that shelter excellent wine museums are the region's mainstay. The Frank Gehry–designed Hotel Marqués de Riscal, close to Elciego, has been likened to Bilbao's Guggenheim in architectural scale and ambition.

Pyrenees

Spectacular mountains and Spain's best hiking

Spain is a walker's destination of exceptional variety, but the Pyrenees (p259) in Navarra, Aragón and Catalonia offer the finest hiking country. Aragón's Parque Nacional de Ordesa y Monte Perdido is one of the Pyrenees' highlights, while its glories are mirrored at Parc Nacional d'Aigüestortes i Estany de Sant Maurici in Catalonia. It's tough but rewarding terrain, a world of great rock walls and glacial cirques, animated by elusive but soulful Pyrenean wildlife.

Plan Your Trip
Need to Know

When to Go

Santiago de Compostela
GO May–Sep

Barcelona
GO year-round

Madrid
GO Mar–May, Sep & Oct

Valencia
GO year-round

Seville
GO Oct–Apr

Dry climate
Warm to hot summers, cold winters
Mild to hot summers, cold winters
Cold climate

High Season (Jun–Aug, public holidays)

- Accommodation books out and prices increase by up to 50%.

- Low season in parts of inland Spain.

- Expect warm, dry and sunny weather; more humid in coastal areas.

Shoulder (Mar–May, Sep & Oct)

- Mild weather and fewer crowds; good for travel.

- Local festivals can send prices soaring.

Low Season (Nov–Feb)

- Cold in central Spain. Mild temperatures in Andalucía and the Mediterranean coast.

- High season in ski resorts.

- Beach-area hotels may be closed but elsewhere prices plummet.

Currency
Euro (€)

Language
Spanish (Castilian). Also Catalan, Basque and Galician.

Visas
Generally not required for stays up to 90 days per 180 days; some nationalities need a Schengen visa.

Money
ATMs widely available. Visa and Mastercard are widely accepted; American Express is less common.

Mobile Phones
Local SIM cards widely available and can be used in European and Australian mobile phones.

Time
GMT/UTC plus one hour during winter and GMT/UTC plus two hours during daylight saving.

Daily Costs

Budget: Less than €80

- Dorm bed: €20–30

- Double room in *hostal* (budget hotel): €50–65 (€60–75 in Madrid, Barcelona and Balearics)

- Self-catering and lunch *menú del día* (set menu): €20–30

Midrange: €80–175

- Double room in midrange hotel: €65–140 (€75–200 in Madrid, Barcelona and Balearics)

- Lunch and/or dinner in local restaurant: €20–40

- Car rental: per day from €25

Top end: More than €175

- Double room in top-end hotel: €140 and up (over €200 in Madrid, Barcelona and Balearics)

- Fine dining for lunch and dinner: €150–250

- Admission to Museo del Prado: €15

Useful Websites

All You Can Read (www.allyoucanread.com/spanish-newspapers/) Links to Spain's top 30 news sites.
Lonely Planet (www.lonelyplanet.com/spain) Destination information, hotel bookings, traveller forums and more.
Paradores (www.parador.es) Spain's finest hotel experiences.
Renfe (Red Nacional de los Ferrocarriles Españoles; www.renfe.com) Spain's rail network.
Turespaña (www.spain.info) Spanish tourist office's site.

Opening Hours

Standard opening hours are for high season only and tend to shorten outside that time.

Banks 8.30am to 2pm Monday to Friday
Central post offices 8.30am to 9.30pm Monday to Friday, 8.30am to 2pm Saturday
Nightclubs Midnight or 1am to 5am or 6am Friday and Saturday
Restaurants Lunch 1pm to 4pm; dinner 8.30pm to 11pm or midnight
Shops 10am to 2pm and 4.30pm to 7.30pm or 5pm to 8pm Monday to Friday or Saturday

See p304 for more on opening hours.

Arriving in Spain

Adolfo Suárez Madrid-Barajas Airport (Madrid) The Metro (€4.50, 30 minutes to the centre) runs from 6.05am to 1.30am; the Exprés Aeropuerto bus (€5; 30 to 40 minutes) runs 24 hours between the airport and Puerta de Atocha train station/Plaza de Cibeles. Taxis cost €30.
El Prat Airport (Barcelona) Buses cost €5.90 and run every five to 10 minutes from 5.35am to 1.05am; it's 30 to 40 minutes to the centre. Trains (€4.60, 25 to 30 minutes to the centre) run half-hourly from 5.42am to 11.38pm. Taxis cost €25 to €35.

Getting Around

Spain's public transport system is one of the best in Europe, with a fast and super-modern train system, an extensive domestic air network, an impressive and well-maintained road network, and buses that connect villages in the country's remotest corners.

Train Extremely efficient rail network, from slow intercity regional trains to some of the fastest trains on the planet. More routes are added to the network every year.

Car Vast network of motorways radiating out from Madrid to all corners of the country, shadowed by smaller but often more picturesque minor roads.

Bus The workhorses of the Spanish roads, from slick express services to stop-everywhere village-to-village buses.

For more on **getting around**, see p310. ➡

Plan Your Trip
Hotspots for...

Spanish Food

Spain's food is among the most varied and innovative on earth, and sampling it will likely be one of your trip's most memorable experiences.

JONATHAN STOKES/LONELY PLANET©

San Sebastián (p223)
One of Europe's gastronomic stars, from Michelin-starred restaurants to Spain's best tapas scene.

Casco Viejo
Enjoy a *pintxo* (tapas) in the *casco viejo*. (p210)

Barcelona (p69)
Catalan cooking is a bastion of tradition and a laboratory for weird-and-wonderful creations.

Tickets
Tapas bar overseen by master chef Ferran Adrià. (p102)

Madrid (p35)
Madrid brings Spain's regional cuisines together, from fabulous tapas to the world's oldest restaurant.

Mercado de San Miguel
Sample fine foods and Spanish-style eating. (p42)

Moorish Architecture

Almost seven centuries of Islamic rule on Iberian soil left behind a legacy of architectural magnificence. Andalucía's cities, in particular, house numerous glittering jewels.

NETRUN78/SHUTTERSTOCK©

Granada (p123)
No city in Spain feels more like the Middle East, from the Albayzín to Europe's most beautiful palace.

Alhambra
Captures the sophistication of Al-Andalus. (p126)

Córdoba (p183)
Once the Moorish heartland, it remains whitewashed and awash in monuments from the age.

Mezquita
The forest of columns is simply sublime. (p186)

Seville (p163)
Seville's Islamic monuments are worthy complements to the stars of Granada and Córdoba.

Alcázar
Exquisite Moorish detail dominates the Alcázar. (p170)

Hiking

Fabulous hiking trails criss-cross Spain's mountain regions; the possibilities are endless, from the Pyrenees and Picos de Europa to the Sierra Nevada.

GLENN NEVIS/SHUTTERSTOCK©

Las Alpujarras (p142)
Hike from one charming whitewashed village to the next in the Sierra Nevada.

Barranco de Poqueira
Explore its most appealing corner on foot. (p142)

Parc Nacional d'Aigüestortes i Estany de Sant Maurici (p262)
Peaks, lakes and Romanesque churches.

Estany Llong
Natural amphitheatre surrounded by mountains. (p263)

Parque Nacional de Ordesa y Monte Perdido (p264)
This stunning park has some of Spain's most celebrated hikes.

Circo de Soaso
A seven-hour trek takes you to the heart of the range. (p265)

Medieval Villages

Spain's pretty pueblos (villages) are something special, from stone-and-wood villages in the north to luminous white hamlets clinging to rocky crags in the Andalusian south.

MARC VENEMA/SHUTTERSTOCK©

The Aragonese Pyrenees (p269)
The Pyrenean foothills shelter numerous candidates for the title of Spain's most beautiful village.

Sos del Rey Católico
Twisting cobblestone lanes climb along a ridge. (p270)

Western Andalucía (p139)
The villages of Andalucía's west have few peers when it comes to hill towns.

Arcos de la Frontera
The postcard-perfect hill town. (p144)

Sierra de Grazalema (p151)
Set in rolling hill country, the villages surrounding Grazalema are, thankfully, little-known.

Zahara de la Sierra
Overlooked by a mountain-top castle. (p153)

Plan Your Trip
Essential Spain

LUKASZ JANYST/SHUTTERSTOCK©

Activities

Spain's landscapes provide the backdrop to some of Europe's best hiking, most famously the Camino de Santiago. The Pyrenees, too, is a stellar place to hike, while walking from one Las Alpujarras village to the next is a memorable way to explore the white villages of the south. Skiing in the Pyrenees is a much-loved Spanish pastime, but the Sierra Nevada, accessible from Granada, is also brilliant. Other highlights include surfing Spain's northwestern coast, wildlife-watching in the north and south, and snorkelling off the Costa Brava.

Shopping

Shopping in Spain will take you from one extreme to the other. Frilly flamenco dresses or bullfighting posters with your name on them seem to overflow from souvenir shops across the country. But look harder and you'll find high-quality crafts and ceramics, genuine flamenco memorabilia and the finest Spanish foods.

Spain is one of Europe's most style-conscious places and its designers are some of the most accessible and innovative you'll find. Madrid and Barcelona offer the most choice, but shopping here is almost a national sport and you're never far from a small shop selling the perfect gift.

Entertainment

While it can be tempting to think that the relentless stream of people filling Spain's streets is entertaining enough, there is far more to Spain's entertainment scene. Live flamenco is an undoubted highlight, but the breadth of Spain's live music scene is almost as appealing. Watching Real Madrid or FC Barcelona live alongside almost 100,000 passionate fans is another experience that features on many bucket lists.

Eating

Spain is one of Europe's culinary powerhouses. So much of Spain's cuisine has colonised the world, from tapas, paella, *jamón* and

JAPATINO/GETTY IMAGES©

churros to Spanish wines and olive oils. But in Spain you're at the source and can enjoy Spanish cooking in all its infinite variety. Better still, you'll experience the unique Spanish culture of eating, a passion for good food that can be as enjoyable as the food itself.

Barcelona and the Basque Country are the undoubted stars of the show, while Galicia and Andalucía are known for their love of tradition and fine seafood. Anywhere along Spain's Mediterranean coast is good for paella, while tapas is a highlight in Barcelona, Madrid, San Sebastián, Seville, Granada and Bilbao. Madrid also deserves special mention – its own cuisine may be unremarkable, but you can find here all that's wonderful about the Spanish kitchen.

Drinking & Nightlife

Spanish nightlife is the stuff of legend – Madrid, for example, has more bars per capita than any other city on earth. There are times when it seems there is a bar on every street corner, and even the smallest village will likely have at least one local wa-

★ Best Flamenco

Casa de la Memoria (p180)

Casa Patas (p64)

Centro Flamenco Fosforito (p189)

Museo del Baile Flamenco (p173)

tering hole. While these bars are places to drink, they're also so much more – they're meeting places, places to order tapas, hubs of community life and the starting point of seemingly endless Spanish nights.

Nightclubs, something of a Spanish speciality, will keep you going until dawn (and sometimes beyond), from mega-clubs to indie hangouts for people-in-the-know. Most Spanish cities have nonstop nightlife, none more so than Madrid, Barcelona and Valencia.

From left: Parque Nacional de Ordesa y Monte Perdido (p264); Flamenco dancers

Plan Your Trip
Month by Month

January

In January, ski resorts in the Pyrenees and the Sierra Nevada are in full swing. Snow in Catalonia is usually better in the second half of January. School holidays run until around 8 January.

March

With the arrival of spring, Spain shakes off its winter blues (such as they are), the weather starts to warm up ever so slightly and Spaniards start dreaming of a summer by the beach.

🎊 Festival de Jerez

One of Spain's most important flamenco festivals (p158) takes place in the genre's heartland in late February or early March.

🎊 Las Fallas de San José

The extraordinary festival of Las Fallas consists of several days of all-night dancing and drinking, first-class fireworks and processions from 15 to 19 March. Its principal stage is Valencia City, and the festivities culminate in the ritual burning of effigies in the streets.

April

Spain has a real spring in its step, with wildflowers in full bloom, Easter celebrations and school holidays. It requires some advance planning (book ahead), but it's a great time to be here.

🎊 Semana Santa (Holy Week)

Easter (the dates change each year) entails parades of *pasos* (holy figures), hooded penitents and huge crowds. It's extravagantly celebrated in Seville.

🎊 Feria de Abril (April Fair)

This week-long party, held in Seville in the second half of April, is the biggest of Andalucía's fairs. *Sevillanos* dress up in their traditional finery, ride around on horseback

Above: Feria de Abril, Seville

LAKISHA BEECHAM/SHUTTERSTOCK ©

and in elaborate horse-drawn carriages, and dance late into the night.

May

A glorious time to be in Spain, May sees the countryside carpeted with spring wildflowers and the weather can feel like summer is just around the corner.

⊙ Córdoba's Courtyards Open Up

Scores of beautiful private courtyards in Córdoba are opened to the public for the Fiesta de los Patios de Córdoba. It's a rare chance to see an otherwise-hidden side of Córdoba, strewn with flowers and freshly painted.

❄ Fiesta de San Isidro

Madrid's major fiesta celebrates the city's patron saint with parades, concerts and more. Locals dress up in traditional costumes, and some of the events, such as the bullfighting season, last for a month.

★ Best Festivals

Bienal de Flamenco, September

Feria de Abril, April

Las Fallas de San José, March

Semana Santa (Holy Week), usually March or April

La Tomatina, August

June

By June, the north is shaking off its winter chill and the Camino de Santiago's trails are becoming crowded. In the south, it's warming up as the coastal resorts ready themselves for the summer onslaught.

♚ Wine Battle

Haro, one of the premier wine towns of La Rioja, enjoys the Batalla del Vino on 29 June. Participants squirt wine all over the

Above: Haro Wine Festival

place in one of Spain's messiest play fights, pausing only to drink the good stuff.

☆ Electronica Festival

Performers and spectators come from all over the world for Sónar, Barcelona's two-day celebration of electronic music, which is said to be Europe's biggest festival of its kind. Dates vary each year.

July

Temperatures in Andalucía and much of the interior can be fiercely hot, but July is a great time to be at the beach and is one of the best months for hiking in the Pyrenees.

☆ Festival de la Guitarra de Córdoba

Córdoba's contribution to Spain's impressive calendar of musical events, this fine international guitar festival ranges from flamenco and classical to rock, blues and beyond. Headline performances take place in the city's theatres.

✤ Running of the Bulls

The Fiesta de San Fermín is the week-long non-stop festival and party in Pamplona with the daily *encierro* (running of the bulls) as its centrepiece. Animal-rights activists underline the stress – and eventual death – suffered by the bulls, and PETA (www.peta. org) organises protests.

✤ Fiestas del Apóstol Santiago

The Día de Santiago on 25 July marks the day of Spain's national saint (St James) and is spectacularly celebrated in Santiago de Compostela. With so many pilgrims around, it's the city's most festive two weeks of the year.

August

Spaniards from all over the country join other Europeans in converging on the coastal resorts of the Mediterranean. Although the weather can be unpredictable, Spain's northwestern Atlantic coast offers a more nuanced summer experience.

✤ La Tomatina

Buñol's massive tomato-throwing festival, held in late August, must be one of the messiest get-togethers in the country. Thousands of people launch about 100 tonnes of tomatoes at one another in just an hour or so!

September

This is the month when Spain returns to work after a seemingly endless summer. Numerous festivals take advantage of the fact that weather generally remains warm until late September at least.

☆ Bienal de Flamenco

There are flamenco festivals all over Spain throughout the year, but this is the most prestigious of them all. Held in Seville in even-numbered years (and Málaga every other year), it draws the biggest names in the genre.

♟ La Rioja's Grape Harvest

Logroño celebrates the feast day of St Matthew (Fiesta de San Mateo) and the year's grape harvest. There are grape-crushing ceremonies and endless opportunities to sample the fruit of the vine in liquid form.

✤ Barcelona's Big Party

Barcelona's co-patron saint, the Virgin of Mercy, is celebrated with fervour in the massive four-day Festes de la Mercè around 24 September. The city stages special exhibitions, free concerts and street performers galore.

December

The weather turns cold, but Navidad (Christmas) is on its way. There are Christmas markets, *turrón* (nougat), a long weekend at the beginning of the month and a festive period that lasts until early January.

Get Inspired

Read

Don Quijote (Miguel de Cervantes; 1605) Spain's best-known novel, about a lovably deluded knight.

Three Plays (Federico García Lorca; 1930s) Spain's greatest playwright's three great tragedies.

For Whom the Bell Tolls (Ernest Hemingway; 1941) Terse tale of the civil war, full of Spanish atmosphere.

A Late Dinner: Discovering the Food of Spain (Paul Richardson; 2007) Erudite journey through Spain's culinary culture.

After the Fall (Tobias Buck; 2019) An excellent study of *la crisis* and everything that came after.

Watch

Jamón, jamón (1992) Dark comedy that brought Penélope Cruz and Javier Bardem to prominence.

Todo sobre mi madre (All About My Mother; 1999) Pedro Almodóvar romp through sex and death.

Mar adentro (The Sea Inside; 2004) Alejandro Amenabar's study of a Galician quadriplegic.

Volver (2006) Lush Almodóvar classic and love letter to Penélope Cruz.

Vicky Cristina Barcelona (2008) Woody Allen comedy about American girls in Spain.

Ocho apellidos vascos (Spanish Affair; 2014) Comic sideways glance at Spain and the Basque Country.

Listen

Fuente y caudal (Paco de Lucía; 1973) Top album by the flamenco-guitar maestro.

Concierto de Aranjuez (Joaquín Rodrigo; 1939) This classical-guitar concerto breathes 'Spain'.

La leyenda del tiempo (Camarón de la Isla; 1979) The great flamenco voice of modern times.

Pokito a Poko (Chambao; 2005) Where flamenco meets electronica.

Indestructible (Diego El Cigala; 2016) The heir to Camarón de la Isla's throne.

El mal querer (Rosalia; 2018) Hugely successful flamenco pop, including genre-busting 'Malamente'.

Above: Illustration from *The History of Don Quixote* (1880), drawings by Gustave Dore

Plan Your Trip
Five-Day Itineraries

Madrid, Barcelona & the Costa Brava

There are few more dynamic cities on earth than Madrid and Barcelona. While you could spend a lifetime in either, throw in a day trip to the Costa Brava for good measure.

Costa Brava (p109) Visit Cadaqués to understand how Salvador Dalí made the region his own, then return to Barcelona by night.

Barcelona (p69) Modernista architecture, fabulous food and a sense that anything is possible: welcome to Barcelona.
🚗 2 hrs to Figueres

Madrid (p35) Madrid has mastered the art of living the good life with galleries and feel-good streets.
✈ 1 hr or 🚗 2½ hrs to Barcelona

Andalucía's Moorish Heartland

Andalucía's trio of vibrant, soulful cities – Seville, Córdoba and Granada – serve as a backdrop to some of the finest Islamic architecture anywhere on the planet.

Córdoba (p183)
Córdoba's medieval heart is filled with reminders of the city's sophisticated past, with the Mezquita its centrepiece.
🚆 2¾ hrs to Granada

Seville (p163)
When most people think of Andalucía at its passionate, beautiful, traditional best, they're probably thinking of Seville. 🚆 1 hr to Córdoba

Granada (p123) Filled with echoes of Al-Andalus and framed by the snowcapped mountains of the Sierra Nevada, Granada is unlike anywhere else in Spain.

FROM LEFT MARGARET STEPIEN/LONELY PLANET © VR2000/SHUTTERSTOCK©

10-Day Itinerary

The Best of Spain

Spain's two most compelling cities (Madrid and Barcelona), a duo of Andalucian beauties (Seville and Granada), and the pick of the hill towns of the south. Put them all together and this itinerary is Spain at its most memorable.

Barcelona (p69) Spend two days here and you'll soon be making plans to return. Focus on food and Gaudí. 🚆 2 hrs to Madrid

Madrid (p35) Take your pick of the art galleries, spend time soaking up the atmosphere in its plazas and go on a tapas crawl. 🚆 2½ hrs to Seville

Seville (p163) Two days is a minimum for getting the most out of this gutsy, beautiful cliché of the Andalusian south. 🚆 3 hrs to Granada

Granada (p123) A day in the Alhambra and Albayzín should leave a day for exploring the town's tapas culture and fine Christian buildings. 🚗 2 hrs to Las Alpujarras

Las Alpujarras (p142) Spend a day exploring the whitewashed villages and pretty valleys that inhabit the Sierra Nevada's southern flank. 🚗 2-3 hrs to Ronda

Ronda (p146) Ronda has gravitas, great food and marvellous views from atop its impossibly high perch.

Plan Your Trip
Two-Week Itinerary

Spain's North

This journey across the country's north takes in the Pyrenees, the Basque Country and Spain's most rugged and most beautiful stretch of coast. En route, you'll enjoy some of the best food of your trip and spend time in gorgeous medieval villages.

Cudillero (p245) Perhaps Spain's loveliest fishing village, Cudillero lies close to some of the country's finest beaches too.
🚗 5-7 hrs to Cabo Ortegal

Cabo Ortegal (p246) Wild, windswept and downright dramatic, the coast around Cabo Ortegal will simply take your breath away.
🚗 5-6 hrs to Santiago de Compostela

Santiago de Compostela (p240) The end point of many a pilgrim's journey, Santiago has loads of charm, glorious architecture and fine food to enjoy at the end of this epic trip.

Santillana del Mar (p242) An impossibly picturesque place, Santillana del Mar is many visitors' choice for Spain's prettiest *pueblo* (village).
🚗 1-2 hrs to Cudillero

Bilbao (p212) A couple of days in Bilbao should allow enough time for the Guggenheim Museum Bilbao and some serious tapas indulgence. 🚗 2-3 hrs to Santillana del Mar

San Sebastián (p223) Beautiful beyond compare and Spain's undisputed culinary capital, San Sebastián is worth at least two days...at *least*. 🚗 2 hrs to Bilbao

Aínsa (p269) There are no more beautiful mountain villages than stone-built Aínsa, with its splendid panoramic views. 🚗 2-3 hrs to Sos del Rey Católico

Taüll (p267) The pick of Catalonia's Pyrenean hamlets, Taüll has Romanesque churches and is the gateway to a stunning national park. 🚗 4 hrs to Aínsa

Sos del Rey Católico (p270) Just when you run out of superlatives, you arrive in Sos del Rey Católico, the essence of a medieval mountain village. 🚗 6 hrs to San Sebastián

Barcelona (p69) The starting point of so many wonderful journeys and a destination in itself, Barcelona is Spain's most celebrated city. 🚗 6 hrs to the Pyrenees

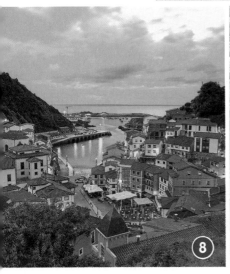

Plan Your Trip
Family Travel

Spain is a family-friendly destination with excellent transport and accommodation infrastructure, food to satisfy even the fussiest of eaters, and an extraordinary range of attractions that appeal to both adults and children. Visiting as a family does require careful planning, but no more than for visiting any other European country.

Practicalities

Look out for the 👪 icon for family-friendly suggestions throughout this guide.

Hotel cots Most hotels (but rarely budget places) have cots, although most only have a handful, so reserve one when booking your room. If asking for a *cuna* (cot), ask for a larger room. Cots sometimes cost extra; other hotels offer them for free.

Playgrounds Most towns and some top-end hotels and resorts have children's play areas and/or swimming pools.

Emergency supplies Spain is likely to have everything you need (eg baby formula, disposable nappies, milk), but bring a small supply of items you're used to having back home in case of emergency (eg Sunday, when most pharmacies are closed).

High chairs You cannot rely on restaurants having *tronas* (high chairs), although many do. Those that do, however, rarely have more than one (a handful at most).

Nappy-changing Facilities Very few restaurants (or other public facilities) have nappy-changing facilities.

Eating Hours When kids get hungry between meals, zip into the nearest tapas bar or super-market; carry emefgency snack supplies for those times when there's simply nothing open.

Transport

Spain's transport infrastructure is world-class, and high-speed AVE trains render irrelevant the distances between many major cities. Apart from anything else, most

ALBERTO LOYO/SHUTTERSTOCK©

kids love the idea that they're travelling at nearly 300km/h.

You can hire a *silla infantil* (car seat; usually for an additional cost) for infants and children from most car-hire firms, but you should always book them in advance. This is especially true during busy travel periods, such as Spanish school holidays, Navidad (Christmas) and Semana Santa (Holy Week).

It's extremely rare that taxis have child seats – unless you're carrying a portable version from home, you're expected to sit the child on your lap, with the seatbelt around you both.

Tips

● Expect your children to be kissed, offered sweets, have their cheeks pinched and their hair ruffled at least once a day.

● Always ask for extra tapas in bars, such as bread, olives or cut, raw carrots.

● Adjust your children to Spanish time (ie late nights) as quickly as you can;

★ Best for Kids

Park Güell (p92), Barcelona

Parque del Buen Retiro (p49), Madrid

Estadio Santiago Bernabéu (p50), Madrid

Costa Brava (p109)

otherwise they'll miss half of what's worth seeing.

● Crayons and paper are rarely given out in restaurants – bring your own.

● If you're willing to let your child share your bed, you won't incur a supplement. Extra beds usually incur a €20 to €30 charge.

● Always ask the local tourist office for the nearest children's playgrounds.

From left: Park Güell (p92); Playa de la Concha (p225)

Detail of *Las Meninas* by Velázquez

Museo del Prado

Welcome to one of the world's elite art galleries. Visiting is the ultimate artistic indulgence, with Spanish masters (Goya, Velázquez and El Greco) and big names from across Europe.

The more than 7000 paintings held in the Museo del Prado's collection (only around 1500 are currently on display) are like a window onto the historical vagaries of the Spanish soul, at once grand and imperious in the royal paintings of Velázquez, darkly tumultuous in *Las pinturas negras* (The Black Paintings) of Goya, and outward looking with sophisticated works from across Europe.

Goya

Francisco José de Goya y Lucientes (Goya) is found on all three floors, but start at the southern end of the ground or lower level. In Room 65, Goya's *El dos de mayo* (The 2nd of May) and *El tres de mayo* (The 3rd of May) rank among Madrid's most emblematic paintings. In Rooms 67 and 68 are some of his darkest and most disturbing works, *Las pinturas negras*.

Great For...

Don't Miss

Goya's *Las pinturas negras* or his *El dos de mayo*.

Palacio Real (p45)

Arriving in Madrid

Aeropuerto de Barajas (Adolfo Suárez Madrid-Barajas Airport; p66) Metro (6.05am to 1.30am; €4.50), bus (€5) and minibus (both 24 hours) to central Madrid; taxis €30.

Puerta de Atocha (Atocha Train Station; p66) Metro and bus to central Madrid (6.05am to 1.30am); taxi from €8.

Estación de Chamartín (Chamartín Train Station; p66) Metro and bus to central Madrid (6.05am to 1.30am); taxi around €15.

Where to Stay

Madrid has high-quality accommodation at prices that haven't been seen in the centre of other European capitals in decades. Five-star temples to good taste and a handful of buzzing hostels bookend a fabulous collection of mid-range hotels and cheaper family-run *hostales* (cheap hotels); most of the midrangers are creative originals.

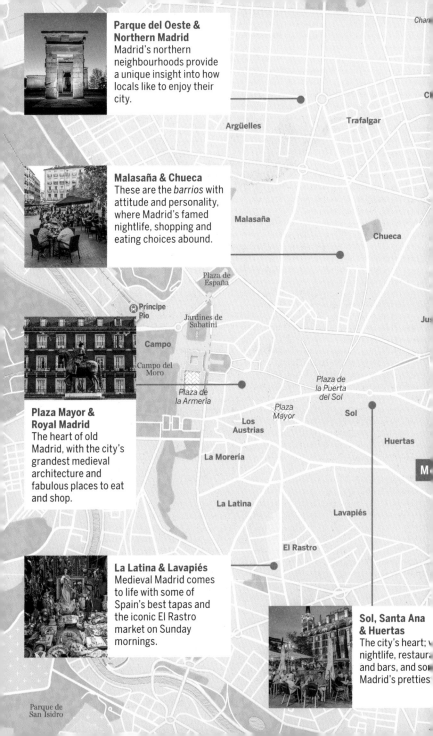

Parque del Oeste & Northern Madrid
Madrid's northern neighbourhoods provide a unique insight into how locals like to enjoy their city.

Chan

Argüelles

Trafalgar

C

Malasaña & Chueca
These are the *barrios* with attitude and personality, where Madrid's famed nightlife, shopping and eating choices abound.

Malasaña

Chueca

Plaza de España

Príncipe Pío

Jardines de Sabatini

Ju

Campo

Campo del Moro

Plaza de la Armería

Plaza de la Puerta del Sol

Plaza Mayor

Sol

Los Austrias

Huertas

La Morería

M

Plaza Mayor & Royal Madrid
The heart of old Madrid, with the city's grandest medieval architecture and fabulous places to eat and shop.

La Latina

Lavapiés

El Rastro

La Latina & Lavapiés
Medieval Madrid comes to life with some of Spain's best tapas and the iconic El Rastro market on Sunday mornings.

Sol, Santa Ana & Huertas
The city's heart; nightlife, restaur and bars, and so Madrid's pretties

Parque de San Isidro

0 — 1 km
0 — 0.5 miles

Castellana

amberí

Almagro

Salamanca

*Adolfo Suárez
Madrid-Barajas
Airport (10km)*

Jardines de
Descubrimiento

Recoletos

Goya

Recoletos

Recoletos

ticia

*Plaza de la
Independencia*

Paseo del
Prado

Jerónimos

Retiro

*Parque del
Buen Retiro*

JSEO DEL PRADO

Real Jardín
Botánico

Atocha

Salamanca
Upmarket, quiet
neighbourhood; fine
boutiques, designer
tapas bars and trendy
food stores make this
Madrid's home of
style.

**El Retiro &
the Art Museums**
Spain's golden mile of
temples to high culture
and art, with a glorious
park thrown in.

Estación
de Atocha

ith
nts
e of
streets.

Madrid Centro (p46)
El Retiro & the Art Museums (p48)
Malasaña, Chueca & Salamanca (p52)

*Estación Sur
de Autobuses (50m)*

Madrid at a Glance...

Madrid is a miracle of human energy and peculiarly Spanish passions, a beguiling place with a simple message: this city knows how to live. Madrid doesn't have the immediate cachet of Paris, the monumental history of Rome or the reputation for cool of that other city up the road. But it's the perfect expression of Europe's most passionate country writ large. Madrid's calling cards are many: astonishing art galleries, relentless nightlife, a feast of fine restaurants and tapas bars, and a population that's mastered the art of the good life. It's not that other cities don't have these things, it's just Madrid has them in bucketloads.

Madrid in Two Days

On day one, visit the **Plaza Mayor** (p44), **Plaza de la Villa** (p45) and **Palacio Real** (p45), then linger in **Plaza de Santa Ana** (p47), before enjoying the incomparable **Museo del Prado** (p39) and lovely **Parque del Buen Retiro** (p49). Hit up Chueca's nightlife at day's end. On day two, visit the **Mirador de Madrid** (p49), **Centro de Arte Reina Sofía** (p49) and go on a tapas crawl in **La Latina** (p55).

Madrid in Four Days

Try to be in Madrid on a Sunday for the **El Rastro flea market** (p43). Go shopping in **Salamanca**, marvel at the Goya frescoes in **Ermita de San Antonio de la Florida** (p44) and complete your trio of art galleries at the **Museo Thyssen-Bornemisza** (p49). Get a taste of local life at **Plaza de Olavide** (p50) and spend time exploring **Malasaña**.

Interior of Museo del Prado

❶ Need to Know

Map p48; www.museo delprado.es; Paseo del Prado; adult/concession/child €15/7.50/free, 6-8pm Mon-Sat & 5-7pm Sun free, audioguide €3.50, admission plus official guidebook €24; ⏱10am-8pm Mon-Sat, to 7pm Sun; Ⓜ Banco de España

✕ Take a Break

The Prado's in-house cafeteria is next to the bookshop. Otherwise, cross the road to Estado Puro (p59).

★ Top Tip

Purchase your ticket online and avoid the queues.

There are more Goyas on the 1st floor in Rooms 34 to 37 – these include the enigmatic *La maja vestida* (The Clothed Maja), and *La maja desnuda* (The Naked Maja).

Velázquez

Diego Rodriguez de Silva y Velázquez (Velázquez) is another of the grand masters of Spanish art who brings so much distinction to the Prado. Of all his works, *Las meninas* (Room 12) is what most people come to see. The rooms surrounding *Las meninas* contain more fine works by Velázquez: watch in particular for his paintings of various members of royalty who seem to spring off the canvas – *Felipe II*, *Felipe IV*, *Margarita de Austria* (a younger version of whom features in *Las meninas*), *El Príncipe Baltasar Carlos* and *Isabel de Francia* – on horseback.

Spanish & Other European Masters

If Spanish painters have piqued your curiosity, look for the stark figures of Francisco de Zurbarán or the vivid, almost surreal works by the 16th-century master and adopted Spaniard El Greco.

Another alternative is the Prado's outstanding collection of Flemish art, with highlights including the fulsome figures and bulbous cherubs of Peter Paul Rubens (1577–1640), *The Triumph of Death* by Pieter Bruegel, Rembrandt's *Artemisa*, and works by Anton Van Dyck. And on no account miss the weird and wonderful *The Garden of Earthly Delights* (Room 56A) by Hieronymus Bosch (c 1450–1516).

And then there are the paintings by Dürer, Rafael, Tiziano (Titian), Tintoretto, Sorolla, Gainsborough, Fra Angelico, Tiepolo...

Museo del Prado

PLAN OF ATTACK

Begin on the 1st floor with ❶ **Las meninas** by Velázquez. Although it alone is worth the entry price, it's a fine introduction to the 17th-century Golden Age of Spanish art; nearby are more of Velázquez' royal paintings and works by Zurbarán and Murillo. While on the 1st floor, seek out Goya's ❷ **La maja vestida and La maja desnuda**, with more of Goya's early works in neighbouring rooms. Downstairs at the southern end of the Prado, Goya's anger is evident in the searing ❸ **El dos de mayo and El tres de mayo**, and the torment of Goya's later years finds expression in the adjacent rooms with ❹ **pinturas negras** (Black Paintings). Also on the lower floor, Hieronymus Bosch's weird and wonderful ❺ **The Garden of Earthly Delights** is one of the Prado's signature masterpieces. Returning to the 1st floor, El Greco's ❻ **Adoration of the Shepherds** is an extraordinary work, as is Peter Paul Rubens' ❼ **Las tres gracias**, which forms the centrepiece of the Prado's gathering of Flemish masters. A detour to the 2nd floor takes in some lesser-known Goyas, but finish in the ❽ **Edificio Jerónimos**, with a visit to the cloisters and the outstanding bookshop.

TOP TIPS

➡ Purchase your ticket online (www.museodelprado.es) and avoid the queues.

➡ Best time to visit is as soon as possible after opening time.

➡ The website (www.museodelprado.es/coleccion/que-ver) has self-guided tours for one- to three-hour visits.

➡ Nearby are Museo Thyssen-Bornemisza and Centro de Arte Reina Sofía. Together they form an extraordinary trio of galleries.

IMAGNO / GETTY IMAGES ©

Las meninas (Velázquez)

This masterpiece depicts Velázquez and the Infanta Margarita. According to some experts, the images of the king and queen appear in mirrors behind Velázquez.

Goya Entrance

Main Ticket Office

Edificio Jerónimos

Opened in 2007, this state-of-the-art extension has rotating exhibitions of Prado masterpieces held in storage for decades for lack of wall space, and stunning 2nd-floor granite cloisters that date back to 1672.

Adoration of the Shepherds (El Greco)

There's an ecstatic quality to this intense painting. El Greco's distorted rendering of bodily forms came to characterise much of his later work.

Las tres gracias (Rubens)

A late Rubens masterpiece, *The Three Graces* is a classical and masterly expression of Rubens' preoccupation with sensuality, here portraying Aglaia, Euphrosyne and Thalia, the daughters of Zeus.

La maja vestida & La maja desnuda (Goya)

These enigmatic works scandalised early-19th-century Madrid society, fuelling the rumour mill as to the woman's identity and drawing the ire of the Spanish Inquisition.

El dos de mayo & El tres de mayo (Goya)

Few paintings evoke a city's sense of self quite like Goya's portrayal of Madrid's valiant but ultimately unsuccessful uprising against French rule in 1808.

Las pinturas negras (Goya)

Las pinturas negras are Goya's darkest works. *Saturno devorando a su hijo* evokes a writhing mass of tortured humanity, while *La romería de San Isidro* and *El aquelarre* are profoundly unsettling.

Edificio Villanueva

① ⑦ ②

Jerónimos Entrance (Main Entrance)

Information Counter & Audioguides

Gift Shop

Cafeteria

Murillo Entrance

⑤ ③ ④

Velázquez Entrance

The Garden of Earthly Delights (Bosch)

A fantastical painting in triptych form, this overwhelming work depicts the Garden of Eden and what the Prado describes as 'the lugubrious precincts of Hell' in exquisitely bizarre detail.

Sardine tapas, Mercado de San Miguel

DIEGYMS/SHUTTERSTOCK ©

Markets of Madrid

Madrid's markets lie at the centre of local life, from the daily Mercado de San Miguel or the Sunday El Rastro institution, to neighbourhood markets where food is a centrepiece.

Mercado de San Miguel

Mercado de San Miguel (p53) is one of Madrid's oldest and most beautiful markets, an inviting space strewn with tables within early-20th-century glass walls. You can order tapas and sometimes more substantial plates at most of the counter bars, and everything here (from caviar to chocolate) is as tempting as the market is alive.

All the stalls are outstanding, but you could begin with *pintxos* (Basque tapas) atop mini toasts at **La Casa de Bacalao** (Stalls 16–17), follow it up with some *jamón* or other cured meats at **Carrasco Guijuelo** (Stall 18), cheeses at Stalls 20–21, all manner of pickled goodies at Stall 22, or the gourmet tapas of **Lhardy** (Stalls 61–62).

Great For...

🍽️ 💬 🛍️

☑ **Don't Miss**

La hora del vermút (vermouth hour) at 1pm Sunday in La Latina bars near El Rastro.

El Rastro flea market

ANASTASIA PETROVA/SHUTTERSTOCK©

El Rastro

A Sunday morning at **El Rastro flea market** (Calle de la Ribera de los Curtidores; ⊙8am-3pm Sun; ⓂLa Latina), Europe's largest, is a Madrid classic. You could easily spend the entire morning inching your way down the hill and the maze of streets. Cheap clothes, luggage, old flamenco records, even older photos of Madrid, faux-designer purses, grungy T-shirts, household goods and electronics are the main fare. For every 10 pieces of junk, there's a real gem (a lost masterpiece, an Underwood typewriter) waiting to be found.

The crowded Sunday flea market was, back in the 17th and 18th centuries, largely a meat market (*rastro* means 'stain', in reference to the trail of blood left behind by animals dragged down the hill). The road leading through the market, Calle de la Ribera de los Curtidores, translates as 'Tanners' Alley'. On Sunday mornings it's the place to be, with all of Madrid here in search of a bargain.

Neighbourhood Markets

In Chueca, the remodelled **Mercado de San Antón** (Map p52; ☎91 330 07 30; www.mercadosananton.com; Calle de Augusto Figueroa 24; tapas from €1.50, mains €5-20; ⊙10am-midnight; ⓂChueca) has fresh produce downstairs, while upstairs there's all manner of appealing tapas varieties from Japan, the Canary Islands and other corners of the country/globe.

Over in Salamanca, **Mercado de la Paz** (☎91 435 07 43; www.mercadodelapaz.com; off Calle de Ayala; ⊙9am-8pm Mon-Fri, to 2.30pm Sat; ⓂSerrano) is one of few Madrid markets not to have been gentrified in recent years and remains a thoroughly local market with fresh produce, delis, and a handful of popular bars.

◎ SIGHTS

Madrid has three of the finest art galleries in the world. Beyond museum walls, there is nowhere easier to access the combination of stately architecture and feel-good living than in the beautiful plazas, where *terrazas* (cafes or bars with outdoor tables) provide a front-row seat for Madrid's fine cityscape and endlessly energetic street life. Throw in areas like Chueca, Malasaña and Salamanca, each with their own personality, and you'll see why this place is so worth spending some time.

◎ Plaza Mayor & Royal Madrid

These *barrios* (districts) are where the story of Madrid began. As the seat of royal power, this is where the splendour of imperial Spain was at its most ostentatious and where Spain's overarching Catholicism was at its most devout – think expansive palaces, elaborate private mansions, ancient churches and imposing convents amid the clamour of modern Madrid.

Plaza Mayor   Square

(Map p46; MSol) Madrid's grand central square, a rare but expansive opening in the tightly packed streets of central Madrid, is one of the prettiest open spaces in Spain, a winning combination of imposing architecture, picaresque historical tales and vibrant street life. At once beautiful in its own right and a reference point for so many Madrid days, it also hosts the city's main tourist office, a Christmas market in December and arches leading to laneways out into the labyrinth.

Ermita de San Antonio de la Florida   Gallery

(Panteón de Goya; ☑91 542 07 22; www. sanantoniodelaflorida.es; Glorieta de San Antonio de la Florida 5; ◔9.30am-8pm Tue-Sun mid-Sep–mid-Jun, 9.30am-2pm Tue-Fri, to 7pm Sat & Sun mid-Jun–mid-Sep; MPríncipe Pío) **FREE** The frescoed ceilings of the restored Ermita de San Antonio de la Florida are one of Madrid's most surprising secrets. The southern of the two small chapels is one of the few places to see Goya's work in its original setting, as painted by the master in

From left: Plaza Mayor; Goya fresco at Ermita de San Antonio de la Florida; Palacio Real; Plaza de la Villa

MATTEO COLOMBO/GETTY IMAGES©

VIVVI SMAK/SHUTTERSTOCK ©

1798 on the request of Carlos IV. It's simply breathtaking.

Palacio Real
Palace

(Map p46; ☎91 454 87 00; www.patrimonio nacional.es; Calle de Bailén; adult/concession €10/5, guide/audioguide €4, EU citizens free last 2hr Mon-Thu; ☺10am-8pm Apr-Sep, to 6pm Oct-Mar; ⓂÓpera) Spain's jewel-box Palacio Real is used only occasionally for royal ceremonies; the royal family moved to the modest Palacio de la Zarzuela years ago.

When the *alcázar* (Muslim fortress) burned down in 1734, Felipe V, the first of the Bourbon kings, decided to build a palace that would dwarf all its European counterparts. Felipe died before the palace was finished, which is perhaps why the Italianate baroque colossus has a mere 2800 rooms, just one-quarter of the original plan.

Plaza de Oriente
Square

(Map p46; ⓂÓpera) This graceful square is one of central Madrid's most beautiful, home as it is to a royal palace that once had aspirations to be the Spanish Versailles, sophisticated cafes watched over by apartments that cost the equivalent of a royal salary, and the **Teatro Real** (Map p46; ☎902 244848; www.teatro-real.com), Madrid's opera house and one of Spain's temples to high culture.

Plaza de la Villa
Square

(Map p46; ⓂÓpera) The intimate Plaza de la Villa is one of Madrid's prettiest. Enclosed on three sides by wonderfully preserved examples of 17th-century *barroco madrileño* (Madrid-style baroque architecture – a pleasing amalgam of brick, exposed stone and wrought iron), it was the permanent seat of Madrid's city government from the Middle Ages until recent years, when Madrid's city council relocated to the grand Palacio de Cibeles on **Plaza de la Cibeles** (Map p52; ⓂBanco de España).

Convento de las Descalzas Reales
Convent

(Convent of the Barefoot Royals; Map p46; www. patrimonionacional.es; Plaza de las Descalzas 3; €6, incl Convento de la Encarnación €8, free for EU citizens 4-6.30pm Wed & Thu; ☺10am-2pm & 4-6.30pm Tue-Sat, 10am-3pm Sun; ⓂÓpera, Sol) The grim plateresque walls of the Convento de las Descalzas Reales offer no

CRIBE/SHUTTERSTOCK ©

OLEG ZNAMENSKIY/SHUTTERSTOCK ©

Madrid Centro

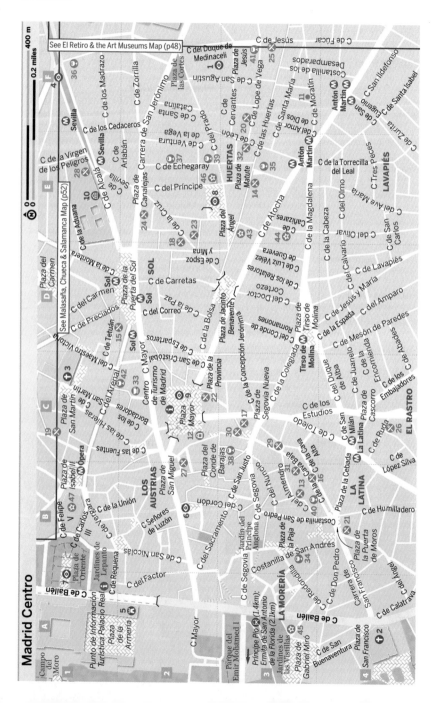

See El Retiro & the Art Museums Map (p48)

See Malasaña, Chueca & Salamanca Map (p52)

400 m
0.2 miles

C del Duque de Medinaceli
C de Jesús
C de Fúcar
Plaza de Jesús
Costanilla de los Desamparados
C de San Ildefonso
C de Santa Isabel
C de Zurita
C de San Eugenio
Antón Martín
LAVAPIÉS
C de la Torrecilla del Leal
C de San Carlos
C del Ave María
C Tres Peces
C del Olmo
C de la Cabeza
C de la Magdalena
Antón Martín
C de Santa María
C de las Huertas
C de Lope de Vega
C de San Agustín
Plaza de las Cortes
C de San Jerónimo
Plaza de la Paja
HUERTAS
C de Echegaray
Plaza Matute
C de Ventura de la Vega
C del Prado
C de Santa Catalina
C de los Madrazo
C de Zorrilla
C de Cervantes
C de León
C del Amor de Dios
Sevilla
C de los Cedaceros
C de la Virgen de los Peligros
C de Alcalá
C de Sevilla
C de Arlabán
Carrera de San Jerónimo
Plaza de Canalejas
C del Príncipe
Plaza del Ángel
Plaza del Carmen
C de la Aduana
C de la Montera
C del Carmen
C de Preciados
Sol
Puerta del Sol
C de Carretas
C de Espoz y Mina
C de la Cruz
C de Atocha
C de Cañizares
C de Relatores
C del Doctor Cortezo
C de la Colegiada
Tirso de Molina
C del Conde de Romanones
Plaza de Jacinto Benavente
C de la Bolsa
C de la Paz
C del Correo
Centro de Turismo de Madrid
Plaza Mayor
Plaza de la Provincia
C Mayor
C de San Cristóbal
C de Esparteros
C de la Concepción Jerónima
C de Segovia Nueva
Tirso de Molina
C de la Espada
C de Jesús y María
C del Amparo
C de Lavapiés
C del Calvario
C del Duque de Alba
C de los Estudios
C de Toledo
C de Juanelo
C de la Encomienda
C de los Embajadores
C de Abades
EL RASTRO
C de Mesón de Paredes
C de San Millán
La Latina
Plaza de Cascorro
C de Ruda
LA LATINA
C de San Pedro
C de Segovia
C del Nuncio
C de San Justo
C del Cordón
Plaza del Conde de Barajas
Plaza de San Miguel
LOS AUSTRIAS
Ópera
C de San Nicolás
C de la Unión
C de Vergara
C de Carlos III
C de Felipe V
Plaza de Isabel II
Plaza de Oriente
Palacio Real
Punto de Información Turística
Plaza de la Armería
Jardines de Lepanto
C de Requena
C del Factor
C de Bailén
C Mayor
Parque del Emir Mohamed I
Jardines de las Vistillas
Plaza de Gabriel Miró
C de San Buenaventura
C de San Francisco
Plaza de San Francisco
C de Calatrava
LA MORERÍA
Costanilla de San Andrés
Plaza de San Andrés
Carrera de San Francisco
C de Don Pedro
C del Ángel
Plaza de la Puerta de Moros
C de Humilladero
C de López Silva
Plaza de la Cebada
Costanilla de San Pedro
C de Don Pedro
C de la Redondilla
C de la Cava Alta
C de la Cava Baja
C del Almendro
C del Nuncio
Jardín del Príncipe Anglona
Plaza de la Paja

Campo del Moro

Príncipe Pío (1.4km);
Ermita de San Antonio de la Florida (2.1km)

Madrid Centro

hint that behind the facade lies a sumptuous stronghold of the faith. The compulsory guided tour (in Spanish) leads you up a gaudily frescoed Renaissance stairway to the upper level of the cloister. The vault was painted by Claudio Coello, one of the most important artists of the Madrid School of the 17th century.

◉ La Latina & Lavapiés

Basílica de San Francisco El Grande   Church

(Map p46; Plaza de San Francisco 1; adult/concession €5/3; ⏰Mass 8-10.30am Mon-Sat, museum 10.30am-12.30pm & 4-6pm Tue-Sun Sep-Jun, 10.30am-12.30pm & 5-7pm Tue-Sun Jul & Aug; ⓂLa Latina, Puerta de Toledo) Lording it over the southwestern corner of La Latina, this imposing baroque basilica is one of Madrid's grandest old churches. Its extravagantly frescoed dome is, by some estimates, the largest in Spain and the fourth largest in the world, with a height of 56m and diameter of 33m.

◉ Sol, Santa Ana & Huertas

Plaza de Santa Ana   Square

(Map p46; ⓂSevilla, Sol, Antón Martín) Plaza de Santa Ana is a delightful confluence of elegant architecture and irresistible energy. It presides over the upper reaches of the **Barrio de las Letras** (District of Letters; Map p46; ⓂAntón Martín) and this literary personality makes its presence felt with the statues of the 17th-century writer Calderón de la Barca and Federíco García Lorca, and in the **Teatro Español** (Map p46; ☎91 360 14 84; www.teatroespanol.es; Calle del Príncipe 25; ⓂSevilla, Sol, Antón Martín) at the plaza's eastern end. Apart from anything else, the plaza is the starting point for many a long Huertas night.

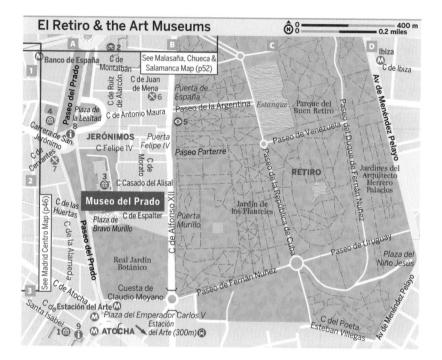

El Retiro & the Art Museums

Real Academia de Bellas Artes de San Fernando   Museum

(Map p46; ☎91 524 08 64; www.realacademia
bellasartessanfernando.com; Calle de Alcalá 13;
adult/child €8/free, Wed free; ☺10am-3pm Tue-
Sun Sep-Jul; Ⓜ Sol, Sevilla) The Real Academia
de Bellas Artes, Madrid's 'other' art gallery,
has for centuries played a pivotal role in
the artistic life of the city. As the royal fine
arts academy, it has nurtured local talent,
thereby complementing the royal penchant
for drawing the great international artists
of the day into their realm. The pantheon
of former alumni reads like a who's who of
Spanish art, and the collection that now
hangs on the academy's walls is a suitably
rich one.

Edificio Metrópolis   Architecture

(Map p46; Gran Vía; Ⓜ Banco de España, Sevilla)
Among the more interesting buildings
along Gran Vía is the stunning, French-
designed Edificio Metrópolis, built in 1905,
which marks the southern end of Gran Vía.
The winged victory statue atop its dome
was added in 1975 and is best seen from

Calle de Alcalá or Plaza de la Cibeles. It's magnificent when floodlit, and for some it's Madrid's most beautiful building.

El Retiro & the Art Museums

Centro de Arte Reina Sofía   Museum
(Map p48; ☑91 774 10 00; www.museoreina sofia. es; Calle de Santa Isabel 52; adult/concession €10/free, 1.30-7pm Sun, 7-9pm Mon & Wed-Sat free; ⏰10am-9pm Mon & Wed-Sat, to 7pm Sun; Ⓜ Estación del Arte) Home to Picasso's *Guernica,* arguably Spain's most famous artwork, the Centro de Arte Reina Sofía is Madrid's premier collection of modern and contemporary art. In addition to plenty of paintings by Picasso, other major drawcards are works by Salvador Dalí and Joan Miró. The collection principally spans the 20th century up to the 1980s. The occasional non-Spanish artist makes an appearance (including Francis Bacon's *Lying Figure;* 1966), but most of the collection is strictly peninsular. Tickets are cheaper if purchased online.

Museo Thyssen-Bornemisza   Museum
(Map p48; ☑902 760511; www.museothyssen. org; Paseo del Prado 8; adult/child €13/free, Mon free; ⏰10am-7pm Tue-Sun, noon-4pm Mon; Ⓜ Banco de España) The Thyssen is one of the most extraordinary private collections of predominantly European art in the world. Where the Prado or Reina Sofía enable you to study the body of work of a particular artist in depth, the Thyssen is the place to immerse yourself in an incredible breadth of artistic styles. Most of the big names are here, sometimes with just a single painting, but the Thyssen's gift to Madrid and the art-loving public is to have them all under one roof.

Parque del Buen Retiro   Gardens
(Map p48; Plaza de la Independencia; ⏰6am-midnight Apr-Sep, to 10pm Oct-Mar; Ⓜ Retiro, Príncipe de Vergara, Ibiza, Atocha) **FREE** The glorious gardens of El Retiro are as beautiful as any you'll find in a European city. Strewn with marble monuments, landscaped lawns, the occasional elegant building (the Palacio de Cristal is especially worth seeking out) and

abundant greenery, it's quiet and contemplative during the week but comes to life on weekends. Put simply, this is one of our favourite places in Madrid.

Mirador de Madrid   Viewpoint
(Map p48; www.centrocentro.org; Plaza de la Cibeles, 8th fl Palacio de Comunicaciones; adult/ child €3/1.50; ⏰10.30am-2pm & 4-7.30pm Tue-Sun; Ⓜ Banco de España) The views from the summit of the Palacio de Comunicaciones are among Madrid's best, sweeping out over Plaza de la Cibeles, up the hill towards the sublime Edificio Metrópolis and out to the mountains. Buy your ticket up the stairs then take the lift to the 6th floor, from where the gates are opened every half-hour. You can either take another lift or climb the stairs up to the 8th floor.

Salamanca

Museo Lázaro Galdiano   Museum
(☑91 561 60 84; www.flg.es; Calle de Serrano 122; adult/concession/child €7/4/free, last hour free; ⏰10am-4.30pm Tue-Sat, to 3pm Sun; Ⓜ Gregorio Marañón) This imposing early-20th-century Italianate stone mansion, set discreetly back from the street, belonged to Don José Lázaro Galdiano (1862–1947), a successful businessman and passionate patron of the arts. His astonishing private collection, which he bequeathed to the city upon his death, includes 13,000 works of art and objets d'art, a quarter of which are on show at any time.

Plaza de Toros   Stadium
(☑91 356 22 00; www.las-ventas.com; Calle de Alcalá 237; ⏰10am-5.30pm; Ⓜ Ventas) **FREE** East of central Madrid, the Plaza de Toros Monumental de Las Ventas (Las Ventas) is the most prestigious bullring in the world, and a visit here is a good way to gain an insight into this controversial Spanish tradition. The **Museo Taurino** (☑91 725 18 57; https://lasventastour.com/en/the-bullfighting-museum; Calle de Alcalá 237; ⏰10am-7pm May-Oct, to 6pm Nov-Apr; Ⓜ Ventas) **FREE** is also here, and the architecture will be of interest even to those with no interest in *las corridas* (bullfights). Bullfights are still held

regularly here during the season, which runs roughly mid-May to September.

◎ Chamberí, Moncloa & Northern Madrid

Estadio Santiago Bernabéu Stadium

(🕿tours 91 398 43 70; www.realmadrid.com; Avenida de Concha Espina 1; tours adult/child €25/18; ⊗tours 10am-7pm Mon-Sat, 10.30am-6.30pm Sun, except match days; Ⓜ︎Santiago Bernabéu) Football fans and budding Madridistas (Real Madrid supporters) will want to make a pilgrimage to the Estadio Santiago Bernabéu, a temple to all that's extravagant and successful in football. Self-guided tours take you up into the stands for a panoramic view of the stadium, then through the presidential box, press room, dressing rooms, players' tunnel and even onto the pitch. The tour ends in the extraordinary Exposición de Trofeos (trophy exhibit). Better still, attend a game alongside 80,000 delirious fans.

For tours of the stadium, buy your ticket at window 10 (next to gate 7).

Plaza de Olavide Square

(Ⓜ︎Bilbao) Plaza de Olavide is one of Madrid's most agreeable public spaces, a real *barrio* special. There are park benches, two children's playgrounds, and bars with outdoor tables all around the perimeter.

⚙ COURSES

Cooking Point Cooking

(Map p46; 🕿91 011 51 54; https://cooking point. es; Calle de Moratín 11; adult/child €70/35; ⊗9.30am-9.30pm Mon-Sat; Ⓜ︎Antón Martín) This excellent cooking school includes a trip to the local market and English-language classes on how to cook paella or prepare traditional tapas.

⚙ TOURS

Devour Madrid Food Tour Food & Drink

(🕿695 111 832; www.madridfoodtour.com; tours €50-130) With five tours for different tastes and budgets, Devour Madrid shows you the best of Spanish food and wine in the centre

Trophies on display in Estadio Santiago Bernabéu

B·HIDE THE SCENE/SHUTTERSTOCK©

of Madrid. Tours are themed: wine and tapas, flamenco, authentic local markets, history or (for the most serious foodies) the Ultimate Spanish Cuisine tour, which takes you to eight tasting stops in four hours.

Adventurous Appetites   Food & Drink
(☏639 331073; www.adventurousappetites. com; 4hr tours €50; ⏰8pm-midnight Mon-Sat) English-language tapas tours through central Madrid. Prices include the first drink but exclude food.

Spanish Tapas Madrid   Food & Drink
(☏672 301231; www.spanishtapasmadrid.com; tours from €70) Local boy Luis Ortega takes you through some iconic Madrid tapas bars, as well as offering tours that take in old Madrid, flamenco and the Prado.

Wellington Society   History
(☏609 143203; www.wellsoc.org; tours from €95) A handful of quirky historical tours laced with anecdotes, led by the inimitable Stephen Drake-Jones.

🔒 SHOPPING

Loewe   Fashion & Accessories
(Map p52; ☏91 522 68 15; www.loewe.com; Gran Vía 8; ⏰10am-8.30pm Mon-Sat, 11am-8pm Sun; Ⓜ Gran Vía) Born in 1846 in Madrid, Loewe is arguably Spain's signature line in high-end fashion and its landmark store on Gran Vía is one of the most famous and elegant stores in the capital. Classy handbags and accessories are the mainstays. Prices can be jaw-droppingly high, but it's worth stopping by, even if you don't plan to buy.

Antigua Casa Talavera   Ceramics
(Map p52; ☏91 547 34 17; www.antiguacasa talavera.com; Calle de Isabel la Católica 2; ⏰10am-1.30pm & 5-8pm Mon-Fri; Ⓜ Santo Domingo) The extraordinary tiled facade of this wonderful old shop conceals an Aladdin's cave of ceramics from all over Spain. This is not the mass-produced stuff aimed at a tourist market, but instead comes from the small family potters of Andalucía and Toledo, ranging from the decorative (tiles)

🍽 Madrid Culinary Specialities

When the weather turns chilly, in Madrid that traditionally means *sopa de ajo* (garlic soup) and *legumbres* (legumes) such as *garbanzos* (chickpeas), *judías* (beans) and *lentejas* (lentils). Hearty stews are the order of the day and there are none more hearty than *cocido a la madrileña*; it's a kind of hotpot or stew that starts with a noodle broth and is followed by or combined with carrots, chickpeas, chicken, *morcilla* (blood sausage), beef, lard and possibly other sausage meats – there are as many ways of eating *cocido* as there are *madrileños* (residents of Madrid). *Repollo* (cabbage) sometimes makes an appearance. Madrid shares with much of the Spanish interior a love of roasted meats. More specifically, *asado de cordero lechal* (spring lamb roasted in a wood-fired oven) is a winter obsession in Madrid. Less celebrated (it's all relative) is *cochinillo asado* (roast suckling pig) from the Segovia region northwest of Madrid.

Cocido a la madrileña
NITO/SHUTTERSTOCK ©

to the useful (plates, jugs and other kitchen items).

El Arco Artesanía   Arts & Crafts
(Map p46; ☏91 365 26 80; www.artesania elarco. com; Plaza Mayor 9; ⏰11am-9pm Mon-Sat, noon-8pm Sun; Ⓜ Sol, La Latina) This original shop in the southwestern corner of Plaza Mayor sells an outstanding array of homemade designer souvenirs, from stone, ceramic and glass work to jewellery and home

Malasaña, Chueca & Salamanca

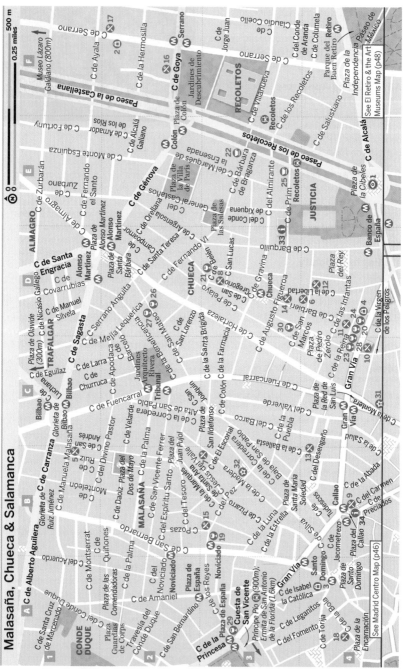

Malasaña, Chueca & Salamanca

fittings. The papier-mâché figures are gorgeous, but there's so much else here to turn your head. It sometimes closes earlier in the depths of winter.

Agatha Ruiz de la Prada
Fashion & Accessories

(Map p52; ☎91 319 05 01; www.agatharuiz delaprada.com; Calle de Serrano 27; ⊙10am-8.30pm Mon-Sat; Ⓜ Serrano) This boutique has to be seen to be believed, with pinks, yellows and oranges everywhere you turn. It's fun and exuberant, but not just for kids. It also has serious and highly original fashion. Agatha Ruiz de la Prada is one of the enduring icons of *la movida madrileña*, Madrid's 1980s outpouring of creativity.

✖ EATING

✖ Plaza Mayor & Royal Madrid

Casa Revuelta
Tapas €

(Map p46; ☎91 366 33 32; Calle de Latoneros 3; tapas from €3; ⊙10.30am-4pm & 7-11pm Tue-Sat, 10.30am-4pm Sun, closed Aug; Ⓜ Sol, La Latina) Casa Revuelta puts out some of Madrid's finest tapas of *bacalao* (cod) bar none –

unlike elsewhere, *tajadas de bacalao* don't have bones in them and slide down the throat with the greatest of ease. Early on a Sunday afternoon, as the Rastro crowd gathers here, it's filled to the rafters. Other specialities include *torreznos* (bacon bits), *callos* (tripe) and *albóndigas* (meatballs).

Mercado de San Miguel
Tapas €

(Map p46; ☎91 542 49 36; www.mercadode sanmiguel.es; Plaza de San Miguel; tapas from €1; ⊙10am-midnight Sun-Thu, to 1am Fri & Sat; Ⓜ Sol) This is one of Madrid's oldest and most beautiful markets, and one of our favourite experiences in the city.

La Ideal
Spanish €

(Map p46; ☎91 365 72 78; Calle de Botoneras 4; bocadillos from €3; ⊙9am-11pm Sun-Thu, to midnight Fri & Sat; Ⓜ Sol) Spanish bars don't come any more basic than this, but it's the purveyor of that enduring and wildly popular Madrid tradition – the *bocadillo de calamares* (a roll stuffed with deep-fried calamari). If it's closed, which is rare, plenty of bars elsewhere around the plaza offer the same deal.

Gourmet Experience   Food Hall €€

(Map p52; www.elcorteingles.es/aptc/gourmet-experience; Plaza del Callao 2, 9th fl; mains €8-20; ⊙10am-10pm; MCallao) Ride the elevator up to the 9th floor of the El Corte Inglés department store for one of downtown Madrid's best eating experiences. The food is excellent, with everything from top-notch tapas or Mexican to gourmet hamburgers, and the view is fabulous, especially over Plaza del Callao and down Gran Vía.

Taberna La Bola   Spanish €€

(Map p52; ☑91 547 69 30; www.labola.es; Calle de la Bola 5; mains €16-25; ⊙1.30-4.30pm & 8.30-11pm Mon-Sat, 1.30-4.30pm Sun, closed Aug; MSanto Domingo) Going strong since 1870 and run by the sixth generation of the Verdasco family, Taberna La Bola is a much-loved bastion of traditional Madrid cuisine. If you're going to try *cocido a la madrileña* (meat-and-chickpea stew; €21) while in Madrid, this is a good place to do so. It's busy and noisy and very Madrid.

El Pato Mudo   Spanish €€

(Map p46; ☑91 559 48 40; elpatomudo@hotmail.es; Calle Costanilla de los Ángeles 8; mains €13-24; ⊙1-4pm & 8-11.30pm Wed-Sun; MÓpera) El Pato Mudo isn't the most famous paella restaurant in Madrid, but it's known to locals for its variety of outstanding rice dishes at reasonable prices. Specialities include black rice with squid ink, soupy rice, authentic *paella valenciana* and shellfish paella. Served directly from the pan for two or more people, they go well with the local wines.

Restaurante Sobrino de Botín   Castilian €€€

(Map p46; ☑91 366 42 17; www.botin.es; Calle de los Cuchilleros 17; mains €18-28; set menus €46.50; ⊙1-4pm & 8pm-midnight; MLa Latina, Sol) It's not every day that you can eat in the oldest restaurant in the world (as recognised by the *Guinness Book of Records* – it was established in 1725). The secret of its staying power is fine *cochinillo asado* (roast suckling pig) and *cordero asado* (roast lamb) cooked in wood-fired ovens. Eating in the vaulted cellar is a treat.

From left: Restaurante Sobrino de Botín; Taberna La Bola; Malacatín; *Pintxos*

🍽 La Latina & Lavapiés

La Latina is Madrid's best *barrio* for tapas, complemented by plenty of fine sit-down restaurants. Calle de la Cava Baja and its surrounding streets is where it all happens. Lavapiés is more eclectic and multicultural and, generally speaking, the further down the hill you go, the better it gets, especially along Calle de Argumosa.

Almendro 13   Tapas €

(Map p46; 📞91 365 42 52; Calle del Almendro 13; mains €8-17; ⏱1-4pm & 7.30pm-midnight Sun-Thu, 1-5pm & 8pm-1am Fri & Sat; Ⓜ La Latina) Almendro 13 is a charming *taberna* (tavern) for traditional Spanish tapas with an emphasis on quality rather than frilly elaborations. Cured meats, cheeses and omelettes dominate the menu. It serves both *raciones* (full-plate) and half-sized plates – a full *ración* of the famously good *huevos rotos* ('broken eggs') served with *jamón* and thin potato slices is a meal in itself.

Juana La Loca   Tapas €€

(Map p46; 📞91 366 55 00; www.juanalaloca madrid.com; Plaza de la Puerta de Moros 4; tapas from €4.50, mains €10-30; ⏱1.30-5.30pm Tue-Sun, 7pm-midnight Sat-Wed, to 1am Thu-Fri; Ⓜ La Latina) Juana La Loca does a range of creative tapas with tempting options lined up along the bar, and more on the menu that is prepared to order. But we love it above all for its brilliant *tortilla de patatas* (potato-and-onion omelette), which is distinguished from others of its kind by the caramelised onions – simply wonderful.

Taberna Txakolina   Tapas €€

(Map p46; 📞91 366 48 77; Calle de la Cava Baja 26; tapas from €4.50; ⏱8pm-midnight Tue, 1-4pm & 8pm-midnight Wed-Sat, 1-4pm Sun; Ⓜ La Latina) Taberna Txakolina calls its *pintxos* 'high cuisine in miniature'. If ordering tapas makes you nervous, it couldn't be easier here – they're lined up on the bar, Basque style, in all their glory, and you can simply point. Whatever you order, wash it down with a *txacoli*, a sharp Basque white.

Malacatín   Spanish €€

(Map p46; 📞91 365 52 41; www.malacatin.com; Calle de Ruda 5; mains €11-17; ⏱11am-5.30pm Mon-Wed & Sat, 11am-5.30pm & 8.15-11pm Thu & Fri, closed Aug; Ⓜ La Latina) If you want to see

🍴 Perfect Catalan Cuisine

Arguably Madrid's best Catalan restaurant, classy **Casa Jorge** (📞91 416 92 44; www.casajorge.com; Calle de Cartagena 104; mains €13-22, set menus €39; ⏱1.30-4.30pm & 8.45pm-midnight Mon-Thu, 8.45pm-1am Fri & Sat, 1.30-4pm Sun, closed Aug; MCartagena) serves up exquisite specialities from Spain's northwest, including *caracoles* (snails), perfectly executed rice dishes and, in season (roughly December to March or April), *calçots con salsa romescu* (big spring onions served with a tomato and red-pepper sauce); you eat the latter with a bib, and they're extraordinarily delicious.

Calçots
NUA ESTUDIO/SHUTTERSTOCK ©

madrileños (residents of Madrid) enjoying their favourite local food, this is one of the best places to do so. The clamour of conversation bounces off the tiled walls of the cramped dining area adorned with bullfighting memorabilia. The speciality is as much *cocido* (meat-and-chickpea stew) as you can eat (€21).

The *degustación de cocido* (taste of *cocido;* €5.50) at the bar is a great way to try Madrid's favourite dish. It's a popular stop for a vermouth.

Casa Lucio
Spanish €€€

(Map p46; 📞91 365 82 17; www.casalucio.es; Calle de la Cava Baja 35; mains €15-30; ⏱1-4pm & 8.30pm-midnight, closed Aug; MLa Latina) Casa Lucio is a Madrid classic and has been wowing *madrileños* since 1974 with its

light touch, quality ingredients and home-style local cooking such as eggs (a Lucio speciality) and roasted meats in abundance. There's also *rabo de toro* (bull's tail) during the Fiestas de San Isidro Labrador and plenty of Rioja to wash away the mere thought of it.

The lunchtime *guisos del día* (stews of the day), including *cocido* on Wednesday, are also popular. Casa Lucio draws an august, well-dressed crowd, which has included the former king of Spain, former US president Bill Clinton and Penélope Cruz.

Posada de la Villa
Spanish €€€

(Map p46; 📞91 366 18 80; www.posadadela villa. com; Calle de la Cava Baja 9; mains €19-33; ⏱1-4pm & 8pm-midnight Mon-Sat, 1-4pm Sun, closed Aug; MLa Latina) This wonderfully restored 17th-century *posada* (inn) is something of a local landmark. The atmosphere is formal, the decoration sombre and traditional (heavy timber and brickwork), and the cuisine decidedly local – roast meats, *cocido* (which usually needs to be pre-ordered), *callos* and *sopa de ajo*.

🜚 Sol, Santa Ana & Huertas

Casa Toni
Spanish €

(Map p46; 📞91 532 25 80; Calle de la Cruz 14; mains €8-15; ⏱noon-4.30pm & 7pm-midnight; MSol) Locals flock to Casa Toni, one of Madrid's best old-school Spanish bars, for simple, honest cuisine fresh off the griddle. Specialities include cuttlefish, gazpacho and offal – the crispy (some would say gristly) pork ear is out of this world. While you're here, you can try one of the local Madrid wines. The prices are great and the old Madrid charm can't be beat.

Casa Labra
Tapas €

(Map p46; 📞91 531 00 81; www.casalabra.es; Calle de Tetuán 11; tapas from €1.10; ⏱11am-3.30pm & 6-11pm; MSol) Casa Labra has been going strong since 1860, an era that the decor strongly evokes. Locals love their *bacalao* and ordering it here – either as deep-fried tapas (*una tajada de bacalao* goes for €1.65) or *una croqueta de bacalao* (€1.10) – is a Madrid rite of initiation. As the lunchtime queues attest, they go through more than 700kg of cod every week.

This is also a bar with history – it was where the Partido Socialista Obrero Español (PSOE; Spanish Socialist Party) was formed on 2 May 1879. It was a favourite of poet and playwright Federíco García Lorca as well as appearing in Pío Baroja's novel *La Busca*.

Las Bravas Tapas **€**

(Map p46; ☎91 522 85 81; www.lasbravas.com; Callejón de Álvarez Gato 3; raciones €4.55-16.60; ⏰12.30-4.30pm & 7-11.30pm Mon-Thu, 12.30-5pm & 7pm-12.30am Fri & Sat, 12.30-5pm & 7-11.30pm Sun; Ⓜ Sol, Sevilla) Las Bravas has long been the place for a *caña* (small glass of beer) and some of the best *patatas bravas* (fried potatoes with a spicy tomato sauce) in town. In fact, its version of the *bravas* sauce is so famous that it's patented; you can buy takeaway tubs.

Casa Alberto Tapas **€€**

(Map p46; ☎91 429 93 56; www.casaalberto.es; Calle de las Huertas 18; tapas €3.50-12, raciones €7-17, mains €16-23; ⏰restaurant 1.30-4pm & 8pm-midnight Tue-Sat, 1.30-4pm Sun, bar noon-1.30am Tue-Sat, 12.30-4pm Sun, closed Sun Jul & Aug; Ⓜ Antón Martín) One of the most atmospheric old *tabernas* of Madrid, Casa Alberto has been around since 1827 and occupies a building where Cervantes is said to have written one of his books. The secret to its staying power is vermouth on tap, excellent tapas at the bar and fine sit-down meals.

Vinos González Tapas **€€**

(Map p46; ☎91 429 56 18; www.casagonzalez.es; Calle de León 12; tapas from €5, raciones €9-18; ⏰9.30am-midnight Mon-Thu, to 1am Fri & Sat, 11.30am-5pm Sun; Ⓜ Antón Martín) This is our sort of deli, one that combines the full-display benefits of a deli with the sit-down comforts of a tapas bar. On offer is a tempting array of local and international cheeses, cured meats and other typically Spanish delicacies. The tables are informal, cafe style, and we recommend lingering.

Los Gatos Tapas **€€**

(Map p46; ☎91 429 30 67; Calle de Jesús 2; tapas from €4; ⏰11am-2am; Ⓜ Antón Martín) Tapas you can point to without deciphering the

Casa Toni

Calle de Ponzano

There is no more happening street in Madrid right now than Chamberí's Calle de Ponzano. For drinking, **El Sainete** (☎91 445 63 62; https://elsainete.com; Calle de Ponzano 6; �ww11pm-1am Tue-Thu, to 2am Fri & Sat, to 5pm Sun; ⓂAlonso Cano), with its craft beers, and **Taberna Averías** (☎91 603 34 50; www.tabernaaverias.com; Calle de Ponzano 16; � 7pm-12.30am Mon-Wed, 12-4pm & 7pm-12.30am Thu, 12pm-1am Fri-Sun; ⓂAlonso Cano) for wine are good choices. **Catarsis** (☎663 725124; Calle de Ponzano 14; ☐5pm-2am Tue-Sun; ⓂAlonso Cano) is one of Madrid's more creative cocktail bars.

For tapas, start with **Bodega de la Ardosa** (☎91 446 58 94; Calle de Santa Engracia 70; raciones from €7; ☐9am-3pm & 6-11.30pm Thu-Tue; Ⓜ Iglesia) or **Alma Cheli** (☎91 517 28 27; www.almacheli.com; Calle de Santa Engracia 103; mains €8-20; ☐noon-midnight Sun-Thu, to 1.30am Fri & Sat; ⓂAlonso Cano). **Sala de Despiece** (☎91 752 61 06; www.saladedespiece.com; Calle de Ponzano 11; mains €7.50-25; ☐1-5pm & 7.30pm-midnight Sun-Thu, 1-5.30pm & 7.30pm-1am Fri & Sat; ⓂAlonso Cano) and **Le Qualité Tasca** (☎683 510538; www.lequalitetasca.com; Calle de Ponzano 48; raciones €15-25; ☐8.30-11.30pm Tue & Wed, 1pm-midnight Thu, 1pm-1.30am Fri & Sat, 1-11pm Sun; ⓂRíos Rosas) are among the street's best. For a slice of urban Andalucía in Madrid, there's **Bienmesabe** (☎91 827 52 42; https://tabernasbienmesabe.com/en; Calle de Santa Engracia 72; mains €11-23; ☐1pm-1am Sun-Wed, to 2am Thu-Sat; Ⓜ Iglesia, Alonso Cano).

Bodega de la Ardosa

menu and eclectic old-world decor (from bullfighting memorabilia to a fresco of skeletons at the bar) make this a popular choice down the bottom end of Huertas. The most popular orders are the *canapés* (tapas on toast), which, we have to say, are rather delicious.

Gran Clavel   Spanish €€
(Map p52; ☎91 524 23 05; www.granclavel. com; Gran Vía 11; mains €9-19; ☐1-4pm Mon-Sat; ⓂGran Vía) The mainstay of lunches for many *madrileños* are called *casas de comidas* – restaurants serving home cooking. This *casa de comidas* is an upmarket version of the genre, serving high-class *cocido*, rice dishes and *bacalao*. It's inside the Iberostars hotel, and it's one of our favourite lunch choices in the centre.

Lhardy   Spanish €€€
(Map p46; ☎91 521 33 85; www.lhardy.com; Carrera de San Jerónimo 8; mains €26-40, set menus €59-78; ☐1-3.30pm & 8.30-11pm Mon-Sat, 1-3.30pm Sun, closed Aug; ⓂSol, Sevilla) This Madrid landmark (since 1839) is an elegant treasure trove of takeaway gourmet tapas downstairs and six dining areas upstairs that are the upmarket preserve of traditional Madrid dishes with an occasional hint of French influence. House specialities include *cocido a la madrileña* (€36.50), pheasant, and wild duck in an orange perfume. The quality and service are unimpeachable.

Paco Roncero Restaurante   Spanish €€€
(Map p46; ☎91 532 12 75; www.casinode madrid. es; Calle de Alcalá 15; mains €44-56, set menus €80-195; ☐1-4pm & 9pm-midnight Mon-Sat; ⓂSevilla) Perched atop the lavish Casino de Madrid building, this temple of haute cuisine is the proud bearer of two Michelin stars and is presided over by celebrity chef Paco Roncero. It's all about culinary experimentation, with a menu that changes as each new idea emerges from the laboratory and moves into the kitchen. The *menú de degustación* (€155) is a fabulous avalanche of tastes.

Gofio
Spanish €€€

(Map p46; ☑91 599 44 04; www.gofiorestaurant.com; Calle de Lope de Vega 9; set menus €50-80; ⊗1.30-4pm & 8.30pm-midnight Wed-Sun; Ⓜ Antón Martín) Michelin-starred Gofio brings to the capital a whole cookbook full of innovative takes on traditional recipes from the Canary Islands. Two set menus take you on different journeys through the islands' cuisine, as conceived by chef Cícero Canary. Advance reservations recommended.

🍴 El Retiro & the Art Museums

Condumios
Tapas €

(Map p48; ☑91 805 74 04; www.condumios.es; Calle de Juan de Mena 12; mains €8-17; ⊗8am-5pm Mon, 10am-midnight Tue-Sat; Ⓜ Banco de España) One of our favourite bars anywhere in the area, this terrific place does all manner of Spanish staples – try the *croquetas de jamón y gambas al ajillo* (ham and garlic-prawn croquettes). The wine list is excellent.

Estado Puro
Tapas €€

(Map p48; ☑91 330 24 00; www.tapasenestadopuro.com; Plaza de Neptuno (Plaza de Cánovas del Castillo) 4; tapas €4-14; ⊗noon-midnight; Ⓜ Banco de España, Estación del Arte) A slick but casual tapas bar, Estado Puro serves up fantastic tapas that push the boundaries of traditional recipes. It's known for many things, among them splendid *croquetas* (with *jamón*, bull's tail or wild mushrooms). The kitchen is overseen by Paco Roncero, head chef at Paco Roncero Restaurante, who learned his trade with master chef Ferran Adrià.

🍴 Salamanca

Casa Dani
Spanish €

(☑91 575 59 25; Calle de Ayala 28, Mercado de la Paz; tapas/mains from €3/8; ⊗7am-8pm Mon-Fri, to 5pm Sat; Ⓜ Serrano) Deep in Salamanca's Mercado de la Paz, Casa Dani is a wildly popular spot for lunch and it gets going earlier than most: most weekdays, there's a queue at 1pm. But any time is good for the homemade *tortilla de patatas* (potato-and-onion omelette), which is

ℹ What's On in Madrid?

EsMadrid Magazine (www.esmadrid.com) Monthly tourist-office listings.

Guía del Ocio (www.guiadelocio.com) Weekly magazine available for €1 at news kiosks.

Metrópoli (www.elmundo.es/metropoli) *El Mundo* newspaper's Friday supplement magazine.

La Noche en Vivo (www.lanocheenvivo.com) Live-music listings.

Newstand in Madrid
MACH PHOTOS/SHUTTERSTOCK ©

among Madrid's best. Pull up a bar stool if you don't fancy waiting for a table.

Street XO
Tapas €€

(Map p52; ☑91 531 98 84; www.streetxo.com; Calle de Serrano 52, El Corte Inglés; mains €8-30; ⊗1.30-4pm & 8.30-11pm Mon-Wed, 1.30-4pm & 8-11.30pm Thu, 1.30-4.30pm & 8-11.30pm Fri & Sat, 1.30-4.30pm & 8.30-11pm Sun; Ⓜ Serrano) After the success of his Michelin-starred DiverXO, Dabiz Muñoz has opened a more accessible but equally creative street-food version. There's always a queue (cocktail orders are taken while you wait), and the dishes are an endless cast of surprises, as you'd expect from one Spain's most restless and talented chefs.

Platea
Spanish €€

(Map p52; ☑91 577 00 25; www.plateamadrid.com; Calle de Goya 5-7; ⊗noon-12.30am Sun-Wed, to 2.30am Thu-Sat; Ⓜ Serrano, Colón) The ornate Carlos III cinema opposite the Plaza de Colón has been artfully transformed into a dynamic culinary scene with more than a hint of burlesque. There are 12 restaurants, three gourmet food stores and cocktail bars.

Astrolabius
Fusion €€

(✐91 562 06 11; www.astrolabiusmadrid.com; Calle de Serrano 118; mains €7-22; ⊙1-4pm & 8.30pm-midnight Tue-Sat, closed Aug; MNúñez de Balboa) This terrific family-run place in Salamanca's north has a simple philosophy – take grandmother's recipes and filter them through the imagination of the grandchildren. The result is a fabulous mix of flavours that changes regularly. The atmosphere is edgy and modern, but casual in the best Madrid sense.

Malasaña & Chueca

Bazaar
Spanish €

(Map p52; ✐91 523 39 05; Calle de la Libertad 21; mains €8.30-14; ⊙1-11.30pm Sun-Wed, to midnight Thu-Sat; MChueca) Bazaar's popularity among the well-heeled Chueca set shows no sign of abating. Its pristine white interior design, with theatre-style lighting and wall-length windows, may draw a crowd that looks like it stepped out of the pages of ¡Hola! magazine, but the food is extremely well priced and innovative, and the atmosphere is casual.

Pez Tortilla
Tapas €

(Map p52; ✐653 919984; www.peztortilla.com; Calle del Pez 36; tapas from €4; ⊙6pm-1am Mon-Wed, noon-1.30am Thu, to 2.30am Fri & Sat, to 1am Sun; MNoviciado) Every time we come here, this place is full to bursting, which is not surprising given its philosophy of great tortilla (15 kinds!), splendid croquetas (croquettes) and craft beers (more than 70 varieties, with nine on tap). The croquetas with black squid ink or the tortilla with truffle brie and jamón (ham) are two stars among many.

Casa Julio
Spanish €

(Map p52; ✐91 522 72 74; Calle de la Madera 37; 6/12 croquetas €6/12; ⊙1.30-3.30pm & 6.30-11pm Mon-Sat Sep-Jul; MTribunal) A citywide poll for the best croquetas (croquettes) in Madrid would see half of those polled voting for Casa Julio and the remainder not doing so only because they haven't been yet. They're that good that celebrities and mere mortals from all over Madrid come here to sample the traditional jamón (ham) variety or more creative versions such as spinach with gorgonzola.

Albur
Tapas €€

(Map p52; ✐91 594 27 33; www.restaurante albur.com; Calle de Manuela Malasaña 15; mains €13-26; ⊙12.30-5pm & 7.30pm-midnight Mon-Thu, 12.30-5pm & 7.30pm-1.30am Fri, 1pm-1.30am Sat, to midnight Sun; ᐟ; MBilbao) One of Malasaña's best deals, this place has a wildly popular tapas bar and a classy but casual restaurant out the back. The restaurant waiters never seem to lose their cool, and the well-priced rice dishes are the stars of the show, although in truth you could order anything here and leave satisfied.

La Carmencita
Spanish €€

(Map p52; ✐91 531 09 11; www.tabernala carmencita.es; Calle de la Libertad 16; mains €14-25; ⊙9am-2am; MChueca) Around since 1854, La Carmencita is the bar where legendary poet Pablo Neruda was once a regular. The folk of La Carmencita have taken 75 of their favourite traditional Spanish recipes and brought them to the table, sometimes with a little updating but more often safe in the knowledge that nothing needs changing.

La Barraca
Valencian €€

(Map p52; ✐91 532 71 54; www.labarraca.es; Calle de la Reina 29; mains €15-22; ⊙1.30-4pm & 8-11.30pm; MGran Vía) The place to come for a real paella, not the tourist version too often found in Madrid, La Barraca has been serving down-home Valencian cooking in the capital since 1935. Try el esgarrat con aceite de oliva (roasted red peppers with cod) and, of course, what many believe to be the best paella in Madrid.

Frida
International €€

(Map p52; ✐91 704 82 86; http://frida madrid. com; Calle de San Gregorio 8; mains €10-17; ⊙9am-1am Mon-Fri, 10am-2am Sat & Sun;

MChueca) What a lovely little spot this is. Set on a tiny square, its wooden tables flooded with natural light through the big windows, Frida is ideal for a casual bite, a quietly intimate meal or simply an afternoon spent reading the papers. Food is simple but tasty – designer pizzas, tajine, kebab...

La Tasquita de Enfrente
Spanish €€€

(Map p52; ☑91 532 54 49; Calle de la Ballesta 6; mains €24-38, set menus €79; ☺1.30-4.30pm & 8.30pm-midnight Mon-Sat; MGran Vía) It's difficult to overstate how popular this place is among people in the know in Madrid's food scene. The seasonal menu prepared by chef Juanjo López never ceases to surprise while also combining simple Spanish staples to stunning effect. The *menú de degustación* (tasting menu; €79) would be our choice for first-timers. Reservations are essential.

🍷 DRINKING & NIGHTLIFE

Nights in the Spanish capital are the stuff of legend. They're invariably long and loud most days of the week, rising to a deafening crescendo as the weekend nears. Two excellent options are hitting the cocktail bars of Chueca or heading for beers and tapas on happening Calle de Ponzano (see p58).

🍸 Plaza Mayor & Royal Madrid

Teatro Joy Eslava
Club

(Joy Madrid; Map p46; ☑91 366 37 33; www.joy-eslava.com; Calle del Arenal 11; €10-18; ☺11.30pm-6am; MSol) The only things guaranteed at this grand old Madrid dance club (housed in a 19th-century theatre) are a crowd and the fact that it'll be open (it's operated just about every day since 1981). The music and the crowd are a mixed bag, but queues are long and invariably include locals, tourists and the occasional *famoso* (celebrity).

🍸 Chueca Cocktail Bars

A defining feature of a night out in Chueca is the proliferation of high-end cocktail bars. **Museo Chicote** (Map p52; ☑91 532 67 37; www.museochicote.com; Gran Vía 12; ☺1pm-3am Mon-Sat, to 1am Sun; MGran Vía), as famous for its history at the cutting-edge of cocktail mixing as for its A-list clientele down through the decades, continues to be the king of Madrid cocktail bars, with a really cool soundtrack thrown in. Just around the corner, **Bar Cock** (Map p52; ☑91 532 28 26; www.barcock.com; Calle de la Reina 16; ☺7pm-3am Mon-Thu, to 3.30am Fri & Sat; MGran Vía) and **Del Diego** (Map p52; ☑91 523 31 06; www.deldiego.com; Calle de la Reina 12; ☺7pm-3am Mon-Thu, to 3.30am Fri & Sat; MGran Vía) both draw a similar crowd, with top-class cocktails and bow-tied waiters to serve them. If your tastes are a little more specific, there's **Gin Club** (El Mercado de la Reina; Map p52; ☑91 521 31 98; www.grupomer cadodelareina.com; Gran Vía 12; ☺1.30pm-2am Sun-Thu, to 2.30am Fri & Sat; MBanco de España) just down the street, or **Cafe Belén** (Map p52; ☑91 308 27 47; www.elcafebelen.com; Calle de Belén 5; ☺3.30pm-3am Tue-Thu, to 3.30am Fri & Sat, to 10pm Sun; ☎; MChueca) for some of Madrid's best *mojitos*.

For something a little more experimental and hand-made cocktails of the utmost quality and originality, it has to be **Macera** (Map p52; ☑91 011 58 10; www.maceradrinks.com; Calle de San Mateo 21; ☺1pm-1am Tue & Wed, to 2am Thu, to 3.30am Fri & Sat, 4-11pm Sun; MAlonso Martínez). Just across the road, **Lola09** (Map p52; ☑91 310 66 95; www.lola09.com; Calle de San Mateo 28; ☺5.30pm-1am Mon, to 1.30am Tue & Wed, to 2am Thu, 4.30pm-2.30am Fri & Sat, 5pm-1am Sun; MAlonso Martínez) has a cult following for its in-house creations.

From left: Teatro Joy Eslava (p61); Chocolatería de San Ginés; Estadio Santiago Bernabéu (p65)

Chocolatería de San Ginés   Cafe

(Map p46; ☎91 365 65 46; www.chocolateria
sangines.com; Pasadizo de San Ginés 5; ◷24hr;
Ⓜ Sol) One of the grand icons of the Madrid
night, this *chocolate con churros* (Spanish
doughnuts with chocolate) cafe sees a
sprinkling of tourists throughout the day,
but locals pack it out in their search for
sustenance on their way home from a
nightclub somewhere close to dawn. Only
in Madrid...

Plaza Menor   Cocktail Bar

(Map p46; ☎665 813821; Calle de Gómez de Mora
3; ◷6pm-1am Mon-Fri, 4pm-2.30am Sat & Sun;
Ⓜ La Latina, Sol) Killer cakes backed by killer
cocktails served in a subterranean cavern
frequented by in-the-know locals – Plaza
Menor is a fab place for an intimate drink;
good tapas as well.

🅞 La Latina & Lavapiés

Taberna El Tempranillo   Wine Bar

(Map p46; ☎91 364 15 32; Calle de la Cava
Baja 38; ◷1-4pm Mon, 1-4pm & 8pm-midnight
Tue-Sun; Ⓜ La Latina) You could come here
for the tapas, but we recommend Taberna

El Tempranillo especially for its wines, of
which it has a selection that puts numerous
Spanish bars to shame. It's not a late-night
place, but it's always packed in the early
evening and on Sunday after El Rastro.
Many wines are sold by the glass.

Delic   Bar

(Map p46; ☎91 364 54 50; www.delic.es; Costanilla de San Andrés 14; ◷11am-2am Sun & Tue-
Thu, to 2.30am Fri & Sat; Ⓜ La Latina) We could
go on for hours about this long-standing
cafe-bar, but we'll reduce it to its most
basic elements: nursing an exceptionally
good mojito or three on a warm summer's
evening at Delic's outdoor tables on one
of Madrid's prettiest plazas is one of life's
great pleasures. Bliss.

🅞 Sol, Santa Ana & Huertas

La Venencia   Bar

(Map p46; ☎91 429 73 13; Calle de Echegaray
7; ◷12.30-3.30pm & 7.30pm-1.30am; Ⓜ Sol,
Sevilla) La Venencia is a *barrio* classic, with
manzanilla (chamomile-coloured sherry)
from Sanlúcar and sherry from Jeréz
poured straight from the dusty wooden

barrels, accompanied by a small selection of tapas with an Andalucian bent. There's no music, no flashy decorations; here it's all about you, your *fino* (sherry) and your friends.

Taberna La Dolores — Bar

(Map p46; ☎91 429 22 43; Plaza de Jesús 4; ⏱11am-1am; Ⓜ Antón Martín) Old bottles and beer mugs line the shelves behind the bar at this Madrid institution (1908), known for its blue-and-white-tiled exterior and a 30-something crowd that often includes the odd *famoso* or two. It claims to be 'the most famous bar in Madrid' – that's pushing it, but it's invariably full most nights of the week, so who are we to argue?

La Azotea — Lounge

(Map p46; ☎91 530 17 61; www.azoteadelcir culo.com; Calle Marqués de Casa Riera 2, 7th fl; €4; ⏱9am-2am Mon-Thu, to 2.30am Fri, 11am-2.30am Sat & Sun; Ⓜ Banco de España, Sevilla) Order a cocktail, then lie down on the cushions and admire the vista from this fabulous rooftop terrace. It's a brilliant place to chill out, with the views at their best close to sunset.

Salmón Gurú — Cocktail Bar

(Map p46; ☎91 000 61 85; www.salmonguru.es; Calle de Echegaray 21; ⏱5pm-2.30am Wed-Sun; Ⓜ Antón Martín) When Sergi Arola's empire collapsed and the celebrated Le Cabrera cocktail bar went with it, Madrid lost one of its best cocktail maestros, Diego Cabrera. Thankfully, he's back with a wonderful multifaceted space where he serves up a masterful collection of drinks – work your way through his menu of 25 Cabrera *clásicos* to get started.

El Imperfecto — Cocktail Bar

(Map p46; ☎680 904436; www.facebook.com/ elimperfectobar; Plaza de Matute 2; ⏱3pm-2am; Ⓜ Antón Martín) Its name notwithstanding, the 'Imperfect One' is our ideal Huertas bar, with occasional live jazz and a drinks menu as long as a saxophone, ranging from cocktails and spirits to milkshakes, teas and creative coffees. Its pina colada is one of the best we've tasted and the atmosphere is agreeably buzzy yet chilled.

🍸 Malasaña & Chueca

1862 Dry Bar
Cocktail Bar

(Map p52; 📞609 531151; www.facebook.
com/1862DryBar; Calle del Pez 27; ⏰3.30pm-
2am Sun-Thu, to 2.30am Fri & Sat; Ⓜ Noviciado)
Great cocktails, muted early-20th-century
decor and a refined air make this one of our
favourite bars down Malasaña's southern
end. Prices are reasonable, the cocktail list
extensive and new cocktails appear every
month.

Café-Restaurante El Espejo
Cafe

(Map p52; 📞91 308 23 47; Paseo de los Recoletos
31; ⏰8am-midnight Mon-Fri, from 9am Sat &
Sun; Ⓜ Colón) Once a haunt of writers and
intellectuals, this architectural gem blends
Modernista and art-deco styles, and its interior could well overwhelm you with all the
mirrors, chandeliers and bow-tied service
of another era. The atmosphere is suitably
quiet and refined, although our favourite
corner is the elegant glass pavilion out on
Paseo de los Recoletos.

Gran Café de Gijón
Cafe

(Map p52; 📞91 521 54 25; www.cafegijon.
com; Paseo de los Recoletos 21; ⏰7am-1.30am;
Ⓜ Chueca, Banco de España) This graceful old
cafe has been serving coffee and meals
since 1888 and has long been favoured by
Madrid's literati for a drink or a meal – *all* of
Spain's great 20th-century literary figures
came here for coffee and *tertulias* (literary
and philosophical discussions). You'll find
yourself among intellectuals, conservative
Franco diehards and young *madrileños*
looking for a quiet drink.

Nice to Meet You
Bar

(Map p52; 📞638 908559; www.dearhotel
madrid.com/en/nice-to-meet-you; Gran Vía 80,
Dear Hotel, 14th fl; ⏰noon-1.30am Sun-Thu,
to 2.30am Fri & Sat; Ⓜ Plaza de España) This
rooftop bar occupying the top floor of
Dear Hotel has a spectacular view of Plaza
España and Malasaña. Come any time of
day to sit down with a cocktail and enjoy
the view, or try something to eat – food
specialities include Mediterranean staples

like cod and ox steak. The ultra-cool lounge
opens from 9pm.

Why Not?
Club

(Map p52; 📞91 521 80 34; Calle de San Bartolomé
7; €10; ⏰10.30pm-6am; Ⓜ Chueca) Underground, narrow and packed with bodies,
gay-friendly Why Not? is the sort of place
where nothing's left to the imagination (the
gay and straight crowd who come here are
pretty amorous) and it's full nearly every
night of the week. Pop and Top 40 music
are the standard, and the dancing crowd is
mixed but all serious about having a good
time.

🎭 ENTERTAINMENT

⭐ Live Music & Flamenco

Teatro Flamenco Madrid
Flamenco

(Map p52; 📞91 159 20 05; www.teatroflamenco
madrid.com; Calle del Pez 10; adult/student &
senior/child €27/18/14; ⏰6.30pm & 8.15pm
Sun-Fri, 6.30pm, 8.15pm & 10pm Sat; Ⓜ Noviciado) This excellent new flamenco venue
is a terrific deal. With a focus on quality
flamenco (dance, song and guitar) rather
than the more formal meal-and-floor-show
package of the *tablaos* (choreographed
flamenco shows), and with a mixed crowd
of locals and tourists, it generates a terrific
atmosphere most nights for the hour-long
show. Prices are also a notch below what
you'll pay elsewhere.

Casa Patas
Flamenco

(Map p46; 📞91 369 04 96; www.casapatas.com;
Calle de Cañizares 10; admission incl drink €40;
⏰shows 10.30pm Mon-Thu, 8pm & 10.30pm Fri &
Sat; Ⓜ Antón Martín, Tirso de Molina) One of the
top flamenco stages in Madrid, this *tablao*
always offers flawless quality that serves as
a good introduction to the art. It's not the
friendliest place in town, especially if you're
only here for the show, and you're likely to
be crammed in a little, but no one complains
about the standard of the performances.

Corral de la Morería
Flamenco

(Map p46; 📞91 365 84 46; www.corraldela
moreria.com; Calle de la Morería 17; admission incl

drink from €50; ⊘shows 7.30pm & 9.30pm Sun-Thu, 8pm & 10.45pm Fri & Sat; MÓpera) This is one of the most prestigious flamenco stages in Madrid, with 50 years of experience as a leading venue and top performers most nights. The stage area has a rustic feel, and tables are pushed up close. Unusually for Madrid's *tablaos*, the Michelin-starred restaurant is excellent. Set menus from €44 (additional to the admission fee).

Las Tablas   Flamenco
(☑91 542 05 20; www.lastablasmadrid.com; Plaza de España 9; admission incl drink/meal from €29/66; ⊘shows 7pm & 9pm; MPlaza de España) Las Tablas has a reputation for quality flamenco and reasonable prices; it's among the best choices in town. Most nights you'll see a classic flamenco show, with plenty of throaty singing and soul-baring dancing. Antonia Moya and Marisol Navarro, leading lights in the flamenco world, are regular performers here.

Café Central   Jazz
(Map p46; ☑91 369 41 43; www.cafecentral madrid.com; Plaza del Ángel 10; €15-20; ⊘11.30pm-2.30am Sun-Thu, to 3.30am Fri & Sat, shows 9pm; MAntón Martín, Sol) In 2011, the respected jazz magazine *Down Beat* included this art-deco bar on its list of the world's best jazz clubs, the only place in Spain to earn the prestigious accolade (said by some to be the jazz equivalent of earning a Michelin star). With well over 1000 gigs under its belt, it rarely misses a beat.

Sala El Sol   Live Music
(Map p52; ☑91 532 64 90; www.salaelsol.com; Calle de los Jardines 3; admission incl drink €10, concert tickets €6-30; ⊘midnight-5.30am Tue-Sat Jul-Sep; MGran Vía) Madrid institutions don't come any more beloved than the terrific Sala El Sol. It opened in 1979, just in time for *la movida madrileña*, and quickly established itself as a leading stage for all the icons of the era, such as Nacha Pop and Alaska y los Pegamoides.

⚽ Football
Estadio Santiago Bernabéu   Football
(☑902 324324; www.realmadrid.com; Avenida de Concha Espina 1; tickets from €40; MSantiago Bernabéu) Watching Real Madrid play is one of football's greatest experiences, but tickets are difficult to find. They can be purchased online, by phone or in person from the ticket office at gate 42 on Avenida de Concha Espina; turn up early in the week before a scheduled game. Numerous online ticketing agencies also sell tickets. Otherwise, you'll need to take a risk with scalpers. Tours are also available.

ℹ INFORMATION
Centro de Turismo de Madrid (Map p46; ☑91 578 78 10; www.esmadrid.com; Plaza Mayor 27; ⊘9.30am-9.30pm; MSol) The Madrid government's Centro de Turismo is terrific. Housed in the Real Casa de la Panadería on the north side of the Plaza Mayor, it has helpful staff. The website offers free downloads of the metro map to your mobile phone.

Punto de Información Turística Plaza del Callao (Map p52; www.esmadrid.com; Plaza del Callao; ⊘9.30am-8.30pm; MCallao)

Punto de Información Turística Palacio Real (Map p46; Calle de Bailén; ⊘9.30am-8.30pm; MÓpera, Plaza de España)

Punto de Información Turística CentroCentro (Map p48; ☑91 454 44 10; Plaza de la Cibeles 1; ⊘10am-8pm Tue-Sun; MBanco de España)

Punto de Información Turística Paseo del Prado (Map p48; ☑91 578 78 10; Plaza de Neptuno; ⊘9.30am-9.30pm; MAtocha)

Punto de Información Turística Reina Sofía (Map p48; www.esmadrid.com; Calle de Santa Isabel 52; ⊘9.30am-8.30pm; MEstación del Arte)

Punto de Información Turística Estadio Santiago Bernabéu (Paseo de la Castellana 138; ⊘9.30am-8.30pm; MSantiago Bernabéu)

Punto de Información Turística Adolfo Suárez Madrid-Barajas T2 (between Salas 5 & 6; ⊘9am-8pm; MAeropuerto T1, T2 & T3)

Metro & Bus Tickets

When travelling on Madrid's metro and bus services, visitors have two options.

Tarjeta Multi (Visitors)

Visitors travelling on the city's public transport system require a **Tarjeta Multi**, a rechargeable card that can be purchased for a one-off €2.50 at machines in all metro stations, *estancos* (tobacconists) and other authorised sales points. Like with London's Oyster Card, you top up your account at machines in all metro stations and *estancos*, and touch-on and touch-off every time you travel. Options include 10 rides (bus and metro) for €12.20 or a single-journey ticket for €1.50.

Tarjeta Turística

The handy **Tarjeta Turística** (Tourist Pass) allows for unlimited travel on public transport across the Comunidad de Madrid (Community of Madrid) for tourists. You'll need to present your passport or national identity card and tickets can be purchased at all metro stations. Passes are available for one/two/three/five/seven days for €8.40/14.20/18.40/26.80/35.40.

IVAN MARC/SHUTTERSTOCK ©

Punto de Información Turística Adolfo Suárez Madrid-Barajas T4 (Salas 10 & 11; ⊙9am-8pm; Ⓜ Aeropuerto T4)

🛈 GETTING THERE & AWAY

AIR

Madrid's **Adolfo Suárez Madrid-Barajas Airport** (☑902 404704; www.aena.es; Ⓜ Aeropuerto T1, T2 & T3, Aeropuerto T4) lies 15km northeast of the city and it's Europe's sixth-busiest hub, with almost 50 million passengers passing through every year.

Barajas has four terminals. Terminal 4 (T4) deals mainly with flights by Iberia and its partners, while the remainder leave from the conjoined T1, T2 and (rarely) T3.

There are car-rental services, ATMs, money-exchange bureaus, pharmacies, tourist offices, left luggage offices and parking services at T1, T2 and T4.

BUS

Estación Sur de Autobuses (☑91 468 42 00; Calle de Méndez Álvaro 83; Ⓜ Méndez Álvaro), just south of the M30 ring road, is the city's principal bus station. It serves most destinations to the south and many in other parts of the country. Most bus companies have a ticket office here, even if their buses depart from elsewhere.

TRAIN

Madrid is served by two main train stations. The bigger of the two is **Puerta de Atocha** (Avenida de la Ciudad de Barcelona; Ⓜ Atocha Renfe), at the southern end of the city centre, while **Chamartín** (☑91 243 23 43; Paseo de la Castellana; Ⓜ Chamartín) lies in the north of the city. The bulk of trains for Spanish destinations depart from Atocha, especially those going south. International services arrive at and leave from Chamartín. For bookings, contact **Renfe** (☑91 232 03 20; www.renfe.com).

There are different types of service, but remember that saving a couple of hours on a faster train can mean a big hike in the fare. Most trains have *preferente* (1st class) and *turista* (2nd class) and have dining cars. High-speed **Tren de Alta Velocidad Española (AVE)** services connect Madrid with Albacete, Barcelona, Burgos, Cádiz, Córdoba, Cuenca, Huesca, León, Lérida, Málaga, Palencia, Salamanca, Santiago de

Compostela, Seville, Valencia, Valladolid, Zamora and Zaragoza. In coming years, Madrid–Bilbao should also start up, and travel times to Galicia should fall. The same goes for Madrid–Granada and Madrid–Badajoz. AVE trains can reach speeds of 350km/h.

❶ GETTING AROUND

Passes for the bus and metro can be bought in stations and some shops (see p65)

TO/FROM THE AIRPORT

BUS

The **Exprés Aeropuerto** (Airport Express; www. emtmadrid.es; per person €5; ⊙24hr; ☎) runs between Puerta de Atocha train station and the airport. From 11.30pm until 6am, departures are from the Plaza de Cibeles, not the train station. Departures take place every 13 to 20 minutes from the station or at night-time every 35 minutes from Plaza de Cibeles.

A free bus service connects all four airport terminals.

METRO

One of the easiest ways into town from the airport is line 8 of the metro to the Nuevos Ministerios transport interchange, which connects with lines 10 and 6 and the local overground *cercanías* (local trains serving suburbs and nearby towns). It operates from 6.05am to 1.30am. A single ticket costs €4.50 including the €3 airport supplement. If you're charging your public transport card with a 10-ride Metrobús ticket (€12.20), you'll need to top it up with the €3 supplement if you're travelling to/from the airport. The journey to Nuevos Ministerios takes around 15 minutes, around 25 minutes from T4.

TAXI

A taxi to the centre (around 30 minutes, depending on traffic; 35 to 40 minutes from T4) costs a fixed €30 for anywhere inside the M30 motorway (which includes all of downtown Madrid). There's a minimum €20, even if you're only going to an airport hotel.

BUS

Buses operated by **Empresa Municipal de Transportes de Madrid** (EMT; ☎902 507850; www.emtmadrid.es) travel along most city routes regularly between about 6.30am and 11.30pm. Twenty-six night-bus *búhos* (owls) routes operate from 11.45pm to 5.30am, with all routes originating in Plaza de la Cibeles.

METRO

Madrid's modern metro (www.metromadrid.es), Europe's second largest, is a fast, efficient and safe way to navigate the city, and generally easier than getting to grips with bus routes. There are 11 colour-coded lines in central Madrid, in addition to the modern southern suburban MetroSur system, as well as lines heading east to the population centres of Pozuelo and Boadilla del Monte. Colour maps showing the metro system are available from any metro station or online. The metro operates from 6.05am to 1.30am.

TAXI

The daytime meter starts at €2.40 in Madrid, and €2.90 between 9pm and 7am and on weekends and holidays. You then pay €1.05 to €1.20 per kilometre depending on the time of day. Several supplementary charges, usually posted inside the taxi, apply. These include: €5.50 to/from the airport (if you're not paying the fixed rate); €3 from taxi ranks at train and bus stations; €3 to/from the Parque Ferial Juan Carlos I; and €6.70 on New Year's Eve and Christmas Eve from 10pm to 6am. There's no charge for luggage.

Among the 24-hour taxi services is **Tele-Taxi** (☎91 371 21 31; www.tele-taxi.es; ⊙24hr).

A green light on the roof means the taxi is *libre* (available). Usually a sign to this effect is also placed in the lower passenger side of the windscreen.

Tipping taxi drivers is not common practice, though rounding fares up to the nearest euro or two doesn't hurt.

Barcelona at a Glance...

Barcelona is a mix of sunny Mediterranean charm and European urban style. The city bursts with art and architecture, Catalan cooking is among the country's best, summer sun seekers fill the beaches in and beyond the city, and the bars and clubs heave year-round. Vestiges of Barcelona's days as a middle-ranking Roman town remain, and its old centre has one of Europe's richest concentrations of Gothic architecture. Elsewhere are some of the world's more bizarre buildings: surreal spectacles capped by Gaudí's La Sagrada Família. Equally worth seeking out are the city's avant-garde chefs, who compete with old-time classics for the gourmet's attention.

Barcelona in Two Days

Start with the Barri Gòtic. After a stroll along **La Rambla** (p76), admire **La Catedral** (p87) and the **Museu d'Història de Barcelona** (p87) on historic **Plaça del Rei** (p86), then visit the **Basilica de Santa Maria del Mar** (p91), and the nearby **Museu Picasso** (p91). Round off with a meal and cocktails in El Born. On day two, experience **Park Güell** (p92) and **La Sagrada Família** (p73). Afterwards, go for dinner at **Casa Delfín** (p98) followed by drinks at **Bar Marsella** (p103).

Barcelona in Four Days

Start the third day with more Gaudí, visiting **Casa Batlló** (p80) and **La Pedrera** (p80), followed by beachside relaxation and seafood in Barceloneta. Day four should be dedicated to Montjuïc, with its museums, galleries, fortress, gardens and Olympic stadium.

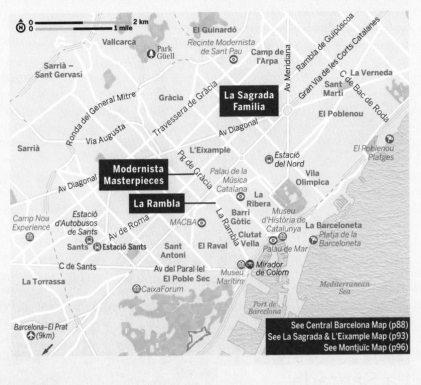

N
2 km
1 mile

El Guinardó

Vallcarca
Park Güell

Recinte Modernista de Sant Pau

Camp de l'Arpa

Rambla de Guipúscoa

Gran Via de les Corts Catalanes

Sarrià – Sant Gervasi

La Verneda

Sant Martí

Ronda del General Mitre

Gràcia

Travessera de Gràcia

La Sagrada Família

Av Meridiana

C de Bac de Roda

El Poblenou

Via Augusta

Av Diagonal

Sarrià

L'Eixample

El Poblenou Platges

Av Diagonal

Pg de Gràcia

Estació del Nord

Modernista Masterpieces

Palau de la Música Catalana

Vila Olímpica

La Rambla

La Ribera

Camp Nou Experience

Estació d'Autobusos de Sants

Av de Roma

MACBA

Barri Gòtic

Museu d'Història de Catalunya

La Barceloneta

Platja de la Barceloneta

Sants

Estació Sants

Sant Antoni

El Raval

Ciutat Vella

Palau de Mar

C de Sants

Av del Paral·lel

El Poble Sec

Museu Marítim

Mirador de Colom

Mediterranean Sea

La Torrassa

CaixaForum

Port de Barcelona

Barcelona–El Prat (9km)

See Central Barcelona Map (p88)
See La Sagrada & L'Eixample Map (p93)
See Montjuïc Map (p96)

Arriving in Barcelona

El Prat airport (p106) Frequent *aerobúses* make the 35-minute run into town (€5.90) from 6am to 1am. Taxis cost €25 to €35.

Barcelona Sants Long-distance trains arrive at this large station near the centre of town, which is linked by metro to other parts of the city.

Where to Stay

Barcelona has some fabulous accommodation, but never – and we repeat never – arrive in town without a reservation. Designer digs are something of a Barcelona speciality, with midrange and top-end travellers particularly well served. Apartments are also widespread and a fine alternative to hotels. Prices in Barcelona are generally higher than elsewhere in the country.

MARCO RUBINO/SHUTTERSTOCK ©

La Sagrada Família

If you can only visit one place in Barcelona, this should be it. Still under construction, La Sagrada Família inspires awe by its sheer verticality in the manner of the medieval cathedrals.

Great For...

Don't Miss

The extraordinary pillars and stained glass, the Nativity Facade, the Passion Facade.

Gaudí's Vision

The Temple Expiatori de la Sagrada Família (Expiatory Temple of the Holy Family) was Antoni Gaudí's all-consuming obsession. Commissioned by a conservative society that wished to build a temple as atonement for the city's sins of modernity, Gaudí saw its completion as his holy mission.

He devised a temple 95m long and 60m wide, able to seat 13,000 people, with a central tower 170m high above the transept (representing Christ) and another 17 of 100m or more. The 12 along the three facades represent the Apostles, while the remaining five represent the Virgin Mary and the four evangelists. With his characteristic dislike for straight lines, Gaudí gave his towers swelling outlines inspired by the weird peaks of the holy mountain Montserrat outside Barcelona. At Gaudí's death,

Facade detail

VINDNA CAV/SHUTTERSTOCK©

❶ Need to Know

Map p93; 📞93 208 04 14; www.sagradafamil-ia.org; Carrer de la Marina; adult/child €20/free; ⊙9am-8pm Apr-Sep, to 7pm Mar & Oct, to 6pm Nov-Feb; Ⓜ Sagrada Família

✕ Take a Break

There is nothing of note in the immediate area (it's a hell of tourist pizza joints).

★ Top Tip

Book tickets online to avoid what can be very lengthy queues.

only the crypt, the apse walls, one portal and one tower had been finished.

The Nativity Facade

The Nativity Facade is the artistic pinnacle of the building, mostly created under Gaudí's personal supervision. You can climb high up inside some of the four towers by a combination of lifts and narrow spiral staircases – a vertiginous experience. The towers are destined to hold tubular bells capable of playing complex music at great volume. Their upper parts are decorated with mosaics spelling out 'Sanctus, Sanctus, Sanctus, Hosanna in Excelsis, Amen, Alleluia'.

Passion Facade

The southwest Passion Facade, theme around Christ's last days and death, was built between 1954 and 1978 based on sur-

viving drawings by Gaudí, with four towers and a large, sculpture-bedecked portal. The main series of sculptures, on three levels, are in an S-shaped sequence, starting with the Last Supper at the bottom left and ending with Christ's burial at the top right.

Glory Facade

The Glory Facade is under construction and will, like the others, be crowned by four towers – a total of 12 representing the Twelve Apostles. Gaudí wanted it to be the most magnificent facade of the church. Inside will be the narthex, a kind of foyer made up of 16 'lanterns', a series of hyperboloid forms topped by cones.

Museu Gaudí

The Museu Gaudí, below ground level, includes interesting material on Gaudí's life and other works, as well as models and photos of La Sagrada Família.

La Sagrada Família

A TIMELINE

1882 Construction begins on a neo-Gothic church designed by Francisco de Paula del Villar y Lozano.

1883 Antoni Gaudí takes over as chief architect, completes the ❶ **crypt** and plans a far more ambitious church to hold 13,000.

1909 The Escoles de Gaudí are completed.

1926 Gaudí dies; work continues under Domènec Sugrañes i Gras. Much of the ❷ **apse** and ❸ **Nativity Facade** is complete.

1930 ❹ **Bell towers** of the Nativity Facade completed.

1936 Construction interrupted by Spanish Civil War; anarchists destroy Gaudí's plans.

1939–40 Architect Francesc de Paula Quintana i Vidal restores the crypt and meticulously reassembles many of Gaudí's lost models, some of which can be seen in the ❺ **museum**.

1976 ❻ **Passion Facade** steeples completed.

1986–2006 Sculptor Josep Maria Subirachs adds sculptural details to the Passion Facade, amid much criticism for employing a style far removed from what was thought typical of Gaudí.

2000 ❼ **Central nave vault** completed.

2010 Pope Benedict XVI consecrates the church; work begins on a high-speed rail tunnel that will pass beneath the church's ❽ **Glory Facade**.

2016-2019 Work continues on the five central towers; the Passion Facade is completed in 2018.

2026 Projected completion date.

TOP TIPS

➡ The best light through the stained-glass windows of the Passion Facade bursts into the heart of the church in the late afternoon.

➡ Visit at opening time on weekdays to avoid the worst of the crowds.

➡ Head up the Nativity Facade bell towers for the views.

Spiral Staircase

Nativity Facade
Gaudí used plaster casts of local people and even of the occasional corpse from the local morgue as models for the portraits in the Nativity scene.

Central Nave Vault
30m wide, with lateral naves of 7.5m bringing the total width to 60m. The central dome reaches 65m in height.

Apse
Building started just after the crypt in mostly neo-Gothic style. It is capped by pinnacles that show a hint of the genius that Gaudí would later deploy in the rest of the church.

Bell Towers

The towers of the three facades will represent the Twelve Apostles. Eight are completed. Lifts whisk visitors up one tower of the Nativity and Passion Facades (the latter gets longer queues) for fine views.

NIKADA / GETTY IMAGES ©

4

Completed Church

Along with the Glory Facade, six other towers remain to be completed. They will represent the four evangelists, the Virgin Mary and, soaring above them all over the transept, a 170m colossus symbolising Christ.

3

7

Glory Facade

This will be the most fanciful facade of all, with a narthex boasting 16 hyperboloid lanterns topped by cones that will look something like an organ made of melting ice cream.

8

Museu Gaudí

Jammed with old photos, drawings and restored plaster models that bring Gaudí's ambitions to life, the museum also houses an extraordinarily complex plumb-line device he used to calculate his constructions.

6

5

Escoles de Gaudí

Crypt

The first completed part of the church, the crypt is in largely neo-Gothic style and lies under the transept. Gaudí's burial place here can be glimpsed from the Museu Gaudí.

Passion Facade

See the story of Christ's last days from Last Supper to burial in an S-shaped sequence from bottom to top of the facade. Check out the cryptogram in which the numbers always add up to 33, Christ's age at his death.

YURIY DMITRIENKO / SHUTTERSTOCK ©

MARK PELF/SHUTTERSTOCK©

La Rambla

One of the world's most famous thoroughfares, La Rambla is a stirring vision of Barcelona's polyglot soul. With the Barri Gòtic on one side and gritty El Raval on the other, there's interest at every turn.

Barcelona's most famous street is both a tourist magnet and a window into Catalan culture, with cultural centres, theatres and architecturally intriguing buildings lining its sides. Set between narrow traffic lanes and flanked by plane trees, the middle of La Rambla is a broad pedestrian boulevard, crowded every day until the wee hours with a wide cross section of society. A stroll here is pure sensory overload, with souvenir hawkers, buskers, pavement artists, mimes and living statues all part of the ever changing street scene.

La Font de Canaletes

From Plaça de Catalunya, La Rambla unfurls down the hill to the southeast. Its first manifestation, La Rambla de Canaletes, is named after a pretty 19th-century, wrought-iron fountain, La Font de Canal-

Great For...

Don't Miss

The Mercat de la Boqueria (p86), one of the world's most celebrated markets, on La Rambla's western shore.

Detail of La Font de Canaletes

❶ Need to Know

Metro stations include Catalunya (north), Liceu (middle) and Drassanes (south).

✕ Take a Break

Bar Pinotxo (p97) is a brilliant tapas bar at the Mercat de la Boqueria.

★ Top Tip

Pickpockets and con artists love La Rambla – keep your wits about you.

etes. Local legend says anyone who drinks from its waters will return to Barcelona. More prosaically, delirious football fans gather here to celebrate whenever FC Barcelona wins something.

Bird Market

In keeping with its numerous contradictory impulses, La Rambla changes personality as it gains momentum down the hill. Stalls crowd in from the side as the name changes to La Rambla dels Estudis (officially) or La Rambla dels Ocells (Birds, unofficially) in Barcelona's twittering bird market (under threat from ice-cream and pastry stands), where you'll be serenaded by birdsong.

Plaça de la Boqueria

At around La Rambla's midpoint lies one of Europe's greatest markets, the Mercat de la Boqueria (p86), while almost opposite is your chance to walk on a Miró: the colourful **Mosaïc de Miró** (Map p88; Ⓜ Liceu) in the pavement, with one tile signed by the artist. Look also for the grandiose Gran Teatre del Liceu (p86), then rest in the lovely **Plaça Reial** (Map p88; Ⓜ Liceu). The lamp posts by the central fountain are Antoni Gaudí's first known works in the city.

La Rambla de Santa Monica

The final stretch of La Rambla, La Rambla de Santa Mònica, widens out to approach the **Mirador de Colom** (☑ 93 285 38 34; www.barcelonaturisme.com; Plaça del Portal de la Pau; adult/child €6/4; ⊗ 8.30am-8.30pm; Ⓜ Drassanes) overlooking Port Vell. And just off La Rambla's southwestern tip, don't miss the sublime Museu Marítim (p91).

Casa Amatller and Casa Batlló

ℹ Need to Know

Four metro lines criss-cross L'Eixample, with Passeig de Gràcia and Diagonal the most useful.

✕ Take a Break

Tapas 24 (p100), one of Barcelona's best tapas bars, is close to Casa Batlló.

Modernista Masterpieces

The elegant, if traffic-filled, district of L'Eixample (pronounced 'lay-sham-pluh') is a showcase for Modernista architecture, including some of Gaudí's most treasured masterpieces.

Great For

Don't Miss

Casa Batlló is quite simply one of the weirdest and most wonderful buildings in Spain.

La Pedrera

This undulating beast is another madcap Gaudí **masterpiece** (Casa Milà; Map p93; ✆93 214 25 76; www.lapedrera.com; Passeig de Gràcia 92; adult/child 7-12yr from €25/14; ⊗9am-8.30pm & 9-11pm Mar-Oct, 9am-6.30pm & 7-9pm Nov-Feb; Ⓜ Diagonal), built from 1905 to 1910 as a combined apartment and office block. Formally called Casa Milà it, it is better known as La Pedrera (the Quarry) because of its uneven grey stone facade.

The Fundació Caixa Catalunya has opened the top-floor apartment, attic and roof, together called the Espai Gaudí (Gaudí Space), to visitors. The roof is the most extraordinary element, with its giant chimney pots looking like multicoloured medieval knights. Gaudí wanted to put a tall statue of the Virgin up here, too: when the Milà family said no, he resigned from the project in disgust. The next floor down is the apartment (El Pis de la Pedrera), done up in the style of a well-to-do family in the early 20th century.

Casa Batlló

One of the strangest residential **buildings** (Map p93; ✆93 216 03 06; www.casabatllo. es; Passeig de Gràcia 43; adult/child over 6yr €29/26; ⊗9am-8pm, last admission 7pm; Ⓜ Passeig de Gràcia) in Europe, this is Gaudí at his hallucinatory best. The facade, sprinkled with blue, mauve and green tiles and studded with wave-shaped window frames and balconies, rises to an uneven blue-tiled roof. Locals know Casa Batlló variously as the *casa dels ossos* (house of bones) or *casa del drac* (house of the dragon). The balconies look like the bony jaws of some strange beast and the roof represents Sant Jordi (St George) and the dragon. The

Palau de la Música Catalana

internal light wells shimmer with tiles of deep-sea blue. Everything swirls: the ceiling is twisted into a vortex around its sunlike lamp; the doors, window and skylights are dreamy waves of wood and coloured glass.

Casa Amatller

One of Puig i Cadafalch's most striking flights of Modernista fantasy, **Casa Amatller** (Map p93; ☑93 216 01 75; www.amatller.org; Passeig de Gràcia 41; adult/child 7-12yr 1hr guided tour €24/12, 40min multimedia tour €19/9.50; ⏱10am-6pm; Ⓜ Passeig de Gràcia) combines Gothic window frames and Romanesque flourishes with a stepped gable borrowed from Dutch urban architecture. But the

★ **Top Tip**

Get started early in the day to stay one step ahead of the crowds.

busts and reliefs of dragons, knights and other characters dripping off the main facade are pure caprice. The beautifully tiled pillared foyer and staircase lit by stained glass feel like some romantic castle.

Casa Lleó Morera

Domènech i Montaner's 1905 contribution to the Illa de la Discòrdia, with Modernista carving outside and a bright, tiled lobby, **Casa Lleó Morera** (Map p93; Passeig de Gràcia 35; Ⓜ Passeig de Gràcia) is perhaps the least odd-looking of the three main buildings on the block. It's now occupied by luxury fashion store Loewe.

Palau Montaner

Though fascinating on the outside and made all the more enticing by its leafy gardens, **Palau Montaner** (Map p93; ☑93 317 76 52; www.fundaciotapies.org; Carrer de Mallorca 278; adult/child €7/free; ⏱by reservation; Ⓜ Passeig de Gràcia), a 1893 creation by Domènech i Montaner, is especially spectacular on the inside, laden as it is with sculptures, mosaics and fine woodwork, and a grand staircase beneath an ornamental skylight.

Palau de la Música Catalana

A fantastical symphony in tile, brick, sculpted stone and stained glass, this Unesco-listed, 2146-seat **concert hall** (☑93 295 72 00; www.palaumusica.cat; Carrer Palau de la Música 4-6; adult/concession/under 10yr €20/16/free; ⏱guided tours 10am-3.30pm Sep-Jun, to 6pm Easter & Jul, 9am-6pm Aug; Ⓜ Urquinaona) is a high point of Barcelona's Modernista architecture. Built by Domènech i Montaner between 1905 and 1908 for the Orfeo Català musical society, it was conceived as a temple for the Catalan Renaissance. The richly coloured auditorium has a ceiling of blue-and-gold stained glass and a shimmering 1000kg skylight that looks like a giant, crystalline, downward-thrusting nipple.

Walking Tour: Hidden Treasures in the Barri Gòtic

This scenic walk will take you back in time, from the early days of Roman Barcino to the medieval era.

Start La Catedral
Distance 1.5km
Duration 1½ hours

Classic Photo: La Catedral

1 Before entering the cathedral, look at the three Picasso friezes on the building facing the square. Next, wander through the magnificent **La Catedral** (p87).

2 Pass through the city gates; turn right into **Plaça de Sant Felip Neri**. The shrapnel-scarred church was damaged by pro-Franco bombers in 1938.

3 Head west to the looming 14th-century **Basílica de Santa Maria del Pi** (Map p88), famed for its magnificent rose window.

C del Petritxol
Plaça del Pi
Plaça de St Josep Oriol
La Rambla de Sant Josep
C d'en Roca
3
Plaça de Sant Josep Oriol
C del Cardenal Casañas
La Rambla
C de la Boqueria
C d'en Quintana
Plaça de la Boqueria
Ⓜ Liceu
C d'en Aroles
C de Sant Pau
La Rambla dels Caputxins
C de la Unió

4 Follow the curving road to pretty **Plaça Reial** (p77). Flanking the fountain are Gaudí-designed lamp posts.

7 The final stop is picturesque **Plaça del Rei** (p86). The former palace located here houses a superb history museum, with significant Roman ruins.

6 Cross Plaça de Sant Jaume and turn left after Carrer del Bisbe. You'll pass the entrance to **Temple d'August** (www.muhba.cat; Carrer del Paradis 10), a ruined roman temple with four columns hidden in a small courtyard.

Take a Break...
In the heart of El Call, **Alcoba Azul** (Map p84; ☎ 93 302 81 41; Carrer de Sant Domènec del Call 14; ⏾ 6pm-midnight) is a jewelbox of tasty delights.

5 Nearby is El Call, the medieval Jewish quarter. Here you'll find **Sinagoga Major** (Map p88), one of Europe's oldest synagogues.

Walking Tour: Touchstone of Barcelona Life

Barcelona has an irresistible energy but also numerous quiet refuges – immersing yourself in both is essential if you want to unlock the city's secrets.

Start: Mercat de la Boqueria
Distance: 4km
Duration: two hours

6 A real local's market, **Mercat de Santa Caterina** combines fine food with fine architecture.

Ⓜ Urquinaona

3 Plaça de Sant Josep Oriol is one of Barcelona's loveliest small squares and a real slice of local life.

1 The epicentre of so much Barcelona life, **Mercat de la Boqueria** is filled with intriguing food options.

Classic Photo: Gaudí's lamp posts in Plaça Reial

2 Plaça Reial is among the busiest hubs of Barcelona life. It's also pretty as a postcard.

Ronda Universitat
Ⓜ Universitat
C de Pelai
Ⓐ Ⓜ Catalunya
C dels Tallers
La Rambla
C de la Canuda
Francesc Cambó
6 FINISH
Via Laietana
C de la Tapineria
Plaça de la Seu
Jaume Ⓜ
C de la Portaferrissa
C de la Palla
3
C de Jaume I
Plaça de Sant Jaume
START **1**
La Rambla
C de la Boqueria
Ⓜ Liceu
C de Ferran
C d'en Quintana
Plaça de Sant Miquel
Plaça Reial **2**
C d'Avinyó
C dels Escudellers
La Rambla
La Rambla de Santa Mònica
C de Josep Anselm Clavé
Ⓜ Drassanes

Arc de
Triomf Ⓜ Ⓜ

4 There's silence and beauty within **Basílica de Santa Maria del Mar** – perfect for escaping the crowds.

C dels Almogàvers

Av Meridiana

C de la Marina

C de Ramon Trias Fargas

C de Wellington

Pg de Pujades

Pg de Picasso

Parc de la Ciutadella **5**

Ⓜ Ciutadella
Vila Olímpica

Zoo de Barcelona

Plaça del Pou de la Figuera

Plaça de Pons i Clerch

C dels Carders

C dels Assaonadors

C de la Princesa

C de Montcada

C dels Banys Vells

C de l'Argenteria

C del Comerç

Pg del Born

Plaça Comercial

Av del Marqués de l'Argentera

4

Plaça de Santa Maria del Mar

Via Laietana

Pla del Palau

Pla del Palau

Barceloneta Ⓜ

🍴

5 Parc de la Ciutadella is a city oasis beloved by locals for its beauty and green open spaces.

Take a Break...
Grab a table on the terrace of **La Vinya del Senyor** (p103) and work your way through the wine list.

Mediterranean Sea

From left: Gran Teatre del Liceu; Mercat de la Boqueria; La Catedral

⊙ SIGHTS

Barcelona's medieval heart is picture-postcard perfect, and complemented by soaring avant-garde buildings from the world's greatest architects. There is no shortage of museums large and small, but what makes the city truly unique is Modernisme – the Catalan version of art nouveau.

◉ La Rambla & Barri Gòtic

Mercat de la Boqueria　　　Market

(Map p88; ☎93 318 20 17; www.boqueria.bar celona; La Rambla 91; ☺8am-8.30pm Mon-Sat; Ⓜ Liceu) Barcelona's most central fresh-produce market is one of the greatest sound, smell and colour sensations in Europe. It's housed in a packed-out Modernista-influenced building every bit as impressive, built from 1840 to 1914 under architect Josep Mas i Vila on the site of the former Sant Josep monastery. La Boqueria may have taken a tourist-oriented turn in recent years, but towards the back you'll discover what it's really about: bountiful fruit and vegetables, and seemingly limitless sea critters, cheeses and meats.

Gran Teatre del Liceu　　　Architecture

(Map p88; ☎93 485 99 00; www.liceubarcelo na.cat; La Rambla 51-59; 45min tour adult/child €9/free; Ⓜ Liceu) If you can't catch a night at the opera (p104), you can still take in the awe-inspiring architectural riches of one of Europe's greatest opera houses. Opened in 1847, the Liceu launched Catalan stars such as Josep (José) Carreras and Montserrat Caballé, and seats up to 2300 people in its grand auditorium. Standard 45-minute tours of classic spaces (the foyer, Saló dels Miralls and auditorium) run in Catalan, Spanish and English; check updated schedules online.

Plaça del Rei　　　Square

(Map p88; Ⓜ Jaume I) The courtyard of the Gothic former Palau Reial Major, this picturesque, almost entirely walled-in square is where the Reyes Católicos (Catholic Monarchs) are thought to have received Columbus following his first New World voyage. Today, part of the palace houses a superb history museum, with significant Roman

KRZYSZTOF DYDYNSKI/LONELY PLANET ©

ruins. The 14th-century **Capella Reial de Santa Àgata** (⊙10am-7pm Tue-Sat, to 8pm Sun) and 16th-century **Palau del Lloctinent** (Carrer dels Comtes; ⊙10am-7pm) `FREE` overlook the square, as does the 1555 (off-limits) **Mirador del Rei Martí** lookout tower, now part of the Arxiu de la Corona d'Aragón.

La Catedral   Cathedral

(Map p88; ☎93 342 82 62; www.catedralbcn. org; Plaça de la Seu; €7, roof or choir €3, chapter house €2; ⊙worship 8.30am-12.30pm & 5.45-7.30pm Mon-Fri, 8.30am-12.30pm & 5.15-8pm Sat, 8.30am-1.45pm & 5.15-8pm Sun, tourist visits 12.30-7.45pm Mon-Fri, 12.30-5.30pm Sat, 2-5.30pm Sun; MJaume I) Barcelona's central place of worship presents a magnificent image. The richly decorated main facade, dotted with gargoyles and the kinds of stone intricacies you would expect of northern European Gothic, sets it quite apart from other Barcelona churches. The facade was actually added from 1887 to 1890. The rest of the building dates to between 1298 and 1460. Its other facades are sparse in decoration, and the octagonal, flat-roofed towers are a clear reminder that, even here,

Catalan Gothic architectural principles prevailed.

Museu d'Història de Barcelona   Museum

(MUHBA; Map p88; ☎93 256 21 00; http://ajuntament.barcelona.cat/museuhistoria; Plaça del Rei; adult/concession/child €7/5/free, 3-8pm Sun & 1st Sun of month free; ⊙10am-7pm Tue-Sat, to 8pm Sun; MJaume I) One of Barcelona's most fascinating museums travels back through the centuries to the very foundations of Roman Barcino. You'll stroll over ruins of the old streets, sewers, laundries, baths and wine- and fish-making factories that flourished here following the town's founding by Emperor Augustus around 10 BCE. Equally impressive is the building itself, which was once part of the Palau Reial Major (Grand Royal Palace) on Plaça del Rei, among the key locations of medieval princely power in Barcelona.

◉ El Raval

MACBA   Gallery

(Museu d'Art Contemporani de Barcelona; ☎93 412 08 10; www.macba.cat; Plaça dels Àngels 1;

Central Barcelona

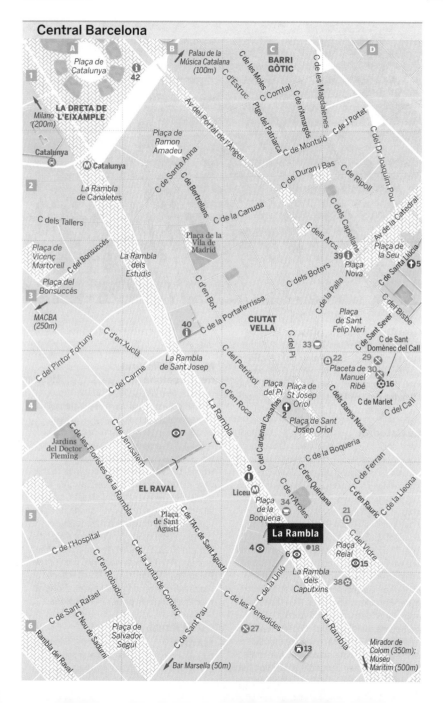

Plaça de Catalunya
42 i

LA DRETA DE L'EIXAMPLE
Milano (200m)

Palau de la Música Catalana (100m)

C de les Moles
BARRI GÒTIC
C d'Estruc
Ptge del Patriarca
C Comtal
C de n'Amargós
C de les Magdalenes
C del J Portet

Av del Portal de l'Àngel

Catalunya
Ⓜ Catalunya

Plaça de Ramon Amadeu

C de Montsió
C de Duran i Bas
C del Dr Joaquim Pou
C del Ripoll

La Rambla de Canaletes

C de Santa Anna
C de Bertrellans
C de la Canuda

C dels Tallers

C dels Capellans
C dels Arcs
Av de la Catedral

Plaça de Vicenç Martorell
C del Bonsuccés
La Rambla dels Estudis

Plaça de la Vila de Madrid

Plaça de la Seu
39 i
Plaça Nova
C de Santa Llúcia
5 ①

Plaça del Bonsuccés

C en Bot
C dels Boters
C de la Palla
C del Bisbe

MACBA (250m)

C del Pintor Fortuny
C d'en Xuclà
C de la Portaferrissa
CIUTAT VELLA
40 i
C del Pi
Plaça de Sant Felip Neri
C de Sant Sever
C de Sant Domènec del Call

La Rambla de Sant Josep
C del Petritxol
33 🚻
22 ⓐ
29 ✕
Placeta de Manuel Ribé
30
16 ①

C del Carme
C d'en Roca
Plaça del Pi
Plaça de St Josep Oriol
2 ①
C dels Banys Nous
C de Marlet
C del Call

La Rambla

C del Cardenal Casañas
Plaça de Sant Josep Oriol

Jardins del Doctor Fleming
C de les Floristes de la Rambla
C de Jerusalem
7 👁
C de la Boqueria
C de Ferran

EL RAVAL
9 i
Liceu Ⓜ
Plaça de la Boqueria
C d'en Quintana
C d'en Rauric
C de la Lleona

Plaça de Sant Agustí
C de l'Arc de Sant Agustí
34 ♨
C de n'Aroles
21 🔒

La Rambla

C de l'Hospital
C d'en Robador
C de la Junta de Comerç
4 👁
6
18 ●
Plaça Reial
C del Vidre
15 ①

C de Sant Rafael
C Nou de Sadurní
La Rambla dels Caputxins
38 ✿

Plaça de Salvador Seguí
C de Sant Pau
C de les Penedides
C de la Unió
27 ✕

Rambla del Raval
Bar Marsella (50m)
13 🏠
La Rambla

Mirador de Colom (350m);
Museu Marítim (500m)

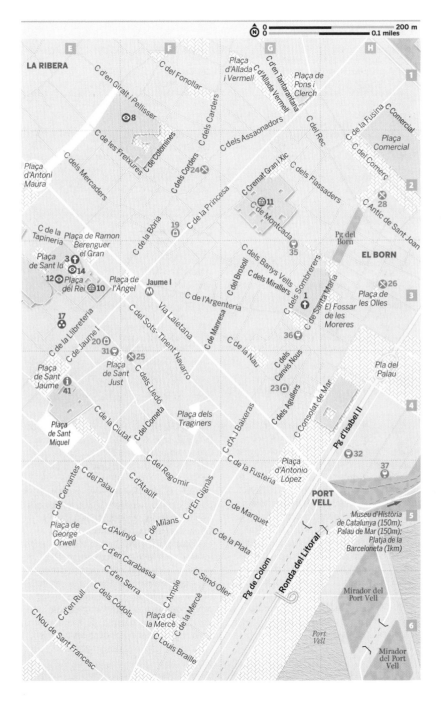

LA RIBERA

C d'en Giralt i Pellisser

C del Fonollar

Plaça d'Allada i Vermell

C d'en Tantarantana

C d'Allada Vermell

Plaça de Pons i Clerch

C del Rec

C de la Fusina

C Comercial

Plaça Comercial

C del Comerç

8

C de les Freixures

C de Colomines

C dels Corders

C dels Carders

C dels Assaonadors

C dels Mercaders

Plaça d'Antoni Maura

C dels Corders

24

C de la Princesa

C Cremat Gran i Xic

C dels Flassaders

C Antic de Sant Joan

28

11

C de Montcada

Pg del Born

EL BORN

C de la Bòria

19

35

C de la Tapineria

Plaça de Ramon Berenguer el Gran

C dels Banys Vells

C dels Miralles

C del Brosoli

C dels Sombrerers

C de Santa Maria

Plaça de les Olles

26

Plaça de Sant Iu

3

14

Plaça del Rei

10

12

Plaça de l'Àngel

Jaume I

C de l'Argenteria

1

El Fossar de les Moreres

3

17

Via Laietana

C de Manresa

C de la Nau

36

Pla del Palau

C de la Llibreteria

C del Sots- Tinent Navarro

C dels Canvis Nous

C de Jaume I

20

31

25

23

C dels Aguilers

C Consolat de Mar

Plaça de Sant Just

C dels Lledó

Pg d'Isabel II

Plaça de Sant Jaume

41

Plaça de Sant Miquel

C de la Ciutat

C del Cometa

Plaça dels Traginers

C d'A J Baixeras

32

37

C de Cervantes

C del Palau

C del Regomir

C d'Ataülf

C d'En Gignàs

C C de la Fusteria

Plaça d'Antonio López

PORT VELL

Plaça de George Orwell

C d'Avinyó

C de Milans

C de Marquet

Museu d'Història de Catalunya (150m); Palau de Mar (150m); Platja de la Barceloneta (1km)

C d'en Carabassa

C de la Plata

C d'en Serra

C Simó Oller

C Ample

C de la Mercè

Pg de Colom

Ronda del Litoral

C d'en Rull

C dels Còdols

Plaça de la Mercè

Mirador del Port Vell

C Nou de Sant Francesc

C Louis Braille

Port Vell

Mirador del Port Vell

Central Barcelona

adult/concession/child under 14yr €11/8.80/ free, 4-8pm Sat free; ⊙11am-7.30pm Mon & Wed-Fri, 10am-8pm Sat, 10am-3pm Sun & public holidays; Ⓜ Universitat) An extraordinary all-white, glass-fronted creation by American architect Richard Meier, opened in 1995, the MACBA has become the city's foremost contemporary art centre, with captivating exhibitions for the serious art lover. The permanent collection is dedicated to Spanish and Catalan art from the second half of the 20th century, with works by Antoni Tàpies, Joan Brossa, Miquel Barceló and Joan Rabascall. International artists, such as Paul Klee, Bruce Nauman, Alexander Calder, John Cage and Jean-Michel Basquiat, are also represented.

Palau Güell   Palace

(Map p88; ☏93 472 57 75; www.palauguell.cat; Carrer Nou de la Rambla 3-5; adult/concession/ child under 10yr incl audio guide €12/9/free, 1st Sun of month free; ⊙10am-8pm Tue-Sun Apr-Oct, to 5.30pm Nov-Mar; Ⓜ Drassanes) Built off La Rambla in the late 1880s for Gaudí's wealthy patron, the industrialist Eusebi Güell, the Palau Güell is a magnificent example of the early days of the architect's fevered architectural imagination. This extraordinary neo-Gothic mansion (one of few major buildings of that era raised in Ciutat Vella) gives an insight into its maker's prodigious genius, and, though a little sombre compared with some of his later whims, it's a characteristic riot of styles (Gothic, Islamic, art nouveau) and materials.

La Ribera

Basílica de Santa Maria del Mar · Church

(Map p88; ☑93 310 23 90; www.santamariadel marbarcelona.org; Plaça de Santa Maria del Mar; guided tour €8.50-10; ☺9am-8.30pm Mon-Sat, 10am-8pm Sun, tours 1-5pm Sat, from 2pm Sun; Ⓜ Jaume I) At the southwestern end of Passeig del Born stands Barcelona's finest Catalan Gothic church, Santa Maria del Mar (Our Lady of the Sea). Begun in 1329, under the watch of architects Berenguer de Montagut and Ramon Despuig, the church is remarkable for its architectural harmony and simplicity. Famously the parishioners themselves gave up their time to help construct the church, particularly the stevedores from the nearby port.

Museu Picasso · Museum

(Map p88; ☑93 256 30 00; www.museupicas so.bcn.cat; Carrer de Montcada 15-23; adult/ concession/under 18yr permanent collection & temporary exhibit €14/7.50/free, 6-9.30pm Thu & 1st Sun of month free; ☺10am-5pm Mon, 9am-8.30pm Tue, Wed & Fri-Sun, to 9.30pm Thu; Ⓜ Jaume I) The setting alone, in five con- tiguous medieval stone mansions, makes Barcelona's Museu Picasso unique (and worth the queues). While the collection concentrates on Pablo Picasso's formative years – potentially disappointing lovers of his better-known later works – there is enough material from subsequent periods to showcase the artist's versatility and genius. Above all, you come away feeling that Picasso was the true original, always one step ahead of himself (let alone anyone else) in his search for new forms of expression.

Mercat de Santa Caterina · Market

(Map p88; ☑93 319 57 40; www.mercatsanta caterina.com; Avinguda de Francesc Cambó 16; ☺7.30am-3.30pm Mon, Wed & Sat, to 8.30pm Tue, Thu & Fri, closed afternoons except Fri Aug; Ⓜ Jaume I) **FREE** Come shopping for your tomatoes or pop in for lunch at this extraordinary-looking produce market, de- signed by forward-thinking architects Enric Miralles and Benedetta Tagliabue to replace its 19th-century predecessor. Completed in 2005 (sadly after Miralles' death in 2000), it's distinguished by its undulating, kalei- doscopic roof, suspended above bustling produce stands, restaurants, cafes and bars by twisting slender branches of what look like grey steel trees.

La Barceloneta & the Waterfront

Museu Marítim · Museum

(☑93 342 99 20; www.mmb.cat; Avinguda de les Drassanes; adult/child €10/5, from 3pm Sun free; ☺10am-8pm; Ⓜ Drassanes) The city's maritime museum occupies the mighty Gothic Reials Drassanes (Royal Shipyards) – a remarkable relic from Barcelona's days as the seat of a seafaring empire. Highlights include a full-scale 1970s replica of Don Juan de Austria's 16th-century flagship, fishing vessels, antique navigation charts and dioramas of the Barcelona waterfront.

Museu d'Història de Catalunya · Museum

(☑93 225 47 00; www.mhcat.cat; Plaça de Pau Vila 3; adult/child €6/free, 1st Sun of month 10am-2.30pm free; ☺10am-7pm Tue & Thu-Sat, to 8pm Wed, to 2.30pm Sun; Ⓜ Barceloneta) Within the revitalised 1880s **Palau de Mar**, this excellent museum travels from the Stone Age through to the arrival of Modernisme in Catalonia and the Spanish Civil War (touch- ing heavily on the cultural and political re- pression felt across Catalonia postwar) and into the 21st century. It's a busy multimedia hotchpotch of dioramas, artefacts, videos, models, documents and interactive bits: all up, a thoroughly entertaining exploration of 2000 years of Catalan history. Signage is in Catalan, Spanish and English.

El Poblenou Platges · Beach

(Ⓜ Ciutadella Vila Olímpica, Llacuna, Poblenou, Selva de Mar) A series of beautiful, broad, sandy golden beaches dotted with *xiringui- tos* (seasonal beach bars) stretches north- east from the Port Olímpic marina. They're largely artificial, but that doesn't deter the millions of sunseekers and swimmers from descending in summer, especially for beach

 Park Güell

Around 1km north of Gràcia, the Unesco-listed **Park Güell** (☏93 409 18 31; www.parkguell.barcelona; Carrer d'Olot 7; adult/child €10/7; ☉8am-9.30pm May-Aug, to 8.30pm Apr, Sep & Oct, to 6.15pm Nov–mid-Feb, to 7pm mid-Feb–Mar; ☐H6, D40, V19, Bus Güell; ⓜLesseps, Vallcarca, Alfons X) is where Antoni Gaudí turned his hand and imagination to landscape gardening. It's a surreal, enchanting place where the great Modernista's passion for natural forms really took flight, and the artificial almost seems more real than the natural.

The park is extremely popular, and access to the central area is limited to 400 people every half-hour – book ahead online. The rest of the park is free and can be visited without booking.

ISMEL LEAL PICHS/SHUTTERSTOCK©

volleyball – and they're still quieter than the sandy strands closer to the city centre.

◉ L'Eixample

Casa de les Punxes   Architecture

(Casa Terrades; Map p93; ☏93 018 52 42; www.casadelespunxes.com; Avinguda Diagonal 420; adult/child €13.50/10, tour €20/16; ☉10am-7pm; ⓜDiagonal) Puig i Cadafalch's 1905 Casa Terrades is known as the Casa de les Punxes (House of Spikes) because of its pointed tile-adorned turrets. Resembling a medieval castle, this former apartment block is the only fully detached building in

L'Eixample, and opened to the public only in 2017. Visits (with multilanguage audio guide) take in its stained-glass bay windows, handsome iron staircase, hydraulic floors, pillars and arches with floral motifs, and rooftop. Guided midday tours run in Spanish (Saturday) and Catalan (Sunday).

Recinte Modernista
de Sant Pau   Architecture

(☏93 553 78 01; www.santpaubarcelona.org; Carrer de Sant Antoni Maria Claret 167; adult/child €15/free, audio guide €4; ☉9.30am-6.30pm Mon-Sat, to 2.30pm Sun Apr-Oct, 9.30am-4.30pm Mon-Sat, to 2.30pm Sun Nov-Mar; ⓜSant Pau/ Dos de Maig) Domènech i Montaner outdid himself as architect and philanthropist with the Modernista Hospital de la Santa Creu i de Sant Pau, renamed the 'Recinte Modernista' in 2014. Built between 1902 and 1930, it was long considered one of Barcelona's most important hospitals, but was repurposed into cultural centres, offices and a monument in 2009. A joint Unesco World Heritage Site together with the Palau de la Música Catalana (p81), the 27-building complex is lavishly decorated and each of its 16 pavilions unique.

◉ Camp Nou, Pedralbes & La Zona Alta

Barça Stadium
Tour & Museum   Museum

(☏902 189900; www.fcbarcelona.com; Gate 9, Avinguda de Joan XXIII; adult/child 4-10yr self-guided tour €29.50/23.50, guided tour €45/37; ☉9.30am-7.30pm mid-Apr–mid-Oct, 10am-6.30pm Mon-Sat, to 2.30pm Sun mid-Oct–mid-Apr; ⓜPalau Reial) A pilgrimage site for football fans around the world, Camp Nou (p105) is a must for FC Barcelona fans. On this tour, which can be guided or self-guided, you'll get an in-depth look at the club, starting with a museum filled with multimedia exhibits, trophies and historical displays, followed by a tour of the stadium. Set aside at least 1½ hours.

La Sagrada & L'Eixample

Sights
1 Casa Amatller	C3
2 Casa Batlló	C3
3 Casa de les Punxes	B2
4 Casa Lleó Morera	C3
5 La Pedrera	B3
6 La Sagrada Família	D1
7 Palau Montaner	C2

Eating
8 Lasarte	B3
9 Tapas 24	C3

Drinking & Nightlife
10 Les Gens Que J'Aime	C3

Montjuïc

Museu Nacional d'Art de Catalunya · Museum

(MNAC; Map p95; ☎93 622 03 60; www.museunacional.cat; Mirador del Palau Nacional, Parc de Montjuïc; adult/child €12/free, after 3pm Sat & 1st Sun of month free, audio guide €4, rooftop viewpoint only €2; ◷10am-8pm Tue-Sat, to 3pm Sun May-Sep, 10am-6pm Tue-Sat, to 3pm Sun Oct-Apr; ☒55, ⓂEspanya) The spectacular neobaroque silhouette of the Palau Nacional can be seen on Montjuïc's slopes from across the city. Built for the 1929 World Exhibition and restored in 2005, it houses a vast collection of mostly Catalan art stretching from the early Middle Ages to the early 20th century. The high point is the unique collection of extraordinary Romanesque frescoes.

Fundació Joan Miró · Gallery

(Map p95; ☎93 443 94 70; www.fmirobcn.org; Avinguda de Miramar; adult/child €13/free, multimedia guide €5; ◷10am-8pm Tue-Sat, to 3pm Sun Apr-Oct, 10am-6pm Tue-Sat, to 3pm Sun Nov-Mar; ☒55, 150, ⓗfrom Paral·lel) Joan Miró, the city's best-known 20th-century artistic progeny, bequeathed this art foundation to his home town in 1971. The light-filled buildings, designed by close friend and architect Josep Lluís Sert (who also built Miró's Mallorca studios), are crammed with seminal works, from Miró's timid earliest sketches to paintings from his last years.

CaixaForum   Gallery

(Map p95; ☑93 476 86 00; www.caixaforum. es; Avinguda de Francesc Ferrer i Guàrdia 6-8; adult/child €4/free, 1st Sun of month free; ⊙10am-8pm year-round, to 11pm Wed Jul & Aug; ⓂEspanya) The La Caixa building society prides itself on its involvement in (and ownership of) art, in particular all that is contemporary. The bank's premier expo space in Barcelona hosts part of its extensive global collection, as well as fascinating temporary international exhibitions, in the completely renovated former Casaramona factory, an outstanding brick Modernista creation by Josep Puig i Cadafalch. From 1940 to 1993, the building housed the First Squadron of the police cavalry unit.

Castell de Montjuïc   Fortress

(☑93 256 44 40; https://ajuntament.barcelona. cat; Carretera de Montjuïc 66; adult/child €5/3, after 3pm Sun & 1st Sun of month free; ⊙10am-8pm Mar-Oct, to 6pm Nov-Feb; ☐150, ☐Telefèric de Montjuïc, Castell de Montjuïc) Enjoying commanding views over the Mediterranean, this forbidding fortress dominates the southeastern heights of Montjuïc. It dates, in its present form, from the late 17th and 18th centuries, though there's been a watchtower here since 1073. For most of its dark history, it has been used as a political prison and killing ground. Anarchists were executed here around the end of the 19th century, fascists during the civil war and Republicans after it – most notoriously Republican Catalan president Lluís Companys in 1940.

⊙ COURSES

Barcelona Cooking   Cooking

(Map p88; ☑93 119 19 86; www.barcelona cooking.net; La Rambla 58, Principal 2; adult/ child 5-13yr/child under 5yr €65/32.50/free, with market visit €78/39; ⚐; ⓂLiceu) Founded by three Galician friends, Barcelona Cooking hosts hands-on, four-hour culinary classes with bilingual chefs. Kick off with an expedition to the celebrated Mercat de la Boqueria, after which you'll be sizzling up a four-course meal (typically including paella), or try a wine-pairing class focused on traditional Catalan tapas. Thoughtful vegetarian, vegan and gluten-free adaptations on request. Book ahead.

⊙ TOURS

Devour Barcelona   Tours

(☑944 58 10 22; www.devourbarcelonafoodtours. com; tours €79-119) Knowledgeable guides lead terrific food tours around Gràcia, the Old City, Sant Antoni and La Barceloneta, mixing gastronomy with history. The various tastings and spots visited are especially focused on small, local producers and family-run joints, with vermouth, *cava* and local culinary specialities highlighted. Most tours last three to four hours – and include more than enough for a full meal!

Barcelona Turisme Walking Tours   Walking

(Map p88; ☑93 285 38 32; www.barcelonaturisme.com; Plaça de Catalunya 17; ⓂCatalunya) The Oficina d'Informació de Turisme de Barcelona (p106) organises one- to two-hour guided tours (in Spanish, Catalan, English and/or French) exploring the Barri Gòtic (adult/child €18/free; wheelchair-accessible option €13.95), Picasso's footsteps (€25/10) and the main jewels of Modernisme (€18/free). It also books tours with private operators (from gourmet food jaunts to cycling tours). Check schedules and book online (with a 10% discount).

Montjuïc

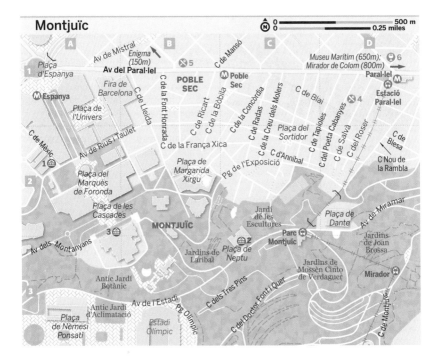

0 — 500 m
0 — 0.25 miles

Montjuïc

Sights
1 CaixaForum A2
2 Fundació Joan Miró C3
3 Museu Nacional d'Art de Catalunya A2

Eating
4 Quimet i Quimet D1
5 Tickets B1

Drinking & Nightlife
6 La Confiteria D1

Wanderbeak   Food & Drink
(📞93 22 06 101; www.wanderbeak.com; Carrer del Comerç 29; group tour per person €79-99; 🕙9am-10pm; Ⓜ️Jaume I, Barceloneta) Founded by a food-loving duo, Wanderbeak runs fun-filled, in-depth, small-group (maximum eight people) gastronomic experiences taking in Barcelona's history and foodie highlights; most dietary requirements are happily catered for on request, and there are cooking classes too. The signature Born to Eat tour leads you through El Born's buzzy lanes via three food stops and a relaxed wine-tasting session.

My Favourite Things   Tours
(📞637 265405; www.myft.net; tours from €30 per person) Offers tours (with no more than 10 participants) based on numerous themes: street art, shopping, food, movies, musical journeys and forgotten neighbourhoods are among the options, and there are tours of Poble Sec and Sant Antoni. Other activities include flamenco and salsa classes, cooking workshops, and bicycle rides in and out of Barcelona. Book online.

Shopping Strips

Avinguda del Portal de l'Àngel This broad pedestrian avenue is lined with high-street chains, shoe shops, book-shops and more. It feeds into Carrer dels Boters and Carrer de la Portafer-rissa, characterised by stores offering light-hearted costume jewellery and youth-oriented streetwear.

Avinguda Diagonal This boulevard is loaded with international fashion names and design boutiques, suitably interspersed with cafes to allow weary shoppers to take a load off.

Carrer d'Avinyó Once a fairly squalid old city street, Carrer d'Avinyó has morphed into a dynamic young fashion strip.

Carrer de la Riera Baixa The place to look for a gaggle of shops flogging preloved threads.

Carrer del Petritxol Best for chocolate shops and art.

Carrer dels Banys Nous Along with nearby Carrer de la Palla, this is the place to look for antiques.

Passeig de Gràcia This is the premier shopping boulevard, chic with a capital 'C', and mostly given over to big-name international brands.

Avinguda del Portal de l'Àngel
RESUL MUSLU/SHUTTERSTOCK ©

🔒 SHOPPING

Herboristeria del Rei   Cosmetics
(Map p88; ☑93 318 05 12; www.herboristeria delrei.com; Carrer del Vidre 1; ⊙3-8.30pm

Tue-Thu, 11am-8.30pm Fri & Sat; Ⓜ Liceu)
Once patronised by Queen Isabel II, this timeless corner store flogs all sorts of weird and wonderful herbs, spices and medicinal plants. It's been doing so since 1823 and the decor (with stained glass and watercolour landscapes) has barely changed since the 1860s – some of the products have, however, and nowadays you'll find everything from fragrant soaps to massage oils.

El Rei de la Màgia   Magic
(Map p88; ☑93 319 73 93; www.elreidelamagia. es; Carrer de la Princesa 11; ⊙4-7.30pm Mon-Wed, 11am-2pm & 4-7.30pm Thu-Sat; Ⓜ Jaume I)
Should you decide to stay in Barcelona and make a living as a magician, this rust-red world of make-believe is the place to buy levitation brooms, glasses of disappearing milk and decks of magic cards. The owners have been keeping locals both astounded and amused for almost 140 years.

Vila Viniteca   Food & Drinks
(Map p88; www.vilaviniteca.es; Carrer dels Agullers 7; ⊙8.30am-8.30pm Mon-Sat; Ⓜ Jaume I)
One of Barcelona's best wine stores (and there are a few...), Vila Viniteca has been hunting down the finest local and imported wines since 1932. There are year-round on-request tastings and a handful of bar tables, and on several November evenings it organises an almost riotous wine-tasting event at which cellars from across Spain present their young new wines.

L'Arca   Clothing
(Map p88; ☑93 302 15 98; www.larca.es; Carrer dels Banys Nous 20; ⊙11am-2pm & 4-8pm Mon-Sat; Ⓜ Liceu) Step inside this enchanting vintage boutique for beautifully crafted apparel from the past, mostly sourced from local homes: 18th-century embroidered silk vests, elaborate silk kimonos and 1920s shawls and wedding dresses, plus old-style earrings made by artisans in southern Spain. The incredible collection has provid-ed fashion for films like *Titanic*, *Talk to Her* and *Perfume: The Story of a Murderer*.

Formatgeria La Seu Food

(Map p88; ☎93 412 65 48; www.formatgeria
laseu.com; Carrer de la Dagueria 16; ⏱10am-2pm
& 5-8pm Tue-Sat; Ⓜ Jaume I) ✐ Dedicated
to artisan cheeses from across Spain,
this small shop is run by the oh-so-
knowledgable Katherine McLaughlin. The
antithesis of mass production, it sells only
the best from small-scale farmers and the
stock changes regularly. Wine-and-cheese
tastings (€9.50 to €32) in the cosy back
room are fun, and the team has a great little
wine bar, **Bar Zim** (Map p88; www.formatgeri
alaseu.com; Carrer de la Dagueria 20; ⏱6-11pm
Mon-Sat; Ⓜ Jaume I), next door.

🍴 EATING

🍴 La Rambla & Barri Gòtic

Bar Pinotxo Tapas €€

(Map p88; ☎93 317 17 31; www.pinotxobar.com;
La Rambla 89, Mercat de la Boqueria; tapas €4-16;
⏱6.30am-4pm Mon-Sat; Ⓜ Liceu) Arguably
La Boqueria's most brilliant tapas bar,
standing strong since 1940. Ever-charming
owner Juanito Bayén serves up superb
Catalan classics: chickpeas with pine nuts
and raisins, *cargols* (snails), smoky *escalivada* (grilled vegetables), soft baby squid
with cannellini beans, or a quivering cube
of caramel-sweet pork belly. Long-running
and unpretentious, Pinotxo is also famous
for its *forquilles* (traditional cooked breakfasts). Arrive early!

Cafè de l'Acadèmia Catalan €€

(Map p88; ☎93 319 82 53; cafedelaacademia@
hotmail.com; Carrer dels Lledó 1; mains €10-20;
⏱1-4pm & 8-11pm Mon-Fri, closed Aug; 🛜;
Ⓜ Jaume I) Smartly executed traditional
Catalan dishes with the odd creative twist
and excellent regional wines make this
wood-beamed, stone-walled spot a packed-
out local favourite, with tables also on Plaça
de Sant Just. City-hall workers pounce on
the lunchtime *menú del día* (€16 – or €12
at the bar!), which might mean pear-and-
parmesan salad, vegetable rice with Mahón
cheese or grilled sole.

🍴 Catalan Starters

Calçots amb romesco Sweet and juicy
spring onions cooked up on a barbecue.

Escalivada Red peppers and aubergines grilled, cooled, peeled, sliced and
served with an olive oil, salt and garlic
dressing.

Esqueixada Salad of *bacallà/bacalao*
(shredded salted cod) with tomatoes,
red peppers, onions, white beans, olives,
olive oil and vinegar.

Esqueixada
FANFO/SHUTTERSTOCK ©

La Vinateria del Call Spanish €€

(Map p88; ☎93 302 60 92; www.lavinateria
delcall.com; Carrer Salomó Ben Adret 9; raciones
€7-18; ⏱7.30pm-1am; 🛜; Ⓜ Jaume I) In a
magical, rambling setting in the former
Jewish quarter, this tiny candlelit jewel
box of a wine bar serves up divine Iberian
sharing plates from Galician-style octopus
and cider-cooked chorizo to perfect *truites*
(omelettes) and Catalan *escalivada*. Spot-
on service, super-fresh local ingredients
and a wonderful selection of wines and
artisan cheeses from across Spain.

🍴 El Raval

Cañete Tapas €€

(Map p88; ☎93 270 34 58; www.barcanete.
com; Carrer de la Unió 17; tapas €2-15, sharing
plates €7-22; ⏱1pm-midnight Mon-Sat; 🛜;
Ⓜ Liceu) Epitomising the ongoing trend
in smartened-up versions of traditional
tapas bars, much-loved and always-busy
Cañete centres on a bustling open kitchen
with a marble-topped bar. The long list

🍽️ Catalan Main Courses

Arròs a la cassola/arroz a la catalana Catalan paella, cooked without saffron.

Arròs negre Rice cooked in black cuttlefish ink.

Bacallà a la llauna Salted cod baked in tomato, garlic, parsley, paprika and wine.

Botifarra amb mongetes Pork sausage with fried white beans.

Cargols/Caracoles Snails, often stewed with *conill/conejo* (rabbit) and chilli.

Fideuà Similar to paella but with vermicelli noodles as the base. Often accompanied by *allioli* (pounded garlic with olive oil), which you can mix in as you wish.

Fricandó Pork and vegetable stew.

Sarsuela/zarzuela Mixed seafood cooked in *sofregit* (fried onion, tomato and garlic sauce) with seasonings.

Suquet de peix Fish and potato hotpot.

Sarsuela
HLPHOTO/SHUTTERSTOCK©

of uber-fresh tapas and *platillos* (sharing plates) packs in modern twists (such as wild-tuna tataki with seaweed) alongside traditional favourites, including gooey tortilla and Andalucian classics like *boquerones* (anchovies) and *tortillitas de camarones* (shrimp fritters). Reservations recommended.

Can Lluís   Catalan €€

(🌙93 441 11 87; www.restaurantcanlluis.cat; Carrer de la Cera 49; mains €10-22; ⊘1-4pm &

8.30-11.30pm Mon-Sat; Ⓜ️Sant Antoni) Three generations have kept this spick-and-span old-time classic in business since 1929. Beneath olive-green beams in the back dining room you can see the spot where an anarchist's bomb went off in 1946, killing the then-owner. Can Lluís is still going strong, however, with excellent seafood, succulent meats, a good *menú del dia* (€12) and almost exclusively Catalan wines.

🍴 La Ribera

Casa Delfín   Catalan €€

(Map p88; 🌙93 319 50 88; www.casadelfin restaurant.com; Passeig del Born 36; tapas €6-11, mains €12-20; ⊘noon-midnight Sun-Thu, to 1am Fri & Sat; 🛜; Ⓜ️Jaume I) One of El Born's culinary delights, Casa Delfín is everything you dream about traditional Catalan-Mediterranean cooking. Lined with wine bottles inside, the service is spot-on and creative presentation lends a contemporary touch. Menus change depending on market produce, but might offer salt-strewn Padrón peppers, plump anchovies from L'Escala, big seafood paellas or *suquet dels pescadors* (Catalan fish stew) for two.

Bar del Pla   Tapas €€

(Map p88; 🌙93 268 30 03; www.bardelpla.cat; Carrer de Montcada 2; tapas €4-11, mains €9-15; ⊘noon-11pm Mon-Thu, to midnight Fri & Sat; 🛜; Ⓜ️Jaume I) A bright and buzzy favourite, with glorious Catalan tiling, a vaulted ceiling and bottles of wine lining the walls. At first glance, the tapas at informal Bar del Pla are traditionally Spanish, but the riffs on the theme display an assured touch of creativity. Try the ham croquettes, wasabi mushrooms, T-bone steak or rice of the day.

Cal Pep   Tapas €€

(Map p88; 🌙93 310 79 61; www.calpep.com; Plaça de les Olles 8; mains €10-20; ⊘7.30-11.30pm Mon, 1-3.45pm & 7.30-11.30pm Tue-Sat, closed last 3 weeks Aug; Ⓜ️Barceloneta) It's getting a foot in the door of this legendary tapas and seafood restaurant that's the problem – queues spread out into the square. Most people are happy elbowing their way to the bar for some of the tastiest

Herboristeria del Rei (p96)

seafood tapas in town. Pep recommends *cloïsses amb pernil* (clams and ham), the *trifàsic* (calamari, whitebait and prawns) or the supersmooth tortilla.

🍴 La Barceloneta & the Waterfront

Can Recasens   Catalan €€
(📞93 300 81 23; www.canrecasens.restaurant; Rambla del Poblenou 102; mains €8-21; ⏰restaurant 8pm-1am, delicatessen 8.15am-1.30pm & 5pm-1am Mon-Fri, 8.15am-1.30pm Sat; Ⓜ Poblenou) One of El Poblenou's most romantic settings, century-old Can Recasens conceals a warren of warmly lit rooms full of oil paintings, flickering candles, fairy lights and fruit baskets. The food is outstanding, with a mix of salads, smoked meats, fondues, and open sandwiches topped with delicacies like wild mushrooms and Brie, *escalivada* and Gruyère, or *sobrasada* (spicy cured sausage) with rosemary honey.

Minyam   Seafood €€
(📞93 348 36 18; www.facebook.com/minyam cisco; Carrer de Pujades 187; tapas €2-10, mains €15-25; ⏰1-11pm Tue-Thu, to 11.30pm Fri & Sat, to 5pm Sun; Ⓜ Poblenou) Billowing with smoke beneath a tajine-like metal lid, smouldering herbs infuse the rice of Minyam's signature Vulcanus (smoked seafood paella with squid ink). Tapas dishes at this stylish, contemporary El Poblenou restaurant are equally inventive and include asparagus fritters, oysters with sea urchin and lemon, prawn omelettes and fondue with truffle oil. There's a popular €12.50 *menú del dia*.

Can Solé   Seafood €€€
(📞93 221 50 12; www.restaurantcansole.com; Carrer de Sant Carles 4; mains €15-40; ⏰1-4pm & 8-11pm Tue-Thu, 1-4pm & 8.30-11pm Fri & Sat, 1-4pm Sun; Ⓜ Barceloneta) Behind imposing wooden doors, this elegantly old-school restaurant with white-cloth tables, white-jacketed waiters and photos of celebrity customers has been serving terrific seafood since 1903. Freshly landed catch stars in traditional dishes such as *arròs caldòs* (rice broth with squid and langoustines) and 'grandmother'-style dishes such as *zarzuela*.

La Barra de Carles Abellán
Seafood €€€

(☑93 295 26 36; www.carlesabellan.com; Plaça de la Rosa dels Vents 1, W Barcelona; tapas €5-25, mains €18-36; ۩7-11am & 7-11.30pm Mon-Thu, 7-11am, 1.30-4pm & 7-11.30pm Fri & Sat, 7-11.30am & 1.30-4pm Sun; ☒V15, V19, MBarceloneta) Star Catalan chef Carles Abellán's stunning glass-encased, glossy-tiled restaurant (designed by favourite local interiorist Lázaro Rosa-Violán) celebrates seafood. Stellar tapas might include pickled octopus and papas aliñás (potato salad) with mackerel. Even more show-stopping are the mains: grilled razor clams with ponzu citrus sauce, squid filled with spicy poached egg yolk, and hake kokotxas (jowls) in a pil pil (garlic, chilli and oil) sauce.

⊗ L'Eixample

Tapas 24
Tapas €

(Map p93; ☑93 488 09 77; www.carlesabellan.com; Carrer de la Diputació 269; tapas €4-12; ۩9am-midnight; ☎; MPasseig de Gràcia) Hotshot chef Carles Abellán runs this basement tapas haven known for its gour-met renditions of old faves, including the bikini (toasted ham-and-cheese sandwich, here with truffle and cured ham), freshly cooked tortilla and zesty lemon-infused boquerones. You can't book, but it's worth the wait. For dessert, try the creamy payoyo cheese. Before 1pm, pop in for superb entrepans (filled rolls) and omelettes.

Disfrutar
Modern European €€€

(☑93 348 68 96; www.disfrutarbarcelona.com; Carrer de Villarroel 163; tasting menus €155-195; ۩1-2.15pm & 8-9.15pm Mon-Fri; ☑; MHospital Clínic) Two-Michelin-star Disfrutar ('Enjoy') is among the city's finest restaurants. Run by alumni of Ferran Adrià's game-changing El Bulli, nothing is as it seems, such as black and green olives that are actually chocolate ganache with orange-blossom water. The Mediterranean-inspired decor is fabulously on point, with latticed brickwork and trademark geometric ceramics from Catalan design team Equipo Creativo, and service is faultless.

Lasarte
Modern European €€€

(Map p93; ☑93 445 32 42; www.restaurantlasarte.com; Carrer de Mallorca 259; mains €52-70;

From left: Cañete (p97); Disfrutar; La Vinateria del Call (p97); Seafood tapas at Quimet i Quimet

🕐1.30-3pm & 8.30-10pm Tue-Sat; Ⓜ Diagonal)
One of Barcelona's pre-eminent restaurants – and its first to gain three Michelin stars (in 2016) – Lasarte is overseen by lauded chef Martín Berasategui and headed up by Paolo Casagrande. From Duroc pig's trotters with Jerusalem artichoke to squid tartare with kaffir consommé, this is seriously sophisticated, seasonally inspired cookery, served in an ultra-contemporary dining room by staff who could put the most overawed diners at ease.

🍽 Montjuïc & Poble Sec

Quimet i Quimet   Tapas €
(Map p95; 📞93 442 31 42; www.quimetquimet.com; Carrer del Poeta Cabanyes 25; tapas €4-10, montaditos €3-4; 🕐noon-4pm & 8-10.30pm Mon-Fri, closed Aug; Ⓜ Paral·lel) Now led by its fourth generation, family-run Quimet i Quimet has been passed down since 1914. There's barely space to swing a *calamar* (squid) in this bottle-lined, standing-room-only place, but it's a treat for the palate. Try delectable made-to-order

ⓘ Tickets to FC Barcelona Matches

A match at Barça's Camp Nou (p105) can be breathtaking; the season runs from September to May, and tickets can be bought at www.fcbarcelona.com or FC Botiga. If you can't make it to see Barça play, a trip to the multimedia museum (p92) with a tour through the locker room and out on to the field is a good secondary option.

Camp Nou stadium
NATURSPORTS/SHUTTERSTOCK©

MATT MUNRO/LONELY PLANET©

MICHAEL HEFFERNAN/LONELY PLANET©

montaditos (tapas on bread), such as salmon with greek yoghurt or tuna belly with sea urchin, with a house wine or vermouth.

Agust Gastrobar · Bistro €€

(☑93 162 67 33; www.agustbarcelona. com; Carrer del Parlament 54; mains €16-24; ⊘7pm-midnight Mon-Thu, 2-4pm & 7pm-midnight Fri-Sun; MPoble Sec) Set up by two French chefs (one of whom trained under Gordon Ramsay), Agust occupies a fabulous mezzanine space with timber beams, exposed brick and textured metro tiles. Scallops gratinéed with asparagus and prawn-and-avocado stuffed cannelloni are savoury standouts, with housemade vermouth and inventive cocktails alongside. Desserts include the extraordinary 'el cactus' (chocolate-crumble soil, mojito mousse, lemon sorbet), in a terracotta pot.

Tickets · Tapas €€€

(Map p95; ☑93 292 42 52; www.elbarri. com; Avinguda del Paral·lel 164; tapas €3-30; ⊘6.30pm-midnight Tue-Fri, 1-3.30pm & 7pm-midnight Sat; MPoble Sec) A flamboyant affair playing with circus images and theatre lights, this is one of the restaurant world's sizzling tickets: a Michelin-starred tapas bar by Albert Adrià, of the legendary (now closed) El Bulli, starring dishes that veer towards the deliciously surreal. Bookings are only taken online 60 days ahead, but you can hop on the waiting list for last-minute cancellations.

Enigma · Gastronomy €€€

(☑616 696322; www.elbarri.com; Carrer de Sepúlveda 38-40; tasting menu €220; ⊘7-9.30pm Tue-Fri, 1-2.30pm & 7-9.30pm Sat; MEspanya) Resembling a 3D art installation, this conceptual Michelin-star creation from the famed Adrià brothers is a 40-course tour de force of cutting-edge gastronomy across six dining spaces. A meal takes 3½ hours and includes customised cocktail pairings (you can order additional drinks). There's a minimum of two diners; reserve months in advance (€100 non-refundable deposit per guest).

🍷 DRINKING & NIGHTLIFE

Barcelona is a nightlife lover's town, with an enticing spread of candlelit wine bars, old-school taverns, stylish lounges and kaleidoscopic nightclubs where the party continues until daybreak. For something a little more sedate, the city's atmospheric cafes and teahouses make a fine retreat when the skies turn grey.

🍵 La Rambla & Barri Gòtic

Caelum · Cafe

(Map p88; ☑93 302 69 93; www.facebook.com/ CaelumBarcelona; Carrer de la Palla 8; ⊘10am-8.30pm Mon-Thu, to 9pm Fri-Sun; 🐾; MLiceu) Centuries of heavenly Spanish gastronomic tradition collide at this exquisite medieval space in the heart of the city, which stocks sweets made by nuns across the country (including irresistible Toledo marzipan). The ground-floor cafe is a dainty setting for decadent cakes and pastries. In the stone-walled underground chamber, flickering candles cast a glow on the ruins of a medieval bathhouse.

Cafè de l'Òpera · Cafe

(Map p88; ☑93 317 75 85; www.cafeopera bcn. com; La Rambla 74; ⊘8.30am-2.30am; 🐾; MLiceu) Opposite the Gran Teatre del Liceu, La Rambla's most traditional cafe has been operating since 1929 and remains popular with opera-goers. It's pleasant enough for an early evening drink or, in the morning, coffee and croissants. Head upstairs for a seat overlooking the busy boulevard, and try the house speciality, the *cafè de l'Òpera* (with chocolate mousse).

🍵 El Raval

La Confiteria · Bar

(Map p95; ☑93 140 54 35; www.confiteria.cat; Carrer de Sant Pau 128; ⊘7pm-2am Mon-Thu, 6pm-3am Fri & Sat, 5pm-2am Sun; 🐾; MParal·lel) This evocative tile-covered cocktail hangout is a trip back to the 19th century. Until the 1980s it was a confectioner's shop, and though the original cabinets are now bursting with booze, the look barely changed with its conversion courtesy of one of

Cafè de l'Òpera

Barcelona's foremost teams in nightlife wizardry. The scene these days is lively and creative (drinks €8 to €10).

Bar Marsella — Bar

(☑93 442 72 63; Carrer de Sant Pau 65; ⊙6pm-2am Mon-Thu, 10pm-3am Fri, 6pm-2.30am Sat, 10pm-2.30am Sun; MLiceu) Bar Marsella has been in business since 1820, and has served the likes of Dalí, Picasso, Gaudí and Hemingway. The latter was known to slump here over an *absenta* (absinthe) amid the tiled floors and glinting chandeliers. The bar still specialises in absinthe (€5), a drink to be treated with respect.

🍷 La Ribera

La Vinya del Senyor — Wine Bar

(Map p88; ☑93 310 33 79; www.facebook. com/vinyadelsenyor; Plaça de Santa Maria del Mar 5; ⊙noon-1am Sun-Thu, to 2am Fri & Sat; ☎; MJaume I) Relax on the terrace in the shadow of the Basílica de Santa Maria del Mar or crowd into the tiny bottle-lined bar. From Priorat to Languedoc, the wine list is as long as *War and Peace*, with 20 drops by the glass. Cheese platters and cold meats keep you going. There's an even more intimate space up the twirling staircase.

El Xampanyet — Wine Bar

(Map p88; ☑93 319 70 03; www.elxampanyet. es; Carrer de Montcada 22; ⊙noon-3.30pm & 7-11pm Tue-Sat, noon-3.30pm Sun; ☎; MJaume I) Nothing has changed for decades at chaotic El Xampanyet, one of Barcelona's best-known *cava* (sparkling wine) bars. It's usually packed, but plant yourself at the bar or grab a table against the decoratively tiled walls for a glass or three of the house *cava* and delicious homemade tapas such as tangy *boquerones* in vinegar or perfectly gooey tortilla.

🍷 La Barceloneta & the Waterfront

Perikete — Wine Bar

(Map p88; ☑93 024 22 29; www.gruporeini.com; Carrer de Llauder 6; ⊙noon-1am; MBarceloneta) Since opening in 2017, this fabulous wine spot has been jam-packed with *barcelonins* and visitors. Jabugo hams hang from the

From left: Bar Marsella (p103); El Xampanyet (p103); Gran Teatre del Liceu

ceiling, vermouth barrels sit above the bar and wine bottles cram every available shelf space. There are over 200 varieties by the glass or bottle, accompanied by excellent tapas (€4 to €10) like made-to-order tortilla.

Bodega Vidrios y Cristales   Wine Bar

(Map p88; ☑93 250 45 01; www.gruposagardi. com; Passeig d'Isabel II 6; ☺noon-midnight; Ⓜ Barceloneta) In a history-steeped, stone-floored 1840 building, this atmospheric little jewel recreates an old-style neigh-bourhood bodega with tins of sardines, anchovies and other delicacies lining the shelves (and used in exquisite tapas, €3 to €15), house-made vermouth and a wonderful array of wines, including Anda-lucian *manzanilla* (sherry from Sanlúcar de Barrameda). A handful of upturned wine barrels let you rest your glass.

🍷 L'Eixample

Les Gens Que J'Aime   Bar

(Map p93; ☑93 215 68 79; www.facebook. com/lesgensquejaime.pub; Carrer de València 286; ☺6pm-2.30am Sun-Thu, 7pm-3am Fri &

Sat; Ⓜ Passeig de Gràcia) Atmospheric and intimate, this basement relic of the 1960s follows a deceptively simple formula: chilled jazz music in the background, minimal lighting from an assortment of flea-market lamps, classic cocktails, and a cosy, cramped scattering of red-velvet-backed loungers around tiny dark tables. Tarot readings are also thrown into the mix.

✪ ENTERTAINMENT

Gran Teatre del Liceu   Theatre

(Map p88; ☑902 787397; www.liceubarcelona. cat; La Rambla 51-59; tickets €15-250; Ⓜ Liceu) Barcelona's grand old opera house, skilfully restored after a fire in 1994, is one of the world's most technologically advanced theatres. Taking a seat in its grand audito-rium, returned to all its 19th-century glory but with the very latest in acoustics, you'll time-travel to another age, or join a guided tour (p86) to explore its architectural beauty.

Palau de la Música Catalana   Classical Music

(☑93 295 72 00; www.palaumusica.cat; Carrer Palau de la Música 4-6; tickets from €15; ☺box

IAROV FILIMONOV/SHUTTERSTOCK©

office 9.30am-9pm Mon-Sat, 10am-3pm Sun; MUrquinaona) A feast for both the eyes and ears, this Modernista confection doubles as the city's most traditional venue for classical and choral music, though the wide-ranging programme also takes in flamenco, pop and – particularly – jazz. Just being here for a performance is an experience. Sip a pre-concert tipple in the foyer, its tiled pillars all a-glitter.

Camp Nou   Football

(☑902 189900; www.fcbarcelona.com; Carrer d'Arístides Maillol; MPalau Reial) The massive stadium of Camp Nou ('New Field' in Catalan) is home to the legendary FC Barcelona. Attending a game amid the roar of the loyal crowds is an unforgettable experience; the season runs from August to May. Alternatively, get a taste of all the excitement at the interactive Barça Stadium Tour & Museum (p92).

Tarantos   Dance

(Map p88; ☑93 301 75 64; www.tarantosbar celona.com; Plaça Reial 17; tickets from €17; ☺shows 7.30pm, 8.30pm & 9.30pm Oct-Jun, plus 10.30pm Jul-Sep; MLiceu) Since 1963, this basement locale has been the stage for up-and-coming flamenco groups performing in Barcelona, with stars such as Antonio Gades and Maruja Garrido having graced the space. These days Tarantos is a mostly tourist-centric affair, with reliable half-hour shows three or four times nightly. Still, it's a good introduction to flamenco, and not a bad setting for drinks.

ℹ INFORMATION

SAFE TRAVEL

● Violent crime is rare in Barcelona, but petty crime (bag-snatching, pickpocketing) is a major problem, especially along crowded La Rambla and the touristed city centre. Report thefts to the **Guàrdia Urbana** (Local Police; ☑93 256 24 77, 092; www.bcn.cat/ guardiaurbana; La Rambla 43; ☺24hr; MLiceu).

● You're especially vulnerable when dragging luggage to/from hotels; make sure you know your route.

● Avoid walking around El Raval and the southern end of La Rambla late at night.

○ Take nothing of value to the beach and don't leave anything unattended.

TOURIST INFORMATION

A couple of general tourist information phone numbers are 010 (for Barcelona) and 012 (for all Catalonia, run by the Generalitat) , or see www. barcelonaturisme.com.

Aeroport del Prat (☑93 285 38 32; Aeroport de Barcelona–El Prat, Terminal 2; ☺8.30am-8.30pm)

Catedral (Map p88; ☑93 368 97 00; Plaça Nova, Col·legi d'Arquitectes; ☺9am-7pm Mon-Sat, to 3pm Sun)

Estació Sants (☑93 285 38 34; Barcelona Sants; ☺8.30am-8.30pm daily Apr-Oct, 8.30am-8.30pm Mon-Fri, to 2.30pm Sat & Sun Nov-Mar; ☒Sants Estació)

Oficina de Turisme de Catalunya (Regional Tourist Office; Map p93; ☑93 238 80 91; https:// escasateva.catalunya.com; Passeig de Gràcia 107, Palau Robert; ☺9am-8pm Mon-Sat, to 2.30pm Sun; ☒Diagonal)

Palau Moja (Barri Gòtic) (Map p88; ☑93 285 38 34; Carrer de la Portaferrisa 1; ☺10am-9pm; ☒Liceu)

Plaça de Catalunya (Map p88; ☑93 285 38 34; Plaça de Catalunya 17-S, underground; ☺8.30am-9pm; ☒Catalunya)

Plaça Sant Jaume (Map p88; ☑93 285 38 34; Plaça de Sant Jaume; ☺8.30am-8pm Mon-Fri, 9am-3pm Sat & Sun; ☒Catalunya)

🛈 GETTING THERE & AWAY

AIR

After Madrid, Barcelona is Spain's busiest international transport hub. A host of airlines, including many budget carriers, fly directly to Barcelona from around Europe. Ryanair also uses Girona and Reus airports (buses link Barcelona to both).

Most intercontinental flights require passengers to change flights in Madrid or another major European hub.

Iberia, Air Europa, Spanair and Vueling all have dense networks across the country.

PIO3/SHUTTERSTOCK ©

Barcelona's main airport is **El Prat** (☎91 321 10 00; www.aena.es; 📶), with the majority of international flights arriving here. In addition, there are two other airports in nearby cities, which are used by some budget airlines.

BUS

Long-distance buses leave from **Estació del Nord** (☎93 706 53 66; www.barcelonanord.cat; Carrer d'Alí Bei 80; ℳArc de Triomf). A plethora of companies service different parts of Spain; many come under the umbrella of **ALSA** (☎902 422242; www.alsa.es). For other companies, ask at the bus station. There are frequent services to Madrid, Valencia and Zaragoza (20 or more a day) and several daily departures to distant destinations such as Burgos, Santiago de Compostela and Seville.

Eurolines, in conjunction with local carriers all over Europe, is the main international carrier; its website provides links to national operators. It runs services across Europe and to Morocco from Estació del Nord, and from **Estació d'Autobusos de Sants** (Carrer de Viriat; ℳSants Estació), next to Estació Sants Barcelona.

Much of the Pyrenees and the entire Costa Brava are served only by buses, as train services are limited to important railheads such as Girona, Figueres, Lleida, Ripoll and Puigcerdà.

TRAIN

Train is the most convenient overland option for reaching Barcelona from major Spanish centres like Madrid and Valencia (though it can be a long haul from other parts of Europe). The high-speed TGV train takes around 6½ hours to/from Paris.

A network of *rodalies/cercanías* run by Renfe (www.renfe.com) serves towns around Barcelona (and the airport).

Frequent high-speed Tren de Alta Velocidad Española (AVE) trains between Madrid and Barcelona run daily in each direction, several in under three hours. After the AVE, Euromed and other similarly modern trains, the most common long-distance trains are the slower, all-stops Talgo.

❶ GETTING AROUND

Barcelona is generally best explored on foot. For heading across the city, the excellent metro can get you most places, with buses and trams filling in the gaps. Taxis are the best option late at night.

Bus Covers most of the city, especially where the metro doesn't. The hop-on, hop-off Bus Turístic, from Plaça de Catalunya, is handy on limited time.

Metro The most convenient option. Runs 5am to midnight Sunday to Thursday, to 2am on Friday and 24 hours on Saturday. Targeta T-Casual (10-ride passes; €11.35) are the best value; otherwise, it's €2.40 per ride in Zone 1.

Taxi You can hail taxis on the street (try La Rambla, Via Laietana, Plaça de Catalunya and Passeig de Gràcia) or at taxi stands, or book online/via app.

COSTA BRAVA

Costa Brava at a Glance...

Stretching north to the French border, the Costa Brava, or 'rugged coast', is perhaps Spain's prettiest holiday coast. A handful of tourist developments aside, there are unspoilt coves, charming seaside towns, spectacular scenery, and some of Spain's best diving around the Illes Medes. In the hilly backcountry (green and covered in umbrella pine in the south, barer and browner in the north) are charming stone villages. Further inland, Girona has a sizeable and strikingly well-preserved medieval centre, and Figueres is famous for its bizarre Teatre-Museu Dalí, foremost of a series of sites associated with Salvador Dalí.

Costa Brava in Two Days

Base yourself in Cadaqués (p115) and fall in love with the town that Dalí made his own, most memorably in the **Casa Museu Dalí** (p115) in nearby Port Lligat. Use the town as a base for exploring Cap de Creus (p117) and visit the **Teatre-Museu Dalí** (p112) in Figueres.

Costa Brava in Four Days

With a couple of extra days, spend at least a night in Girona (p119), basing yourself within its medieval core to immerse yourself in its storied history. To complete a triumvirate of Dalí masterpieces, visit **Castell de Puból** (p117), then sleep in the charming coastal town of Tossa de Mar (p114).

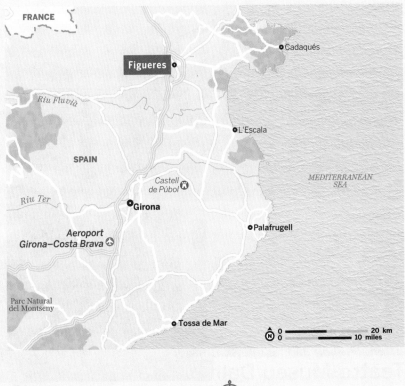

FRANCE

Cadaqués

Figueres

Riu Fluvià

L'Escala

SPAIN

MEDITERRANEAN
SEA

Castell
de Púbol

Riu Ter

Girona

Aeroport
Girona–Costa Brava

Palafrugell

Parc Natural
del Montseny

Tossa de Mar

0 ____ 20 km
N 0 ____ 10 miles

Arriving in Costa Brava

Girona–Costa Brava airport (p120), a Ryanair hub, is 13km southwest of central Girona, with Sagalés (www.sagales. com) connecting it to Girona's main bus/train station (€2.75, 30 minutes, hourly). Direct buses from Barcelona go to most towns on or near the Costa Brava. If driving, the AP7 tollway and the NII highway both run from Barcelona via Girona and Figueres to the French border.

Where to Stay

The Costa Brava has outstanding accommodation, from beachfront hotels to boutique-style places in the old centre of Girona. Girona draws visitors year-round, but many of the coastal towns are very quiet – and we mean very quiet – outside of the peak summer months. Carnaval in February/March is the exception. During weekends and public holidays, particularly in peak season, accommodation should be booked well ahead of time.

Interior of Teatre-Museu Dalí

IAKOV FILIMONOV/SHUTTERSTOCK ©

Teatre-Museu Dalí

Welcome to one of the weirdest, most wonderful art museums anywhere on earth. 'Theatre-museum' is an apt label for this trip through the incredibly fertile imagination of one of the great showmen of the 20th century.

From the moment you lay eyes on this place, the building aims to surprise – from its entrance watched over by medieval suits of armour balancing baguettes on their heads, to bizarre sculptures outside the entrance on Plaça de Gala i Salvador Dalí, to the pink wall along Pujada del Castell. The Torre Galatea, added in 1983, is where Dalí spent his final years. Exhibits within these walls range from enormous installations to the more discreet, such as a mysterious tiny room with a mirrored flamingo.

The interior contains a substantial portion of Dalí's life's work, though you won't find his most famous pieces here: they are scattered around the world. Even so, it's an entirely appropriate final resting place for the master of surrealism, and has helped assure his immortality.

Great For...

Don't Miss

Dalí's heavenly re-imagining of the Sistine Chapel in the Palace of the Wind Room.

Giant eggs outside the museum building

KIEV.VICTOR/SHUTTERSTOCK©

ⓘ Need to Know

www.salvador-dali.org; Plaça de Gala i Salvador Dalí 5, Figueres; adult/child under 9yr €15/free; ⊙9am-8pm Apr-Jul & Sep, 9am-8pm & 10pm-1am Aug, 9.30am-6pm Tue-Sun Oct & Mar, 10.30am-6pm Tue-Sun Nov-Feb

✕ Take a Break

A block away, **Integral** (☎972 51 63 34; www.facebook.com/integral.figueres; Carrer de la Jonquera 30; mains €10-15; ⊙1-3.30pm Mon & Tue, 1-3.30pm & 8-10.30pm Wed-Sat; 🖉) serves excellent vegetarian cooking made from organic ingredients.

★ Top Tip

This is one museum where you'll need to book ahead online.

The Essentials

Where to start? Choice exhibits include *Taxi Plujós* (Rainy Taxi), incorporating an early Cadillac; put a coin in the slot and water washes all over the occupant of the car. The Sala de Peixateries (Fishmongers' Hall) holds a collection of Dalí oils, including the famous *Autoretrat Tou amb Tall de Bacon Fregit* (Soft Self-Portrait with Fried Bacon) and *Retrat de Picasso* (Portrait of Picasso). Beneath the former stage of the theatre is the crypt with Dalí's plain tomb, located at 'the spiritual centre of Europe' as Dalí modestly described it.

Gala, Dalí's wife and lifelong muse, is seen throughout – from the *Gala Mirando el Mar Mediterráneo* (Gala Looking at the Mediterranean Sea) on the 2nd level, which also appears to be a portrait of Abraham Lincoln from afar, to the classic *Leda Atómica* (Atomic Leda).

Other Highlights

After you've seen the more notorious pieces, such as climbing the stairs in the famous Mae West Room, see if you can find a turtle with a gold coin balanced on its back, peepholes into a mysterious tiny room with a mirrored flamingo amid fake plants, and Dalí's re-imagining of the Sistine Chapel in the Palace of the Wind Room.

A separate entrance (same ticket and opening times) leads into Dalí Joies, a collection of 37 jewels designed by Dalí. He designed these on paper (his first commission was in 1941) and the jewellery was made by specialists in New York. Each piece, ranging from the disconcerting Ull del Temps (Eye of Time) through to the Cor Reial (Royal Heart), is unique.

Tossa de Mar

Tossa de Mar curves around a boat-speckled bay, guarded by a headland crowned with impressive defensive medieval walls and towers. Tourism has bolted a larger, modern extension onto this picturesque village of crooked, narrow streets, though its old town and clifftop views retain their magic.

◉ SIGHTS

The deep-ochre fairytale walls and towers on pine-dotted **Mont Guardí**, the headland at the southern end of Tossa's main beach, were built between the 12th and 14th centuries. They encircle the **Vila Vella** (old town), which reached peak splendour in the 15th century; it's now crammed with steep cobbled streets and whitewashed houses garlanded with flowers. A 1917 **lighthouse** crowns Mont Guardí.

> *it's the artist Salvador Dalí who truly gave Cadaqués its sparkle*

From left: Vila Vella; Street statue in Tossa de Mar; Cadaqués boat landing; *Suquet de peix*

⊗ EATING

Keep an eye out for *cim i tomba*, a hearty one-pot fish-and-vegetable stew traditionally prepared out at sea by Tossa's fishermen.

La Cuina de Can Simón Catalan €€€

(☑972 34 12 69; www.cuinacansimon.com; Carrer del Portal 24; mains €28-42, tasting menus €70-100; ⊙1-3.30pm & 8-10.30pm, closed Mon Apr-Jul & Sep, closed Sun night, Mon & Tue Oct-Mar) This is the standout of a slew of restaurants hugging the old wall along Carrer del Portal. Within an 18th-century fisher's stone house, Michelin-starred La Cuina de Can Simón credits its innovative dishes to a dual heritage: the owners' grandparents were a fisherman and an artist. Flavoursome seasonal fusions include meunière sole with Iberian ham, or a seafood-packed bouillabaisse.

ⓘ INFORMATION

Oficina de Turisme de Tossa de Mar (☑972 34 01 08; www.infotossa.com; Avinguda del Pelegrí 25; ⊙9am-9pm Mon-Sat, 10am-2pm & 5-8pm Sun

KAVALENKAVA/SHUTTERSTOCK ©

ISA_FERNANDEZ_FERNANDEZ/SHUTTERSTOCK ©

Jun-Sep, 9.30am-2pm & 4-7pm Mon-Sat, 10am-2pm Sun Oct-May, closed Sun Nov-Mar) Next to Tossa's bus station.

❶ GETTING THERE & AWAY

From Tossa's **bus station** (Plaça de les Nacions Sense Estat), **Sarfa** (www.sarfa.com) runs to/from Barcelona's Estació del Nord (€12.35, 1¼ hours, five to six daily) and airport (€14.50, 2¼ hours, two to five daily), plus Girona airport from mid-June to October (€10.10, 55 minutes, two daily).

Cadaqués

Cadaqués gleams above the cobalt-blue waters of a rocky bay on Catalonia's most easterly outcrop. This whitewashed village owes its allure in part to its windswept pebble beaches and meandering lanes, and the easygoing atmosphere that draws throngs of summer visitors. But it's the artist Salvador Dalí who truly gave Cadaqués its sparkle.

◎ SIGHTS

Casa Museu Dalí   Notable House
(📞972 25 10 15; www.salvador-dali.org; Port Lligat; adult/child under 8yr €12/free; ◷9.30am-9pm mid-Jun–mid-Sep, 10.30am-6pm mid-Sep–early Jan & mid-Feb–mid-Jun, closed early Jan–mid-Feb, plus Mon Nov–mid-Mar) Overlooking a peaceful cove in Port Lligat, a tiny fishing settlement 1km northeast of Cadaqués, this magnificent seaside complex was the residence and sanctuary of Salvador Dalí, who lived here with his wife Gala from 1930 to 1982. The splendid whitewashed structure is a mishmash of cottages and sunny terraces, linked by narrow labyrinthine corridors and containing an assortment of offbeat furnishings. Access is by semi-guided eight-person tour; book well ahead, by phone or online.

✖ EATING

Cadaqués' signature dish is *suquet de peix*, a potato-based fish-and-shellfish stew. Book in advance to dine in busy July and August.

MARTIN SILVA COSENTINO/SHUTTERSTOCK ©

SHEBEKO/SHUTTERSTOCK ©

Enoteca MF
Tapas €€

(Plaça des Poal 3; small sharing plates €6-13; ⊙noon-10pm Mon, Tue & Thu-Sat, to 4pm Sun) A short walk east of the main beach, this wine-centric gastrobar serves up outstanding tapas to tables on a small terrace facing the waterfront. Standouts include sea bass ceviche with thyme, tender razor clams, decadent foie with figs, and beef cheeks with truffle mashed potatoes. Go early, as there are no reservations.

Lua
Fusion €€

(☑972 15 94 52; www.facebook.com/lua.cdqs; Carrer Santa Maria 1; dishes €9-20; ⊙1-4pm & 8pm-midnight May-Sep, closed Tue Oct-Apr, may close Jan-Mar; ☑) A mango-yellow door sets the jazzy tone for delicious, creative Mediterranean-Asian 'soul food' at this laid-back, Italian-run eatery with beer-barrel tables and benches on an old-town alley. It's perfect for vegetarians; try a veggie Venus bowl of black rice, hummus and babaganoush, or lighter bites like cheese platters and original ceramic-bowl salads. Excellent seafood too (tuna tartare and salmon poke bowls).

Compartir
Fusion €€€

(☑972 25 84 82; www.compartircadaques.com; Riera Sant Vicenç; mains €22-30; ⊙1-3.15pm & 8-10.15pm, closed Mon Jul & Aug, closed Mon & Tue Oct, Nov, Apr & May, closed Mon & Sun Nov-Mar) Headed up by a trio of El Bulli alumni, this terrace restaurant revolves around innovative, gourmet sharing plates ('*compartir*' means 'to share'), yet retains a (comparatively) laid-back feel. The always-evolving menu fuses traditional Catalan flavours into contemporary delights like Thai-style turbot or marinated sardines with raspberry, beetroot and pistachios. The setting is a 300-year-old house, and bookings are essential.

ℹ INFORMATION

Oficina de Turisme (☑972 25 83 15; www.visit cadaques.org; Carrer del Cotxe 2; ⊙9am-9pm Mon-Sat, 10am-1pm & 5-8pm Sun Jul–mid-Sep, 9am-1pm & 3-6pm Mon-Sat, 10am-1pm Sun mid-Sep–Jun, closed Sun Oct-Mar)

Oficina de Turisme (www.visitcadaques.org; Port Lligat; ⊙10am-1pm & 4-7pm Tue-Sat, 10am-

Cap de Creus coastal landscape

3pm Sun mid-Jul–mid-Sep) Summer booth next to the Casa Museu Dalí.

ℹ️ GETTING THERE & AWAY

Sarfa (www.sarfa.com) buses connect Cadaqués to Barcelona's Estació del Nord (€25, 2¾ hours, one to two daily) and airport (€27, 3½ hours, one to two daily), plus Figueres (€5.60, one hour, four daily) and Girona (€11, 1¾ hours, one week-days, plus weekends in summer) via Castelló d'Empúries (€4.25, 45 minutes, six daily).

Cap de Creus

Cap de Creus is the most easterly point of the Spanish mainland and is a place of sublime, rugged beauty, battered by the merciless *tramuntana* wind and reach-able by a lonely, 8km-long road that winds its way through the moonscapes. With a steep, rocky coastline indented by coves of turquoise water, it's an especially wonderful place to be at dawn or sunset.

The odd-shaped rocks, barren plateaux and deserted shorelines that litter Dalí's famous paintings were not just a product of his fertile imagination. This is the landscape that inspired the artist, which he described as a 'grandiose geological delirium'.

🏃 ACTIVITIES

The Cap de Creus peninsula is much loved for the walking trails along its craggy cliffs; pick up route maps at the information centre (p118) or Cadaqués' tourist office (p116). **Itinerari 17**, from the Paratge de Tudela car park to Cala Culop (4km return), weaves past the huge Roca Cavallera, which morphed into the subject of Dalí's painting *The Great Masturbator*.

The Cap de Creus peninsula is much loved for the walking trails along its craggy cliffs

🏰 Castell de Púbol

If you're intrigued by Dalí, the **Castell de Púbol** (www.salvador-dali.org; Plaça de Gala Dalí, Púbol; adult/student €8/6; ⊘10am-8pm mid-Jun–mid-Sep, to 6pm Tue-Sun mid-Mar–mid-Jun & mid-Sep–Oct, to 5pm Tue-Sun Nov-early Jan) is an essential piece of the puzzle. Between Girona and Palafrugell (22km northwest of the latter, south off the C66), this 14th-century castle was Dalí's gift to his wife and muse Gala, who is buried here. The Gothic-Renaissance building, with creeper-covered walls, spiral stone staircases and a shady garden, was decorated to Gala's taste, though there are surrealist touches like a grimacing anglerfish fountain and a pouting-lips sofa.

To get here, catch a bus to La Pera from Girona (€3.05, 40 minutes, six to nine daily) or Palafrugell (€3.15, 30 minutes, seven to 10 daily), and alight at the stop on the C66 then walk 2km south to the castle. Alternatively, take a train from Girona to Flaça (€3.30, 15 minutes, at least 15 daily), then taxi the last 5km.

🍴 EATING

Perched atop the cape, the **Bar Restaurant Cap de Creus** (☑972 19 90 05; www.facebook. com/pg/restaurante.capdecreus; mains €11-20; ⊘10am-7pm Mon-Thu, to midnight Fri-Sun Nov-Apr, 9am-midnight daily May-Oct, hours vary) ca-ters to exhausted hikers and beach-goers with an unexpected combination of Catalan and Indian food.

ℹ️ INFORMATION

Espai Cap de Creus (http://parcsnaturals. gencat.cat/ca/cap-creus; ⏲10am-2pm & 3-6pm late-Jun–mid-Sep, 10am-3pm May-late Jun & 2nd half Sep) The park's main information centre has walking route maps and displays about local fauna and flora, inside the cape's lighthouse.

ℹ️ GETTING THERE & AWAY

Cap de Creus is most easily accessed by car, along an 8km gravel road winding northeast from Cadaqués via Port Lligat. Many visitors hike to the cape from Cadaqués (8km, 2½ hours).

Figueres

Fourteen kilometres inland from Catalonia's glistening Golf de Roses lies Figueres, birthplace of Salvador Dalí and now home to the artist's flamboyant theatre-museum. Although Dalí's career took him to Madrid, Barcelona, Paris and the USA, Figueres remained close to his heart. In the 1960s and '70s he created the extraordinary Teatre-Museu Dalí (p113) – a monument to surrealism and a legacy that outshines any other Spanish artist in terms of both popularity and sheer flamboyance. Whatever your feelings about this complex, egocentric man, this museum is worth every cent and minute you can spare.

🎯 SIGHTS

Castell de Sant Ferran   Fort
(www.lesfortalesescatalanes.info; Pujada del Castell; adult/child €3.50/free; ⏲10am-8pm Jul–mid-Sep, 10.30am-6pm mid-Sep–Oct & Apr-Jun, to 3pm Tue-Sun Nov-Mar) Figueres' sturdy 18th-century fortress commands the surrounding plains from a low hill 1km northwest of the centre. The complex is a wonder of military engineering: it sprawls over 32 hectares, with the capacity for

6000 men to march within its walls and snooze in military barracks.

Museu de l'Empordà   Museum
(www.museuemporda.org; La Rambla 2; adult/child €4/free; ⏲11am-8pm Tue-Sat May-Oct, to 7pm Tue-Sat Nov-Apr, 11am-2pm Sun year-round) Extending over four floors, the local museum time travels from ancient amphorae to 7th-century sculptures to rotating installations of contemporary art. You'll find some exceptional early 20th-century works, including lush charcoal drawings by Juan Núñez Fernández, who was Dalí's drawing teacher. Other highlights include landscapes by the watercolour master Ramon Reig Corominas and portraits and still lifes by Marià Baig Minobis.

🍴 EATING

El Motel   Catalan €€
(📞972 50 05 62; www.hotelemporda.com; Hotel Empordà, Avinguda Salvador Dalí 170; mains €15-29; ⏲12.45-3.30pm Sun & Mon, 12.45-3.30pm & 8.30-10.30pm Wed-Sat; 🅿️🛜) Jaume Subirós, the chef and owner of this smart roadside hotel-restaurant 1km north of Figueres' centre, is a seminal figure of the transition from traditional Catalan home cooking to the polished, innovative affair it is today. Local, seasonal ingredients star on the menu, which may feature highlights like salted Rose shrimp, roasted rabbit, or a salad of figs, goat's cheese, mint and pistachio.

Restaurant Durán   Catalan €€
(📞972 50 12 50; www.hotelduran.com; Carrer Lasauca 5; mains €17-28; ⏲12.45-4pm & 8-10.30pm) Dine under the same roof as Salvador Dalí once did at this top-class, chandelier-lit restaurant, where smart service and plush decor are matched by such expertly prepared delights as smoked-salmon tartare, sole in orange sauce and pineapple carpaccio topped by mango ice cream. There's a €25, three-course set menu, along with a seasonal tasting menu (€40).

ℹ️ INFORMATION

Oficina de Turisme Figueres (📞972 50 31 55; www.visitfigueres.cat; Plaça de l'Escorxador 2; ⏰9am-8pm Mon-Sat, 10am-3pm Sun Jul-Aug, 9.30am-6pm Mon-Fri, 10am-5pm Sat, to 2pm Sun Sep-Jun)

ℹ️ GETTING THERE & AWAY

Sarfa (www.sarfa.com) buses serve Cadaqués (€5.60, one hour, four to seven daily) from Figueres' bus station.

Figueres train station, 800m southeast of the centre, has half-hourly trains to/from Girona (€4.10 to €6.90, 30 to 40 minutes) and Barcelona (€12 to €16, 1¾ to 2½ hours).

Girona

Northern Catalonia's largest city, Girona is a jewellery box of museums, galleries and Gothic churches, strung around a web of cobbled lanes and medieval walls. Reflections of Modernista mansions shimmer in the Riu Onyar, which separates the walkable historic centre on its eastern bank from the gleaming commercial centre on the west.

With Catalonia's most diverse nightlife and dining scene outside Barcelona, Girona makes a delicious distraction from the coast.

◎ SIGHTS

Catedral de Girona   Cathedral
(www.catedraldegirona.cat; Plaça de la Catedral; adult/concession incl Basílica de Sant Feliu €7/5; ⏰10am-7.30pm Jul & Aug, to 6.30pm Apr-Jun, Sep & Oct, to 5.30pm Nov-Mar) Towering over a flight of 86 steps rising from Plaça de la Catedral, Girona's imposing cathedral is far more ancient than its billowing baroque facade suggests. Built over an old Roman forum, parts of its foundations date from the 5th century. Today, 14th-century Gothic styling – added over an 11th-century Romanesque church – dominates, though a beautiful, double-columned Romanesque

🍽️ The World's Best Restaurant?

Ever-changing avant-garde takes on Catalan dishes have catapulted **El Celler de Can Roca** (📞972 22 21 57; www.cellercanroca.com; Carrer Can Sunyer 48; degustation menus €190-220, with wine pairing €265-330; ⏰8-9.30pm Tue, 12.30-2pm & 8-9.30pm Wed-Sat) to global fame. Holding three Michelin stars, it's been named one of the best restaurants in the world numerous times by The World's 50 Best. Each year brings new innovations, from molecular gastronomy to multi-sensory food-art interplay, all with mama's home cooking as the core inspiration.

Run by the three Girona-born Roca brothers, El Celler is set in a refurbished country house, 2km northwest of central Girona. Closed some holidays; check the website for availability. Book online 11 months in advance or join the standby list.

Fig stuffed with foie-gras at El Celler de Can Roca
WESTEND61/GETTY IMAGES©

cloister dates from the 12th century. With the world's second-widest Gothic nave, it's a formidable sight to explore, but audio guides are provided.

Museu d'Història dels Jueus   Museum
(www.girona.cat/call; Carrer de la Força 8; adult/child €4/free; ⏰10am-8pm Mon-Sat, to 2pm Sun Jul & Aug, 10am-6pm Tue-Sat, to 2pm Mon & Sun Sep-Jun) Until 1492, Girona was home to Catalonia's second-most important medieval Jewish community, after Barcelona, and

one of the country's finest Jewish quarters. This excellent museum takes pride in this heritage, without shying away from less salubrious aspects such as Inquisition persecution and forced conversions. You also see a rare 11th-century *miqvé* (ritual bath) and a 13th-century Jewish house.

Museu d'Art de Girona
Gallery

(www.museuart.com; Pujada de la Catedral 12; €6, incl Catedral and Basílica de Sant Feliu €10; ⊙10am-7pm Tue-Sat May-Sep, to 6pm Oct-Apr, to 2pm Sun year-round) Next to the cathedral, in the 12th- to 16th-century Palau Episcopal, this art gallery impresses with the scale and variety of its collection. Around 8500 pieces of art, mostly from this region, fill its displays, which ranges from Romanesque woodcarvings and murals to paintings of the city by 20th-century Polish-French artist Mela Muter, early-20th-century sculptures by influential Catalan architect Rafael Masó i Valentí, and works by leading Modernista artist Santiago Rusiñol.

Banys Àrabs
Ruins

(www.banysarabs.org; Carrer de Ferran el Catòlic; adult/child €2/1; ⊙10am-7pm Mon-Sat Mar-Oct, to 6pm Mon-Sat Nov-Feb, to 2pm Sun year-round) Although modelled on earlier Islamic and Roman bathhouses, the Banys Àrabs are a finely preserved, 12th-century Christian affair in Romanesque style (restored in the 13th century). The baths contain an *apodyterium* (changing room), with a small octagonal pool framed by slender pillars, followed by a *frigidarium* and *tepidarium* (with respectively cold and warm water) and a *caldarium* (a kind of sauna) heated by an underfloor furnace.

Muralles de Girona
Walls

(Girona City Walls; Carrer de Ferran el Catòlic; ⊙dawn-dusk) **FREE** A walk along Girona's majestic medieval walls is a wonderful way to soak up the city landscape. There are several access points, including a lane east of the cathedral that leads into the thick greenery of the **Jardins dels Alemanys** (Carrer dels Alemanys). Nearby, you can clamber up a spiral staircase inside the

Torre Gironella (Carrer dels Alemanys) for a fantastic lookout (and an excellent spot to watch the sunset). From there, you can continue along high above the rooftops to the Jardins de la Muralla, where the wall ends.

✪ EATING

La Fábrica
Cafe €

(www.lafabricagirona.com; Carrer de la Llebre 3; dishes €3-9; ⊙9am-3pm; 🖥🥤) ✔ Girona's culinary talents morph into top-quality coffee and Catalan-inspired brunchy favourites starring local ingredients at this energetic German-Canadian–owned cycle-themed cafe. Pillowy artisan *torrades* (toasts) – perhaps topped with avocado, feta and peppers – arrive on wooden sliders, washed down with expertly poured brews made with beans sourced from eco-conscious suppliers.

8de7
Catalan €€

(✆972 10 44 30; Carrer de les Hortes 10; 3-course meal €18, tapas €4-9; ⊙1-4pm & 9-11pm Tue-Sat) It's well worth venturing across the river to this low-key dining room serving up market-fresh daily specials like mouthwatering paella and grilled Iberian pork, as well as a fantastic tapas selection (which can make a fine assorted meal). On clear nights, dine al fresco at the tables in front. Reserve ahead.

ⓘ INFORMATION

Oficina de Turisme de Girona (✆972 01 00 01; www.girona.cat/turisme; Rambla de la Llibertat 1; ⊙9am-8pm Mon-Fri, 9am-2pm & 4-8pm Sat Apr-Oct, 9am-7pm Mon-Fri, 9am-2pm & 3-7pm Sat Nov-Mar, 9am-2pm Sun year-round) Helpful, multilingual office by the river.

ⓘ GETTING THERE & AWAY

AIR

Girona–Costa Brava airport (www.aena.es) is 13km southwest of the centre, with **Sagalés** (www.sagales.com) connecting it to Girona's

KAROL KOZLOWSKI/GETTY IMAGES©

Banys Àrabs

main bus/train station (€2.75, 20 to 30 minutes, hourly), as well as Barcelona's Estació del Nord (one way/return €16/25, 1¼ hours). A taxi to central Girona costs around €25/35 during the day/night.

BUS

Sarfa (www.sarfa.com) serves Cadaqués (€11, 1¾ hours, one weekdays, plus weekends in summer) and other coastal destinations. The bus station is next to the train station, 1km southwest of the old town.

TRAIN

Girona is on the train line between Barcelona (€11.25 to €31.30, 40 minutes to 1¼ hours, at least half-hourly), Figueres (€4.10 to €6.90, 30 to 40 minutes, at least half-hourly) and Portbou, on the French border (€6.15 to €8.25, one hour, 11 to 15 daily).

GRANADA

Granada at a Glance...

Revered for its lavish Alhambra palace, and enshrined in medieval history as the last stronghold of the Moors in Western Europe, Granada is the darker, more complicated cousin of Seville. Twenty-first-century Granada is anything but straightforward. Instead, this stunning city set spectacularly in the crook of the Sierra Nevada is an enigmatic place where – if the mood is right – you sense you might find something that you've long been looking for. A free tapa, perhaps? A flamenco performance that finally unmasks the spirit of duende? Granada has all of this and more.

Granada in Two Days

Spend the best part of a day in the **Alhambra** (p126) – no matter how long you spend here, it won't be enough. Near sunset, head up to the **Mirador San Nicolás** (p131) for wonderful views back across the valley to the Alhambra. Devote the second day to the **Albayzín** (p130), exploring its palaces, teahouses and restaurants.

Granada in Four Days

With more time, dive into the city's tapas culture, especially along Calle de Elvira and Calle Navas, and explore the magnificent Christian monuments of the **Catedral de Granada** (p133), **Capilla Real** (p133) and the gilded **Basílica San Juan de Dios** (p133). Make sure you leave time to explore the signposts to the poet Lorca's legacy. For sustenance, don't miss **El Bar de Fede** (p134), **La Fábula Restaurante** (p135) and **Arrayanes** (p135).

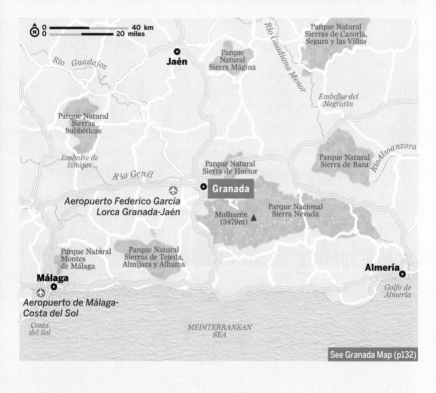

See Granada Map (p132)

Arriving in Granada

Granada is well connected to the rest of Spain by air, bus, train and a network of motorways. Aeropuerto Federico García Lorca is 17km west of the city, to which it is connected by Autocares J González (www.autocaresjosegonzalez.com) buses. The train station, 1.5km northwest of the centre, is connected to the centre by regular buses.

Where to Stay

Granada has accommodation that ranges from brilliant boutique conversions of medieval mansions to business hotels, from flower-strewn, family-run *hostales* (cheap hotels) to palatial digs fit for a king. High season can be any time of the year, but weekends and festivals are particularly busy. And unlike Seville and Córdoba, which bake in summer, Granada is lovely at any time.

Patio de los Leones

Alhambra

The Alhambra is part palace, part fort and a World Heritage Site that's a lesson in medieval architecture. It is unlikely that, as a historical monument, it will ever be surpassed.

Great For...

Don't Miss

Patio de los Leones, the Alhambra's centrepiece and gateway to the inner sanctum.

Palacios Nazaríes

The central palace complex, the Palacios Nazaríes, is the pinnacle of the Alhambra's design. Highlights include the Patio de Arrayanes, where rooms look onto a rectangular pool edged in myrtles, and the Salón de los Embajadores, where the marvellous domed marquetry ceiling uses more than 8000 cedar pieces to create its intricate star pattern representing the seven heavens.

The adjacent Patio de los Leones (Courtyard of the Lions), built in the 14th century, has a fountain that channelled water through the mouths of 12 marble lions as its centrepiece. The stucco work hits its apex here, with almost lace-like detail. On the patio's northern side is the Sala de Dos Hermanas (Hall of Two Sisters), whose dizzying ceiling is a fantastic *muqarnas* dome with some 5000 tiny cells. A reflecting pool

Plasterwork detail

JOSEPPIZARRO/SHUTTERSTOCK ©

🚉 Train Station

Gran Vía de Colón

Alhambra

🛈 Need to Know

📞958 02 79 71, tickets 858 95 36 16; www. alhambra-patronato.es; adult/12-15yr/under 12yr €14/8/free, Generalife & Alcazaba only adult/under 12yr €7/free; ⏰8.30am-8pm Apr–mid-Oct, to 6pm mid-Oct–Mar, night visits 10-11.30pm Tue & Sat Apr–mid-Oct, 8-9.30pm Fri & Sat mid-Oct–Mar

✖ Take a Break

Bring a picnic and behave like royalty by relaxing in the Generalife gardens.

★ Top Tip

Buy tickets online at https://tickets. alhambra-patronato.es/en.

and terraced garden front the small Palacio del Partal (Palace of the Portico), the oldest surviving palace in the Alhambra, from the time of Mohammed III (r 1302–09).

Generalife

From the Arabic *jinan al-'arif* (the overseer's gardens), the Generalife is a soothing arrangement of pathways, patios, pools, fountains, tall trees and, in season, flowers. At the north end is the emirs' summer palace, a whitewashed structure on the hillside facing the Alhambra. The courtyards here are particularly graceful; in the second courtyard, the trunk of a 700-year-old cypress tree suggests what delicate shade once graced the patio. Climb the steps outside the courtyard to the Escalera del Agua, a delightful bit of garden engineering, where water flows along a shaded staircase.

Alcazaba & Christian Buildings

The western end of the Alhambra grounds are the remnants of the Alcazaba, chiefly its ramparts and several towers including the Torre de la Vela (Watchtower), with a narrow staircase leading to the top terrace where the cross and banners of the Reconquista were raised in January 1492.

By the Palacios Nazaríes, the hulking Renaissance-era Palacio de Carlos V, built in 1527 after the Reconquista, clashes spectacularly with its surroundings. Inside, the **Museo de la Alhambra** (⏰8.30am-8pm Wed-Sat, to 2.30pm Sun & Tue mid-Mar–mid-Oct, 8.30am-6pm Wed-Sat, to 2.30pm Sun & Tue mid-Oct–mid-Mar) **FREE** has a collection of Alhambra artefacts and the **Museo de Bellas Artes** (📞958 56 35 08; EU/non-EU citizens free/€1.50; ⏰9am-8pm Tue-Sat Apr–mid-Oct, 9am-6pm Tue-Sat mid-Oct–Mar, 9am-3pm Sun year-round) displays paintings and sculptures from Granada's Christian history.

Alhambra

A TIMELINE

900 CE The first reference to *al-qala'a al-hamra* (the Red Castle) atop the Sabika hill.

1237 Mohammed I, founder of the Nasrid dynasty, moves his court to Granada. Threatened by belligerent Christian armies he builds a new defensive fort, the **❶ Alcazaba**.

1302–09 Designed as a summer palace and country estate for Granada's rulers, the bucolic **❷ Generalife** is begun by Mohammed III.

1333–54 Yusuf I initiates the construction of the **❸ Palacios Nazaríes**, still considered the highpoint of Islamic culture in Europe.

1350–60 Up goes the **❹ Palacio de Comares**, taking Nasrid lavishness to a whole new level.

1362–91 The second coming of Mohammed V ushers in even greater architectural brilliance, exemplified by the construction of the **❺ Patio de los Leones**.

1527 The Christians add the **❻ Palacio de Carlos V**. Inspired Renaissance palace or incongruous crime against Moorish art? You decide.

1829 The languishing, half-forgotten Alhambra is 'rediscovered' by American writer Washington Irving during a protracted sleepover.

1954 The Generalife gardens are extended southwards to accommodate an outdoor theatre.

TOP TIPS

➡ Booking tickets as far ahead as possible is essential; by phone or online.

➡ You can visit the general areas of the palace free of charge any time by entering through the Puerta de la Justicia.

➡ Within the Alhambra grounds, the lavish Parador de Granada is a fabulous (and pricey) place to stay, or just pop in for a drink or meal.

CHOI HYEKYUNG / SHUTTERSTOCK ©

Sala de la Barca
Throw your head back in the anteroom to the Comares Palace, where the gilded ceiling is shaped like an upturned boat. Destroyed by fire in the 1890s, it has been painstakingly restored.

Palacio de Carlos V
It's easy to miss the stylistic merits of this Renaissance palace, added in 1527. Check out the ground-floor Museo de la Alhambra for artefacts directly related to the palace's history.

Mexuar

Patio de Machuca

Palacios Nazaríes

Illustration Detail

Puerta de la Justicia

Alcazaba
Find time to explore the towers of the original citadel, the most important of which – the Torre de la Vela – takes you, via a winding staircase, to the Alhambra's best viewpoint.

EMPERORCOSAR / SHUTTERSTOCK ©

Palacio de Comares

The largest room in the Palacio de Comares, renowned for its rich geometric ceiling, is the Salón de los Embajadores – a negotiating room for the emirs and a masterpiece of Moorish design.

Patio de los Arrayanes

If only you could linger longer beside the rows of *arrayanes* (myrtle bushes) that border this calming rectangular pool. Shaded porticos with seven harmonious arches invite further contemplation.

Salón de los Embajadores

Baños Reales

Washington Irving Apartments

Sala de Dos Hermanas

Focus on the *dos hermanas* – two marble slabs either side of the fountain – before enjoying the intricate cupola embellished with 5000 tiny moulded stalactites. Poetic calligraphy decorates the walls.

(4)

Patio de los Arrayanes

Patio de la Lindaraja

(5)

Sala de los Reyes

Sala de los Abencerrajes

Jardines del Partal

Palacio del Partal

Generalife

A coda to most people's visits, the 'architect's garden' is no afterthought. While Nasrid in origin, the horticulture is relatively new: the pools and arcades were added in the early 20th century.

Patio de los Leones

Count the 12 lions sculpted from marble, holding up a gurgling fountain. Then pan back and take in the delicate columns and arches built to signify an Islamic vision of paradise.

Alhambra Practicalities

Some parts of the Alhambra can be visited free of charge, but for the main areas you'll need a ticket. There are several types: a General ticket (€14) covers all areas; a Gardens ticket (€7) gives entry to all areas except the Palacios Nazaríes; Night Visit Palacios Nazaríes (€8) allows year-round night visits to the Nasrid Palaces; Night Visit Gardens & Generalife tickets (€5) are available from April to May and September to mid-October; Dobla de Oro (€19.65) covers admission to the Alhambra and several sites in the Albayzín neighbourhood.

You can buy tickets from two hours to three months in advance, online, by phone or at the Alhambra ticket office. Rarely, a few 'leftover' tickets may be available at the ticket office on the day.

If you've booked a ticket, you can either print it yourself or pick it up at the ticket office at the Alhambra Entrance Pavilion or the Corral del Carbón, where there's a ticket machine. All children's tickets must be collected at the Alhambra ticket office as you'll need to prove your kids' ages.

Audio guides are available for €6. No outside food is allowed.

By foot, walk up the Cuesta de Gomérez from Plaza Nueva through the woods to the Puerta de la Justicia. Bus C3 runs to the ticket office from a bus stop just off Plaza Isabel la Católica.

Detail from Palacios Nazaríes
MEGSTANTON/BUDGET TRAVEL©

◉ SIGHTS

North of Plaza Nueva (Granada's main square), the Albayzín district is demarcated by Gran Vía de Colón and the Río Darro. Over the river is the Alhambra hill, whose southwest slopes are occupied by the Realejo, Granada's former Jewish quarter. West of the Albayzín, the centre is home to the cathedral.

◎ Alhambra & Realejo

Centro de la Memoria Sefardí   Museum

(☑610 060255; museosefardidegranada@gmail.com; Placeta Berrocal 5; tour €5; ⊙10am-2pm & 5-8pm Sun & Tue-Thu, 10am-2pm Fri Apr-Oct, 10am-2pm & 4-8pm Sun & Tue-Thu, 10am-2pm Fri Nov-Mar) The Sephardic Jews were expelled en masse in 1492, and there are very few left living in Granada. But this didn't stop one enterprising couple from opening a museum to their memory in 2013, the year the Spanish government began offering Spanish citizenship to any Sephardic Jew who could prove their Iberian ancestry. The owners also do Realejo tours on advance request.

◎ Near Plaza Nueva

Baños Árabes El Bañuelo   Architecture

(Carrera del Darro 31; €5, Sun free; ⊙9.30am-2.30pm & 5-8.30pm May–mid-Sep, 10am-5pm mid-Sep–Apr) Sitting by the Río Darro, this well-preserved Moorish bathhouse dates to the 11th or 12th century. Light beams into its vaulted brick rooms through octagonal star-shaped shafts, illuminating columns, capitals and marble-tiled floors. The ticket includes entrance to the Palacio de Dar-al-Horra.

◎ Albayzín

On the hill facing the Alhambra across the Darro valley, Granada's old Muslim quarter (the Albayzín) is a place for aimless wandering; you'll get lost regularly whatever map you're using. The cobblestone streets are lined with signature only-in-Granada *cármenes* (large mansions with walled gardens, from the Arabic '*karm*' for garden). The Albayzín survived as the Muslim quarter for several decades after the Christian conquest in 1492.

Bus C1 runs circular routes from Plaza Nueva around the Albayzín about every seven to nine minutes, from 7.30am to 11pm.

Palacio de Dar-al-Horra   Palace

(671 563553; Callejón de las Monjas; €5, Sun free; 9.30am-2.30pm & 5-8.30pm May–mid-Sep, 10am-5pm mid-Sep–Apr) Up high in the Albayzín – down a lane off Placeta de San Miguel Bajo and Callejón del Gallo – this 15th-century Nasrid palace was the home of sultana Aixa, the mother of Boabdil, Granada's last Muslim ruler. It's surprisingly intimate, with rooms set around a central courtyard and fabulous views across the surrounding neighbourhood and over to the Alhambra. After the Reconquista, it was incorporated into the adjacent Monasterio de Santa Isabel la Real. Admission includes entry to the El Bañuelo Moorish baths.

For those classic shots of the Alhambra...wander up to this well-known lookout

Calle Calderería Nueva   Street

Linking the upper and lower parts of the Albayzín, Calle Calderería Nueva is a narrow street famous for its *teterías* (teahouses). It's also a good place to shop for slippers, hookahs, jewellery and North African pottery from an eclectic cache of shops redolent of a Moroccan souk.

Mirador San Nicolás   Viewpoint

(Plaza de San Nicolás) For those classic sunset shots of the Alhambra sprawled along a wooded hilltop with the Sierra Nevada mountains looming in the background, wander up through the Albayzín to this well-known lookout (reached via Callejón de San Cecilio). Expect pastel-hued sunsets and crowds of camera-toting tourists, students and buskers; it's also a haunt of pickpockets and bag-snatchers, so keep your wits about you. Other fab viewpoints pop up across the surrounding streets.

Calle Calderería Nueva

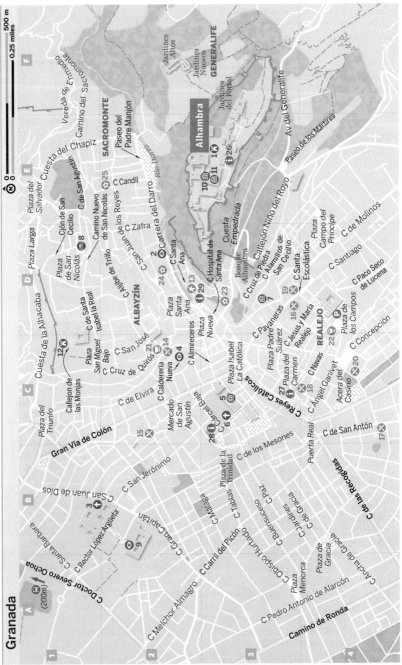

Granada

N

0.25 miles

500 m

GENERALIFE

Jardines
Altos

Jardines
Nuevos

Jardines
del Portal

Alhambra 1

i 26

Av del Generalife

Paseo de los Mártires

Paseo del Padre Manjón

SACROMONTE

Camino del Sacromonte

Vereda de Enmedio

Cuesta del Chapiz

Cuesta del Salvador

Plaza del
Salvador

C de San Agustín 25

Camino Nuevo
de San Nicolás

C Candil

C Zafra

Carretera del Darro 2

Río Darro

10 11

Cuesta
Empedrada

Callejón Niño del Royo

Plaza del
Príncipe

Campo del

C de Molinos

Cjón de San
Cecilio

Plaza Larga

Plaza
de San
Nicolás 8

C Santa
Ana

24 13

C Hospital de
Santa Ana

Bosque
Alhambra

Cuesta de Piedra

C Alamillos de
San Cecilio

C Santa
Escolástica

C Santiago

C Paco Seco
de Lucena

C Aljibe de Trillo

ALBAYZÍN

C San Juan de los Reyes

Plaza
Santa
Ana

29

Plaza
Nueva

23

7 19

C Santa

16

REALEJO

22

Plaza de
los Campos

C de Santa
Isabel la Real

C de San José

Plaza
San Miguel
Bajo

C Calderería
Nueva 14

21 4

C Almireceros

C Payaneras

Plaza Padre
Suárez

C Jesús y María

C Navas

C Concepción

Cuesta de la Alhacaba

12

Callejón de
las Monjas

C Cruz de Quirós

Plaza Isabel
La Católica

C Reyes Católicos

27 Plaza del
Carmen 18

Acera del
Casino 20

Plaza de
Gracia

Plaza del
Triunfo

Gran Vía de Colón

C de Elvira

Mercado
de San
Agustín

15

Cárcel Baja

5

28 6

C Ángel Ganivet

C de San Antón 17

C San Jerónimo

Puerta Real

C de las Recogidas

Plaza de la
Trinidad

C de los Mesones

San Juan de Dios

3

C Málaga

C Tablas

C Buensuceso

Obispo Hurtado

C Carril del Picón

C Melchor Almagro

C Rector López-Argüeta

C Gran Capitán

9

C de Santa Bárbara

C Doctor Severo Ochoa

(200m)

Plaza
Menorca

C Pedro Antonio de Alarcón

Ancha de Gracia

Camino de Ronda

Granada

◎ Plaza Bib-Rambla & Around

Capilla Real
Historic Building

(☏958 22 78 48; www.capillarealgranada.com; Calle Oficios; adult/child €5/free; ◷10.15am-6.30pm Mon-Sat, 11am-6pm Sun) The Royal Chapel is the last resting place of Spain's Reyes Católicos (Catholic Monarchs), Isabel I de Castilla (1451–1504) and Fernando II de Aragón (1452–1516), who commissioned the elaborate Isabelline-Gothic-style mausoleum that was to house them. Commenced in 1505, it wasn't completed until 1517, hence the royals' interment in the Alhambra's Convento de San Francisco (p127) until 1521. Their monumental marble tombs (and those of their heirs) lie behind a 1520 gilded wrought-iron screen by Bartolomé de Jaén.

Catedral de Granada
Cathedral

(☏958 22 29 59; www.catedraldegranada. com; Plaza de las Pasiegas; adult/child €5/ free; ◷10am-6.30pm Mon-Sat, 3-5.45pm Sun) From street level, it's difficult to appreciate the immensity of Granada's cavernous, boxed-in cathedral. But it's nonetheless a monumental work of architecture, and one of Spain's largest cathedrals. Built atop Granada's former mosque, it was originally

intended to be Gothic, but over the two centuries of its construction (1523–1704) it underwent major modifications. Most notably, architect Diego de Siloé changed its layout to a Renaissance style, and Alonso Cano added a magnificent 17th-century baroque facade.

◎ Outside the Centre

Basílica San Juan de Dios
Basilica

(☏958 27 57 00; www.basilicasanjuandedios. es; Calle San Juan de Dios 19; adult/child €5/free; ◷10am-8pm Mon-Sat, 2-8pm Sun Jun-Sep, to 7pm Oct-May) Built between 1737 and 1759, this spectacular basilica unveils a blinding display of opulent baroque decor. Barely an inch of its interior lacks embellishment, most of it in gleaming gold and silver. Frescos by Diego Sánchez Sarabia and Italian artists Corrado Giaquinto and Tomás Ferrer adorn the ceilings and side chapels, while up above the basilica's dome soars to 50m. The highlight, however, is the extraordinary gold altarpiece in the Capilla Mayor (main chapel). Audio guides bring the details to life.

Monasterio de San Jerónimo
Monastery

(☏958 27 93 37; Calle Rector López Argüeta 9; €4; ◷10am-1.30pm & 4-7.30pm Apr-Oct, 10am-1.30pm

Granada Card

The five-day **Granada Card** (www.
granadatur.com; adult €36 to €40, child
€11) covers admission to 10 city monuments, including the Alhambra, and nine
free trips on local city buses.

Palacio de Carlos V, Alhambra (p127)
MARQUES/SHUTTERSTOCK©

& 3-6.30pm Nov-Mar) With Gothic cloisters,
fragrant orange trees and a lavishly decorated interior, this 16th-century monastery
is one of Granada's most stunning Catholic
buildings. Behind a plateresque entrance by
Diego de Siloé, the church mixes late-Gothic
and Renaissance styling, and reveals a
profusion of painted sculptures and vivid
colours, most spectacularly on the apse's
immense eight-level gilt retable.

⊕ ACTIVITIES

Hammam Al Ándalus   Hammam
(☎958 22 99 78; www.granada.hammamal
andalus.com; Calle Santa Ana 16; baths €38, with
massage from €50; ☉10am-midnight) With
three pools of different temperatures, plus
a steam room and the option of skin-
scrubbing massages, this is the best of Granada's Moorish-style baths. Its dim, tiled

*this is the best of Granada's
Moorish-styled baths.*

rooms are suitably sybaritic and relaxing.
Reservations required.

⊗ EATING

Hicuri Art Restaurant   Vegan €
(☎858 98 74 73; www.restaurantehicuriartvegan.
com; Plaza de los Girones 3; mains €7.50-10,
menú del día €14; ☉noon-11pm Mon-Sat; ☞) ✿
Granada's leading street artist, El Niño de
las Pinturas, has been let loose inside Hi-
curi, creating a psychedelic backdrop to the
wonderful vegan food and organic wines
served at this easy-going, hugely popular
restaurant. Zingy salads, creative veggie
burgers and curried seitan sit alongside
plant-based renditions of Andalucian faves,
like shiitake croquettes or *pisto* (ratatouille)
with *patatas a lo pobre*.

Picoteca 3Maneras   Andalucian €€
(☎958 22 68 18; www.facebook.com/pico
teca3maneras; Calle Santa Escolástica 19;
mains €12-17; ☉1-4.30pm & 8pm-midnight
Tue-Sat, 1-4.30pm Sun; ☞) ✿ Glorious
fresh produce, spot-on service, chic
whitewashed decor, excellent Spanish
wines and a deliciously creative approach
to local cuisine make Picoteca a Realejo
gem. South American and various Asian
flavours infuse ambitiously reimagined
dishes such as pork-and-wild-mushroom
risotto, pear-and-pancetta gnocchi, and
tuna in orange sauce; every Sunday there's
a special *arroz*.

El Bar de Fede   Andalucian €€
(☎958 28 88 14; www.facebook.com/Elbar
deFede1; Calle Marqués de Falces 1; raciones €9-
15; ☉9am-2am Mon-Thu, to 3am Fri & Sat, 11am-
2am Sun) 'Fede' refers to hometown poet
Federico García Lorca, whose free, creative
spirit seems to hang over this chicly styled,
gay-friendly bar. Patterned wallpaper, stone
arches and high tables set around a ceram-
ic-tiled island create a casual feel, and the
food is a joy. Standouts include aubergines
drizzled with honey, chicken in orange
sauce and perfect garlic-parsley squid.

Arrayanes
Moroccan €€

(✆619 076862, 958 22 84 01; www.rest-arra
yanes.com; Cuesta Marañas 7; mains €10-17;
⊙1.30-4.30pm & 7.30-11.30pm Wed-Sun, closed
mid-Jan–mid-Feb; 🖌) Granada hosts some
excellent Moroccan kitchens, especially
in the Albayzín, and long-established Arrayanes one of its best. Tinkling fountains,
ceramic tiles and ornate arches set the
stage for superb North African staples,
from *bisara* split-pea soup to steaming tagines and flaky *pastelas* (savoury pies). No
alcohol, but the mint lemonade is perfect.

Los Diamantes
Tapas €€

(✆958 227 070; www.barlosdiamantes.com; Calle
Navas 26; raciones €10-14; ⊙12.15-5.30pm &
7.15pm-midnight) A Granada institution, going
strong since 1942, this scruffy, always-busy
joint is one of the best tapas hangouts on
bar-packed Calle Navas. It's standing room
only, but the seafood – fried squid, grilled
prawns, *boquerones* – is excellent and
there's a sociable scene. Branches around
town, including on Plaza Nueva.

La Fábula
Restaurante
Gastronomy €€€

(✆958 25 01 50; www.restaurantelafabula.com;
Calle de San Antón 28, Hotel Villa Oniria; mains
€23-30, tasting menus €80-125; ⊙2-3.30pm &
8.30-10.30pm) 🍴 A formal fine-dining restaurant set in a stylishly restored 1909 *palacete*
(now the Hotel Villa Oniria), La Fábula is the
domain of star chef Ismael Delgado López,
whose artfully composed plates of contem-
porary-Spanish cuisine with strong, seasonal
Granada flavours impress: fresh fish from
Motril, *ibérico* pork cheeks, Riofrío caviar,
smoked-cheese ravioli with garlic and honey.
The terrace garden is lovely for a drink.

Restaurante Chikito
Andalucian €€€

(✆958 22 33 64; www.restaurantechikito.com;
Plaza Campillo 9; mains €18-28; ⊙12.30-4.30pm
& 7.30-11.30pm Thu-Tue) Lorca hung out at this
restaurant back in the day, when it was called
the Café Alameda. Nowadays, its woody,
faux-medieval interior caters to a mix of visitors and smartly dressed locals who come
to dine on timeless favourites such as oxtail

🍽 Free Tapas

Granada – bless its generous heart – is
one of the last bastions of that fantastic
practice of free tapas with every drink.
Place your drink order at the bar and,
hey presto, a plate will magically appear
with a generous portion of something
delicious-looking on it. Order another
drink and another plate will materialise.
The process is repeated with every
round you buy – and each time the
tapa gets better. Packed shoulder-to-
shoulder with tapas institutions, Calle
de Elvira and Calle Navas are good
places for bar crawls.

JAYME WISEMAN/SHUTTERSTOCK©

stew, roast lamb and *remojón* (orange-and-
cod salad).

🍷 DRINKING & NIGHTLIFE

The best street for drinking is the rather
scruffy Calle de Elvira, but other chilled bars
line Río Darro at the base of the Albayzín
and Calle Navas. Just north of Plaza de Trinidad are a bunch of cool, hipster-ish bars.

Taberna La Tana
Wine Bar

(✆958 22 52 48; www.facebook.com/Taberna
LaTana; Placeta del Agua 3; ⊙12.30-4pm &
8.30pm-midnight, closed Sat & Sun Jul & Aug)
With bottles stacked to the rafters and a
small wood-and-brick interior, friendly La
Tana is one of Granada's greatest wine bars.
It specialises in Spanish labels (over 400 of
them!), backed up with beautifully paired
tapas. Ask about the wines of the month.

From left: Montaditos tapas; Hammam in Granada; Peña La Platería

Abaco Té Teahouse

(www.abacote.com; Calle Álamo de Marqués 5; ⏱3-9.30pm; 📶) Hidden up in the Albayzín, outrageously popular Abaco puts an arty contemporary spin on the traditional *tetería* (no hookahs). Choose from an encyclopaedic list of infusions (€2.50 to €4), fresh juices, excellent cakes and vegetarian snacks (crepes, salads, *montaditos*). The roof terrace is irresistible.

😄 ENTERTAINMENT

Do not miss the nightly shows (€30; 8pm) in the **Palacio de los Olvidados** (📞958 19 71 22; www.flamencolosolvidados.com; Cuesta de Santa Inés 6; adult/child €18/12; ⏱shows 8.15pm & 9.30pm), which combine Lorca's plays with some magnificent self-penned flamenco. Best night out in Granada. No contest!

Peña La Platería Flamenco

(📞603 473228, 958 21 06 50; www.laplateria.org. es; Placeta de Toqueros 7) Founded in 1949, La Platería claims to be Spain's oldest flamenco club. Unlike some of Andalucía's more private clubs, it regularly opens its doors to nonmembers for soulful, foot-stomping performances on Thursday nights at 10pm, as well as on other sporadic occasions. Tapas and drinks are available. Book ahead!

Casa del Arte Flamenco Flamenco

(www.casadelarteflamenco.com; Cuesta de Gomérez 11; shows €20; ⏱shows 7.30pm & 9pm) A small flamenco venue that is neither a *tablao* (choreographed flamenco show) nor a *peña* (private club), but something in between. The performers are invariably top-notch, managing to conjure a highly charged mood in the intimate space.

ℹ INFORMATION

Oficina de Información Turística (Alhambra) (📞958 02 79 71; www.granadatur.com; Calle Real de la Alhambra; ⏱7.30am-8.30pm May-Oct, to 6.30pm Nov-Apr) In the Alhambra.

Oficina de Turismo Municipal (📞958 24 82 80; www.granadatur.com; Plaza del Carmen 9; ⏱9am-6pm Mon-Sat, to 2pm Sun) The official city tourist office.

Oficina de Turismo Provincial (📞958 24 71 28; www.turgranada.es; Calle Cárcel Baja 3; ⏱9am-

8pm Mon-Fri Mar-Oct, to 7pm Nov-Feb, 10am-7pm Sat, 10am-3pm Sun year-round) Information on Granada province.

Oficina de Turismo Regional (☑958 57 52 02; www.andalucia.org; Calle Santa Ana 2; ☺9am-7.30pm Mon-Fri, 9.30am-3pm Sat & Sun) For information on the whole Andalucía region.

ⓘ GETTING THERE & AWAY

AIR

Aeropuerto Federico García Lorca Granada-Jaén (Map p137; ☑913 211000; www.aena.es) is 17km west of the city, near the A92. Direct flights connect with Madrid, Barcelona, Bilbao, Palma de Mallorca, London, Manchester and Milan.

Alsa (☑902 42 22 42; www.alsa.es) bus 245 runs to the city centre (€3, 20 to 40 minutes) at 6am and then at least hourly between 9.20am and 10pm.

BUS

Granada's **bus station** (Avenida Juan Pablo II) is 3km northwest of the city centre. Alsa (p137) runs

buses across the region, including to/from Las Alpujarras, and has one to two daily direct connections to Madrid's Barajas airport (€47, 4¾ hours).

TRAIN

The train station is 1.5km northwest of the centre, off Avenida de la Constitución. For the centre, walk straight ahead to Avenida de la Constitución and turn right to pick up the LAC bus to Gran Vía de Colón. There are regular services to Madrid (€37 to €81, 3¼ hours), Barcelona (€36 to €75, 6¼ to 7½ hours), Córdoba (€15 to €49, 1¼ to 2 hours) and Seville (€29 to €62, 2¼ to 4 hours).

ⓘ GETTING AROUND

Individual bus tickets are €1.40 (€1.50 at night); pay the bus driver with notes or coins. The most useful lines are C1, which departs from Plaza Nueva and does a full circuit of the Albayzín; C2, which runs from Plaza Nueva up to Sacromonte; and C3, which goes from Plaza Isabel II up through the Realejo quarter to the Alhambra.

ANDALUCIAN HILL TOWNS

Andalucian Hill Towns at a Glance...

Andalucía's hill towns rank among Spain's most memorable attractions, from the Moorish echoes of the high-altitude hamlets of Las Alpujarras in the east to Arcos de la Frontera in the west. These pueblos blancos (white villages) cling to impossibly steep hillsides and rocky crags, ancient village fortresses rising from the plains. Up close, in the twisting laneways and pretty squares, there is an intimacy to the experience, a hidden world unchanged in centuries.

Andalucía's Hill Towns in Three Days

Las Alpujarras (p142) has the densest concentration of whitewashed hill towns anywhere in Andalucía – spend at least two days exploring the area, mixing in some short day hikes with driving between the villages to sample the local cuisine. On your third day, make a bee-line for **Ronda** (p146), one of the most beautiful villages anywhere in Spain.

Andalucía's Hill Towns in One Week

After visiting Las Alpujarras and Ronda, spend at least a night in **Arcos de la Frontera** (p144), preferably sleeping in the *parador* (state-owned hotel). Add a couple of extra nights exploring the **Sierra de Grazalema** (p151) – Zahara de la Sierra, Olvera and Grazalema are stunning hill towns with some great hiking in the vicinity. Don't miss **Carmona** (p158) and **Vejer de la Frontera** (p160) to round out your week.

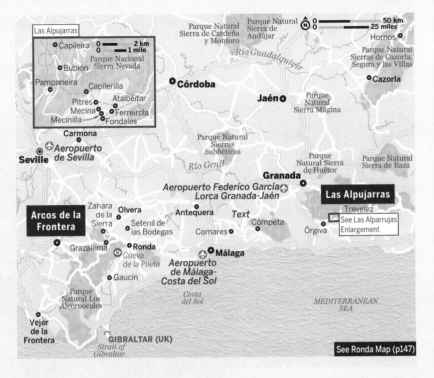

Arriving in Andalucía's Hill Towns

There are numerous gateways to Andalucía's hill towns. Málaga is ideal if Ronda is your starting point; it receives flights from all over Europe. Granada works for Las Alpujarras, while Seville or Jerez de la Frontera are convenient for Arcos de la Frontera. All of these airports and train stations have car-rental offices, although we recommend reserving your vehicle in advance.

Sleeping

Every village and town across the region has accommodation, from peerless *paradors* to welcoming, family-run *hostales* (cheap hotels) and *casas rurales* (rural homes), with plenty of midrange places in between. Ronda, Arcos de la Frontera, Vejer de la Frontera and the villages of Las Alpujarras have the widest selection.

Trevélez

Las Alpujarras

The icy sentinels of the Sierra Nevada lord it over Las Alpujarras, a jumble of deep green valleys and stunning white, pocket-sized villages. Together they represent some of the most breathtaking scenery in Spain.

Great For...

Don't Miss

Trevélez, home to some of Andalucía's finest *jamón serrano*.

Las Alpujarras' 70km-long jumble of valleys consists of arid hillsides split by deep ravines, its oasis-like white villages set beside rapid streams and surrounded by gardens, orchards and woodlands. Las Alpujarras has a historical personality all its own: Las Alpujarras was the last part of Spain to retain a strong Muslim population and it shows in everything from the architecture to the cuisine.

Barranco de Poqueira

When seen from the bottom of the Poqueira gorge, the three villages of Pampaneira, Bubión and Capileira, 14km to 20km northeast of Órgiva, look like splatters of white paint flicked Jackson Pollock–style against the grey stone behind. They're the most beautiful and most visited villages of the Alpujarras. The Poqueira is famous for its

Jámon shop

PHILIP LEE HARVEY/LONELY PLANET©

❶ Need to Know

You'll need your own wheels around here. Spring and autumn are the best months to visit.

✖ Take a Break

Taberna Restaurante La Tapa (☑618 307030; Calle Cubo 6; mains €8-18; ⊙noon-4pm & 8pm-midnight; 🚲) 🐚 in Capileira serves Moorish dishes in a lovely setting.

★ Top Tip

The further east you go along the valleys, the fewer tourists you're likely to find.

multitude of artisan crafts; leather, weaving and tilework are all done using age-old methods. Then there is the unique cuisine made using locally produced ham, jam, cheese, honey, mushrooms and grapes. Equally alluring are the hiking trails that link the villages, many of them perfectly doable in a day.

Trevélez

To gastronomes, Trevélez equals ham – or *jamón serrano* to be more precise – one of Spain's finest cured hams that matures perfectly in the village's rarefied mountain air. It is the second-highest village in Spain, sited at 1486m on the almost treeless slopes of the Barranco de Trevélez.

La Tahá

In the next valley east from Poqueira, life gets substantially more tourist-free. Still known by the Arabic term for the administrative districts into which the Islamic caliphate divided the Alpujarras, this region consists of the town of Pitres and its six outlying villages – Mecina, Capilerilla, Mecinilla, Fondales, Ferreirola and Atalbéitar – in the valley just below, all of Roman origin. Day trippers are few.

Las Alpujarras Walking Trails

The alternating ridges and valleys of Las Alpujarras are criss-crossed with a network of mule paths, irrigation ditches and hiking routes, for a near-infinite number of good walks between villages or into the wild. The villages in the Barranco de Poqueira are the most popular starting point, but even there, you'll rarely pass another hiker on the trail. Colour-coded routes ranging from 4km to 23km (two to eight hours) run up and down the gorge, and you can also hike to Mulhacén (3479m; mainland Spain's highest peak) from here.

Arcos de la Frontera

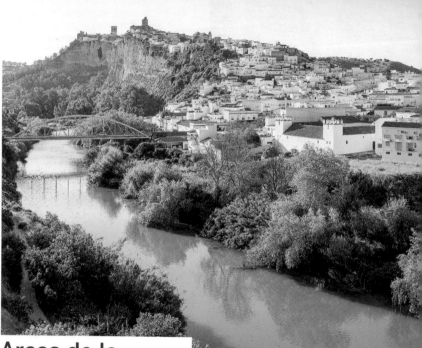

STEFANO_VALERI/SHUTTERSTOCK ©

Arcos de la Frontera

Everything you've ever dreamed a pueblo blanco (white town) to be materialises in Arcos de la Frontera, with its thrilling clifftop location and old town full of winding streets and mystery.

The appeal of Arcos de la Frontera lies in walking its stunning streets and catching glimpses of the glorious views out across the plains that surround the town. There are, however, a few attractions worth seeking out as you explore the town.

Basílica Menor de Santa María de la Asunción

This Gothic-cum-baroque **creation** (Plaza del Cabildo; €2; ⊙10am-12.45pm & 4-6.30pm Mon-Fri, 10am-1.30pm Sat Mar–mid-Dec) is one of Andalucía's more beautiful and intriguing small churches, built over several centuries on the site of a mosque. Check out the ornate gold-leaf altarpiece (a miniature of the one in Seville cathedral) carved between 1580 and 1608, a striking painting of San Cristóbal (St Christopher), a 14th-century

---

Great For...

Don't Miss

The lookout on Plaza del Cabildo at the heart of the old town.

Bell tower at Basílica Menor de Santa María de la Asunción

Need to Know

Park in Plaza de España, then take the half-hourly 'microbus' up to the old town.

Take a Break

Atmospheric **Aljibe** (622 83 65 27; Calle Cuesta de Belén; mains €10-19; 12.30-4pm & 7.30-11.30pm Wed-Mon;) serves Moroccan-inspired cuisine in a re-imagined 18th-century cistern.

★ Top Tip

Even if you don't stay in the parador, wander into its public areas for fabulous views.

mural uncovered in the 1970s, an ornate wood-carved choir and the lovely Isabelline ceiling tracery.

Plaza de Cabildo

Lined with fine ancient buildings, Plaza del Cabildo is the centre of the old town, its vertiginous **mirador** affording exquisite vistas over the Río Guadalete. The 11th-century, Moorish-built **Castillo de los Duques** is closed to the public, but its outer walls frame classic Arcos views. On the square's eastern side, the **Parador de Arcos de la Frontera** (956 70 05 00; www.parador.es; r €120-150;) is a reconstruction of a 16th-century magistrate's house.

Mirador de Abadés

Less famous than the mirador on Plaza del Cabildo, the **Mirador de Abadés** (Calle Abadés) offers a sweeping panorama of Arcos and the surrounding country from the southeastern end of the old town.

Convento de las Mercedarias

It's not often that buying biscuits feels like going to confession, but step into the vestibule of this ancient **convent** (Plaza Boticas), push a bell and a concealed nun on the other side of a wooden partition will invite you to buy a bag of sweet treats. Place your money in a revolving compartment and within a couple of minutes it will flip back round with your order on it.

A Frontier Town

Arcos' strategic position made it an important prize and, for a brief period during the 11th century, Arcos was an independent Berber-ruled *taifa* (small kingdom). In 1255, it was claimed by Christian King Alfonso X El Sabio for Seville and it remained 'de la Frontera' (on the frontier) between Moorish and Christian Spain until the fall of Granada in 1492.

Ronda

Perched on an inland plateau riven by the 100m fissure of El Tajo gorge, Ronda is one of Andalucía's most spectacular towns. It has a superbly dramatic location and owes its name ('surrounded' by mountains) to the encircling Serranía de Ronda.

⊙ SIGHTS

La Ciudad, the historic old town on the southern side of El Tajo gorge, is an atmospheric area for a stroll, with its evocative, still-tangible history, Renaissance mansions and wealth of museums. The newer town, where you'll be deposited if you arrive by bus or train, harbours the emblematic bullring and the leafy Alameda del Tajo gardens. Three bridges crossing the gorge connect the old town with the new.

Puerta de Almocábar   Gate

The old town is surrounded by massive fortress walls pierced by two ancient gates: the Islamic Puerta de Almocábar, which in the 13th century was the main gateway to the castle, and the 16th-century **Puerta de Carlos V**. Inside, the Islamic layout remains intact, but the maze of narrow streets now takes its character from the Renaissance mansions of powerful families whose predecessors accompanied Fernando el Católico in the taking of the city in 1485.

Iglesia de Santa María La Mayor   Church

(Calle José M Holgado; adult/child €4.50/2; ☺10am-8pm Apr-Sep, to 7pm Mar & Oct, to 6pm Nov-Feb, closed 12.30-2pm Sun) The city's original mosque metamorphosed into this elegant church. Just inside the entrance is an arch covered with Arabic inscriptions that was part of the mosque's *mihrab* (prayer niche indicating the direction of Mecca). The church has been declared a national monument, and its interior is a riot of decorative styles and ornamentation. A huge central cedar choir stall divides the church into two sections: aristocrats to the front, everyone else at the back.

Plaza de Toros   Notable Building

(Calle Virgen de la Paz; €8, incl audio guide €9.50; ☺10am-8pm Apr-Sep, to 7pm Mar & Oct, to 6pm Nov-Feb) In existence for more than 200 years, this is one of Spain's oldest bullrings and the site of some of the most important events in bullfighting history. A visit is a way of learning about this deep-rooted Spanish tradition without actually attending a bullfight. The on-site Museo Taurino is crammed with memorabilia such as blood-spattered costumes worn by 1990s star Jesulín de Ubrique. It also includes artwork by Picasso and photos of famous fans such as Orson Welles and Ernest Hemingway.

Baños Árabes   Historic Site

(Calle San Miguel; €3.50, Tue free; ☺10am-3pm Sat & Sun year-round, to 7pm Mon-Fri Apr-Sep, to 6pm Mon-Fri Oct-Mar) Backing onto Ronda's river, these 13th-century Arab baths are among the best-preserved in all of Andalucía, with horseshoe arches, columns and clearly designated divisions between the hot and cold thermal areas. An excellent 10-minute video (in Spanish and English) helps you visualise the baths in their heyday. Enjoy the pleasant walk down here from the centre of town.

Puente Nuevo   Bridge

(New Bridge; interpretive centre adult/reduced €2.50/2; ☺interpretive centre 10am-6pm Mon-Fri, to 3pm Sat & Sun) Straddling the dramatic gorge of the Río Guadalevín (Deep River) is Ronda's most recognisable sight, the towering Puente Nuevo, so named not because it's particularly new (building started in 1759) but because it's newer than the **Puente Viejo** (Old Bridge). A rather lacklustre interpretive centre documenting the bridge's history sits directly underneath. You'll get better bridge views from above, or from the **Sendero Los Molinos**, which runs along the bottom of the gorge. The bridge separates the old and new towns.

Plaza de España   Square

The town's main square was made famous by Ernest Hemingway in *For Whom the Bell Tolls*. Chapter 10 tells how, early in

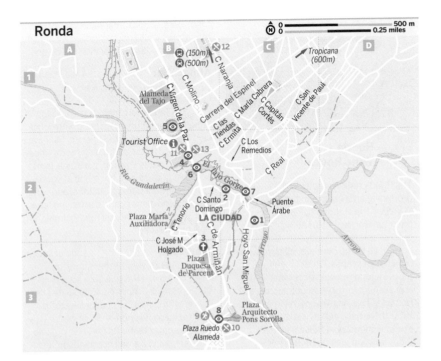

Ronda

the civil war, the 'fascists' of a small town were rounded up in the *ayuntamiento* (town hall), clubbed, and made to walk the gauntlet between two lines of townspeople before being thrown off a cliff. The episode is based on events that took place here in the Plaza de España. What was the *ayuntamiento* is now Ronda's **parador** (☏952 87 75 00; www.parador.es; Plaza de España; r €143-326; P❄@🌐🏊).

Casa del Rey Moro   Gardens

(House of the Moorish King; ☏617 610808; www. casadelreymoro.org; Calle Cuesta de Santo Domingo 9; adult/reduced €6/3; ⊙10am-9.30pm May-Sep, to 8pm Oct-Apr) Several landscaped terraces give access to La Mina, an Islamic stairway of nearly two hundred steps cut into the rock all the way down to the river at the bottom of the gorge. These steps enabled Ronda to maintain water supplies when it was under attack. It was also the

Ronda Wine Route

The Ronda region was a major wine-producing area in Roman times; Ronda la Vieja is the archaeological site of the great Roman city of Acinipo, which means 'among the vineyards'. Coins have been found here embellished with bunches of grapes. Other viticultural relics include remains of ceramic kilns and even a bronze head of Bacchus at a Roman villa in nearby Los Villares. Since 1990 there has been a renaissance of the wine industry in these parts and today you can visit up to 21 wineries in the region (by prior appointment). Check www.ruta-vinos-ronda.com for more details.

JESUS NOGUERA PHOTOGRAPHY/SHUTTERSTOCK ©

point where Christian troops forced entry in 1485. The steps are dark, steep and wet in places. Take care.

✖ EATING

Typical Ronda food is hearty mountain fare, with an emphasis on stews (called *cocido*, *estofado* or *cazuela*), *trucha* (trout), *rabo de toro* (oxtail stew) and game such as *conejo* (rabbit), *perdiz* (partridge) and *codorniz* (quail).

Bodega San Francisco   Tapas €
(www.bodegasanfrancisco.com; Calle Comandante Salvador Carrasco; tapas €1-2, raciones €6-10; ⏱noon-5pm & 7pm-midnight Fri-Wed) This is one of Ronda's cheapest and most Spanish

tapas bars, with a remarkable variety of tapas, plus a full lineup of grilled meats and Iberian hams. It's just north of the centre.

Almocábar   Andalucian €€
(☑952 87 59 77; Calle Ruedo Alameda 5; tapas €2, mains €15-25; ⏱12.30-4.30pm & 8-11pm Wed-Mon) Tapas here include *montaditos* (small pieces of bread) topped with delicacies like duck breast and chorizo. Mains are available in the elegant dining room, where meat dominates – rabbit, partridge, lamb and beef cooked on a hot stone at your table. There's a bodega upstairs, and wine tastings and dinner can be arranged for a minimum of eight people (approximately €50 per person).

Tropicana   Andalucian €€
(☑952 87 89 85; www.facebook.com/tropicana ronda; cnr Avenida Málaga & Calle Acinipo; mains €12-20; ⏱12.30-3.30pm & 7.30-10pm Wed-Sun) A little off the trail in Ronda's new town, the Tropicana has nonetheless garnered a strong reputation for its certified-organic food, served in a small but handsome restaurant with the feel of a modern bistro.

Tragatá   Tapas €€
(☑952 87 72 09; www.tragata.com; Calle Nueva 4; mains €12-25; ⏱1.15-3.45pm & 8-11pm; 🐾) A small outpost for Ronda's gourmet guru, Benito Gómez, who runs the nearby **Bardal** (☑951 48 98 28; www.restaurantebardal.com; Calle José Aparicio 1; 15-course/19-course tasting menu €115/140; ⏱noon-4.30pm & 8-11.30pm Tue-Sat), Tragatá allows you to sample some of the same *cocina alta* (haute cuisine) at a fraction of the price. The eruption of flavours ranges from tomato salad with mint and basil to Japanese *tatakis* to pig's trotter and pig's snout stew.

ℹ INFORMATION

Tourist Office (☑952 18 71 19; www.turismo deronda.es; Paseo de Blas Infante; ⏱9.30am-6pm Mon-Fri, to 5pm Sat, to 2.30pm Sun) Opposite the Plaza de Toros; provides information on the town and region.

Plaza de Toros (p146)

GETTING THERE & AWAY

BUS

From the town's **bus station** (Plaza Concepción García Redondo 2), **Comes** (956 80 70 59; www.tgcomes.es) runs to Cádiz (€18, 3½ hours). **Damas** (959 25 69 00; www.damas-sa.es) goes to Seville (€12.75, 1¾ to 2¾ hours) via Algodonales (€3.60, 40 minutes) and Grazalema (€3, 50 minutes). **Avanzabus/Portillo** (912 72 28 32; www.avanzabus.com) has four daily buses to Málaga (€12.70, 2¾ to three hours) and eight to Marbella (€6.85, 1¼ hours).

CAR

There are a number of underground car parks charging €2.40 per hour or €18 per day. Some hotels offer parking deals for guests, and there's also free street parking on the periphery of town.

TRAIN

Ronda's **train station** (952 87 16 73; www. renfe.com; Avenida de Andalucía) is on the line between Bobadilla and Algeciras. Trains run to Algeciras (€11.50 to €20.10, 1½ to two hours,

five daily) via Gaucín and Jimena de la Frontera. This train ride is one of Spain's finest and worth taking just for the views. Other trains depart for Málaga (€12, two to 2¾ hours, one daily), Madrid (€55.70, four hours, three daily) and Granada (€16.65, 2½ to three hours, three daily). For Seville, change at Bobadilla or Antequera-Santa Ana. It's less than 1km from the train station to most accommodation. A taxi will cost around €7.

Cómpeta

This picturesque village with its panoramic views, steep winding streets and central bar-lined plaza overlooking the 16th-century church has long attracted a large, mixed foreign population. Not only has this contributed to an active cultural scene, but Cómpeta is also home to one or two good restaurants serving contemporary cuisine. It also has a couple of charity shops (rare in Spain) and a foreign-language bookshop. The village is a good base for hiking and other similar outdoor activities.

✪ ACTIVITIES

El Lucero
Walking

An exhilarating long walk from Cómpeta is up the dramatically peaked El Lucero (1779m), from whose summit, on a clear day, you can see both Granada and Morocco. This is a demanding full-day return hike from Cómpeta, but it's possible to drive as far up as Puerto Blanquillo pass (1200m) via a slightly hairy mountain track from Canillas de Albaida.

Los Caballos del Mosquín
Horse Riding

(☏608 658108; www.horseriding-andalucia.com; Canillas de Albaida; half-day trek €90-100) Specialises in guided horse-riding treks in the mountains of La Axarquía ranging from one hour to three days (including full board and accommodation). Located up a steep road between Cómpeta and Canillas de Albaida.

> *Few white towns are as perfect as Grazalema*

✪ EATING

Taberna-Tetería Hierbabuena
Moroccan €

(☏630 916553; www.facebook.com/restaurante tabernahierbabuena; Avenida de la Constitución 35; mains €6-13; ⊙9am-midnight Tue-Sun) Though it has its share of low-slung tables, shapely lampshades and silver teapots, the Hierbabuena isn't your average *tetería* (teahouse): it offers English breakfasts, 'curry nights' and mushy peas, as well as teas and tagines. The combination seems to satisfy the food urges of its largely expat clientele.

El Pilón
International €€

(☏952 55 35 12; www.restaurantelpilon.com; Calle Laberinto 3; mains €11-20; ⊙7-11pm; ☏) This former carpenter's workshop is the village's most popular restaurant – and rightly so. Dishes are created using locally sourced ingredients whenever possible, and the eclectic options include tandoori chicken, swordfish with olive tapenade and some truly creative vegetarian dishes. There's a cocktail lounge with sweeping views, regular entertainment, and sticky toffee pudding for homesick Brits.

From left: Cómpeta; Zahara de la Sierra (p153); Baños Árabes, Ronda (p146); Grazalema

Taberna-Restaurante
Casa Paco   Andalucian €€

(📞952 51 60 77; www.facebook.com/casapaco competa; Plaza Almijara 6; mains €10-26; ⊗9am-midnight Tue-Sat, from 10am Sun) One of three restaurants with alfresco seating under a cluster of umbrellas in the main square, Paco – the one nearest to the church – is the best, with strong coffee, traditional tapas, speedy waitstaff and good crêpes.

ℹ️ INFORMATION

Tourist Office (📞952 55 36 85; Avenida de la Constitución; ⊗10am-2.30pm Mon-Sat, to 2pm Sun) Located beside the bus stop at the foot of the village; has plenty of information about the town and region.

ℹ️ GETTING THERE & AWAY

Three buses travel daily from Málaga to Cómpeta (€4.50, 1½ hours), stopping via Torre del Mar. There's a free car park up the hill from the tourist office.

Sierra de Grazalema

The rugged, pillar-like peaks of the Parque Natural Sierra de Grazalema rise abruptly from the plains northeast of Cádiz, revealing sheer gorges, rare firs, wild orchids and the province's highest summits, against a beautifully green backdrop at altitudes of 260m to 1648m. This is the wettest part of Spain – stand aside, Galicia and Cantabria, Grazalema village logs an average 2200mm annually. It's gorgeous walking country (best months: May, June, September and October), and, for the more intrepid, adventure activities abound.

The 534-sq-km park, named Spain's first Unesco Biosphere Reserve in 1977, extends into northwestern Málaga province, where it includes the **Cueva de la Pileta** (📞666 741775; www.cuevadelapileta.org; Benaoján; adult/child €10/6; ⊗tours 10am-1pm & 4-6pm May-Sep, to 5pm Oct-Apr), a cave with Stone Age paintings near Benaoján.

Grazalema

Few white towns are as perfect as Grazalema, with its spotless whitewashed houses

 Setenil de las Bodegas

While most white towns sought protection atop lofty crags, the people of Setenil did the opposite and burrowed into the dark caves beneath the steep cliffs of the River Trejo. The strategy clearly worked. It took the Christian armies a 15-day siege to dislodge the Moors from their well-defended positions in 1484. Many of the original cave-houses remain and some have been converted into bars and restaurants. Further afield, you can hike along the 6km **Ruta de los Molinos** past ancient mills to the next village of **Alcalá del Valle**.

The tourist office is near the top of the town in the 16th-century **Casa Consistorial**, which exhibits a rare wooden Mudéjar ceiling. A little higher up is the 12th-century **castle** (opening hours are sporadic; check at the tourist office), captured by the Christians just eight years before the fall of Granada.

Setenil has some great tapas bars that make an ideal pit-stop while you study its unique urban framework. Start in Restaurante Palermo in Plaza de Andalucía at the top of town and work your way down.

of rust-tiled roofs and wrought-iron window bars sprinkled on the steep, rocky slopes of its eponymous mountain range. Hikes fan out in all directions, making Grazalema the most popular base for adventures into

the Parque Natural Sierra de Grazalema, and the village is also an age-old producer of blankets, honey, cheese and meat-filled stews, and has its own special mountain charm.

✖ EATING

La Maroma   Tapas €€
(📞956 13 22 79; www.facebook.com/gastrobar lamaroma; Calle Santa Clara; tapas €2-6, mains €6-16; ⏱noon-5pm & 7.30-11pm Tue-Sun; 🛜🍴) The cooking is more fun and inventive than the rustic check cloths, beamed ceiling and bull-festival inspired music suggests at this cosy gastrobar, run by a young family team. Creative local-inspired tapas and *raciones* throw mountain ingredients into tasty bites like mushrooms in honey-and-thyme sauce, wafer-thin chips, *huevos rotos* (fried eggs with potatoes), or *payoyo*-cheese salad with Grazalema-honey dressing. There's a dedicated vegan/vegetarian menu.

Restaurante El Torreón   Andalucian €€
(📞956 13 23 13; Calle del Agua 44; mains €7-18; ⏱1-4pm & 7-10.30pm Thu-Tue; 🛜🍴) This cosy, friendly restaurant with a roaring winter fire specialises in traditional mountain cuisine, from local chorizo and cheese platters to *tagarnina* (thistle) scrambles (a Cádiz delicacy) and sirloin in green-pepper sauce. There's also a meat-free Andalucian-style menu (mushroom risotto, *tagarnina* croquettes, spinach scramble). Tables spill onto the street when it's sunny.

ℹ INFORMATION

Oficina de Turismo (📞956 13 20 52; www. grazalema.es; Plaza de los Asomaderos; ⏱9am-3pm Tue-Sun Jun-Sep, 10am-2pm & 3-5.30pm Tue-Sun Oct-May) Excellent Parque Natural Sierra de Grazalema walking information, plus last-minute, same-day hiking permits (in person only). Probably the province's most helpful tourist office.

Zahara de la Sierra

ⓘ GETTING THERE & AWAY

Damas (☏959 25 69 00; www.damas-sa.es) runs two daily buses to/from Ronda (€3, 1½ hours); two to three daily to/from Ubrique (€2.32, 40 to 60 minutes), two of them via Benaocaz (€1.61, 10 to 30 minutes); and one daily Monday to Friday to/from El Bosque (€1.44, 40 minutes), where you can change for Arcos de la Frontera.

Zahara de la Sierra

Strung around a vertiginous crag at the foot of the Grazalema mountains, over-looking the glittering turquoise Embalse de Zahara (Zahara Reservoir), rugged Zahara hums with Moorish mystery. For over 150 years in the 14th and 15th centuries, it stood on the old medieval frontier facing off against Christian Olvera, clearly visible in the distance. These days Zahara ticks all the classic white-town boxes, its streets framed by tall palms and hot-pink bougain-villea. It's also a great base for hiking the Garganta Verde, so it's popular. During the afternoon siesta, however, you could hear a pin drop.

◎ SIGHTS

Zahara village centres on Calle San Juan; towards its western end stands the 20th-century **Capilla de San Juan de Letrán** (Calle San Juan; ◷11am-1.30pm), with a Moorish-origin clock tower, while at its eastern end is the pastel-pink, 18th-century baroque **Iglesia de Santa María de Mesa** (Plaza del Rey; admission by donation; ◷11am-2pm & 3-6pm). Below the central plaza is a garden of rare *pinsapos* (Mediterranean firs).

⊗ EATING

El Pantalán   Andalucian €
(☏602 298232; www.elmogote.com; Carretera A2300; mains €7-15; ◷10am-11pm daily May-Sep, closed Tue & Wed Oct-Apr; ☕) Fabulous Zahara views across the glassy reservoir make this relaxed restaurant and waterfront lounge bar, 3km north of town, hugely popular on warm days. Barbecued meats, seafood bites like fried *chocos* (cuttlefish) or *tortillitas de camarones* (shrimp fritters), and tapas of local cheese or *tagarnina* stew are

among the classic dishes. It's attached to water sports outfitter El Mogote.

Al Lago
Andalucian €€

(☑956 12 30 32; www.al-lago.es; Calle Félix Rodríguez de la Fuente; mains €8-20; ⊙12.30-4.30pm & 8-10.30pm Thu-Tue Mar-Oct; 🛜🅿) 🍴 At the foot of the village, overlooking Zahara's reservoir, British-American-run Al Lago serves Andalucian cuisine with an inventive, contemporary slant. Seasonal, often organic regional ingredients star in creations ranging from beautifully prepared flatbread pizzas, mountain-cheese platters and local trout to chef Stefan's six-course tasting menus (€42), all expertly paired with Cádiz and Málaga wines. Excellent vegetarian and gluten-free options.

Also here are six subtly chic lake-view rooms and two kitchen-equipped **apartments** (☑956 12 30 32; www.al-lago.es; Calle Félix Rodríguez de la Fuente; incl breakfast d €85-117, f €98-110, apt €82-92; ⊙Mar-Oct; ❄🛜).

GETTING THERE & AWAY

Comes (☑956 80 70 59; www.tgcomes.es) runs two daily weekday buses to/from Ronda (€4.60, 45 to 75 minutes).

Antequera

Known as the crossroads of Andalucía, Antequera sees plenty of travellers pass through but few lingering visitors. But those who choose not to stop are missing out. The town's foundations are substantial: two Bronze Age burial mounds guard its northern approach and Moorish fables haunt its grand Alcazaba. The undoubted highlight here, though, is the opulent Spanish-baroque style that gives the town its character and that the civic authorities have worked hard to restore and maintain. There's also an astonishing number of churches – more than 30, many with wonderfully ornate interiors.

Dolmen de Menga

⊙ SIGHTS

Antequera
Dolmens Site   Archaeological Site

(⊙9am-3pm & 8-10pm Tue-Sat, 9am-3pm Sun
Jul–mid-Sep, hours vary rest of year) **FREE** Antequera's two earth-covered burial mounds –
the **Dolmen de Menga** and the **Dolmen de
Viera** – were built out of megalithic stones
by Bronze Age people around 2500 BC.
When they were rediscovered in 1903, they
were found to be harbouring the remains of
several hundred bodies. Considered to be
some of the finest Neolithic monuments in
Europe, they were named a Unesco World
Heritage site in 2016.

Alcazaba   Fortress

(adult/child €4/2, incl Colegiata de Santa María
la Mayor €6/3; ⊙10am-6pm) Favoured by the
Granada emirs of Islamic times, Antequera's hilltop Moorish fortress has a fascinating history and covers a massive 62,000
sq metres. The main approach to the hilltop
is from Plaza de San Sebastián, up the
stepped Cuesta de San Judas and then
through an impressive archway, the **Arco
de los Gigantes**, built in 1585 and formerly
bearing huge sculptures of Hercules. All
that's left today are the Roman inscriptions
on the stones.

Colegiata de Santa
María la Mayor   Church

(Plaza Santa María; adult/child €3/1.50, incl Alcazaba €6/3; ⊙10am-6pm) Just below the Alcazaba is the large 16th-century Colegiata de
Santa María la Mayor. This church-college
played an important part in Andalucía's
16th-century humanist movement, and
flaunts a beautiful Renaissance facade,
lovely fluted stone columns inside and a
Mudéjar *artesonado* (a ceiling of interlaced
beams with decorative insertions). It also
plays host to some excellent musical events
and exhibitions. Just outside the church
entrance, don't miss the ruins of Roman
baths dating from the 3rd century AD.

Iglesia del Carmen   Church

(Plaza del Carmen; €2; ⊙11am-1.30pm Tue-Sat
Jul–mid-Sep, hours vary rest of year) Only the
most jaded would fail to be impressed by
the Iglesia del Carmen and its marvellous
18th-century Churrigueresque *retablo*
(altarpiece). Magnificently carved in red
pine by Antequera's own Antonio Primo, it's
spangled with statues of angels by Diego
Márquez y Vega, and saints, popes and
bishops by José de Medina. While the main
altar is unpainted, the rest of the interior
is a dazzle of colour and design, painted to
resemble traditional tile work.

⊗ EATING

Welcome to a bastion of traditional
cooking. Antequera specialities include
porra antequerana (a thick and delicious
garlicky soup that's similar to gazpacho),
bienmesabe (literally 'tastes good to me'; a
sponge dessert) and *angelorum* (a dessert
incorporating meringue, sponge and egg
yolk). Antequera also does a fine breakfast
mollete (soft bread roll), served with a
choice of fillings.

Baraka   Tapas €

(☎664 390778; Plaza de las Descalzas; tapas
€2-4; ⊙10am-2am Mon & Wed-Fri, from 11am Sat
& Sun) Sombreros off to the brave staff at
Baraka, who cross a busy road, trays loaded, risking life and limb to serve punters
sitting in a little park opposite. Like all good
Antequera restaurants, Baraka doesn't
stray far from excellent local nosh (*porra
antequerana* calls loudly), although it does
a nice sideline in *pintxos* (Basque tapas)
and serves heavenly bread.

Arte de Cozina   Andalucian €€

(☎952 84 00 14; www.artedecozina.com; Calle
Calzada 27; tapas €2.80-3.50, mains €15-24; ⊙1-
11pm) It's hard not to notice the surrounding agricultural lands as you approach
Antequera, and this fascinating little
hotel-restaurant combo is where you get
to taste what they produce. Slavishly true
to traditional dishes, it plugs little-known
Antequeran specialities such as gazpacho
made with green asparagus or *porra* with
oranges, plus meat dishes that include
lomo de orza (preserved pork loin).

Recuerdos Tapas Bodega   Tapas €€

(☑951 35 63 65; Calle Laguna 5; tapas €1.85-3.90, raciones €8-16; ⊙12.30-5pm & 8pm-midnight) Classy, casual Recuerdos stands out for its innovative home cooking, backed by a varied lineup of wines and cocktails. Three dozen flavourful offerings – Iberian pork loin with pineapple, homemade partridge pâté with rosemary oil and Seville orange marmalade, and shrimp fritters with avocado aioli – all come as tapas, *medias raciones* and *raciones*. It's a 10-minute walk north of the tourist office.

ⓘ INFORMATION

Municipal Tourist Office (☑952 70 25 05; http://turismo.antequera.es; Calle Encarnación 4; ⊙9.30am-7pm Mon-Sat, 10am-2pm Sun) A helpful tourist office with information about the town and region.

ⓘ GETTING THERE & AWAY

Antequera has two train stations. Closest to town is the **Antequera-Ciudad train station** (Avenida de la Estación), 1.5km north of the centre. At research time, work was still underway on a new high-speed train tine that will eventually connect Antequera-Ciudad with Granada and Almería. In the meantime, Antequera-bound train passengers must disembark at **Antequera-Santa Ana station**, 18km northwest of the town, and catch a free Renfe bus transfer into town.

High-speed AVE trains travel from Antequera-Santa Ana to Málaga (€27, 25 minutes, eight daily), Córdoba (€34, 35 minutes, 13 daily) and Madrid (€76, 2½ hours, 10 daily).

Sierra de Cazorla, Segura y Las Villas

One of the biggest drawcards in Jaén province – and, for nature lovers, in all of Andalucía – is the mountainous, lushly wooded Parque Natural Sierras de Cazorla, Segura y Las Villas. This is the largest protected area in Spain – 2099 sq km of craggy mountain ranges, deep, green river valleys, canyons, waterfalls, remote hilltop castles and abundant wildlife, with a snaking, 20km-long reservoir, the Embalse del Tranco, in its midst. The abrupt geography, with altitudes varying between 460m at the lowest point up to 2107m at the summit of Cerro Empanadas, makes for dramatic changes in the landscape.

The best times to visit the park are spring and autumn, when the vegetation is at its most colourful and temperatures are pleasant. The park is hugely popular with Spanish tourists and attracts several hundred thousand visitors each year. The peak periods are Semana Santa, July, August and weekends from April to October.

Cazorla

This picturesque, bustling white town sits beneath towering crags just where the Sierra de Cazorla rises up from a rolling sea of olive trees, 45km east of Úbeda. It makes the perfect launching pad for exploring the beautiful Parque Natural Sierras de Cazorla, Segura y Las Villas, which begins dramatically among the cliffs of Peña de los Halcones (Falcon Crag) directly above the town.

◉ SIGHTS

The heart of town is **Plaza de la Corredera**, with busy bars and the elegant *ayuntamiento*, in a 400-year-old former monastery, looking down from its southeast corner. Canyon-like streets lead south to the **Balcón de Zabaleta**. This little viewpoint is like a sudden window in a brick wall, with stunning views over the white houses up to the picturesque **Castillo de la Yedra** (Museo del Alto Guadalquivir; EU/non-EU citizen free/€1.50; ⊙tours 10.30am, noon, 1.30pm, 4pm, 5.30pm & 7pm Tue-Sat, 10.30am, noon & 1.30pm Sun) and the mountains beyond. From here another narrow street leads down to Cazorla's most picturesque square, **Plaza de Santa María**, dominated by the shell of the 16th-century **Iglesia de Santa María** (Plaza de Santa María; church ad-

Parque Natural Sierras de Cazorla, Segura y Las Villas

mission free, tour €2; ⊘9.30am-1.30pm & 4-8pm Tue-Sun Apr-Oct, to 7pm Nov-Mar).

Castillo de La Iruela — Castle

(Cuesta Santo Domingo, La Iruela; €1; ⊘10am-2pm & 4-8pm Wed-Mon) In a stunningly picturesque and panoramic perch on a rocky pinnacle towering over pretty La Iruela village, this ancient fortification is well worth the 3km drive or 1.5km uphill walk from central Cazorla. It was founded in early Islamic times though the keep and much of the walls date from after the castle's conquest by the Archbishop of Toledo in 1231. Brooding below is the shell of the 16th-century Iglesia de Santo Domingo, torched by Napoleonic troops two centuries ago.

⊗ EATING

La Yedra — Andalucian €

(⊘953 71 02 92; Calle Cruz de Orea 51; mains €9-14; ⊘noon-midnight Mon-Sat) Rub elbows with the locals at this down-to-earth spot near Cazorla's market, where the lunchtime *menú del día* (including appetiser, main

course, dessert and drink) goes for €11. Expect traditional country fare like *sopa de ajo* (garlic soup) followed by filling mains such as stewed pork with tomatoes, peppers and potatoes.

Mesón Leandro — Spanish €€

(⊘953 72 06 32; www.mesonleandro.com; Calle Hoz 3; mains €12-26; ⊘1.30-4pm & 8.30-11pm Wed-Mon) Leandro is a step up in class from most other Cazorla eateries, offering professional but friendly service in a bright dining room with lazy music, and only one set of antlers on the wall. The broad menu of nicely presented dishes ranges from partridge-and-pheasant pâté to *fettuccine a la marinera* and a terrific *solomillo de ciervo* (venison tenderloin).

ⓘ INFORMATION

Oficina Municipal de Turismo (⊘953 71 01 02; www.cazorla.es/turismo; Plaza de Santa María; ⊘10am-1pm & 4-8pm Tue-Sun Apr-Oct, to 7pm Nov-Mar) Inside the remains of Santa María church, with some information on the natural park as well as the town.

Flamenco Festival

Vibrant Jerez de la Frontera, near Cádiz, is the cradle of flamenco. **Festival de Jerez** (www.facebook.com/FestivalDeJerez; ☺late Feb–early Mar) is the city's biggest flamenco celebration, with top-tier performances at venues around town.

ANNA55555/SHUTTERSTOCK ©

Punto de Información Cazorla (☑670 943880; Calle Martínez Falero 11; ☺10am–2pm & 5.30–8.30pm Mon–Sat, 10am–2pm Sun Jul–mid-Sep, hours vary rest of year) Good for information on the park as well as the town and surrounds.

❶ GETTING THERE & AWAY

Alsa (www.alsa.es) runs three to five daily buses to Úbeda (€4.35, one hour), Baeza (€5, 1¼ hours), Jaén (€9.50, two to 2½ hours) and Granada (€18.20, 3½ to four hours). The **bus station** (Calle de Hilario Marco) is 500m north of Plaza de la Corredera via Plaza de la Constitución.

Carmona

Rising above a sea of golden, sun-baked plains 35km east of Seville, Carmona is a delight. Its hilltop centre is packed with noble palaces, majestic Mudéjar churches and two Moorish forts; nearby, a haunting Roman necropolis tells of the town's ancient origins.

The strategically sited town flourished under the Romans, who laid out a street plan that survives to this day: Via Augusta, running from Rome to Cádiz, entered Carmona by the eastern Puerta de Córdoba and left by the western Puerta de Sevilla. The Muslims subsequently built a strong defensive wall, but in 1247 the town fell to Fernando III. Later, Mudéjar and Christian artisans constructed grand churches, convents and mansions.

◎ SIGHTS

Necrópolis Romana   Roman Site
(Roman cemetery; ☑600 143632; www.museosdeandalucia.es; Avenida de Jorge Bonsor 9; EU/non-EU citizens free/€1.50; ☺9am–9pm Tue-Sat, to 3pm Sun Apr–mid-Jun, 9am–3pm Tue-Sun mid-Jun–mid-Sep, 9am–6pm Tue-Sat, to 3pm Sun mid-Sep–Mar) This ancient Roman necropolis is one of the most important of its kind in Andalucía. The site, which is slightly let down by a lack of signage, contains hundreds of tombs, some elaborate and many-chambered, hewn into the rock in the 1st and 2nd centuries CE. Most of the inhabitants were cremated: in the tombs are wall niches for the box-like stone urns. You can enter the huge **Tumba de Servilia** and climb down into several others.

Alcázar de la Puerta de Sevilla   Fortress
(☑954 19 09 55; Plaza de Blas Infante; adult/child €2/1, Mon free; ☺10am–6pm Mon-Sat, to 3pm Sun Sep-Jun, 9am-3pm Mon-Fri, 10am-3pm Sat & Sun Jul & Aug) Carmona's signature fortress is a formidable sight. Set atop the Puerta de Sevilla, the imposing main gate of the old town, it had already been standing for five centuries when the Romans reinforced it and built a temple on top. The Muslim Almohads added an *aljibe* (cistern) to the upper patio, which remains a hawk-like perch from which to admire the typically Andalucian tableau of white cubes and soaring spires.

Buy tickets at the tourist office.

Prioral de Santa María de la Asunción

Alcázar de Arriba Ruins

(Alcázar del Rey Don Pedro; Calle Extramuros de Santiago; adult/student/child €2/1/free; ⏱11am-3pm Mon, Tue, Thu & Fri, to 3pm Sat & Sun) The stark, ruined fortress on the south-eastern edge of Carmona was an Almohad fort that Pedro I turned into a country palace in the 13th century. It was brought down by earthquakes in 1504 and 1755 and its ruins now provide a memorable viewing platform and a backdrop to the luxurious Parador de Carmona hotel.

Prioral de Santa María de la Asunción Church

(☎954 19 14 82; www.santamariacarmona.org; Plaza Marqués de las Torres; adult/child €3/1.80; ⏱9.30am-2pm & 5-7pm Tue-Fri, 9.30am-2pm Sat) This splendid church was built mainly in the 15th and 16th centuries on the site of Carmona's former mosque. The Patio de los Naranjos, through which you enter, has a Visigothic calendar carved into one of its pillars. The interior, crowned by high Gothic vaults, is centred on a towering altarpiece detailed to a mind-boggling degree with 20 panels of biblical scenes framed by gilt-scrolled columns.

Convento de Santa Clara Convent

(☎954 14 21 02; www.clarisasdecarmona. wordpress.com; Calle Torno de Santa Clara; adult/child €2/1; ⏱11am-2pm & 4.30-6.30pm Thu-Mon) With its Gothic ribbed vaulting, carved Mudéjar-style ceiling and dazzling altarpiece – a shining example of Sevillan baroque – the Santa Clara convent appeals to both art and architecture buffs. Take in the bell tower, actually an 18th-century addition, and pretty, arch-lined cloister before picking up some cookies baked by the resident nuns.

🍴 EATING

Casa Curro Montoya Spanish €€

(☎657 903629; Calle Santa María de Gracia 13; tapas from €2.50, raciones €8.50-17; ⏱1.15-5pm & 8.15pm-midnight) This easy-going bar-restaurant occupies a narrow high-ceilinged hall decorated with deep-scarlet walls and classic bullfighting memorabilia. A low-key jazz soundtrack sets the mood

Learn to Cook in Vejer

Annie B's Spanish Kitchen (☑620 560649; www.anniebspain.com; Calle Viñas 11; 1-day course €155) Master the art of Andalucian cooking with sherry educator and local-cuisine expert Annie Mansion, whose popular day classes (Andalucian, Moroccan, seafood) end with lunch by the pool or on the roof terrace at her gorgeous old-town house. Annie also runs multi-day cooking courses, Morocco day trips, and tapas, food and sherry tours of Vejer, Cádiz and Jerez.

Chicharrónes (fried pork)
FUSIONSTOCK/SHUTTERSTOCK ©

for the likes of tuna-belly tapas and plates of plump white asparagus.

Molino de la Romera   Andalucian €€

(☑954 14 20 00; www.molinodelaromera.es; Calle Sor Ángela de la Cruz 8; tapas €3.50-6, mains €12-19; ⊘1-4pm & 8.30-11.30pm Mon-Sat) Housed in a cosy, 15th-century olive-oil mill complete with panoramic terrace, a lovely courtyard and coolly rustic interior, this popular restaurant serves hearty, well-prepped meals with a splash of contemporary flair. Particularly good are its char-grilled meat dishes, including juicy cuts of tender Galician beef.

ℹ INFORMATION

Tourist Office (☑954 19 09 55; www.turismo.carmona.org; Alcázar de la Puerta de Sevilla;

⊘10am-6pm Mon-Sat, to 3pm Sun Sep-Jun, 9am-3pm Mon-Fri, 10am-3pm Sat & Sun Jul & Aug)

ℹ GETTING THERE & AWAY

Casal (☑954 99 92 90; www.autocarescasal.com) runs buses to Seville (€2.85, 1¼ hours, at least seven daily) from a **stop** on Paseo del Estatuto.

ALSA (☑902 42 22 42; www.alsa.es) has three daily buses to Córdoba (€9.83, 1½ hours) via Écija (€4.85, 35 minutes) leaving from a **stop** on the other side of Paseo del Estatuto.

Vejer de la Frontera

Vejer – the jaw drops, the eyes blink, the eloquent adjectives dry up. Looming moodily atop a rocky hill above the busy N340, 50km south of Cádiz, this serene, compact white town is something special. Yes, there's a labyrinth of twisting old-town streets encircled by imposing 15th-century walls, some serendipitous viewpoints, a ruined castle, a booming culinary scene, a smattering of dreamy hotels and a tangible Moorish influence. But Vejer has something else: an air of magic and mystery, an imperceptible touch of *duende* (spirit).

◎ SIGHTS

Enclosing the old town, Vejer's imposing 15th-century **walls** are particularly visible between the Arco de la Puerta Cerrada (of 11th- or 12th-century origin) and the 15th-century Arco de la Segur, two of the four original gateways to survive. The area around the Arco de la Segur and Calle Judería was, in the 15th century, the *judería* (Jewish quarter). Start with the 10th- or 11th-century Puerta de Sancho IV (another surviving gateway) next to Plaza de España and work round.

Plaza de España   Square

With its elaborate 20th-century, Seville-tiled fountain and perfectly white town hall, Vejer's palm-studded, cafe-filled Plaza de

España is a favourite hang-out. There's a small lookout above its western side (via Calle de Sancho IV el Bravo).

Castillo
Castle

(Calle del Castillo; ⊘10am-2pm & 5-9pm approx May-Sep, 10am-2pm & 4-8pm approx Oct-Apr) FREE Vejer's much-reworked castle, once home of the dukes of Medina Sidonia, dates from the 10th or 11th century. You can wander through the Moorish entrance arch, past the original rainwater *aljibe* (cistern), and climb the hibiscus-fringed ramparts for fantastic views across town to the white-sand coastline.

✖ EATING

Mercado de Abastos
Andalucian €

(Calle San Francisco; dishes €2-8; ⊘noon-4pm & 8pm-midnight) Now glammed up gastro-bar-style, Vejer's early-20th-century Mercado de San Francisco has become a buzzy foodie hot spot full of world-wandering stalls. Grab a *vino* and choose between Andalucian classics and contemporary twists: Iberian ham *raciones, tortilla de patatas*, fried fish in paper cups and popular sushi.

Corredera 55
Andalucian €€

(☎956 45 18 48; www.califavejer.com; Calle de la Corredera 55; mains €11-22; ⊘noon-11.30pm; 🅿) ☏ Exquisitely styled with boho-chic Vejer flair, Corredera 55 delivers elegant, inventive seasonal cuisine packed with local, organic ingredients and Cádiz-meets-international flavours. Andalucian wines pair perfectly with creations such as mushroom and garlic risotto, cauliflower

fritters with honey-yoghurt dressing, or *cava*-baked prawn-stuffed fish of the day. Perch at street-side tables (winter blankets provided!) or eat in the cosy dining room amid Vejer paintings.

El Jardín del Califa
Moroccan €€

(☎956 45 17 06; www.califavejer.com; Plaza de España 16; mains €12-18; ⊘1-4pm & 8-11.30pm; 🅿) ☏ Sizzling atmosphere and flawless cooking combine at this beautiful restaurant hidden within a cavernous 16th-century, Moorish-origin house where even finding the bathroom is a full-on adventure; it's also a fabulous **hotel** (☎956 44 77 30; www.califavejer.com; Plaza de España 16; incl breakfast r €100-165, ste €170-250; 🅿❄🛜) and *tetería*. The seasonal, local-produce Moroccan–Middle Eastern menu – tagines, couscous, hummus, falafel – is crammed with Maghreb flavours (saffron, figs, almonds). Book ahead, for the palm-sprinkled garden or the moody interior.

ℹ INFORMATION

Oficina Municipal de Turismo (☎956 45 17 36; www.turismovejer.es; Avenida Los Remedios 2; ⊘10am-2.30pm & 4.30-9pm Mon-Sat, 10am-2pm Sun, reduced hours Oct-Apr)

Getting There & Away

From Avenida Los Remedios, Comes (p154) runs buses to Cádiz, Zahara de los Atunes, Jerez and Seville. All other buses stop at La Barca de Vejer, on the N340 at the bottom of the hill; from here, it's a steep 20-minute walk or €6 taxi up to town.

SEVILLE

Seville at a Glance...

Some cities have looks, other cities have personality. The sevillanos get both, courtesy of their flamboyant, charismatic, ever-evolving Andalucian metropolis founded, according to myth, 3000 years ago by the Greek god Hercules. Drenched for most of the year in spirit-enriching sunlight, this is a city of feelings as much as sights, with different seasons prompting vastly contrasting moods: solemn for Semana Santa, flirtatious for the spring fiesta and soporific for the gasping heat of summer. And one of the most remarkable things about modern Seville is its ability to adapt and etch fresh new brushstrokes onto an ancient canvas.

Seville in One Day

Get moving in the **Barrio de Santa Cruz** (p172), then visit the **Alcázar** (p171). Come up for air in El Centro and brave a crowded tapas bar near Plaza de la Alfalfa. Admire (or not) the whimsical **Metropol Parasol** (p173) and the shopping chaos of **Calle Sierpes** (p173). Then roll up for night-time drinks in the **Alameda de Hércules** (p179).

Seville in Two Days

Buy your ticket for the **Catedral** (p166), which deserves at least two hours. Afterwards have lunch in El Arenal and stroll the river banks down to **Parque de María Luisa** (p177). Take in **Plaza de España** (p177) before finishing the day with a flamenco show at the **Casa de la Guitarra** (p180).

Parque Natural
Sierra de Aracena
y Picos de Aroche

Parque Natural
Sierra Norte
de Sevilla

Parque Natural
Sierra de
Hornachuelos

Córdoba

Río Odiel

Río Tinto

Río Guadalquivir

**Aeropuerto
de Sevilla**

Carmona

Écija

Río Corbones

Seville

Río Guadaira

Río Genil

Huelva

Parque
Nacional
de Doñana

*Golfo de
Cádiz*

*Lucio de los
Ansares*

Antequera

Río Guadiaro

**Arcos de la
Frontera**

Zahara de
la Sierra

*ATLANTIC
OCEAN*

**Jerez de la
Frontera**

Parque Natural
Sierra de
Grazalema

Ronda

Parque Natural
Sierra de
las Nieves

Málaga

*Embalse de
Guadalcacín*

**Aeropuerto
de Málaga-
Costa del Sol**

Cádiz

Parque
Natural Los
Alcornocales

Río Genil

*Costa
de la Luz*

See Seville Map (p174)

50 km
25 miles

Arriving in Seville

Seville's airport has loads of domestic (and some international) flights. The city is also connected by super-fast AVE trains to Madrid and Córdoba. Buses and taxis connect the airport and Estación Santa Justa with the city centre.

Where to Stay

Seville has fine accommodation choices, from boutique marvels to flower-filled *hostales* (budget hotels). High season typically runs from March to June and again in September and October. During Semana Santa and the Feria de Abril, rates are doubled – at least! – and sell out completely. Book well ahead at this time.

Detail from Capilla Mayor

Catedral & Giralda

Seville's immense cathedral, officially the biggest in the world by volume, is awe-inspiring in its scale and sheer majesty. Its former minaret, the Giralda, is an architectural jewel.

Great For...

Don't Miss

The Capilla Mayor contains its greatest treasure, a sublime gold-plated altarpiece.

After Seville fell to the Christians in 1248 the mosque was used as a church until 1401. Then the church authorities decided to knock it down and start again. 'Let's construct a church so large future generations will think we were mad', they quipped (or so legend has it). When it was completed in 1502 after 100 years of hard labour, the Catedral de Santa María de la Sede, as it is officially known, pretty much defined the word 'Gothic'. It's also a veritable art gallery replete with notable works by Zurbarán, Murillo, Goya and others.

Tomb of Columbus

Inside the Puerta de los Príncipes (Door of the Princes) stands the monumental tomb of Christopher Columbus, containing what are believed to be the great explorer's bones, brought here from Cuba in 1898.

Giralda

DAVID PINEDA SVENSKE/SHUTTERSTOCK©

ⓘ Catedral & Giralda

Archivo de Indias ⓜ

Plaza del Triunfo

Av de la Constitución

Río Guadalquivir

Alcázar Gardens

Puerta de Jerez ⓜ ⓜ Puerta de Jerez

ⓘ Need to Know

☎902 09 96 92; www.catedraldesevilla.es; Plaza del Triunfo; adult/child €10/free, incl rooftop guided tours €16, 4.30-6pm Mon free; ⊙11am-3.30pm Mon, to 5pm Tue-Sat, 2.30-6pm Sun Sep-Jun, 10.30am-4pm Mon, to 6pm Tue-Sat, 2-7pm Sun Jul & Aug

✕ Take a Break

Slick Mamarracha (p179) serves up modern tapas in a stylish setting near the cathedral.

★ Top Tip

Take time to admire the cathedral from the outside. It's particularly stunning at night from the Plaza Virgen de los Reyes, and from across the river in Triana.

Even though there were suggestions that the bones kept here were possibly those of his son Diego, recent DNA tests seemed to finally prove that it really is Christopher Columbus.

Capilla Mayor

East of the choir is the Capilla Mayor (Main Chapel). Its Gothic retable is the jewel of the cathedral and reckoned to be the biggest altarpiece in the world. Begun by Flemish sculptor Pieter Dancart in 1482 and finished by others in 1564, this sea of gilt and polychromed wood holds over 1000 carved biblical figures.

Sacrista Mayor

This large room with a finely carved stone dome was created between 1528 and 1547; the arch over its portal has carvings of

16th-century foods. Pedro de Campaña's 1547 *Descendimiento* (Descent from the Cross), above the central altar at the southern end, and Francisco de Zurbarán's *Santa Teresa*, to its right, are two of the cathedral's most precious paintings.

Giralda

In the northeastern corner of the cathedral, you'll find the passage for the climb up to the belfry of the Giralda. The decorative brick tower, which stands 104m tall, was the minaret of the mosque, constructed between 1184 and 1198 at the height of Almohad power. At the very top is El Giraldillo, a 16th-century bronze weather vane representing 'faith' that has become a symbol of Seville.

Seville Cathedral

THE HIGHLIGHTS TOUR

In 1402 the inspired architects of Seville set out on one of the most grandiose building projects in medieval history. Their aim was to shock and amaze future generations with the size and magnificence of the building. It took until 1506 to complete the project, but 500 years later Seville Cathedral is still the largest Gothic cathedral in the world.

To avoid getting lost, orient yourself by the main highlights. To the right of the visitor entrance is the grand **❶ Tomb of Columbus**. Continue into the southeastern corner to uncover some major art treasures: a Goya in the Sacristía de los Cálices, a Zurbarán in the **❷ Sacristía Mayor**, and Murillo's shining *La inmaculada* in the Sala Capitular. Skirt the cathedral's eastern wall past the often-closed **❸ Capilla Real**, home to some important royal tombs. By now it's impossible to avoid the lure of the **❹ Capilla Mayor** with its fantastical altarpiece. Hidden over in the northwest corner is the **❺ Capilla de San Antonio** with a legendary Murillo. That huge doorway nearby is the rarely opened **❻ Puerta de la Asunción**. Make for the **❼ Giralda** next, stealing admiring looks at the high, vaulted ceiling on the way. After looking down on the cathedral's immense footprint, descend and depart via the **❽ Patio de los Naranjos**.

Capilla de San Antonio
One of 80 interior chapels, you'll need to hunt down this little gem notable for housing Murillo's 1656 painting, *Vision of St Anthony of Padua*. The work was pillaged by thieves in 1874 but later restored.

Patio de los Naranjos
Inhale the perfume of 60 Sevillan orange trees in a cool patio bordered by fortress-like walls – a surviving remnant of the original 12th-century mosque. Exit is gained via the horseshoe-shaped Puerta del Perdón.

Puerta del Perdón

8

5

6

Iglesia del Sagrario

Puerta del Bautismo

Puerta de la Asunción
Located on the western side of the cathedral and also known as the Puerta Mayor, these huge, rarely opened doors are pushed back during Semana Santa to allow solemn processions of Catholic *hermandades* (brotherhoods) to pass through.

TOP TIPS

➡ Don't try to visit the Alcázar and cathedral on the same day. There is far too much to take in.

➡ Take time to admire the cathedral from the outside. It's particularly stunning at night from the Plaza de la Virgen de los Reyes, and from across the river in Triana.

➡ Skip the line by booking tickets online or buying them at the Iglesia Colegial del Divino Salvador on Plaza del Salvador.

Giralda
Ascend, not by stairs, but by a series of 35 ramps to the pinnacle of this 11th-century minaret topped by a Gothic-baroque belfry. Standing 104m tall, it has long been the defining symbol of Seville.

El Giraldillo

Capilla Mayor
Behold! The cathedral's main focal point contains its greatest treasure, a magnificent gold-plated altarpiece depicting various scenes in the life of Christ. It constitutes the life's work of one man, Flemish artist Pieter Dancart.

Capilla Real
The atmospheric, but often-closed, Royal Chapel is dedicated to the Virgen de los Reyes. In a silver urn lie the hallowed remains of the city's Christian conqueror Fernando III and his son, Alfonso the Wise.

Sacristía Mayor
Art lovers will adore this large domed room containing some of the city's greatest paintings, including Zurbarán's *Santa Teresa* and Pedro de Campaña's *El descendimiento*. It also guards the city key captured in 1248.

Main Entrance

Tomb of Columbus
Buried in Valladolid in 1506, the remains of Christopher Columbus were moved four times before they arrived in Seville in 1898 encased in an elaborately carved catafalque.

Real Alcázar interior

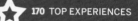

VICHIE81/SHUTTERSTOCK©

Real Alcázar

If heaven really does exist, let's hope it looks a little like the inside of Seville's Alcázar. Built primarily in the 1300s, the castle marks one of history's architectural high points.

Great For...

Don't Miss

The Patio de las Doncellas is the highlight of the peerless Palacio de Don Pedro.

Originally founded as a fort for the Cordoban governors of Seville in 913, the Alcázar has been expanded or reconstructed many times in its 11 centuries of existence. In the 11th century, Seville's prosperous Muslim *taifa* (small kingdom) rulers developed the original fort by building a palace called Al-Muwarak (the Blessed) in what's now the western part of the Alcázar. The 12th-century Almohad rulers added another palace east of this, around what's now the Patio del Crucero. Christian Fernando III moved into the Alcázar when he captured Seville in 1248, and several later Christian monarchs used it as their main residence. Fernando's son Alfonso X replaced much of the Almohad palace with a Gothic one. Between 1364 and 1366, Pedro I created the Alcázar's crown jewel, the sumptuous Mudéjar Palacio de Don Pedro.

Patio de las Doncellas

ⓘ Need to Know

☑954 50 23 24; www.alcazarsevilla.org; Plaza del Triunfo; adult/student/child €11.50/3/ free, 6-7pm Mon Apr-Sep free, 4-5pm Mon Oct-Mar free; ⊘9.30am-7pm Apr-Sep, to 5pm Oct-Mar

✕ Take a Break

Just north of the Alcázar, **Bodega Santa Cruz** (☑954 21 86 18; Calle Rodrigo Caro 1; tapas €2.50; ⊘8am-midnight) is forever crowded and good for tapas.

★ Top Tip

Don't visit the Alcázar and Cathedral on the same day. There is far too much to take in.

First Steps

From the ticket office inside the **Puerta del León** (Lion Gate), you'll emerge into the **Patio del León** (Lion Patio), which was the garrison yard of the original Al-Muwarak palace. Just off here is the **Sala de la Justicia** (Hall of Justice), with beautiful Mudéjar plasterwork and an *artesonado* (ceiling of interlaced beams with decorative insertions).

Palacio de Don Pedro

Posterity owes Pedro I a big thank you for creating the **Palacio de Don Pedro** (also called the Palacio Mudéjar), the most stunning architectural feature in Seville. At its heart is the wonderful **Patio de las Doncellas** (Patio of the Maidens), surrounded by beautiful arches, plasterwork and tiling. The sunken garden in the centre was

uncovered by archaeologists in 2004 from beneath a 16th-century marble covering.

The **Cámara Regia** (King's Quarters), on the northern side of the patio, has stunningly beautiful ceilings and wonderful plaster- and tile work. Its rear room was probably the monarch's summer bedroom. From here you can move west into the little **Patio de las Muñecas** (Patio of the Dolls), the heart of the palace's private quarters, featuring delicate Granada-style decoration. Indeed, plaster work was actually brought here from the Alhambra in the 19th century when the mezzanine and top gallery were added for Queen Isabel II.

Gardens

Formal gardens with pools and fountains sit closest to the palace. The gardens' most arresting feature is the Galeria de Grutesco, a raised gallery with porticoes fashioned in the 16th century out of an old Muslim-era wall.

◎ SIGHTS

◎ Barrio de Santa Cruz

Seville's medieval *judería* (Jewish quarter), east of the cathedral and Real Alcázar, is today a tangle of atmospheric, winding streets and lovely plant-decked plazas perfumed with orange blossom. Among its most characteristic plazas is Plaza de Santa Cruz, which gives the *barrio* (district) its name, and the wonderfully romantic Plaza de Doña Elvira.

Hospital de los Venerables Sacerdotes   Museum

(☎954 56 26 96; www.hospitaldelosvenerables. es; Plaza de los Venerables 8; adult/student/child €10/8/free; ☉10am-8pm Mar-Jun & Sep-Nov, 10am-2pm & 5.30-9pm Jul & Aug, 10am-6pm Dec-Feb) This gem of a museum, housed in a former hospice for priests, is one of Seville's most rewarding. The artistic highlight is the Focus-Abengoa Foundation's collection of 17th-century paintings in the Centro Velázquez. It's not a big collection, but each work is a masterpiece of its genre – highlights include Diego Velázquez' *Santa Rufina*, his *Inmaculada concepción,* and a sharply vivid portrait of *Santa Catalina* by Bartolomé Murillo.

Centro de Interpretación Judería de Sevilla   Museum

(☎954 04 70 89; www.juderiadesevilla.es; Calle Ximénez de Enciso 22; adult/student €6.50/5; ☉11am-7pm) Dedicated to Seville's Jewish history, this small, poignant museum occupies an old Sephardic house. Santa Cruz's Jewish population never recovered from a brutal massacre in 1391. The massacre and other historical happenings are catalogued inside, along with a few surviving mementos including documents, costumes and books.

Plaza de la Virgen de los Reyes   Square

All Seville's monumental beauty is on display at this historic plaza. Set around an ornate 20th-century fountain-lamppost, the square abuts the dramatic bulk of the cathedral and Giralda, both of which are magically lit at night. Also eye-catching is the red facade of the **Palacio Arzobispal** (Archbishop's Palace), a majestic baroque palace housing diocese offices.

From left: Hospital de los Venerables Sacerdotes; House in Barrio de Santa Cruz; Palacio Arzobispal; Calle Sierpes

Opposite, on the plaza's southern flank, is the 16th-century **Convento de la Encarnación**.

El Centro

Museo del Baile Flamenco   Museum

(☏954 34 03 11; www.museoflamenco.com; Calle Manuel Rojas Marcos 3; adult/child €10/6, incl show €26/15; ◷10am-7pm) The brainchild of *sevillana* flamenco dancer Cristina Hoyos, this museum illustrates the dance with interactive displays, paintings, displays of period dresses and photos of revered erstwhile (and contemporary) performers. Even better are the fantastic nightly performances (at 5pm, 7pm and 8.45pm; €22) staged both in the courtyard and the more intimate basement space (€37 including a drink). Combined museum and show tickets are a good option.

Calle Sierpes   Street

Running north from Plaza de San Francisco, pedestrianised Calle Sierpes is Seville's premier shopping street. Along with the parallel Calles Tetuán and Velázquez, it's lined with chain stores, old family-run shops, the occasional independent boutique, and shops selling gaudy traditional fans and flamenco wear. It's busiest between 6pm and 9pm.

Palacio de la Condesa de Lebrija   Palace

(☏954 22 78 02; www.palaciodelebrija.com; Calle Cuna 8; adult/child incl guided tour €12/6, ground fl 6pm & 7pm Mon free; ◷10.30am-7.30pm) This aristocratic 16th-century mansion, set around a beautiful Renaissance-Mudéjar courtyard, boasts an eclectic look that blends a range of decorative elements, including Roman mosaics, Mudéjar plaster work and Renaissance masonry. Its former owner, the late Countess of Lebrija, was an archaeologist; she remodelled the house in 1914, filling many of the rooms with treasures from her travels.

Visits to the top floor are by guided tour only (in English or Spanish), though this is included in the ticket price.

Metropol Parasol   Landmark

(☏606 635214; www.setasdesevilla.com; Plaza de la Encarnación; €3; ◷9.30am-10.30pm Sun-Thu, to 11pm Fri & Sat) The Metropol Parasol,

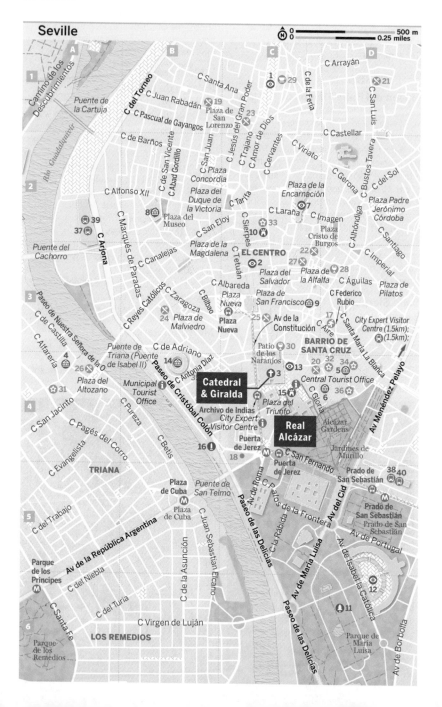

Seville

0 — 500 m
0 — 0.25 miles

Camino de los Descubrimientos

Río Guadalquivir

Puente de la Cartuja

C del Torneo

C Juan Rabadán

C Pascual de Gayangos

C de Barños

C de San Vicente

C Abad Gordillo

C Alfonso XII

C Plaza Concordia

Plaza del Duque de la Victoria

C Santa Ana

Plaza de San Lorenzo

19

23

C Jesús del Gran Poder

C Trajano

C Amor de Dios

C Cervantes

C Arrayán

C de la Feria

C Castellar

C Viriato

C Gerona

C San Luis

C del Sol

C Bustos Tavera

21

Plaza de la Encarnación

C Tarifa

C Laraña

C Imagen

7

Plaza Padre Jerónimo Córdoba

C Alhóndiga

C Santiago

8

Plaza del Museo

C Marqués de Paradas

C Canalejas

C San Eloy

Plaza de la Magdalena

C Sierpes

C Tetuán

10

33

EL CENTRO

2

Plaza Cristo de Burgos

22

27

Plaza del Salvador

Plaza de la Alfalfa

28

C Águilas

Plaza de Pilatos

C Imperial

39

37

C Arjona

Puente del Cachorro

Paseo de Nuestra Señora de la O

C de Castilla

C Alfarería

C Reyes Católicos

C Zaragoza

C Bilbao

C Albareda

Plaza Nueva

Plaza de San Francisco

9

C Federico Rubio

City Expert Visitor Centre (1.5km);
(1.5km);

24

Plaza de Malviedro

Plaza Nueva

25

Av de la Constitución

17

C Aire

C Santa María La Blanca

BARRIO DE SANTA CRUZ

4

26

31

Puente de Triana (Puente de Isabel II)

C de Adriano

14

C Antonia Díaz

Paseo de Cristóbal Colón

Plaza del Altozano

Municipal Tourist Office

Patio de los Naranjos

30

3

13

Catedral & Giralda

15

Plaza del Triunfo

20

32

5

34

36

Central Tourist Office

C Gloria

Real Alcázar

Alcázar Gardens

Jardines de Murillo

Av Menéndez Pelayo

C San Jacinto

C Pagés del Corro

C Pureza

C Betis

Archivo de Indias
City Expert
Visitor Centre

16

18

Puerta de Jerez

M

C San Fernando

Puerta de Jerez

Prado de San Sebastián

38

40

TRIANA

C Evangelista

Plaza de Cuba

Puente de San Telmo

Av de Roma

C Patios de la Frontera

Av del Cid

Prado de San Sebastián

Prado de San Sebastián

Av de Portugal

C del Trabajo

M

Plaza de Cuba

C Juan Sebastián Elcano

Paseo de las Delicias

C la Rábida

Av de María Luisa

Av de Isabel la Católica

12

Parque de los Príncipes

M

Av de la República Argentina

C del Niebla

C de la Asunción

C del Turia

C Virgen de Luján

11

Parque de María Luisa

Parque de los Remedios

C Santa Fe

LOS REMEDIOS

Paseo de las Delicias

Av de Borbolla

Seville

known locally as *Las Setas* (The Mushrooms), is one of Seville's iconic modern landmarks. Built in 2011 to a design by German architect Jürgen Mayer H, the colossal sunshade is a hypnotic sight with its undulating honeycombed canopy – said to be the world's largest wooden-framed structure – and massive support trunks. Lifts run up from the basement to the top, where you can enjoy killer views from a winding walkway.

Museo de Bellas Artes   Museum

(Fine Arts Museum; ☑955 54 29 42; www.museo debellasartesdesevilla.es; Plaza del Museo 9; EU/non-EU citizens free/€1.50; ☺9am-9pm Tue-Sat, to 3pm Sun) Housed in a grand mannerist palace, the former Convento de la Merced, the Museo de Bellas Artes is one of Spain's premier art museums. Its collection of Spanish and Sevillan paintings and sculptures comprises works from the 15th to 20th centuries, but the focus is very much on brooding religious paintings from the city's 17th-century Siglo de Oro (Golden Age).

Works are displayed in chronological order, with the Golden Age masterpieces clustered in *salas* V to X. The most visually arresting room is the convent's former church (*sala* V), hung with paintings by masters of the Sevillan baroque, above all Murillo. His *Inmaculada concepción* (aka *La colosal*; 1650) at the head of the church displays all the curving, twisting movement so central to baroque art. Other artists represented include Pacheco (teacher and father-in-law of Velázquez), Juan de Valdés Leal, Zurbarán (look for his deeply sombre *Cristo crucificado*, c 1630–35) and sculptor Juan Martínez Montañés.

Elsewhere, look out for El Greco's portrait of his son Jorge Manuel (c 1600–05), Velázquez's *Cabeza de apóstol* (1620), and a portrait by Goya in *sala* XI.

For a change of subject matter, push on to *sala* XII where Gonzalo Bilbao's *Las cigarreras* (The Cigarette Makers; 1915) is

one of several canvases depicting scenes of Sevillan life.

◉ El Arenal & Triana

Torre del Oro   Tower

(📋954 22 24 19; Paseo de Cristóbal Colón; adult/6-14 yrs €3/1.50, Mon free; ⊙9.30am-6.45pm Mon-Fri, 10.30am-6.45pm Sat & Sun) This distinctive tower, one of Seville's signature landmarks, has been guarding the Río Guadalquivir since the 13th century. The original dodecagonal structure, built to bolster the city's fortified walls, was subsequently heightened, first in the 14th century and then again in the late 1700s. Over the centuries, the tower has served as a chapel, prison and naval office; nowadays it houses a small maritime museum and a rooftop viewing platform.

It owes its name to the golden light that would reflect off its tiles, though some dispute this, claiming the name is a reference to the gold that was plundered from Spain's New World colonies and stored in the tower.

**Plaza de Toros
de la Real Maestranza**   Museum

(📋954 21 03 15; www.realmaestranza.com; Paseo de Cristóbal Colón 12; tours adult/child €8/3, 3-7pm Mon free; ⊙9.30am-9pm Apr-Oct, to 7pm Nov-Mar, to 3pm bullfight days) In the world of bullfighting, Seville's white and yellow-trimmed bullring is the equivalent of football's Old Trafford or Camp Nou – if you're selected to fight here, you've made it. In addition to having almost religious significance to fans, it's also the oldest ring in Spain – construction started in 1761 and continued on and off until 1881 – and one of the biggest, with a capacity of up to 14,000. A visit enables you to learn about bullfighting's deep-rooted traditions without witnessing a fight.

Centro Cerámica Triana   Museum

(📋954 34 15 82; Calle Antillano Campos 14; adult/child €2.10/free; ⊙11am-5.30pm Tue-Sat, 10am-2.30pm Sun) Housed in a former tile factory, this small museum provides a fascinating introduction to Triana and its industrial past. Exhibits, which include

---

✦ Seville's Festivals

Feria de Abril (https://feriadesevilla.anda lunet.com; El Real de la Feria; ⊙Apr) Seville's celebrated spring fair is held two weeks after Easter on the Real de la Feria fairground in the Los Remedios area west of the Río Guadalquivir. For six days and nights, *sevillanos* dress up in elaborate finery, parade around in horse-drawn carriages (the *paseo de caballos*), eat, drink and dance the *sevillana* (a popular style of fiesta dance).

Bienal de Flamenco (www.labienal.com; ⊙Sep) The big names of the flamenco world descend on Seville for this major flamenco festival. Held in September in even-numbered years, it features a comprehensive program of performances, exhibitions and workshops in venues across town.

Semana Santa (www.semana-santa.org; ⊙Mar/Apr) Every day from Palm Sunday to Easter Sunday, elaborate, life-size *pasos* (floats carrying revered statues of Christ or the Virgin Mary) are paraded across town from their home churches to the cathedral. For the best views, park yourself near the cathedral in the early evening.

Semana Santa
JOSE MANUEL GAVIRA/SHUTTERSTOCK©

❝ the 34-hectare Parque de María Luisa is the perfect place to escape the noise ❞

brick-lined kilns and a comprehensive collection of tiles, chart the methodology and history of ceramic production, cleverly tying it in with the wider history of the neighbourhood and its residents.

South of the Centre

Parque de María Luisa   Park

(⏰8am-10pm Sep-Jun, to midnight Jul & Aug; 🚼🎪) A glorious oasis of green, the 34-hectare Parque de María Luisa is the perfect place to escape the noise and heat of the city, with duck ponds, landscaped gardens and paths shaded by soaring trees. The land, formerly the estate of the Palacio de San Telmo, was donated to the city in the late 19th century and developed in the run-up to the 1929 Exposición Iberoamericana.

Plaza de España   Square

(Avenida de Portugal) This bombastic plaza, designed by architect Aníbal González in the Parque de María Luisa, was the most extravagant of the building projects completed for the 1929 Exposición Iberoamericana. A vast brick-and-tile confection, it's all very over the top, but it's undeniably impressive with its flamboyant neo-Mudéjar architecture, fountains and Venetian-style bridges. A series of ceramic tile panels depict maps and historical scenes from each Spanish province.

You can hire row boats to ply the canal that skirts the plaza for €6 (for 35 minutes).

🏃 ACTIVITIES

Aire Baños Árabes   Hammam

(📞955 01 00 24; www.beaire.com; Calle Aire 15; bath/bath with massage from €37/56; ⏰10am-10pm Sun-Tue, to 11pm Wed & Thu, to midnight Fri & Sat) These smart, Arabic-style baths win prizes for tranquil atmosphere, historic setting (in a centuries-old Mudéjar townhouse) and Moroccan *riad*-style decor. Various bath and massage packages are available – see the website for details. It's always best to book a day or so in advance.

🚲 Seville by Bike

Seville's bike-sharing scheme, **Sevici** (📞900 900722; www.sevici.es), is one of the largest of its kind in Europe with 2500 bikes and 250 docking stations.

Most of Sevici's users are locals, but visitors can use the bikes by getting a seven-day subscription for €15 (plus a €150 returnable deposit). To register, go to a Sevici docking station and follow the on-screen instructions. Seville has around 130km of bike lanes (most painted green and equipped with their own traffic signals) and the first 30 minutes of usage are free. Beyond that, it's €1.03 for the first hour and €2.04 every hour thereafter.

Alternatively, a number of operators offer bike tours and rental, including **Surf the City** (📞693 261910; www. surfthecity.es; Calle Almirante Lobo 2, Edificio Cristina Local 15; kickscooter tours €20-50, bike tour €25; ⏰10am-8pm; 🚼) 🖋.

TRABANTOS/SHUTTERSTOCK©

🎫 TOURS

Pancho Tours   Tours

(📞664 642904; www.panchotours.com) FREE Runs excellent free tours, although you're welcome to tip the hard-working guide who'll furnish you with an encyclopedia's worth of anecdotes, stories, myths and theories about Seville's fascinating past. The 2½-hour tours kick off daily at 11am – check the website for details. Pancho also offers bike tours (€25), skip-the-line

FIONA FLORES WATSON/LONELY PLANET©

El Garlochi

cathedral (€21.25) and Alcázar visits (€17.50), and nightlife tours (from €17).

✖ EATING

Mercado de Triana   Market €
(Plaza del Altozano; snacks €3-4.50; ⊙9am-3pm Mon-Sat) Triana's 19th-century market is not huge but its stalls, richly laden with plump fresh fruit, silvery fish, cheese and hanging hams, are an inviting sight. Pick up picnic provisions or stop by at **Jamonería Jose Luis Romero** at Stall 58 for platters of expertly carved *jamón* and wine by the glass.

Sal Gorda   Andalucian €
(☑955 38 59 72; www.facebook.com/SalGorda Sevilla; Calle Alcaicería de la Loza 23; tapas €3.20-8.50; ⊙1-4.30pm & 8-11.30pm Wed-Mon) Incongruously located in an old shoe shop, this tiny, low-key place serves innovative takes on Andalucian dishes – try *ajo blanco* (white gazpacho soup) with *mojama* (salt-cured tuna), and a first-class version of the ubiquitous tuna tartare. Mushroom risotto with langoustines is a firm favourite, and the wine list features good local whites

such as El Mirlo Blanco from Constantina. Reservations recommended.

La Brunilda   Tapas €€
(☑954 22 04 81; Calle Galera 5; tapas €4-7.50, mains €6.50-15; ⊙1-4pm & 8.30-11.30pm Tue-Sat, 1-4pm Sun) Hidden away in an anonymous Arenal backstreet, this tapas hotspot is a guarantee of good times. The look is modern casual with big blue doors, brick arches and plain wooden tables, and the food is imaginative and brilliantly executed. Arrive promptly or expect long queues.

Bar-Restaurante Eslava   Tapas €€
(☑954 90 65 68; www.espacioeslava.com; Calle Eslava 3; tapas €2.90-4.50, restaurant mains €13.50-26; ⊙bar 12.30pm-midnight Tue-Sat, restaurant 1.30-4pm & 8.30pm-midnight Tue-Sat) You'll almost certainly have to wait for a table at the bar, but it's so worth it, especially if you use the time to start on the excellent wine list. The tapas are superb: contemporary, creative, brilliantly executed and incredible value for money. Standouts include slow-cooked egg served on mush-

room puree, and a filo pastry cigar stuffed with cuttlefish and algae.

conTenedor   Andalucian €€

(☑954 91 63 33; www.restaurantecontenedor. com; Calle San Luis 50; mains €9-22; ☺1.30-4.30pm & 8-11.30pm Mon-Thu, 1.30-4.30pm & 8.30pm-midnight Fri & Sat, 1.30-4.30pm & 8.30-11.30pm Sun) The atmosphere at this slow-food restaurant in boho Macarena is arty and relaxed, with an open kitchen, mismatched furniture and colourful paintings by co-owner Ricardo on the walls. The food is equally appealing, with dishes composed to show off locally sourced organic produce. Try the duck rice, the house speciality, or keep it green with a creative salad.

Mamarracha   Tapas €€

(☑955 12 39 11; www.mamarracha.es; Calle Hernando Colón 1-3; tapas €2.50-12, mains €5.50-14; ☺1-4.30pm & 8.30pm-midnight) Sharp decor, young staff in black T-shirts, cool tunes and an international menu, this is a fine example of the modern tapas bars that Seville so excels at. Its interior sports distressed cement, exposed vents and a vertical garden wall, while its menu reveals some slick combos, including a terrific focaccia with marinated Iberian pork.

La Azotea   Andalucian €€

(☑955 11 67 48; www.laazoteasevilla.com; Calle Conde de Barajas 13; tapas €3.50-6.50, mains €12-22; ☺1.30-4.30pm & 8pm-midnight) A trend-setter on the tapas revival scene that blazed across the city a few years ago, Azotea continues to impress diners, both *sevillanos* and out-of-towners. Its Scandi-inspired interior sets the mood for artfully plated tapas and contemporary creations such as artichokes with fried sweetbreads. Other branches are at Calle Mateos Gago 8 by the cathedral, and Calle Zaragoza 5.

Fargo   Andalucian €€

(☑955 27 65 52; www.facebook.com/fargobio; Calle Pérez Galdós 20; tapas €5-9, mains €10-16; ☺12.30-3pm & 7.30-11pm; ☑) An excellent restaurant in the Alfalfa area serving locally sourced, almost exclusively organic food, with a pleasantly different vibe: relaxed

decor, low lighting and soft music create a calm ambience. Vegetarian and vegans are well catered to with standouts such as quinoa tabouleh spiked with almonds, mint and Andalucian fruit, though meat and fish are served too. Wines are natural.

🍸 DRINKING & NIGHTLIFE

Cafes and bars are a fundamental part of life in Seville and you'll have no trouble finding somewhere to drink. Popular areas abound, including Calle Betis in Triana, Plaza de Salvador, the Barrio de Santa Cruz, and the Alameda de Hércules, host to a lively scene and the city's gay nightlife. In summer, dozens of *terrazas de verano* (open-air bars) pop up on the river's banks.

El Garlochi   Bar

(Calle Boteros 26; ☺9pm-3am Mon-Sat, to midnight Sun) There are few weirder places to drink than this baroque temple of kitsch. Decked out in ultra-camp religious decor, it's dedicated entirely to the iconography, smells and sounds of the Semana Santa (Holy Week). To get in the mood, try the signature cocktail, a *Sangre de Cristo* (Blood of Christ), made from grenadine, sparkling wine and whisky.

El Viajero Sedentario   Cafe

(www.facebook.com/viajerosedentario; Alameda de Hércules 77; ☺9.30am-1am Tue-Sat, 10.30am-11pm Sun) This inviting Alameda cafe is a lovely place to hang out with its bright murals, shady courtyard and tiny book-stacked interior. Early evening is a good time for a relaxed pre-dinner beer, and it's not uncommon to find people dancing to low-key jazz tunes on sultry summer nights.

La Terraza del Eme   Rooftop Bar

(www.emecatedralmercer.com; Calle de los Alemanes 27; ☺2pm-2am Sun-Thu, to 2am Fri & Sat) Enjoy spectacular cathedral close-ups and classic cocktails at the chic roof-terrace bar of the five-star EME Catedral Hotel. Drinks are on the pricey side at around €16 for a

Tablao El Arenal

G&T, but DJs create a lively lounge vibe and the Catedral views really are special.

⊕ ENTERTAINMENT

Museo del Baile Flamenco (p173) also stages excellent nightly concerts.

Casa de la Memoria   Flamenco
(☑954 56 06 70; www.casadelamemoria.es; Calle Cuna 6; adult/student/child €18/15/10; ☺11am-6pm, shows 7.30pm & 9pm) Occupying the old stables of the 16th-century Palacio de la Condesa de Lebrija, this cultural centre stages authentic, highly charged flamenco shows, as well as housing a small exhibition of flamenco memorabilia. The nightly shows are perennially popular, and as space is limited, you'll need to reserve tickets a day or so in advance by calling or visiting the venue.

La Casa del Flamenco   Flamenco
(☑955 02 99 99; www.lacasadelflamencosevilla. com; Calle Ximénez de Enciso 28; adult/student/ child €20/15/10; ☺shows 7pm winter & autumn, 7pm & 8.30pm spring, 8.30pm summer) A beautiful patio in an old Sephardic Jewish mansion in Santa Cruz is home to La Casa del Flamenco. Shows, performed on a stage hemmed in by seating on three sides, are mesmerising.

Casa de la Guitarra   Flamenco
(☑954 22 40 93; www.flamencoensevilla.com; Calle Mesón del Moro 12; adult/child €18/12; ☺shows 7.30pm & 9pm) Ensconced in an 18th-century town house, this is a tiny flamenco venue (no food or drinks served). Its two evening shows are intimate affairs with three on-stage performers and the audience squeezed into a small seating area flanked by display cases full of guitars. To guarantee a place, it's best to book ahead.

Tablao Los Gallos   Flamenco
(☑954 21 69 81; www.tablaolosgallos.com; Plaza de Santa Cruz 11; adult/child €35/20; ☺shows 8pm & 10pm) Located on a pretty Santa Cruz plaza, this is Seville's oldest *tablao* (choreographed flamenco show), dating from 1966. Its twice-nightly shows feature a wider range of performers (all top-notch) than most set-ups, with four dancers, three singers and

three guitarists – hence its above-average admission price. One for aficionados.

Casa Anselma Flamenco

(☑606 162502; Calle Pagés del Corro 49; ⊘11.45pm-2am Mon-Sat) True, the music is often more folkloric than flamenco, but this Triana institution is the antithesis of a showbiz flamenco *tablao* (choreographed show), with cheek-to-jowl crowds, zero amplification and spontaneous outbreaks of dancing. Doors don't open till around midnight, and there's an arbitrary admission policy, so you may be refused entry. Reservations recommended.

Tablao El Arenal Flamenco

(☑954 21 64 92; www.tablaoelarenal.com; Calle Rodo 7; show incl drink/tapas/dinner €39/62/75; ⊘shows 7.15pm & 10pm) Of all the venues offering flamenco 'dinner shows', this is one of the best. With a seating capacity of 100 in an old-school tavern, it lacks the grit and *duende* (flamenco spirit) of the *peñas* (small flamenco clubs), but you can't fault the skill of the performers. Skip the food, though.

ℹ INFORMATION

Tourist information is readily available at official tourist offices throughout the city. Staff generally speak English.

Airport Tourist Office (☑954 78 20 35; www. andalucia.org; Seville Airport; ⊘9am-7.30pm Mon-Fri, 9.30am-3pm Sat & Sun)

Central Tourist Office (☑954 21 00 05; www. turismosevilla.org; Plaza del Triunfo 1; ⊘9am-7.30pm Mon-Fri, 9.30am-7.30pm Sat & Sun; 🛜)

Municipal Tourist Office (☑955 47 12 32; www. visitasevilla.es; Paseo Marqués de Contadero; ⊘9am-2.30pm Mon-Fri)

Train Station Tourist Office (☑954 78 20 02; www.andalucia.org; Estación Santa Justa; ⊘9am-7.30pm Mon-Fri, 9.30am-3pm Sat & Sun)

There are also private City Expert offices providing information and booking services. Two useful offices are in the **centre** (☑900 920 092; https://cityexpert.travel; Avenida de la Constitución 23B; ⊘9.30am-9pm) and at the

train station (www.cityexpert.es; Estación Santa Justa; ⊘9.30am-6pm Mon-Sat, to 2.30pm Sun).

ℹ GETTING THERE & AWAY

AIR

Seville's **airport** (Aeropuerto de Sevilla; Map p181; ☑913 21 10 00; www.aena.es; A4, Km 532) has a fair range of international and domestic flights. A number of international carriers fly in and out of Seville; carrier and schedule information changes frequently, so it's best to check with specific airlines or major online booking agents.

BUS

Estación de Autobuses Plaza de Armas (☑955 03 86 65; www.autobusesplazadearmas.es; Avenida del Cristo de la Expiración) Seville's main bus station. From here, **ALSA** (☑902 42 22 42; www.alsa.es) buses serve Granada (€23 to €30, three hours, 11 to 12 daily) and Córdoba (€12.65, two hours, seven daily).

Estación de Autobuses Prado de San Sebastián (Plaza San Sebastián) Has services to smaller towns in western Andalucía. **Comes** (☑902 19 92 08; www.tgcomes.es) runs to Cádiz, Jerez de la Frontera and some of the harder-to-reach *pueblos blancos* (white towns) in Cádiz province.

TRAIN

Seville's principal train station, **Estación Santa Justa** (Avenida Kansas City), is 1.5km northeast of the centre.

High-speed AVE trains go to/from Madrid (€50 to €88, 2½ to 3¼ hours, hourly) and Córdoba (€14 to €32, 45 minutes to 1¼ hours, up to 35 daily). Slower trains head to Granada (€31 to €61, 2½ to 4¼ hours, nine daily).

ℹ GETTING AROUND

Walking is the best option, especially in the centre. The Sevici (p177) bike-sharing scheme has made cycling easy and bike lanes are now almost as ubiquitous as pavements. Buses are more useful than the metro to link the main tourist sights. Whole roads in the city centre are now permanently closed to traffic; park on the periphery.

CÓRDOBA

Córdoba at a Glance...

Córdoba's mesmerising multi-arched Mezquita is one of the world's greatest Islamic buildings. The Mezquita is a symbol of the sophisticated Islamic culture that flourished here more than a millennium ago when Córdoba was the capital of Islamic Spain, and Western Europe's biggest and most cultured city. But there's much more to this city. Córdoba is a great place for exploring on foot or by bicycle, staying and eating well in old buildings centred on verdant patios, diving into old wine bars and feeling millennia of history at every turn.

Córdoba in Two Days

You could easily spend a day in the **Mezquita** (p186). When you can finally tear yourself away, head for the **Centro Flamenco Fosforito** (p189) and **Alcázar de los Reyes Cristianos** (p189). Otherwise, wander the charming streets of the Judería and dine at **Taberna Salinas** (p190) and **La Boca** (p190).

Córdoba in Four Days

With extra time, make an excursion to evocative **Medina Azahara** (p191). Back in town, take in a flamenco performance at **Centro Flamenco Fosforito** (p189), wander along the riverbank from the **Puente Romano** (p190), visit the **Palacio de Viana** (p189), and eat and drink well at **Bodegas Campos** (p190) and **Bodega Guzmán** (p191).

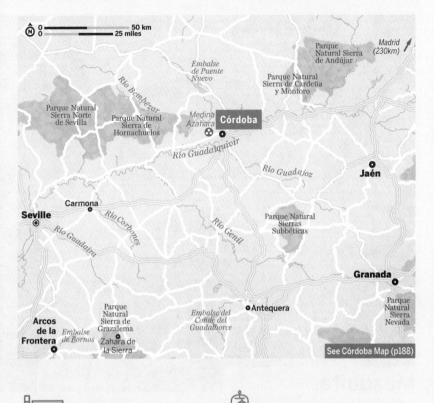

See Córdoba Map (p188)

Arriving in Córdoba

Super-fast AVE train services connect Córdoba with Madrid (€33 to €63, 1¾ hours) and Seville (€14 to €30, 45 minutes). Taxis from the train station to the Mezquita cost around €7.

Where to Stay

Córdoba's many accommodation options span the spectrum of economy to deluxe. Even some of the lower-end places offer elegantly styled and spacious rooms, while others are laden with antiques and history. Booking ahead is essential. Expect prices to rise during Semana Santa, the May festivals and some weekends.

Cathedral

Mezquita

It's impossible to overemphasise the beauty of Córdoba's great mosque. With all its lustrous decoration, it evokes the city's golden age of sophistication and peaceful coexistence between faiths.

Great For...

Don't Miss

The mosque's greatest treasure, the 10th-century *mihrab,* a scallop-shell-shaped prayer niche facing Mecca.

Patio de los Naranjos

This lovely courtyard forms the entrance to the Mezquita. It was formerly the site of ritual ablutions before prayer in the mosque. Its most impressive entrance is the **Puerta del Perdón**, a 14th-century Mudéjar archway in the base of the bell tower. The courtyard can be enjoyed free of charge at any time.

Bell Tower (Minaret)

The 54m-high bell tower reopened to visitors in 2014 after 24 years of intermittent restoration work, and you can climb up to its bells for fine panoramas. Originally built in 951–52, it was encased in a strengthened outer shell and heightened by the Christians in the 16th and 17th centuries. Córdoba's minaret influenced all minarets built thereafter throughout the Western Islamic world.

Bell tower

ⓘ Need to Know

Mosque; ☏957 47 05 12; www.mezquita-cat-edraldecordoba.es; Calle Cardenal Herrero 1; adult/child €10/5, 8.30-9.30am Mon-Sat free; ⊙10am-7pm Mon-Sat, 8.30-11.30am & 3-7pm Sun Mar-Oct, 10am-6pm Mon-Sat, 8.30-11.30am & 3-6pm Sun Nov-Feb

✕ Take a Break

Legendary little **Bar Santos** (Calle Magistral González Francés 3; tapas €2.30-5; ⊙10am-midnight Mon-Fri, from 11am Sat & Sun) serves Córdoba's best *tortilla de patata* (potato omelette) under the Mezquita's walls.

★ Top Tip

Get here early: free entry 8.30am and 9.30am (except Sunday) and no groups before 10am.

Columns & Arches

The main prayer hall consists of 'naves' lined by two-tier arches striped in red brick and white stone. The columns used for the Mezquita used material collected from earlier Visigothic and Roman buildings. Later enlargements of the mosque extended these lines of arches to cover an area of nearly 120 sq metres and create one of the biggest mosques in the world. The arcades are one of the much-loved Islamic architectural motifs. Their simplicity and number give the Mezquita a sense of endlessness.

Mihrab & Maksura

Just past the cathedral's western end, the approach to the glorious *mihrab* begins, marked by heavier, more elaborate arches. Immediately in front of the *mihrab* is the *maksura* (royal prayer enclosure), with its

intricately interwoven arches and lavishly decorated domes created by Caliph Al-Hakam II in the 960s. The decoration of the *mihrab* portal incorporates 1600kg of gold mosaic cubes, a gift from the Christian emperor of Byzantium, Nicephoras II Phocas.

Cathedral

Following the Christian conquest of Córdoba in 1236, the Mezquita was used as a cathedral and remained largely unaltered for nearly three centuries. But in the 16th century, King Carlos I gave the cathedral authorities permission to rip out the centre of the Mezquita in order to construct the Capilla Mayor (the main altar area) and *coro* (choir). Legend has it that when he saw the result, the horrified king exclaimed: 'You have destroyed something that was unique in the world'.

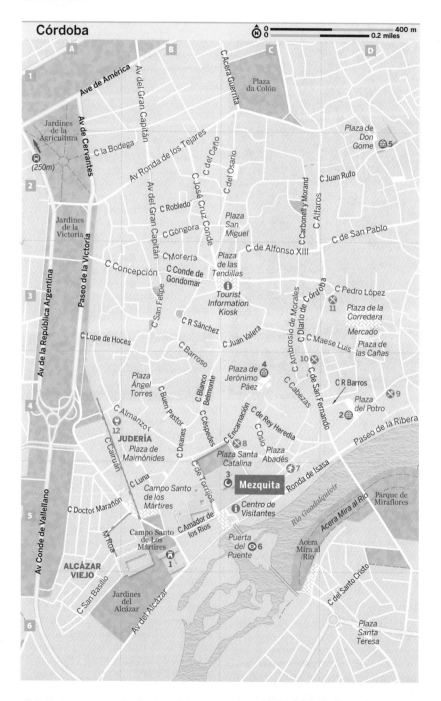

Córdoba

N

0 _____ 400 m
0 _____ 0.2 miles

Plaza da Colón

Ave de América

Av del Gran Capitán

Av de Cervantes

C Acera Guerrita

Jardines de la Agricultura

(250m)

C la Bodega

Av Ronda de los Tejares

Av del Gran Capitán

Plaza de Don Gome 5

C Juan Rufo

C del Caño

C del Osario

Jardines de la Victoria

Paseo de la Victoria

C Robledo

C José Cruz Conde

C Góngora

Plaza San Miguel

C Carbonell y Morand

C Alfaros

C de San Pablo

Av de la República Argentina

C Morería

C Concepción

C Conde de Gondomar

Plaza de las Tendillas

C de Alfonso XIII

Tourist Information Kiosk

C Ambrosio de Morales

C Diario de Córdoba

C Pedro López

11

Plaza de la Corredera

C San Felipe

C R Sánchez

C Juan Valera

C Maese Luis

Mercado

C Barroso

10

Plaza de las Cañas

Plaza Ángel Torres

C Almanzor

C Buen Pastor

C Blanco Belmonte

C Céspedes

Plaza de Jerónimo Páez

4

C de San Fernando

C Cabezas

C R Barros

Plaza del Potro

2

9

C Lope de Hoces

JUDERÍA

12

C Deanes

C Encarnación

C de Rey Heredia

C Osio

8

Plaza Abadés

Paseo de la Ribera

Plaza de Maimónides

C Caìndàn

C de Torrilos

Plaza Santa Catalina

3

Mezquita

7

Ronda de Isasa

Río Guadalquivir

Parque de Miraflores

C Luna

Campo Santo de los Mártires

Centro de Visitantes

Acera Mira al Río

Av Conde de Vallellano

C Doctor Marañón

M Roa

Campo Santo de Los Mártires

C Amador de los Ríos

1

Puerta del Puente 6

Acera Mira al Río

ALCÁZAR VIEJO

C San Basilio

Jardines del Alcázar

Av del Alcázar

C del Santo Cristo

Plaza Santa Teresa

Córdoba

◉ SIGHTS

Alcázar de los Reyes Cristianos *Fortress*

(Fortress of the Christian Monarchs; ☎957 42 01 51; https://cultura.cordoba.es; Calle Caballerizas Reales; adult/student/child €5/2.50/free; ⏰8.30am-2.30pm Tue-Sun mid-Jun–mid-Sep, 8.15am-8pm Tue-Fri, 9.30am-6pm Sat, 8.15am-2.45pm Sun mid-Sep–mid-Jun) This formidable fort-palace dates to the 14th century when it was commissioned by King Alfonso XI and built over an earlier Moorish palace. It was Córdoba's main royal residence and it was here that Fernando and Isabel met Christopher Columbus in 1486. Inside, the highlight is a series of Roman mosaics, discovered under Plaza de la Corredera in the 1950s, while outside, the exquisite Moorish-style gardens are a joy to explore.

Centro Flamenco Fosforito *Museum*

(Posada del Potro; ☎957 47 68 29; www.centro flamencofosforito.cordoba.es; Plaza del Potro; ⏰8.45am-3.15pm Tue-Sun mid-Jun–mid-Sep, 8.15am-8pm Tue-Fri, 9.30am-6pm Sat, 8.15am-2.45pm Sun mid-Sep–mid-Jun) `FREE` Charmingly housed in a historic inn, this passionately curated museum is a must for anyone with even a passing interest in flamenco. Exhibits, which include photos, film footage, recordings and instruments, are combined with information panels in English and Spanish to chart the history of the art form and its great exponents.

Free concerts and flamenco performances are occasionally held here – check the website for upcoming events.

Palacio de Viana *Museum*

(☎957 49 67 41; www.palaciodeviana.com; Plaza de Don Gome 2; whole house/patios €8/5, 2-5pm Wed free; ⏰10am-7pm Tue-Sat, to 3pm Sun Sep-Jun, 9am-3pm Tue-Sun Jul & Aug) A noble Renaissance palace, the Palacio de Viana

📖🖌 Córdoba's Judería

The old Jewish quarter west and north of the Mezquita is a labyrinth of narrow streets and small squares, whitewashed buildings and wrought-iron gates allowing glimpses of plant-filled patios. The importance of the medieval Jewish community is illustrated by the Judería's proximity to the Mezquita and the city's centres of power. Spain had one of Europe's biggest Jewish communities, recorded from as early as the 2nd century CE. Persecuted by the Visigoths, they allied themselves with the Muslims following the Arab conquests. By the 10th century, they were established among the most dynamic members of society, holding posts as administrators, doctors, jurists, philosophers and poets.

Córdoba's Guitar Festival

Festival de la Guitarra de Córdoba
(https://guitarracordoba.es; ⊙early Jul)
A 10-day celebration of the guitar.
Theatres across town stage concerts
of classical, flamenco, rock, blues, and
more by top Spanish and international
names.

is a particular delight in spring when its 12
plant-filled patios are awash with colour.
The much-modified 14th-century mansion
was home to the aristocratic Marqueses
de Viana until 1980, and its stately rooms
are crammed with art and antiques. Visits
to the palace are by guided tour only, but
you're free to explore the pretty courtyards
on your own.

The *palacio* is 800m northeast of Plaza
de las Tendillas.

Puente Romano   Bridge
Spanning the Río Guadalquivir just below
the Mezquita, this handsome 16-arch
bridge originally formed part of Via Augusta, the ancient Roman road that connected
Girona in Catalonia with Cádiz. It has been
rebuilt several times since the 1st century
CE and now makes for a lovely traffic-free
stroll.

For a classic Córdoba view, cross the
bridge and from the far riverside path
look back to the Mezquita dominating the
skyline.

🏃 ACTIVITIES

Hammam Baños Árabes   Hammam
(☑957 48 47 46; http://cordoba.hammamal
andalus.com; Calle del Corregidor Luis de la
Cerda 51; baths & steam room €32, incl massage
€45-99; ⊙10am-midnight) Follow the lead of
the medieval Cordobans and treat yourself
to a soak in the warm, hot and cold pools of
these beautifully renovated Arab baths. You
can also enjoy a range of massages.

🍴 EATING & DRINKING

Taberna Salinas   Andalucian €
(☑957 48 29 50; www.tabernasalinas.com; Calle
Tundidores 3; mains €7.75-11; ⊙12.30-3.30pm
& 8-11pm Mon-Sat, closed Aug) A historic bar-
restaurant (since 1879) with a patio and
several rooms, Salinas is adorned in classic
Córdoba fashion with tiles, wine barrels, art
and photos of bullfighter Manolete. It's popular with tourists, but it retains a traditional
atmosphere and its classic regional food is
reliably good (and served in huge helpings).

Bodegas Campos   Andalucian €€
(☑957 49 75 00; www.bodegascampos.com;
Calle de Lineros 32; mains €12-26; ⊙1-4pm &
8.30-11pm) This atmospheric warren of
rooms and patios is a local institution,
popular with *cordobeses* and visitors alike –
including ex-Brit PM Tony Blair. The restaurant and more informal *taberna* (tavern)
specialise in creatively updated regional
dishes such as avocado purée and beef
tenderloin with foie gras. It also produces
its own house Montilla wine.

La Boca   Fusion €€
(☑957 47 61 40; www.facebook.com/restaur
ante.laboca; Calle de San Fernando 39; mains
€12.50-18.50; ⊙noon-midnight Wed-Mon, to
5pm Tue; 🛜) Local ingredients are given an
international makeover at this inventive
restaurant, appearing in dishes such as
Iberian pork-cheek loaf in red curry or tuna
tataki with soy mayo. Complementing the
fusion cuisine, its *taberna* rooms and more

formal restaurant section sport an arty, casually stylish look. Reservations advisable at weekends.

Bodega Guzmán
Wine Bar

(Calle de los Judíos 7; ☺noon-4pm & 8.30-11.30pm Fri-Wed) This cavernous Judería bar, frequented by both locals and tourists, is straight out of central casting with its ceramic tiling, bullfighting memorabilia and giant wine barrels. Get into the groove by sipping on a bone-dry Montilla *fino*, perhaps accompanied by a tapa of sheep's cheese in olive oil.

❶ INFORMATION

Information on Córdoba and its province is available at www.cordobaturismo.es. There are currently two tourist offices in town:

Centro de Visitantes (Visitors Centre; ☑902 20 17 74; www.turismodecordoba.org; Plaza del Triunfo; ☺9am-7pm Mon-Fri, 9.30am-2.30pm Sat & Sun) The main tourist office near the Mezquita; can provide maps and printed material in English and Spanish.

Municipal Tourist Information Kiosk (www. turismodecordoba.org; Plaza de las Tendillas; ☺9am-1.30pm & 5-7.15pm daily) On Plaza de las Tendillas in the modern part of town.

❶ GETTING THERE & AWAY

Most travellers arrive in Córdoba by train. Its modern train station, 1.2km northwest of Plaza de las Tendillas, is served both by fast AVE services and by some slower regional trains. There

Medina Azahara

Some 8km west of Córdoba stand the ruins of **Medina Azahara** (Madinat al-Zahra; ☑957 10 49 33; www.mu seosdeandalucia. es; Carretera Palma del Río Km 5.5; EU/non-EU citizen free/€1.50, shuttle bus adult/child €2.50/1.50; ☺9am-9pm Tue-Sat Apr–mid-Jun, to 3pm mid-Jun–mid-Sep, to 6pm mid-Sep–Mar, 9am-3pm Sun year-round; ℗), the 10th-century palace-city built by Caliph Abd ar-Rahman III. Only about a tenth of the original city has been excavated and visits, which start in a modern museum some 2km below the hillside ruins, are limited to the central section of the Alcázar, the quarter that comprised the caliph's palace and attendant offices and residential blocks.

DAVID ACOSTA ALLELY/SHUTTERSTOCK©

are services to Madrid (€39 to €63, 1¾ to 2¼ hours, 30 daily) and Seville (€14 to €32, 45 to 75 minutes, up to 35 daily).

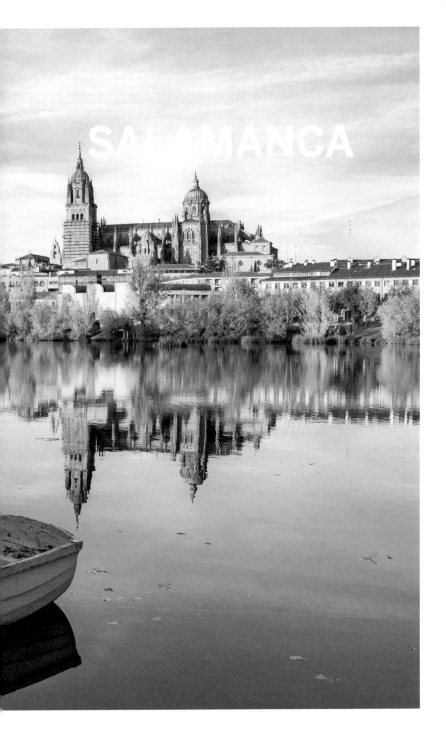

SALAMANCA

Salamanca at a Glance...

Whether floodlit by night or bathed in late afternoon light, there's something magical about Salamanca. This is where one of Europe's oldest universities meets rare beauty in a city awash with golden sandstone overlaid with ochre-tinted Latin inscriptions. The result is an extraordinary virtuosity of plateresque and Renaissance styles without peer anywhere in Spain. The monumental highlights are many, with the exceptional Plaza Mayor an unforgettable highlight, not to mention the exquisite cathedral and university facades. But this is also Castilla's liveliest city, home to a massive student population that courses through the streets day and night.

Salamanca in One Day

Begin in the **Plaza Mayor** (p198), the glorious beating heart of the city. Join the crowds and head for the **Catedral Nueva** (p196), then the staggering altarpiece of the **Catedral Vieja** (p197). Round out your day with visits to the **Universidad Civil** (p198) and **Convento de San Esteban** (p199), sandwiched between meals at **La Cocina de Toño** (p201) and the upmarket **Victor Gutiérrez** (p203).

Salamanca in Two Days

Admire the **Casa de las Conchas** (p200) and **Real Clerecía de San Marcos** (p200), then climb the **Ieronimus** (p197) for exceptional views out over the city's rooftops. Don't miss the outstanding **Museo de Art Nouveau y Art Decó** (p200) or the cloister at the **Convento de las Dueñas** (p201).

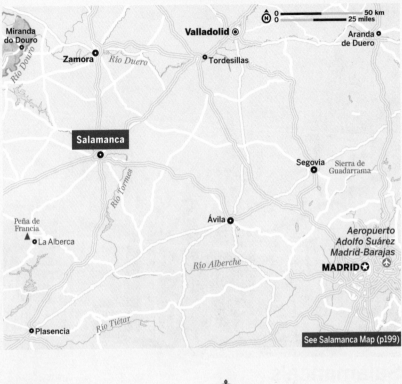

Arriving in Salamanca

Salamanca has no airport. The bus and train stations are a 10- and 15-minute walk, respectively, from Plaza Mayor. Bus 4 runs past the bus station and around the old-city perimeter to Calle Gran Vía, an easy walk from Plaza Mayor. From the train station, the best bet is bus 1, which heads into the centre along Calle de Azafranal.

Where to Stay

Salamanca has excellent accommodation across a range of budgets. In the city centre close to the Plaza Mayor, boutique hotels rub shoulders with simpler, often family-run *hostales* and apartments. The more upmarket hotels aren't far away, but generally inhabit quieter spots south of the more clamorous streets of the centre – even so, you're still within walking distance.

Catedral Nueva

CANADASTOCK/SHUTTERSTOCK ©

Salamanca's Cathedrals

Most Spanish cities can boast one cathedral. Salamanca has two. The city's conjoined old and new cathedrals have virtuoso facades and glorious interiors in keeping with Salamanca's reputation for architectural magic.

Great For...

Don't Miss

The extraordinary altarpiece in the Catedral Vieja. It's one of Spain's most beautiful.

A better name for these twin towers of worship would be the 'old cathedral' and 'even older cathedral' – the Catedral Nueva is a mere babe having been completed in 1733. Then again, Salamanca nearly had no cathedrals at all. The 1755 Lisbon earthquake wrought devastation across the region and you can still see cracks and broken windows from that time. On 31 October every year, locals climb to the cupola to play flutes and drums in riotous commemoration of the day the cathedrals nearly fell.

Catedral Nueva

The tower of this late-Gothic cathedral lords it over the city centre, its compelling Churrigueresque (an ornate style of baroque) dome visible from almost every angle. The interior is similarly impressive, with elaborate choir stalls, main chapel

Catedral Vieja

RENATA SEDMAKOVA SHUTTERSTOCK ©

ⓘ Need to Know

☑923 21 74 76; Plaza de Anaya; adult/child €6/4 (includes audio guide & admission to both cathedrals); ⏱10am-6pm Oct-Mar, 10am-8pm Apr-Sep

✕ Take a Break

You're never far from anywhere in Salamanca. The cool and casual **Mandala Café** (☑923 12 33 42; Calle de Serranos 9-11; set menu €13.50; ⏱8am-11pm; 🚻) is just a few blocks away.

★ Top Tip

Come to the Plaza de Anaya after sunset but before midnight (when they turn the floodlights off) for stunning facade views.

and retrochoir, much of it courtesy of the prolific José Churriguera. The ceilings are also exceptional, along with the Renaissance doorways – particularly the **Puerta del Nacimiento** on the western face, which stands out as one of several miracles worked in the city's native sandstone.

The Puerta de Ramos, facing Plaza de Anaya, contains a 'spotting' challenge. Look for the little astronaut and ice-cream cone chiselled into the portal by stonemasons during restoration work in 1992.

Catedral Vieja

The Catedral Nueva's largely Romanesque predecessor, the Catedral Vieja is adorned with an exquisite 15th-century **altarpiece**, one of the finest outside Italy. Its 53 panels depict scenes from the lives of Christ and Mary and are topped by a haunting

representation of the Final Judgement. The cloister was largely ruined in an earthquake in 1755, but the **Capilla de Anaya** houses an extravagant alabaster sepulchre and one of Europe's oldest organs, a Mudéjar work of art from the 16th century.

The cathedral was begun in 1120 and remains something of a hybrid. There are Gothic elements, while the unusual ribbed cupola, the **Torre del Gallo**, reflects a Byzantine influence.

Ieronimus

For fine views over Salamanca, head to the tower at the southwestern corner of the Catedral Nueva's facade. From here, stairs (€3.75) lead up through the tower, past labyrinthine but well-presented exhibitions of cathedral memorabilia, then along the interior balconies of the sanctuaries of the Catedral Nueva and Catedral Vieja and out onto the exterior balconies.

◎ SIGHTS

Plaza Mayor
Square

Built between 1729 and 1755, Salamanca's exceptional grand square is widely considered to be Spain's most beautiful central plaza. It's particularly memorable at night when illuminated (until midnight) to magical effect. Designed by Alberto Churriguera, it's a remarkably harmonious and controlled baroque display. The medallions placed around the square bear the busts of famous figures.

Universidad Civil
Historic Building

(☑ ext 1150 923 29 44 00; www.salamanca.es; Calle de los Libreros; adult/concession €10/5, audio guide €2; ☺ 10am-7pm Mon-Sat, to 2pm Sun mid-Sep–Mar, 10am-8pm Mon-Sat, to 2pm Sun Apr–mid-Sep) Founded initially as the Estudio General in 1218, the university reached the peak of its renown in the 15th and 16th centuries. The visual feast of the entrance facade is a tapestry in sandstone, bursting with images of mythical heroes, religious scenes and coats of arms. It's dominated by busts of Fernando and Isabel. Behind the facade, the highlight of an otherwise-modest collection of rooms lies upstairs: the extraordinary **university library**, the oldest in Europe.

Containing some 2800 manuscripts gathering dust, the library is a real cemetery of forgotten books. Note the fine late-Gothic features and beautiful *techumbre* (carved wooden ceiling).

Among the small lecture rooms arranged around the courtyard downstairs, the **Aula de Fray Luis de León** was named after the celebrated 16th-century theologian and writer whose statue adorns the Patio de las Escuelas Menores outside. Arrested by the Inquisition for having translated the 'Song of Solomon' into Spanish, the sardonic theologian returned to his class after five years in jail and resumed lecturing with the words, 'As I was saying yesterday...'

The **Escalera de la Universidad** (University Staircase) that connects the two floors has symbols carved into the balustrade, seemingly of giant insects having a frolic with several bishops – to decode

Plaza Mayor

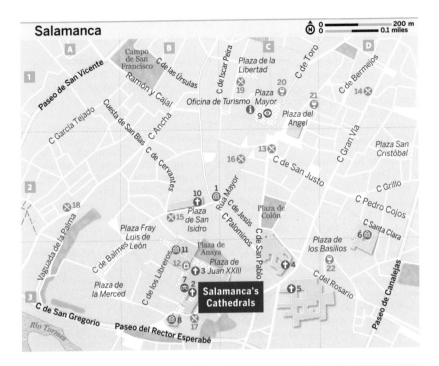

Salamanca

◎ Sights
1 Casa de las Conchas B2
2 Catedral Vieja B3
3 Catedral Nueva B3
4 Convento de las Dueñas C3
5 Convento de San Esteban C3
6 Convento de Santa Clara D2
7 Ieronimus B3
8 Museo de Art Nouveau y Art Decó B3
9 Plaza Mayor C1
10 Real Clerecía de San Marcos B2
11 Universidad Civil B3

🏛 Shopping
12 Mercatus B3

✖ Eating
13 El Pecado C2
14 La Cocina de Toño D1
15 Mandala Café B2
16 Mesón Las Conchas C2
17 Restaurante Lis B3
18 Victor Gutiérrez A2
19 Zazu Bistro C1

○ Drinking & Nightlife
20 Doctor Cocktail C1
21 Tío Vivo C1
22 Vinodiario D3

them was seen as symbolic of the quest for knowledge.

Convento de San Esteban Convent
(☏923 21 50 00; www.conventosanesteban.
es; Plaza del Concilio de Trento; adult/child €4/
free; ⊙10am-1.15pm & 4-7.15pm Apr-Oct, 10am-
1.15pm & 4-5.15pm Nov-Mar) Just down the hill
from the cathedral, the lordly Dominican
Convento de San Esteban's church has an
extraordinary altar-like facade, with the
stoning of San Esteban (St Stephen) as
its central motif. Inside is a well-presented
museum dedicated to the Dominicans, a
splendid Gothic-Renaissance cloister and
an elaborate church built in the form of a

Latin cross and adorned by an overwhelming 17th-century **altar** by José Churriguera.

You can now also climb to the terrace directly above the facade, which is worth doing for the fine Salamanca views. The climb is open at 11.30am, noon, 12.30pm, 7pm and 7.30pm Tuesday to Saturday, 10.30am, 11am and 11.30am on Sundays from April to October, with shorter hours the rest of the year.

Museo de Art Nouveau y Art Decó
Museum

(Casa Lis; ☑923 12 14 25; www.museocasalis. org; Calle de Gibraltar; adult/under 12yr €4/free, 11am-2pm Thu free; ⊘11am-8pm; 👪) Utterly unlike any other Salamanca museum, this stunning collection of sculpture, paintings and art deco and art nouveau pieces inhabits a beautiful, light-filled Modernista (Catalan art nouveau) house. There's abundant stained glass and exhibits that include Lalique glass, toys by Steiff (inventor of the teddy bear), Limoges porcelain, Fabergé watches, fabulous bronze and marble figurines, and a vast collection of 19th-century children's dolls (some strangely macabre),

which kids will love. There's also a cafe and an excellent gift shop.

Real Clerecía de San Marcos
Church

(San Marcos; ☑923 27 71 00; www.torresdela clerecia.com; Calle de la Compañia; San Marcos €3, Scala Coeli €3.75, combined ticket €6; ⊘San Marcos 10.30am-12.45pm & 4-5.30pm Tue-Fri, 10.30am-1.30pm & 4-5.30pm Sat, 10.30am-1.30pm Sun, Scala Coeli 10am-7.15pm) Visits to this colossal baroque church and the attached Catholic university are via obligatory **guided tours** (in Spanish), which run every 45 minutes. You can also climb the **Scala Coeli** (tower) – some 166 steps, including the bell tower – to enjoy superb panoramic views.

Casa de las Conchas
Historic Building

(House of Shells; ☑923 26 93 17; Calle de la Compañia 2; ⊘9am-9pm Mon-Fri, 9am-2pm & 4-7pm Sat, 10am-2pm & 4-7pm Sun) **FREE** One of the city's most endearing buildings, Casa de las Conchas is named after the 300 scallop shells clinging to its facade. The house's original owner, Dr Rodrigo Maldonado de Talavera, was a doctor at the court of Isabel and a member of the Order of Santiago,

From left: Convento de San Esteban (p199); Universidad Civil (p198); Casa de las Conchas; Convento de las Dueñas

whose symbol is the shell. It now houses the public **library**, entered via a charming colonnaded courtyard with a central fountain and intricate stone tracery.

Convento de las Dueñas   Convent
(☎923 21 54 42; Plaza Concilio de Trento; €2; ⏰10.30am-12.45pm & 4.30-7.15pm Mon-Sat) This Dominican convent is home to the city's most beautiful cloister, with some decidedly ghoulish carvings on the capitals.

Convento de Santa Clara   Museum
(☎660 108314; Calle Santa Clara 2; adult/child €3/free; ⏰9.30am-12.45pm & 4.25-6.10pm Mon-Fri, 9.30am-2.10pm Sat & Sun) This much-modified convent started life as a Romanesque structure and now houses a small museum. You can admire the beautiful frescos and climb up some stairs to inspect the 14th- and 15th-century wooden Mudéjar ceiling at close quarters. You can visit only as part of a (Spanish-language) **guided tour**, which runs roughly every hour.

Casa de las Conchas is named after the 300 scallop shells clinging to its facade

🅰 SHOPPING
Mercatus   Gifts & Souvenirs
(☎923 29 46 48; www.mercatus.usal.es; Calle de Cardenal Pla y Deniel; ⏰10am-8.15pm Mon-Sat, 10.15am-2pm Sun) The official shop of the University of Salamanca has a stunning range of stationery items, leather-bound books and other carefully selected reminders of your Salamanca visit.

✖ EATING
La Cocina de Toño   Tapas €€
(☎923 26 39 77; www.lacocinadetoño.es; Calle Gran Via 20; tapas from €1.60, mains €11-23, set menus from €17; ⏰11am-4.30pm & 8-11.30pm Tue-Sat, 11am-4.30pm Sun; 📶) This place owes its loyal following to its creative *pinchos* (tapas) and half-servings of dishes such as escalope of foie gras with roast apple and passionfruit jelly. The restaurant serves more traditional fare as befits the decor, but the bar is one of Salamanca's gastronomic stars. Slightly removed from the old city, it draws a predominantly Spanish crowd.

CORRADO BARATTA/SHUTTERSTOCK ©

Tapas

Zazu Bistro
Italian €€

(923 26 16 90; www.restaurantezazu.com; Plaza de la Libertad 8; mains €11-17; ⊙2-4pm & 8.30pm-midnight) Enjoy a romantic intimate ambience and Italian-inspired dishes like asparagus, mint and cheese risotto or farfalle with tomato, bacon, vodka and parmesan. The culinary surprises extend to desserts, like that delectable British standard, sticky toffee pudding. Every dish is executed to perfection. Snag a table by the window overlooking this tranquil square.

El Pecado
Contemporary Spanish €€

(923 26 65 58; www.elpecadorestaurante.es; Plaza del Poeta Iglesias 12; mains €15-19, menú de degustación €25-35; ⊙1.30-4pm & 8.30-11.30pm; ✍) A trendy place that regularly attracts Spanish celebrities and well-to-do locals, El Pecado (The Sin) has an intimate dining room and a quirky, creative menu. The hallmarks are fresh tastes, a lovely lack of pretension, intriguing combinations and dishes that regularly change according to what is fresh in the market that day. The menú de degustación is outstanding. Reservations recommended.

The marinated wild salmon, passionfruit and yucca should give you an idea of what to expect.

Mesón Las Conchas
Castilian €€

(923 21 21 67; Rúa Mayor 16; mains €12-23; ⊙bar 8am-midnight, restaurant 1-4pm & 8pm-midnight; 🖫) Enjoy a choice of outdoor tables, an atmospheric bar or the upstairs, wood-beamed dining area. The bar caters mainly to locals who know their embutidos (cured meats). For sit-down meals, there's a good mix of roasts, platos combinados and raciones (full-size tapas). The restaurant serves a highly rated oven-baked turbot.

Restaurante Lis
Castilian €€

(923 21 62 60; www.restaurantelis.es; Patio Chico 18; mains €15-19, set menus €30-45; ⊙2-4pm & 8.30pm-late Tue-Sat, 4-8.30pm Sun) This classy restaurant a couple of doors up from the Museo de Art Nouveau y Art Decó specialises in set menus with a choice of five starters for sharing, followed by an elected meat or fish main, and dessert. The atmosphere is intimate and the cooking

assured, with riffs on well-known dishes such as duck hamburger or mango ravioli. Reservations recommended.

Victor Gutiérrez   Contemporary Spanish €€€

(☑923 26 29 73; www.restaurantevictorgutierrez. com; Calle de Empedrada 4; set menus €72-120; ☺1.30-4pm & 8.30-11pm Tue-Fri, 1.30-4pm & 9-11pm Sat, 1.30-4pm Sun; 🛜) This is still the best table in town. Chef Victor Gutiérrez has a Michelin star and his place has a justifiably exclusive vibe, with an emphasis on innovative dishes with plenty of colourful drizzle. The choice of what to order is largely made for you with some excellent set menus that change regularly. Reservations essential.

🍷 DRINKING & NIGHTLIFE

Tío Vivo   Bar

(☑923 215 768; www.tiovivosalamanca.com; Calle del Clavel 3-5; ☺3.30pm-late) Sip drinks by flickering candlelight to a background of '80s music, enjoying the whimsical decor of carousel horses and oddball antiquities. There's live music Tuesday to Thursday from midnight, sometimes with a €5 cover charge.

Doctor Cocktail   Cocktail Bar

(☑923 26 31 51; www.facebook.com/thedoctor salamanca; Calle del Doctor Piñuela 5; ☺4pm-late) Excellent cocktails, friendly bar staff and a cool crowd make for a fine mix just

north of the Plaza Mayor. Apart from the creative list of cocktails, it has over 30 different kinds of gin to choose from and above-average tonic to go with it.

Vinodiario   Wine Bar

(☑923 61 49 25; www.vinodiario.com; Plaza de los Basilios 1; ☺noon-5pm & 8pm-12.30am) Away from the crowds of the old-city centre, this quiet but classy neighbourhood wine bar is run by knowledgeable bar staff and loved by locals who, in summer, fill the outdoor tables for evening drinks. The tapas are good and wine by the glass starts from €2.50.

ℹ️ INFORMATION

Oficina de Turismo (☑923 21 83 42; www.sala manca.es; Plaza Mayor 32; ☺9am-7pm Mon-Fri, 10am-7pm Sat, to 2pm Sun) An audio guide to city sights can be accessed on your phone via www. audioguiasalamanca.es.

ℹ️ GETTING THERE & AWAY

Buses include Madrid (regular/express €17.80/26, 2½ to three hours, hourly) and there's a limited service to smaller towns with just one daily bus – except on Sunday – to La Alberca (€6, around 1½ hours), with stops in the villages of the Sierra de Francia, such as Mogarraz and San Martín del Castañar.

Regular trains run to Madrid's Chamartín station (from €18.40, 1½ to four hours).

BASQUE
COUNTRY

In this Chapter

Basque Country at a Glance...

No matter where you've just arrived from, the Basque Country is different. Known to Basques as Euskadi or Euskal Herria (the land of Basque speakers) and called El Pais Vasco in Spanish, this is where mountain peaks reach for the sky and sublime rocky coves are battered by mighty Atlantic swells. Food is an obsession in this part of the country, whether it's the three-Michelin-starred restaurants of San Sebastián or the fabulous pintxo (Basque tapas) bars there or in Bilbao. And the Basque Country has reinvented itself as one of Spain's style and culture capitals, with Bilbao's Museo Guggenheim leading the way.

Basque Country in Two Days

With so little time, you've little choice but to spend a day in **Bilbao** with the **Museo Guggenheim** (p208) as your visit's centrepiece, as well as spending some time in the town's old centre and food market. Spend your second day in **San Sebastián**, sampling some of the best food Europe has to offer and wandering along the sublime **Playa de la Concha** (p225).

Basque Country in Four Days

Four days would be a minimum to get the best out of the Basque Country. Add an extra day in San Sebastián and factor in a day trip to **Gernika** (p220) or a night in **Vitoria** (p229). Better still, stay a few days longer and do it all.

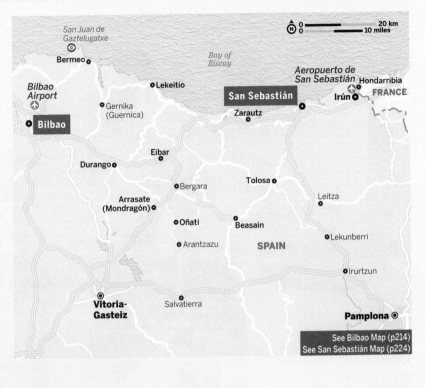

Arriving in Basque Country

Bilbao is connected by air to numerous European and other Spanish cities; an airport bus connects the airport with the city centre. Otherwise, train and bus services connect Bilbao and San Sebastián with other Basque towns and villages, as well as to Madrid, Barcelona and other northern Spanish cities.

Where to Stay

Such is the region's popularity that hotel rooms are at a premium in the Basque Country, particularly in San Sebastián, where advance bookings are essential. Both San Sebastián and Bilbao are popular weekend getaways, so you may have better luck on week-days, although year-round could almost be considered one long high season. Many coastal towns have good-value guesthouses run by families.

Museo Guggenheim Bilbao

Bilbao's shimmering titanium Museo Guggenheim Bilbao is one of modern architecture's most iconic buildings. It almost single-handedly lifted Bilbao into the 21st century and placed it firmly in the international art and tourism spotlight.

Great For...

Don't Miss

The atrium – the interior counterpoint to the facade's flights of fancy.

The Exterior

Canadian architect Frank Gehry's inspired use of flowing canopies, cliffs, promontories, ship shapes, towers and flying fins here is irresistible. Gehry designed the Guggenheim with historical and geographical contexts in mind. The site was an industrial wasteland, part of Bilbao's wretched and decaying warehouse district on the banks of the Ría del Nervión. The city's historical industries of shipbuilding and fishing reflected Gehry's own interests, not least his engagement with industrial materials in previous works. The gleaming titanium tiles that sheathe most of the building like giant herring scales are said to have been inspired by the architect's childhood fascination with fish.

Puppy, by Jeff Koons

DOLORES GIRALDEZ ALONSO/SHUTTERSTOCK ©

ⓘ Need to Know

📞944 35 90 80; www.guggenheim-bilbao. eus; Avenida Abandoibarra 2; adult/child €13/ free; ⊙10am-8pm, closed Mon Sep-Jun

✕ Take a Break

The museum has a high-class restaurant, but try the **Bistró** (📞944 00 04 30; www.neruaguggenheimbilbao.com; Avenida Abandoibarra 2; 5-/9-/14-course menu €85/115/148; ⊙1-3pm Tue & Sun, 1-3pm & 8.30-10pm Wed-Sat May-Sep, 8.30-10pm Thu-Sat Oct-Apr), with menús from €20.

★ Top Tip

The Artean Pass joint ticket for the Guggenheim and Bilbao's Museo de Bellas Artes costs just €14.

Beyond Gehry

Other artists have added their touch to the Guggenheim as well. Lying between the glass buttresses of the central atrium and the Ría del Nervión is a simple pool of water that emits a mist installation by Fuyiko Nakaya. Near the riverbank is Louise Bourgeois' *Maman,* a skeletal spider-like canopy said to symbolise a protective embrace. Jeff Koons' kitsch whimsy *Puppy,* a 12m-tall Highland Terrier made up of thousands of begonias, is on the city side of the museum.

The Interior

The interior of the Guggenheim is purposefully vast. The cathedral-like atrium is more than 45m high, with light pouring in through the glass cliffs. Permanent exhibits fill the ground floor and include such wonders as mazes of metal and phrases of light

reaching for the skies. For many, though, the temporary exhibitions are the main attraction. Recent exhibitions featured the life work of Yoko Ono and the extraordinary sculptures of Brazilian Ernesto Neto.

Guggenheim Essentials

Admission prices vary depending on special exhibitions and the time of year. The last ticket sales are half an hour before closing. Free guided tours in Spanish take place at 12.30pm and 5pm. Tours can be conducted in other languages, but ask at the information desk beforehand. Excellent self-guided audio tours in other languages are free with admission and there is also a special children's audio guide. Entry queues can be horrendous, with wet summer days and Easter almost guaranteeing you a wait of over an hour. The museum is wheelchair accessible.

Pintxos at Gandarias

Pintxos in San Sebastián

San Sebastián stands atop a pedestal as one of the planet's culinary capitals. The city overflows with bars, almost all of which have bar tops weighed down under a mountain of Spain's best pintxos *(Basque tapas).*

Great For...

Don't Miss

Pack in with the locals at tiny **Antonio Bar** (📞943 42 98 15; www.antoniobar.com; Calle de Vergara 3; pintxos €2-4.50, mains €17-24; ⏰1-3.30pm & 7-11pm Mon-Sat).

The following *pintxo* bars all charge between €2.50 to €3.50 for one *pintxo*. Not so bad if you just take one, but is one ever enough?

See p218 for details on the art of eating *pintxos*.

La Cuchara de San Telmo

This **bar** (📞943 44 16 55; Calle 31 de Agosto 28; pintxos €3-5; ⏰7.30-11pm Tue, 12.30-5.30pm & 7.30-11.30pm Wed-Sun) offers miniature Basque nouvelle cuisine from a supremely creative kitchen. Unlike many San Sebastián bars, this one doesn't have any *pintxos* laid out on the bar top; instead, order from the blackboard menu behind the counter.

La Cuchara de San Telmo

MARGARET STEPHEN/LONELY PLANET©

Tue, noon-3pm & 7-11pm Wed-Sun). You can order it a dozen different ways topped with everything from sea urchin roe to black olive paté.

A Fuego Negro

Dark, theatrical and anything but traditional, **A Fuego Negro** (www.afuegonegro.com; Calle 31 de Agosto 31; pintxos €4-6; ⏱noon-4pm & 7-11.30pm) is one of the leading designers of arty *pintxos*. Everything here is a surprise: expect olives stuffed with a burst of vermouth, juicy mini kobe beef burgers on a tomato bun, and tender codfish with pureed cauliflower curry.

Bergara Bar

One of the most highly regarded *pintxo* bars in the Gros neighbourhood, **Bergara Bar** (www.pinchosbergara.es; General Artetxe 8; pintxos €2-4.50; ⏱9.30am-11pm) has a mouthwatering array of delights piled onto the bar counter, as well as others chalked up onto the board.

Gandarias

You'll find all the classics on hand at **Gandarias** (☎943 42 63 62; www.restaurante gandarias.com; Calle 31 de Agosto 23; pintxos €2.50-4.75; ⏱11am-3.30pm & 7pm-midnight), which has a sterling reputation for its artfully prepared *pintxos*. House specials include seared foie gras with redcurrants, Joselito Iberian ham, scrumptious *solomillo* (tenderloin) sandwiches, stuffed mushrooms and delicious crab pie.

Txepetxa

The humble *antxoa* (anchovy) is elevated to royal status at this wood-panelled, old-fashioned local **favourite** (☎943 42 22 27; www.facebook.com/bartxepetxa; Calle de la Pescadería 5; pintxos €2-3.50; ⏱7-11pm

Bilbao

Bilbao isn't the kind of city that knocks you out with its physical beauty – head on over to San Sebastián for that particular pleasure – but it is a city that slowly wins you over. Bilbao, after all, has had a tough upbringing. Surrounded for years by an environment of heavy industry and industrial wastelands, its riverfront landscapes and quirky architecture were hardly recognised or appreciated by travellers on their way to more pleasant destinations. But Bilbao's graft paid off when a few wise investments left it with a shimmering titanium landmark, the Museo Guggenheim.

The Botxo (Hole), as it's fondly known to its inhabitants, has now matured into a major European art centre. But at heart it remains a hard-working town, and one with real character. It's this down-to-earth soul, rather than its art galleries, that is the real attraction of the vital, exciting and cultured city of Bilbao.

📷 Las Siete Calles

Forming the heart of Bilbao's Casco Viejo are seven streets known as the Siete Calles (Basque: Zazpi Kaleak). These dark, atmospheric lanes – Barrenkale Barrena, Barrenkale, Carnicería Vieja, Belostikale, Tendería, Artekale and Somera – date to the 1400s when the east bank of the Ría del Nervión was first developed. They originally constituted the city's commercial centre and river port; these days they teem with lively cafes, *pintxo* bars and boutiques.

⊙ SIGHTS

Museo de Bellas Artes Gallery

(☑944 39 60 60; www.museobilbao.com; Plaza del Museo 2; adult/child €10/free, 6-8pm free; ☺10am-8pm Wed-Mon) The Museo de Bellas Artes houses a compelling collection that includes everything from Gothic sculptures to 20th-century pop art. There are three main subcollections: classical art, with works by Murillo, Zurbarán, El Greco, Goya and Van Dyck; contemporary art, featuring works by Gauguin, Francis Bacon and Anthony Caro; and Basque art, with works of the great sculptors Jorge Oteiza and Eduardo Chillida, and strong paintings by the likes of Ignacio Zuloaga and Juan de Echevarría.

Casco Viejo Old Town

The compact Casco Viejo, Bilbao's atmospheric old quarter, is full of charming streets, boisterous bars and plenty of quirky and independent shops. At the heart of the Casco are Bilbao's original seven streets, **Las Siete Calles**, which date from the 1400s.

The 14th-century Gothic **Catedral de Santiago** (www.catedralbilbao.com; Plaza de Santiago; adult/child €5/free; ☺10am-9pm Jul & Aug, to 8pm Sep-Jun) has a splendid Renaissance portico and pretty little cloister. Further north, the 19th-century arcaded **Plaza Nueva** (Plaza Barria) is a rewarding *pintxo* haunt. There's a small Sunday-morning **flea market** here, which is full of secondhand book and record stalls. Street performers and waiters with trays piled high weave in between, although the market is much more subdued in winter. A sweeter-smelling **flower market** takes place on Sunday mornings in the nearby **Plaza del Arenal**.

Euskal Museoa Museum

(Museo Vasco; ☑944 15 54 23; www.euskal-museoa.eus; Plaza Miguel Unamuno 4; adult/child €3/free, Thu free; ☺10am-7pm Mon & Wed-Fri, 10am-1.30pm & 4-7pm Sat, 10am-2pm Sun) One of Spain's best museums devoted to Basque culture takes visitors on a

Catedral de Santiago

journey from Palaeolithic days to the 21st century, giving an overview of life among the boat builders, mariners, shepherds and artists who have left their mark on modern Basque identity. Displays of clothing, looms, fishing nets, model boats, wood-cutters' axes, sheep bells and navigational instruments illustrate everyday life, while iconic round funerary stones help segue into topics of Basque rituals and beliefs.

Zubizuri Bridge

The most striking of the modern bridges that span the Ría del Nervión, the Zubizuri (Basque for 'White Bridge') has become an iconic feature of Bilbao's cityscape since its completion in 1997. The work of Spanish architect Santiago Calatrava, it has a curved glass-brick walkway (slippery when wet) suspended under a flowing white arch to which it's attached by a series of steel spokes.

🕝 TOURS

There are a number of different city tours available. Some are general-interest tours, others focus on specific aspects of the city such as architecture or food. The following are recommended.

Bilbao Tourist Office (p218) organises 1½-hour walking tours (€4.50) covering either the old town or the architecture in the newer parts of town. At busy times tours can run with more frequency.

Bilbao Greeters (www.bilbaogreeters. com; by donation) One of the more original, and interesting, ways to see the city and get to know a local is through the Bilbao Greeters organisation. Essentially a local person gives you a tour of the city, showing you their favourite sights, places to hang out and, of course, *pintxo* bars. You need to reserve through the website at least a fortnight in advance.

🔒 SHOPPING

For major department stores and big-name fashion labels, trawl the streets of El Ensanche. For more one-of-a-kind, independent boutiques, Casco Viejo is the place to look (although even here the chain shops

Bilbao

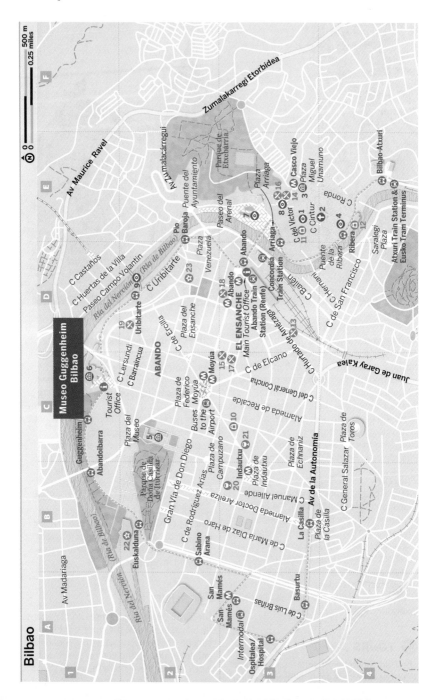

Museo Guggenheim Bilbao

500 m
0.25 miles

Av Maurice Ravel

Av Madariaga

Ría de Bilbao

Parque de Doña Casilda de Iturrizar

Plaza del Museo

Tourist Office

Guggenheim

Abandoibarra

Gran Vía de Don Diego

C de Rodríguez Arias

C de María Díaz de Haro

Alameda Doctor Areilza

Sabino Arana

Euskalduna

San Mamés

C de Luis Briñas

Intermodal / Ospitalea / Hospital

Basurtu

Plaza de la Casilla

La Casilla

C General Salazar

Plaza de Toros

Av de la Autonomía

C Manuel Allende

Plaza de Indautxu

Indautxu

Plaza de Campuzano

Buses to the Airport

Plaza de Federico Moyúa

Moyúa

C de Elcano

Alameda de Recalde

Plaza de Echániz

C del General Concha

Plaza de Ensanche

C de Ercilla

C de Lersundi

C Barraincua

ABANDO

EL ENSANCHE

Main Tourist Office

Abando Train Station (Renfe)

Abando Train Station

Abando

C de Hurtado de Amézaga

C Bailén

Concordia Train Station

Juan de Garay Kalea

C de San Francisco

C de Chemani

Ría del Nervión (Ría de Bilbao)

C Uribitarte

Uribitarte

C de Ercilla

C Campo Volantín

C Huertas de la Villa

C Castaños

Paseo del Arenal

Plaza Venezuela

Plaza Pío Baroja

Puente del Ayuntamiento

Parque de Etxebarria

Zumalakarregi Etorbidea

Av Zumalacárregui

Plaza Arriaga

Casco Viejo

Plaza Miguel Unamuno

C Ronda

C del Victor

C Cintur

Puente de la Ribera

Ribera

Saralegi Plaza

Atxuri Train Station & Eusko Tram Terminus

Bilbao-Atxuri

San Mamés

Bilbao

are increasingly making their presence felt). Bilbao is also a great place for food shopping (of course!).

La Quesaría · Food & Drinks
(www.facebook.com/laqueseriabilbao; Calle Jardines 10; ⏰10.30am-2pm & 5-8.30pm Mon-Sat, 11am-3pm Sun) Cheese lovers shouldn't miss this wondrous shop. You'll find more than 40 varieties of the good stuff, with new selections every week. It's also worth browsing the selection of microbrews (try a pale ale from the Bidassoa Basque Brewery), wines, local jams and other goodies.

Mercado de la Ribera · Market
(www.mercadodelaribera.biz; Calle de la Ribera; ⏰8am-2.30pm Mon & Sat, 8am-2.30pm & 5-8pm Tue-Fri) Overlooking the river, the Mercado de la Ribera is an expansive food market that draws many of the city's top chefs for their morning selection of fresh produce. If you're not planning a picnic, don't miss the *pintxo* counters upstairs (open till 10pm), which offer an excellent spread – plus seating indoors and out.

Chocolates de Mendaro · Chocolate
(www.chocolatesdemendaro.com; Calle de Licenciado Poza 16; ⏰10am-2pm & 4.30-8pm Mon-Fri, 10am-2pm Sat) This old-time chocolate shop spills over with pralines, truffles and nougats in shapes including anchovies and oysters, and stocks its own hot choco-

late mixes. It was founded in 1850 by the Saint-Gerons family, who installed a cocoa mill at their rural property, where chocolates are still made by hand today. Visits to the mill are possible by appointment.

🌟 ENTERTAINMENT

Kafe Antzokia · Live Music
(☎944 24 46 25; www.kafeantzokia.eus; Calle San Vicente 2) Within a former cinema, this is the vibrant heart of contemporary Basque Bilbao, featuring international rock, blues and reggae, as well as the cream of Basque rock-pop. Weekend concerts run from 10pm to 1am, followed by DJs until 5am. During the day, it's a cafe, restaurant and cultural centre with Basque dancing classes (sign up online) all rolled into one.

Euskalduna Palace · Live Music
(☎944 03 50 00; www.euskalduna.eus; Avenida Abandoibarra 4) Built on the riverside former shipyards in 1999, in a style that echoes the great shipbuilding works of the 19th century, this vast venue is home to the Bilbao Symphony Orchestra and the Basque Symphony Orchestra. With a 2164-capacity main hall and 18 smaller halls, it hosts a wide array of operas, concerts, musicals and films.

Pintxo Bars in Bilbao

Although Bilbao lacks San Sebastián's stellar reputation for *pintxos* (Basque tapas), prices are generally slightly lower here (all charge from around €2.50 per *pintxo*) and the quality is about equal. There are literally hundreds of *pintxo* bars throughout Bilbao, but the Plaza Nueva on the edge of the Casco Viejo offers especially rich pickings, as do Calle de Perro and Calle Jardines.

Some of the city's standouts, in no particular order:

Gure Toki (www.guretoki.com; Plaza Nueva 12; pintxos €3-5.50; ⏱9am-11.30pm Mon-Sat, 9.30am-4pm Sun) With a subtle but simple line in creative *pintxos,* including some made with ostrich.

Casa Victor Montes As well known for its *pintxos* as its full meals.

La Viña del Ensanche (☏944 15 56 15; www.lavinadelensanche.com; Calle de la Diputación 10; small plates €5-22.50, tasting menu €35; ⏱8.30am-11pm Mon-Fri, noon-1am Sat) Hundreds of bottles of wine line the walls of this outstanding *pintxos* bar. And when we say outstanding, we mean that it could well be the best place to eat *pintxos* in the city.

El Globo (www.barelglobo.es; Calle de la Diputación 8; pintxos €2.50-4.50; ⏱8am-11pm Mon-Thu, 8am-midnight Fri, 11am-midnight Sat) This is an unassuming but popular bar with favourites such as *txangurro gratinado* (spider crab).

Ledesma No 5 (Calle de Ledesma 5; pintxos €3-5.50; ⏱10am-11.30pm Mon-Wed, 10am-1am Thu, 10am-2.30am Fri, noon-2.30am Sat, noon-11pm Sun) An unmissable spot among the outdoor eateries on pedestrianised Ledesma.

🍴 EATING

Singular   Pintxos €
(☏944 23 17 43; www.singularbar.com; Calle Lersundi 2; pintxos €3-4.50; ⏱9.30am-11pm Mon-Thu, to 1am Fri, 12.15pm-1am Sat) Amid rough-hewn stone walls, vintage iron columns, sleek industrial pipes and venting, and bare-bulbed lights, Singular lays out bite-size morsels of pure perfection on its marble-topped bar. Enjoy high-quality ingredients (grilled sardines with olive oil, sweet potato with anchovies), which you can complement with a craft brew (six on tap and another 50 by the bottle).

Casa Rufo   Basque €€
(☏944 43 21 72; www.casarufo.com; Hurtado de Amézaga 5; mains €16-20; ⏱1.30-4pm & 8.30-11pm Mon-Sat, 1.30-4pm Sun) Tucked in the back of a small deli and wine shop, Casa Rufo feels like a hidden dining spot – albeit one that's terrible at keeping secrets (reserve ahead). Amid shelves packed with top-quality wines, diners tuck into delectable Navarran asparagus, house-smoked duck, baked cod with tomatoes and red peppers, and chargrilled steaks.

Casa Victor Montes   Basque €€€
(☏944 15 70 67; www.victormontes.com; Plaza Nueva 8; mains €19.50-27.50, pintxos €2.80-6; ⏱1-4.45pm & 5-11pm) The 1849-built Victor Montes attracts numerous luminaries but locals also appreciate its exquisite gilding, marble and frescoes, 1000-strong wine list and superb food. *Pintxos* span foie gras with cider jelly to *lomo* (cured pork sausage) with prawns and rum-soaked raisins. If you're planning a full meal, book in advance and savour the house special, *txuleta* (seven-year-old dairy cow T-bone steak for two; €48).

🍷 DRINKING & NIGHTLIFE

In the Casco Viejo, around Calles Barrenkale, Ronda and de Somera, there are plenty of terrific hole-in-the-wall, no-nonsense bars with a generally youthful crowd.

Opposite: Bilbao Casco Viejo (p212)

🍴 The Art of Eating Pintxos

The perfect *pintxo* should have exquisite taste, texture and appearance and should be savoured in two elegant bites. The Basque version of a *tapa*, the *pintxo* transcends the commonplace by the sheer panache of its culinary campiness. In San Sebastián especially, Basque chefs have refined the *pintxo* to an art form.

The choice isn't normally limited to what's on the bar top in front of you: many of the best *pintxos* are the hot ones you need to order. These are normally chalked up on a blackboard on the wall somewhere.

Locals tend to just eat one or two of the house specials at each bar before moving on somewhere else. When it comes to ordering, tell the bar staff what you want first and never just help yourself to a *pintxo* off the counter!

Across the river, in the web of streets around Muelle Marzana and Bilbao la Vieja, are scores more little bars and clubs. This is gritty Bilbao as it used to be in the days before the arty makeover. It's not a great idea for women to walk here alone at night.

Cork Wine Bar
(Calle de Licenciado Poza 45; ⏲11am-4pm & 7-11pm Mon-Thu, to midnight Fri & Sat) Taste your way around some of Spain's finest small artisan vineyards at this cosy wine bar owned and run by Jonathan García, a former Basque sommelier champion.

Its blackboard chalks up 25 whites and 40 reds available by the glass. Selections change every two months but always include lightly sparkling *txakoli* (Basque white wine) and rich reds from La Rioja.

Le Club Rooftop Bar
(www.hotelercilla.com; Hotel Ercilla, Calle de Ercilla 37-39; ⏲noon-midnight; 🛜) Sweeping views over Bilbao's skyline extend from this 12th-floor, glass-walled rooftop bar at the top of the Hotel Ercilla. Especially at sunset and after dark, when its decking is flooded in neon-blue light, it's a spectacular spot for a craft beer, glass of wine or dry martini, accompanied by Basque cheeses and hams, *pintxos* and burgers.

ℹ️ INFORMATION

Main Tourist Office (📞944 79 57 60; www.bilbaoturismo.net; Plaza Circular 1; ⏲9am-8pm; 🛜) At this state-of-the-art office there's free wi-fi access, a bank of touch-screen computers with local information and, best of all, some humans to help answer questions (take a number). There are also branches at the **airport** (📞944 03 14 44; www.bilbaoturismo.net; Bilbao Airport; ⏲9am-9pm) and the **Museo Guggenheim Bilbao** (www.bilbaoturismo.net; Alameda Mazarredo 66; ⏲10am-7pm Jul-Aug, to 3pm Sun Sep-Jun).

ℹ️ GETTING THERE & AWAY

AIR

Bilbao's **airport** (BIO; 📞913 21 10 00; www.aena.es; Loiu; 🛜) is in Loiu, near Sondika, 12km north-east of the city. A number of European carriers serve the city, including low-cost airlines.

BUS

Bizkaibus travels to destinations throughout the rural Basque Country, including coastal communities such as Mundaka (€2.55), Gernika (€2.55) and Lekeitio (€3.35).

If you're heading directly to San Sebastián, there's a direct service from Bilbao airport departing hourly from 6.45am to 11.45pm (€17.10, 1¼ hours).

Bilbao's main bus station, **Intermodal** (944 39 50 77; www.bilbaointermodal.es; Gurtubay 1, San Mamés), is west of the centre. There are regular services to the following destinations:

Destination	Fare (€)	Duration (hr)
Barcelona	26-37	7-8½
Biarritz (France)	5-13	2½
Logroño	10-15	1¾
Madrid	20-55	4½-5½
Oñati	7-8.50	1¼
Pamplona	15-20	2-2½
San Sebastián	6-13.50	1¼
Santander	7-15.50	1¼
Vitoria	8-15	1½

TRAIN

The **Abando train station** (902 43 23 43; Plaza Circular 2) is just across the river from Plaza Arriaga and the Casco Viejo. There are frequent trains to the following destinations:

Tickets & Passes

Save money by purchasing a Barik card for €3 at metro vending machines, topping it up with credit (from €5) and using it on Bilbao's metro, tram and bus lines. One card can be used for multiple people, and the card pays for itself after five uses. Single passes can also be purchased from metro machines.

Destination	Fare (€)	Duration (hr)
Barcelona	33-39	6¾
Burgos	11.50-19	2¾
Madrid	25-48.50	5-6½
Valladolid	15.50-25	4

Nearby is the **Concordia train station** (Calle Bailén 2), with its handsome art-nouveau facade of wrought iron and tiles. It is used by Renfe Feve (www.renfe.com), part of Spain's national Renfe line, which has trains running west into

Abando train station

GUIRDO1088/SHUTTERSTOCK ©

Worth a Trip: San Juan de Gaztelugatxe

One of the most photographed features of the Basque coast, 10km to Bermeo's northwest, is the small, rocky isle of **San Juan de Gaztelugatxe** (www.tiketa. eus/gaztelugatxe; island free, hermitage €1; ☉island year-round, hermitage 11am-6pm Tue-Sat, to 3pm Sun Jul & Aug). Accessed from the mainland by climbing 241 steps via a stone footbridge, it's topped by a hermitage, Ermita de San Juan de Gaztelugatxe, which was built by the Knights Templar in the 10th century. Between Easter and September, island entry is only guaranteed by reserving an allocated time slot ahead of time online.

Local tradition holds that it was named after St John the Baptist, who allegedly visited the island. *Game of Thrones* fans will recognise the setting, which starred as Dragonstone in season seven.

The island is the goal of pilgrimages on 24 June, 31 July and 29 August. Legend has it that by ringing the bell outside the hermitage three times, you will be granted a wish and banish bad spirits. And if you don't believe in such things, the spectacular views along the coast should prove reward enough for the walk out here. Keep in mind that this place gets very crowded in the summer. If coming then, go very early in the morning to beat the worst of the bell-ringing hordes.

UNDERWORLD/SHUTTERSTOCK©

Cantabria. There are three slow daily trains to Santander (from €9, three hours) where you can change for stations in Asturias.

The **Atxuri train station** (☎944 01 99 00; Calle Atxuri 6) is just upriver from Casco Viejo. From here, Euskotren (www.euskotren.es) operates services every half-hour to the following:

Destination	Fare (€)	Duration (hr)
Bermeo	3.40	1¾
Gernika	3.40	1
Mundaka	3.40	1½

❶ GETTING AROUND

TO/FROM THE AIRPORT

The **airport bus** (Bizkaibus A3247; one-way €3) departs from a stand on the extreme right as you leave arrivals. It runs through the northwestern section of the city, passing the Museo Guggenheim Bilbao, stopping at Plaza de Federico Moyúa and terminating at the Intermodal bus station. It runs from the airport every 15 minutes in summer and every 30 minutes in winter from 6.15am to midnight.

Taxis from the airport to the Casco Viejo cost about €25 to €35 depending on traffic.

There is also a direct hourly bus from the airport to San Sebastián (€17.10, 1¼ hours), running from 7.45am to 11.45pm.

METRO

There are metro stations at the city's main focal points, including the Casco Viejo. Tickets cost €1.60 to €1.90 (€0.91 to €1.19 with a Barik card), depending on distance travelled. The metro runs to the north coast from a number of stations on both sides of the river and makes it easy to get to the beaches closest to Bilbao.

Gernika (Guernica)

Gernika (Castillian: Guernica) is a state of mind. At a glance it seems no more than a modern and not-too-attractive country town. Apparently, prior to the morning of 26 April 1937, Gernika wasn't quite so ugly, but the horrifying events of that day meant that the town was later reconstructed as fast as possible, with little regard for aesthetics.

◎ SIGHTS

Museo de la Paz de Gernika Museum

(946 27 02 13; www.museodelapaz.org; Plaza Foru 1; adult/child €5/free, Sun free; 10am-7pm Tue-Sat, 10am-2pm Sun Mar-Oct, 10am-2pm & 4-6pm Tue-Sat, 10am-2pm Sun Nov, Dec & Feb) Gernika's seminal experience is a visit to the Peace Museum, where audiovisual displays calmly reveal the horror of war, both in the Basque Country and around the world. Aside from creating a moving portrait of the events that transpired on 26 April 1937, the museum grapples with the topic of peace and reconciliation with illuminating insights by the Dalai Lama, Adolfo Pérez Esquivel and others.

Displays are mostly in Basque and Spanish; an English-language booklet helps provide a deeper understanding of what's on view.

Parque de los Pueblos de Europa Park

(Calle Allende Salazar) The Parque de los Pueblos de Europa contains a typically curvaceous **sculpture** by Henry Moore and a monumental work by renowned Basque sculptor Eduardo Chillida. The park leads to the attractive **Casa de Juntas**, where the provincial government has met since 1979. Nearby is the **Tree of Gernika**, under which the Basque parliament met from medieval times to 1876.

◎ EATING

Auzokoa Pintxos €

(www.facebook.com/AuzokoaTaberna; Calle Pablo Picasso 9; pintxos €2-3; 8am-4pm & 7-11pm) Set on the restaurant-lined lane in the heart of Gernika, Auzokoa whips up some of the best *pintxos* in town. The highlights are scallop gratin served on the shell, and crab with anchovies and egg.

📖 Gernika's Story

The reasons Franco wished to destroy Gernika are pretty clear. The Spanish Civil War was raging and WWII was looming on the horizon. Franco's Nationalist troops were advancing across Spain, but the Basques, who had their own autonomous regional government consisting of supporters of the Left and Basque nationalists, stood opposed to Franco, and Gernika was the final town between the Nationalists and the capture of Bilbao.

On the morning of 26 April 1937, planes from Hitler's Condor Legion flew forwards and backwards over the town demonstrating their newfound concept of saturation bombing. In the space of a few hours, the town was destroyed and many people were left dead or injured. Exactly how many people were killed remains hard to quantify, with figures ranging from a couple of hundred to well over a thousand. The Museo de la Paz de Gernika claims that around 250 civilians were killed and several hundred injured.

The tragedy of Gernika gained international resonance with Picasso's iconic painting *Guernica,* which has come to symbolise the violence of the 20th century. A copy of the painting now hangs in the entrance hall of the UN headquarters in New York, while the original hangs in the Centro de Arte Reina Sofía (p49) in Madrid.

Tiled reproduction of Picasso's *Guernica*
TICHR/SHUTTERSTOCK©

ⓘ INFORMATION

Tourist Office (🖁946 25 58 92; www.gernika-lumo.org; Artekalea 8; ⊙10am-7pm Mon-Sat, to 2pm Sun Easter-Oct, 10am-6pm Mon-Fri, to 2pm Sat & Sun Nov-Mar) Friendly multilingual staff provide info on Gernika and nearby attractions.

ⓘ GETTING THERE & AWAY

Gernika is an easy day trip from Bilbao by Euskotren train from Atxuri train station (€3.40, one hour). Trains run every half-hour; buses also make the journey.

Lekeitio

Bustling Lekeitio is gorgeous. The attractive old core is centred on the grand basilica and a busy harbour lined by multicoloured, half-timbered old buildings – some of which house fine seafood restaurants and *pintxo* bars. But for most visitors, it's the beaches that are the main draw.

> **Bustling Lekeitio is gorgeous.**

From left: Tree of Gernika (p221); Casa de Juntas, Gernika (p221); Lekeitio; San Sebastián Aquarium (p225)

◎ SIGHTS

Isla de San Nicolás   Island

One of the great attractions of Lekeitio is the rocky island, known in Basque as Garraitz, sitting just offshore of the main beach (Playa Isuntza). When the tides are low, a paved path appears, allowing visitors to stroll straight out to the island, and take a 200m trail to the top for a fine view over the seaside. Be mindful of the tides, so you don't have to swim back! The tourist office posts tidal charts.

Basílica de la Asunción de Santa María   Basilica

(www.basilicadelekeitio.com; Calle Abaroa; ⊙8am-noon & 5-7.30pm Mon-Fri) Looming high over the old centre, this late-Gothic church, complete with flying buttresses topped with pinnacles, offers a vision of grandeur surprising for such a small town. In fact, Lekeitio's prolific whaling industry helped fund such extravagance. Highlights include the frieze-covered west facade, and a staggering Gothic-Flemish altarpiece that's the third-largest in Spain after Seville and Toledo.

KARSOL/SHUTTERSTOCK ©

JARNO GONZALEZ ZARRAONANDIA/SHUTTERSTOCK ©

EATING

Lekeitio has some appealing places to eat, including a handful of bars with outdoor seating across from the harbour. Self-caterers can pick up fish, straight from the boats, from nearby stalls.

Mesón Arropain　　　Seafood €€€
(📞946 24 31 83; Iñigo Artieta Etorbidea 5; mains €23-28; ⏱1-3.30pm & 8-11pm Jun-Aug, 1-3.30pm & 8-10.30pm Fri & Sat, 1-3.30pm Sun Sep-May) Situated 800m south of the centre, Mesón Arropain serves some of the best seafood for miles around. The chef lets the high-quality ingredients speak for themselves in simple but beautifully prepared dishes. Start off with its famous *arrain zopa* (fish soup) and move on to *zapo beltza* (anglerfish with fried Gernika peppers) or *legatzen kokotxak* (hake with prawns and clams).

There's an excellent wine selection.

INFORMATION

The **tourist office** (📞946 84 40 17; www.lekeitio. org; Plaza Independencia; ⏱10am-2pm & 4-8pm Jul & Aug, 10am-2pm Tue-Sun Sep-Jun) is on the main square; stop by for info on self-guided tours of the old town.

GETTING THERE & AWAY

Bizkaibus bus A3512 leaves hourly from Bilbao's Intermodal bus station (€3.35, 1½ hours). Slower buses go via Gernika and Elantxobe (two hours). Buses also run four to five times daily from Lekeitio to San Sebastián (€7.25, 1½ hours).

San Sebastián

It's impossible to lay eyes on stunning San Sebastián (Basque: Donostia) and not fall madly in love. This city is cool and happening by night, charming and well-mannered by day. It's a city filled with people that love to indulge – and with Michelin stars apparently falling from the heavens onto its restaurants, not to mention a *pintxo* (tapas) culture almost unmatched anywhere else in Spain, San Sebastián frequently tops lists of the world's best places to eat.

ARRIETA PHOTO/SHUTTERSTOCK ©

DAVID HERRAEZ CALZADA/SHUTTERSTOCK ©

San Sebastián

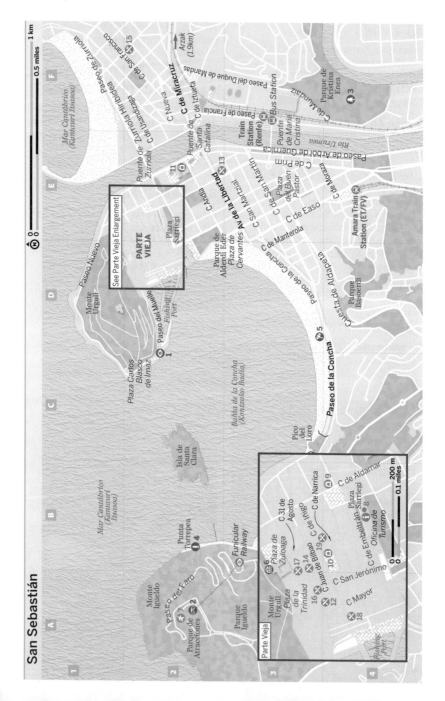

0   1 km
0   0.5 miles

See Parte Vieja Enlargement

PARTE VIEJA

Mar Cantábrico
(Kantauri Itsasoa)

Monte Igueldo

Parque de Atracciones

Paseo del Faro

Funicular Railway

Punta Torrepea 4

Isla de Santa Clara

Bahía de la Concha
(Kontxako Badia)

Monte Urgull

Paseo Nuevo

Plaza Carlos Blasco de Imaz

Fishing Port

Paseo del Muelle 1

Pico del Loro

Paseo de la Concha

Paseo de Zurriola

Paseo de San Francisco

Mar Cantábrico
(Kantauri Itsasoa)

C de San Francisco 15

C Nueva

C de Miracruz

C de Iztueta

Arzak (1.9km)

Puente de Zurriola

Paseo del Duque de Mandas

C de Usandizaga

Puente de Santa Catalina

Plaza Sarriegi

Parque de Alderdi Eder

Plaza de Cervantes

Av de la Libertad 13

C Aldia

11

C de San Martín

C de Prim

Plaza del Buen Pastor

C de Easo

C de Manterola

C de Moraza

Parque de Kristina Enea

C de Mundaiz

Bus Station 3

Train Station (Renfe)

Puente de María Cristina

Paseo de Francia

Río Urumea

Paseo de Árbol de Guernica

Amara Train Station (ET/FV)

Cuesta de Aldapeta

Parque Basoerdi

Paseo de la Concha

5

Av de la Martzal

C de San Martín

C de Eso

Parte Vieja

0   200 m
0   0.1 miles

Monte Urgull

Plaza de la Trinidad

Plaza de Zuloaga

C 31 de Agosto

6

17

14

C de Iñigo

16

J uan de Bilbao 19

12

C San Jerónimo

C de Narrica

C de Aldamar

9

Plaza Sarriegi

Oficina de Turismo 8

C de Embeltrán

10

C Mayor

18

Fishing Port

Plaza de Zuloaga

7

2

Parque de Atracciones

San Sebastián

◎ SIGHTS

Aquarium   Aquarium
(☏943 44 00 99; www.aquariumss.com; Plaza Carlos Blasco de Imaz 1; adult/child €13/6.50; ◷10am-9pm Jul & Aug, 10am-8pm Mon-Fri, to 9pm Sat & Sun Easter-Jun & Sep, 10am-7pm Mon-Fri, to 8pm Sat & Sun Oct-Easter) Fear for your life as huge sharks bear down behind glass panes, or gaze at otherworldly jellyfish. The highlights of a visit to the city's excellent aquarium are the cinema-screen-sized deep-ocean and coral-reef exhibits and the long tunnel, around which swim creatures of the deep. The aquarium also contains a maritime museum section. Allow at least 1½ hours for a visit.

San Telmo Museoa   Museum
(☏943 48 15 80; www.santelmomuseoa.eus; Plaza de Zuloaga 1; adult/child €6/free, Tue free; ◷10am-8pm Tue-Sun) One of the best museums in the Basque Country, San Telmo Museoa has a thought-provoking collection that explores Basque history and culture in all its complexity. Exhibitions are spread between a restored convent dating back to the 16th century and a cutting-edge newer wing that blends into its plant-lined backdrop of Mt Urgull. The collection ranges from historical artefacts to bold fusions of contemporary art. San Telmo also stages some outstanding temporary exhibitions.

Playa de la Concha   Beach
(Paseo de la Concha) Fulfilling almost every idea of how a perfect city beach should be formed, Playa de la Concha (and its wester-ly extension, Playa de Ondarreta) is easily among the best city beaches in Europe. Tanned and toned bodies spread across the sand throughout the long summer months, when a fiesta atmosphere prevails. The swimming is almost always safe. At night, the view of the bay's twinkling lights and illuminated monuments is magical.

Parque de Cristina Enea   Park
(Paseo Duque de Mandas; ◷8am-9pm May-Sep, 9am-7pm Oct-Apr) Created by the Duke of Mandas in honour of his wife, the Parque de Cristina Enea is a favourite escape for locals. This formal park, the most attractive in the city, contains ornamental plants, ducks and peacocks, and open lawns. Its wooded paths make for a scenic stroll, past towering red sequoias and a magnificent Lebanese cedar.

Monte Igueldo   Viewpoint
(www.monteigueldo.es; €2.30; ◷10am-9pm Mon-Fri, to 10pm Sat & Sun Jul, 10am-10pm Aug, 10am-8pm Mon-Fri, to 9pm Sat & Sun Jun & Sep, shorter hours Oct-May) The views from the summit of Monte Igueldo (181m), just west of town, will make you feel like a circling hawk staring down over the vast pano-rama of the Bahía de la Concha and the surrounding coastline and mountains. The

Mundaka's Wave

Universally regarded as the home of the best wave in Europe, Mundaka, a coastal town northeast of Bilbao, is the stuff of legend for surfers across the world. The wave breaks on a perfectly tapering sandbar formed by the outflow of the Río Urdaibai and, on a good day, offers heavy, barrelling lefts that can reel off for hundreds of metres. Fantastic for experienced surfers, Mundaka is not a place for novices to take to the waves.

ALAIN KITER/SHUTTERSTOCK ©

best way to get here is via the old-world **funicular railway** (www.monteigueldo.es; Plaza del Funicular; return adult/child €3.75/2.50; ⊙10am-10pm Jun-Aug, shorter hours Sep-May) to the **Parque de Atracciones** (🖉943 21 35 25; www.monteigueldo.es; Paseo de Igeldo; ⊙11am-11.30pm Aug, hours vary Feb-Jul & Sep-Dec), a small, old-fashioned funfair at the top of the hill. Opening hours vary throughout the year; check schedules online.

Peine del Viento   Sculpture

(Paseo de Eduardo Chillida) A symbol of the city, the *Peine del Viento* (Wind Comb) sculpture, which lies at the far western end of the Bahía de la Concha, below Monte Igueldo, is the work of the famous Basque sculptor Eduardo Chillida and architect Luis Peña Ganchegui. Installed in 1977, the artwork is made of giant iron shapes anchored by pink granite and is spread across three nearby sites. Its powerful but mysterious forms look all the more striking against the wave-battered coastline.

🕙 TOURS

Pintxos of San Sebastián   Tours

(🖉943 48 11 66; www.sansebastianturismo.eus; tours €65; ⊙noon & 7pm) The tourist office runs a two-hour tour in English of some of the city's *pintxo* haunts. Prices include four *pintxos* and four glasses of wine. The meeting point is outside the main tourist office (p228) on the edge of the old town.

🛍 SHOPPING

The Parte Vieja is awash with small independent boutiques, while the Área Romántica has all your brand-name and chain-store favourites. Gros has a handful of boutiques and eye-catching shops that capture the city's most creative side.

Aitor Lasa   Food & Drinks

(www.aitorlasa.com; Calle de Aldamar 12; ⊙8.30am-2pm & 5-8pm Mon-Fri, 8.30am-2.30pm Sat) This high-quality deli is the place to stock up on ingredients for a gourmet picnic, with a heavenly array of cheeses, mushrooms and seasonal fruit and vegetables.

Mimo San Sebastián
Gourmet Shop   Food & Drinks

(🖉943 00 80 70; www.mimofood.com; Paseo de la República Argentina 4, Hotel Maria Cristina; ⊙10am-8pm Mon-Fri, 10am-7pm Sat & Sun) Located inside the regal Hotel Maria Cristina, this is where those with a real appreciation of fine food and wine come to do their shopping. The shop also offers customised hampers and a wide selection of edible souvenirs, tableware and gourmet gifts. International shipping available. Check out Mimo's **foodie tours** and **cooking classes** as well.

Alboka Artesanía   Arts & Crafts

(Plaza de la Constitución; ⊙10.30am-1.30pm & 4-8pm Mon-Fri, 10.30am-8.30pm Sat, 11am-2.30pm Sun) Crafts and objects made in the Basque Country fill this shop on one of the old town's prettiest plazas. You'll find ceramics, tea towels, marionettes, picture frames, T-shirts, pelota balls and of course those iconic oversized berets.

🍴 EATING

With more than a dozen Michelin stars (including three restaurants with the coveted three stars), San Sebastián stands atop a pedestal as one of the culinary capitals of the planet. As if that alone weren't enough, the city is overflowing with bars – almost all of which have bar tops weighed down under a mountain of *pintxos* that almost every Spaniard will (sometimes grudgingly) tell you are the best in the country. Indeed, a raft of the world's best chefs, including such luminaries as Catalan super-chef Ferran Adrià, have said that San Sebastián is quite possibly the best place on the entire planet to eat.

Bar Martinez Pintxos €

(☏943 42 49 65; www.barmartinezdonosti. com; Calle 31 de Agosto 13; pintxos €2-5.50; ☺11am-3.30pm & 6.30pm-midnight Sat-Wed, 6.30pm-midnight Fri Jul & Aug, from 7pm Sep-Jun) Opening its doors in the 1940s, the tiny, character-laden Bar Martinez, with its many dusty bottles of wine, has had plenty of time to get things right, including the award-winning *morros de bacalao* (slices of cod balanced atop a piece of bread) and *brocheta de pulpo* (octopus skewers).

La Fábrica Basque €€

(☏943 43 21 10; www.restaurantelafabrica. es; Calle del Puerto 17; mains €17-25, tasting menu €40; ☺1-3pm & 8.30-10.30pm Mon-Sat, 1-3pm Sun) The red-brick interior walls and white tablecloths lend an air of class to this restaurant, whose modern takes on Basque classics continue to make waves with San Sebastián locals. Multicourse tasting *menús* let you sample various delicacies, such as paprika-marinated octopus or king prawn flan with crab mayonnaise; there are cheaper weekday lunch menus. Advance reservations essential.

Mugaritz Gastronomy €€€

(☏943 52 24 55; www.mugaritz.com; Aldura Aldea 20, Errenteria; tasting menu €220; ☺12.30-2pm & 8-9.30pm Tue-Sat Apr-Nov) Perched high up in the bucolic hills 10km southeast

View of Parque de Atracciones, Monte Igueldo (p225)

SAIKOSP/SHUTTERSTOCK©

of San Sebastián, twin-Michelin-starred Mugaritz' calling card is chef Andoni Luis Aduriz' avant-garde cuisine incorporating produce foraged in the surrounding forest and gastronomic trickery, such as lemon-shaped oysters, edible river stones and even edible cutlery.

The restaurant closes for four months per year, when the chef and his brigade come up with the new year's creations.

Arzak   Gastronomy €€€

(📞943 27 84 65; www.arzak.es; Avenida Alcalde Jose Elósegui 273; tasting menu €242; ⏱1.15-3.15pm & 8.45-10.30pm Tue-Sat) With three shining Michelin stars, acclaimed chef Juan Mari Arzak is king when it comes to Basque nouvelle cuisine, and his restaurant, 3.5km east of San Sebastián, is considered one of the best in the world. Arzak is now assisted by his daughter Elena, and they never cease to innovate.

Boundary-pushing dishes such as cured sweetbreads with prawn-flavoured corn chips, or gingerbread topped with crab and sea grapes, are conceived in research and development kitchen, 'the lab', which draws on over 1000 ingredients to create ingenious creations. The unrivalled wine list runs over 46 pages.

Martín Berasategui
Restaurant   Gastronomy €€€

(📞943 36 64 71; www.martinberasategui.com; Calle Loidi 4, Lasarte-Oria; tasting menu €275; ⏱1-2.45pm & 8.30-10.15pm Wed-Sat, 1-2.45pm Sun) This superlative restaurant, 9km southwest of San Sebastián, is considered by gourmands to be among the world's finest dining addresses. The chef, Martín Berasategui, approaches cuisine as a science and the results are tastes you never knew existed. Try dishes such as crystallised mullet with a squid-ink bonbon, and cod gel with pickled asparagus and caviar.

ℹ INFORMATION

Oficina de Turismo (📞943 48 11 66; www.sansebastianturismo.com; Alameda del Boulevard 8; ⏱9am-8pm Mon-Sat, 10am-7pm Sun Jul-Sep, 9am-7pm Mon-Sat, 10am-2pm Sun Oct-May) This friendly office provides comprehensive

Catedral de Santa María (p230)

SAKOOP/SHUTTERSTOCK©

information on the city and the Basque Country in general.

❶ GETTING THERE & AWAY

AIR

San Sebastián **airport** (EAS; ☑913 21 10 00; www.aena.es; Calle Gabarrari, Hondarribia) is 22km east of town, near Hondarribia. It has regular domestic services to Madrid and Barcelona.

Biarritz Airport (BIQ; www.biarritz.aeroport. fr), 48km northeast of San Sebastián in France, is a convenient arrival point for the region. Destinations served include the UK, Ireland and major continental European cities. Buses (€7, 45 minutes, up to eight daily) link the airport with San Sebastián's bus station.

BUS

San Sebastián's **bus station** (Estación Donostia Geltokia; www.estaciondonostia.com; Paseo Federico García Lorca 1) is 1km southeast of the Parte Vieja, on the east side of the river, below the Renfe train station. All the bus companies have offices and ticket booths here.

There are daily bus services to the following:

Destination	Fare (€)	Duration (hr)
Biarritz (France)	7-13	1¼
Bilbao	6.75-15	1¼
Bilbao airport	17.10	1¼
Madrid	16-53	5-6
Pamplona	8-20	1
Vitoria	12-20	1½

TRAIN

The main **Renfe train station** (Paseo de Francia) is just across Río Urumea, on a line linking Paris to Madrid. There are several services daily to Madrid (€22 to €50, 5½ hours) and two to Barcelona (€32 to €82, six hours).

Oñati

With a flurry of magnificent architecture and a number of interesting sites scattered through the surrounding green hills, the small and resolutely Basque town of Oñati is a great place to get to know the rural Basque heartland.

◉ SIGHTS

Iglesia de San Miguel   Church
(Avenida de Unibertsitate 1; ⊘hours vary) This late-Gothic confection has a cloister built over the river and a 17th-century crypt where the Counts of Guevara are buried. The church faces onto the main square, Foruen Enparantza, dominated by the eye-catching baroque *ayuntamiento* (town hall). Contact the tourist office for opening times and guided tours.

❶ INFORMATION

Tourist Office (☑943 78 34 53; www.oñatituris mo.eus; Calle San Juan 14; ⊘9.30am-2pm & 3.30-7pm Jun-Sep, 10am-2pm & 4-6pm Tue-Sun Oct-Apr) Just west of Iglesia de San Miguel, by the river. It runs various guided tours of the town's attractions, though you'll need to contact it at least several days in advance for an English-speaking guide.

❶ GETTING THERE & AWAY

PESA buses serve Oñati from many destinations in the Basque Country, including Bilbao (€7.25, 60 to 75 minutes, three daily) and Vitoria-Gasteiz (€4.95, one hour, one daily).

Vitoria

Vitoria-Gasteiz – often shortened to simply Vitoria – has a habit of falling off the radar, yet it's actually the capital of the entire Basque Country. With an art gallery whose contents frequently surpass those of the more famous Bilbao galleries, a delightful old quarter, dozens of great *pintxo* bars and restaurants, a large student contingent and a friendly local population, you have the makings of a lovely city.

/BASOTXERRI/SHUTTERSTOCK ©

Pintxos in Saburdi bar

⊙ SIGHTS

Artium
Museum

(☎945 20 90 00; www.artium.eus; Calle de Francia 24; adult/child €5/free, by donation Wed & last weekend of month; ☺11am-2pm & 5-8pm Tue-Fri, 11am-8pm Sat & Sun; 🐾) Art lovers shouldn't miss Vitoria's palace of modern art. The large subterranean galleries are filled with engrossing pieces by artists from the Basque Country (including Eduardo Chillida, Jorge Oteiza and Cristina Iglesias), Spain (Joan Miró, Salvador Dalí) and beyond (such as American Bill Viola and Argentine-Italian Fabian Marcaccio), complemented by thought-provoking temporary exhibitions. Multilingual audio guides are free. There are hands-on activities for kids, periodic film screenings and concerts, and an in-house cafe.

Catedral de Santa María
Cathedral

(☎945 25 51 35; www.catedralvitoria.eus; Plaza Santa María; tours €8.50-10.50; ☺10am-1pm & 4-7pm) At the summit of the old town and dominating its skyline is the Catedral de Santa María. Built between the 13th and 14th centuries in the Gothic style, this medieval masterpiece was declared a cathedral in 1861. Although restoration is ongoing, it is open for guided visits. English-language tours are offered at least once a day; call ahead or book a tour online. The recommended cathedral and tower tour includes underground chambers and the rooftop, with views over the city.

✖ EATING

Internationally, Vitoria might not have the same culinary cachet as San Sebastián, but among in-the-know Spaniards this is a city with serious culinary pedigree. How serious? Well, in 2014 it was awarded the title *Capital Nacional de la Gastronomía* (National Gastronomic Capital) on account of its stellar array of *pintxo* bars and highly creative chefs.

Saburdi
Pintxos €

(www.saburdi.com; Calle de Eduardo Dato 32; pintxos €2-4; ☺8am-midnight Mon-Thu, 8am-1am Fri & Sat, 11am-midnight Sun) One of the best, if somewhat underrated, *pintxo* spots in town, Saburdi serves gourmet morsels of perfection in its stone-walled interior or sunny outdoor tables. Nibble on delicacies such as *txistorra* (Basque chorizo) with apple sauce, pickled anchovies with tomato jelly cubes and black-olive tapenade, or octopus and potato cakes.

PerretxiCo   Pintxos €

(☑945 13 72 21; www.perretxico.es; Calle San Antonio 3; pintxos €2.50-5, mains €8.50-15; ⊙10am-midnight) This award-winning spot packs in the crowds with inspired bites such as octopus and sweet potato tacos, codfish tempura, and goat's-cheese, walnut and honey lollipops. For something more substantial, book a table in the back and linger over roasted whole turbot with mushrooms, or roast Navarran lamb with yellow-pepper relish. Until noon, it serves house-made churros and hot chocolate.

Asador Matxete   Grill €€

(☑945 13 18 21; www.matxete.com; Plaza de Matxete 4-5; mains €15-34; ⊙1-3.45pm & 8.30-11pm Tue-Sat, noon-3.45pm Sun) There are two types of *asador* (restaurants specialising in barbecued meat): smoky old farmhouse-like places, and sleek new urban remakes. This one falls in the second category, firing up grilled steaks and whole fish served in a vaulted stone dining room and lovely summer terrace on a quiet old town plaza.

Andere   Spanish €€€

(☑945 21 49 30; www.restauranteandere.com; Calle Gorbea 8; mains €18-28.50; ⊙1-3.45pm & 8.30-11pm Tue-Sun) This elegant restaurant rambles over several white-clothed dining spaces, including a glass-roofed terrace filled with greenery and flowers. Cutting-edge creations, such as roast wood pigeon with miso-braised quinoa, or hazelnut- and sage-stuffed lamb shoulder with thistle cream sauce, are served alongside such traditional dishes as *carrilleras al vino tinto* (beef cheeks in red wine sauce).

🍷 DRINKING & NIGHTLIFE

The Casco Viejo's main action is at Calle de la Cuchillería/Aiztogile and neighbouring Cantón de San Francísco Javier, both of which are packed with busy bars. There's a heavy Basque nationalist atmosphere in some bars.

ℹ INFORMATION

Tourist Office (☑945 16 15 98; www.vitoria-gasteiz.org/turismo; Plaza de España 1; ⊙10am-8pm Jul-Sep, 10am-7pm Mon-Sat, 11am-2pm Sun Oct-Jun) In the central square of the old town. Guided tours (English available) of the city, its murals and the extensive green spaces and birdwatching sites can be arranged by request.

ℹ GETTING THERE & AWAY

There are car parks by the train station, by the Artium, and just east of the cathedral.

Vitoria's **bus station** (www.vitoria-gasteiz.org; Plaza de Euskaltzaindia) is 2km northwest of the historic centre, reached by tram TG1 from the Parlamento stop near Parque de la Florida. Regular services include the following:

Destination	Fare (€)	Duration (hr)
Barcelona	29-35	7
Bilbao	8-15	1½
Madrid	25-44	4
Pamplona	9-13	1¾
San Sebastián	12-20	1½

The train station is located on Plaza Geltoki, 600m south of the historic centre. Trains go to the following:

Destination	Fare (€)	Duration (hr)	Frequency (per day)
Barcelona	32-65	5	4
Madrid	15-45	4-6	up to 10
Pamplona	6.30-8	1	6
San Sebastián	8-17	1¾	up to 10

NORTHWEST COAST

Northwest Coast at a Glance...

Cantabria, Asturias and Galicia are unlike anywhere else in Spain. The coastline from Santander in the east all the way to the Portuguese border is a succession of sheer cliffs, beautiful beaches and quiet fishing ports. Behind it, at the eastern end, gorgeously green river valleys dotted with stone-built villages rise to the 2000m-plus mountain wall of the Picos de Europa. Away to the west, Galicia is home to Santiago de Compostela, the goal of those who set out yearly on the storied Camino de Santiago pilgrim trail. Throw in some of Spain's best seafood and a host of engaging villages and cities, and you'll want to spend as much time here as you can.

Northwest Coast in Three Days

With three days at your disposal, spend them meandering along the coast of Asturias and Cantabria, perhaps basing yourself in **Santillana del Mar** (p242) or **Cudillero** (p245). Plan for some beach sightseeing (don't expect warm weather – you're more likely to be admiring the view than swimming) and a day excursion into the **Picos de Europa** (p236).

Northwest Coast in One Week

Use your extra time for a half day at the **Museo de Altamira** (p242), then drive slowly along Galicia's coast, taking in the breathtaking scenery around the **Cabo Ortegal** (p246) and pausing at the smaller fishing villages with their fine, fresh-off-the-boat seafood en route. Don't miss the **Costa da Morte** (p245), a dramatic Atlantic coastline, on your way into **Santiago de Compostela** (p240).

Arriving in the Northwest Coast

There are international airports at Santander, the Aeropuerto de Asturias (between Oviedo and Gijón) and Santiago de Compostela, with additional domestic airports at A Coruña and Vigo. Santander has overnight ferries to/from the UK, while all cities in the area are connected to the rest of the country by regular bus and train services.

Where to Stay

There's good accommodation across the region, from Santander to Santiago, with the widest selection in the cities. Summer is the high season and bookings are always recommended in Santiago or anywhere along the coast. The Picos de Europa are also popular in summer and on weekends, but virtually deserted in winter. Oviedo and Gijón can be good value on weekends.

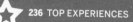

ANIBAL TREJO/SHUTTERSTOCK ©

Picos de Europa

The jagged, deeply fissured Picos de Europa mountains straddle southeast Asturias, southwest Cantabria and northern Castilla y León, and amount to some of the most spectacular country in Spain.

Great For...

Don't Miss

The cable car at Fuente Dé for superlative views.

Western Picos

Approaching the Picos from the Asturian (western) side, the Macizo Occidental (El Cornión) unfolds in a series of gorgeous high-altitude lakes, green pastures and bald rock panoramas. Plain Cangas de Onís is the area's main base, with a host of outdoor activities, while unassuming Arriondas, 8km northwest of Cangas, is the starting point for kayak and canoe rides down the Río Sella. About 10km southeast of Cangas lies Covadonga, famous as the first spot in Spain where the Muslims were defeated. From Covadonga, a twisting mountain road zips up to the beautiful Lagos de Covadonga, where several fine hiking trails begin.

Central Picos

The star attraction of the Picos' central massif is the gorge that divides it from the

ⓘ Need to Know

The area bursts with visitors in July and August. June and September are quieter.

✕ Take a Break

El Molín de la Pedrera (☐985 84 91 09; www.elmolin.com; Calle Río Güeña 2; mains €19-30; ⏱1-4.30pm & 8.30-11.30pm Thu-Tue early Feb-late Dec, closed last week Jun & Sun-Tue evenings approx Oct-May) in Covadonga Asturias serves excellent local cooking.

★ Top Tip

Order *queso de cabrales* (local blue cheese) wherever you find it.

western Macizo El Cornión. The popular Garganta del Cares (Cares Gorge) trail through it gets busy in summer, but the walk is always an exhilarating experience. This part of the Picos, however, also has plenty of less heavily tramped paths and climbing challenges. Arenas de Cabrales, on the AS114 between Cangas de Onís and Panes, is a popular base, but Poncebos, Sotres, Bulnes and Caín also offer facilities.

Eastern Picos

The AS114 east from Cangas de Onís and Arenas de Cabrales in Asturias meets the N621, running south from the coast, at the humdrum town of Panes. South of Panes, the N621 follows the Río Deva upstream through the impressive **Desfiladero de la Hermida** gorge. You cross into Cantabria at Urdón, 2km north of the hamlet of **La Her-**

mida, then continue 18km south to **Potes**, the major base and activity hub for the eastern Picos. About 23km west of Potes lies **Fuente Dé**, with its **cable car** (☐942 73 66 10; www.cantur.com; Fuente Dé; adult/child return €18/7, one way €11/4; ⏱10am-6pm early Feb–mid-Jul & mid-Sep–early Jan, 9am-7pm or 8pm Easter & mid-Jul–mid-Sep; P) providing the main Picos access point in this area.

Bears in the Picos de Europa

The wild mountain area of southwest Asturias and northwestern Castilla y León, including Parque Natural de Somiedo, is the main stronghold of Spain's biggest animal, the *oso pardo* (brown bear). Bear numbers in the Cordillera Cantábrica have climbed to over 200 from as low as 70 in the mid-1990s, including a smaller population of 30 to 40 in a separate easterly area straddling southeast Asturias, southwest Cantabria and northern Castilla y León. You can see bears in semi-liberty at the **Cercado Osero** (☐985 96 30 60; www.osodeasturias.es) 🐾 on the Senda del Oso.

Hiking marker along the Camino de Santiago

Camino de Santiago

For more than 1000 years, people have taken up the Camino de Santiago's age-old symbols (the scallop shell and staff) and walked to the tomb of St James the Apostle, in Santiago de Compostela.

Great For...

Don't Miss

The final march into Santiago de Compostela.

Camino Francés

Although there are many *caminos* (paths) to Santiago in Spain, by far the most popular is, and has always been, the Camino Francés, which originated in France, crossed the Pyrenees at Roncesvalles and then headed west for 783km across the regions of Navarra, La Rioja, Castilla y León and Galicia. Waymarked with cheerful yellow arrows and scallop shells, the 'trail' is a mishmash of rural lanes, paved secondary roads and footpaths all strung together. Starting at Roncesvalles, the Camino takes roughly two weeks cycling or five weeks walking.

Camino History

In the 9th century a remarkable event occurred in the poor Iberian hinterlands: following a shining star, Pelayo, a religious hermit, unearthed the tomb of the

Statue in a church along the Camino Francés

ℹ️ Need to Know

People walk and cycle the Camino year-round, but June to August is most popular.

🍴 Take a Break

There are around 300 *refugios* (pilgrim hostels) along the Camino.

★ Top Tip

Get your *Credencial* (like a pilgrims' passport) stamped at various points along the route.

apostle James the Greater (or, in Spanish, Santiago). The news was confirmed by the local bishop, the Asturian king and later the Pope. Its impact is hard to truly imagine today, but it was instant and indelible: first a trickle, then a flood of Christian Europeans began to journey towards the setting sun in search of salvation.

Compostela later became the most important destination for Christians after Rome and Jerusalem. Its popularity increased with an 11th-century papal decree granting it Holy Year status: pilgrims could receive a plenary indulgence – a full remission of your lifetime's sins – during a Holy Year; the next one is in 2021.

Other Routes

The Camino Francés is by no means the only route and the summer crowds along it have prompted some to look at alternative routes. Increasingly popular routes include the following:

◦ **Camino Portugués** North to Santiago through Portugal.

◦ **Camino del Norte** Via the Basque Country, Cantabria and Asturias.

◦ **Via de la Plata** From Andalucía north through Extremadura, Castilla y León and on to Galicia.

A very popular alternative is to walk only the last 100km (the minimum distance allowed) from Sarria in Galicia in order to earn a *Compostela* certificate of completion given out by the Catedral de Santiago de Compostela.

Another possibility is to continue on beyond Santiago to the dramatic, 'Land's End' outpost of Fisterra (Finisterre), an extra 88km.

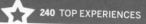

Catedral de Santiago de Compostela

Santiago de Compostela

Locals say the arcaded, stone streets of Santiago de Compostela are most beautiful in the rain, when the old town glistens. However, it's hard to catch Santiago in a bad pose.

Great For...

Don't Miss

The **Museo de San Martiño Pinario** (www.espacioculturalsmpinario.com; Praza da Inmaculada; adult/student, pilgrim & senior €4/3; ⏰10am-8pm Jun-Oct, 11am-7pm Nov-May) is a huge baroque Benedictine monastery with an incredibly ornate main altarpiece.

Catedral de Santiago de Compostela

The grand heart of Santiago, the **cathedral** (www.catedraldesantiago.es; Praza do Obradoiro; Pórtico de la Gloria guided tour adult/senior, student & pilgrim/child €10/8/free; ⏰9am-8pm) soars above the city centre in a splendid jumble of spires and sculpture. Its beauty is a mix of the original Romanesque structure (constructed between 1075 and 1211) and later Gothic and baroque flourishes. The tomb of Santiago beneath the main altar is a magnet for all who come to the cathedral. The artistic high point is the Pórtico de la Gloria inside the west entrance.

Praza do Obradoiro

The grand square in front of the cathedral's western facade earned its name (Workshop Sq) from the stonemasons' workshops set

Entrance to Colexio de San Xerome

LKONYA/SHUTTERSTOCK ©

Praza do
Obradoiro
Catedral de
Santiago de
Compostela
Rúa das Hortas
Museo das
Peregrinacións
e de Santiago
Rúa da Virxe da Cerca
Train Station
(1.4km)

❶ Need to Know

May, June and September are good
months to come.

✕ Take a Break

Mercado de Abastos (www.mercadode
abastosdesantiago.com; Rúa das Ameas 5-8;
⏰8am-2pm Mon-Sat) 🍴, Santiago's main
market and foodie central.

★ Top Tip

Visit the cathedral early in the morning
to avoid the crowds.

Museo das Peregrinacións e de Santiago

Recently installed in a newly converted
premises on Praza das Praterías, the **Museum of Pilgrimages & Santiago** (http://mu
seoperegrinacions.xunta.gal; Praza das Praterías;
adult/pilgrim & student/senior & child €2.40/1.20/
free, free Sun & from 2.30pm Sat; ⏰9.30am-
8.30pm Tue-Fri, 11am-7.30pm Sat, 10.15am-2.45pm
Sun) gives fascinating insights into Santiago
(man and city) down the centuries. There are
great close-up views of some of the cathedral's towers from the 3rd-floor windows.

Santiago's Food Scene

Central Santiago can be a wonderful place
to sample Galicia's celebrated cuisine. Try
O Filandón (Rúa Acibechería 6; medias raciones
€10-12; ⏰1-4pm & 8pm-1am Mon-Sat), **O Curro
da Parra** (www.ocurrodaparra.com; Rúa do
Curro da Parra 7; starters & medias raciones €5-
15, mains €17-23; ⏰1.30-3.30pm & 8.30-11.30pm
Tue-Sun; 🛜) or **Abastos 2.0** (📞654 015937;
www.abastoscompostela.com; Rúa das Ameas;
dishes €7-15, menú from €30; ⏰noon-3.30pm &
8-11pm Mon-Sat).

up here while the cathedral was being built.
Stretching across the northern end of the
plaza, the Renaissance-style **Hostal dos
Reis Católicos** (📞981 58 22 00; www.parador.
es; adult/child €3/free, Mon free; ⏰noon-2pm
& 4-6pm Sun-Fri) was built in the early 16th
century by order of the Catholic monarchs,
Isabel and Fernando, as a recuperation
centre for exhausted pilgrims. Today it's a
parador (luxury hotel).

Along the western side of the plaza
stretches the elegant 18th-century **Pazo
de Raxoi** (Praza do Obradoiro), now Santiago's city hall. At the southern end stands
the **Colexio de San Xerome** (⏰Mon-Fri,
hours vary) **FREE**, a 17th-century building
with a 15th-century Romanesque/Gothic
portal.

Cantabria

Santillana del Mar

This medieval jewel is in such a perfect state of preservation, with its bright cobbled streets, flower-filled balconies and tanned stone-and-brick buildings huddling in a muddle of centuries of history, that it seems too good to be true. People still live here, passing their grand, precious houses down from generation to generation.

Museo de Altamira

The highlight of the **Museo de Altamira** (942 81 80 05; www.culturaydeporte.gob. es/mnaltamira; Avenida Marcelino Sanz de Sautuola , Santillana del Mar; adult/senior, student & child €3.50/free, Sun & from 2pm Sat free; 9.30am-8pm Tue-Sat, to 3pm Sun May-Oct, 9.30am-6pm Tue-Sat, to 3pm Sun Nov-Apr; P) is the **Neocueva**, a dazzling, full-sized re-creation of the real Cueva de Altamira's most interesting chamber, the **Sala de Polícromos** (Polychrome Hall), with its exquisite, 15,000-year-old ochre-and-black bison paintings created using the natural rock relief. The museum's interesting other displays cover prehistoric humanity and cave art worldwide, from Altamira to Australia. The museum is incredibly popular (277,000 visitors in 2019), so it's advisable to book well ahead online, especially from Easter to September.

EATING

La Villa
Cantabrian €€

(942 81 83 64; www.lavillarestaurante.es; Calle La Gándara; menú €18, mains €17-20; 1-3.30pm & 8-10.30pm, closed early Dec–mid-Mar, Tue & Wed mid-Mar–Jun & Oct–mid-Dec, Wed Sep) La Villa's three-course lunch menu, including a full bottle of wine, offers great value for touristy Santillana. Settle into the stone-walled garden courtyard and sample northern classics such as *cocido montañés* (Cantabrian stew with meat and beans) or veal entrecôte with Cabrales cheese, followed by excellent rice pudding for dessert.

Restaurante Gran Duque
Cantabrian €€

(942 84 03 86; www.granduque.com; Calle del Escultor Jesús Otero 7; mains €12-20, menú €20; 1-4pm & 8-11pm Dec-Oct, closed Sun dinner & Mon lunch Sep-Jun) Quality local fare is served in this stone house with noble trappings. There's a good range of both surf and turf options, and a decent *menú del día* available for lunch and dinner.

GETTING THERE & AWAY

Autobuses La Cantábrica (942 72 08 22; www.lacantabrica.net) runs three or more daily buses from Santander to Santillana (€2.70, 40 minutes), continuing to Comillas (€1.55, 30 minutes from Santillana) and San Vicente de la Barquera (€2.25, 50 minutes from Santillana). Buses stop by **Campo del Revolgo** (Calle Revolgo), just south of the main road.

Comillas

Sixteen kilometres west of Santillana through verdant countryside, Comillas is set across hilltops crowned by some of the most original and beautiful buildings in Cantabria. Adding to the town's charms are a lovely golden beach and a pleasant, cobbled old centre.

> The 2km-long, soft-blonde Playa Oyambre, 5km west of Comillas, is a sandy dream

EQROY/SHUTTERSTOCK ©

Palacio de Sobrellano

⊙ SIGHTS

Palacio de Sobrellano
Historic Building

(☎942 72 03 39; http://centros.culturadecan
tabria.com; Barrio de Sobrellano; adult/child
€3/1.50, grounds free; ⊙9.30am-6.30pm Tue-
Sun Apr–mid-Jun & mid-Sep–Oct, 9.45am-7.30pm
mid-Jun–mid-Sep, 9.30am-3.30pm Tue-Fri, to
5.30pm Sat & Sun Nov-Mar) With this marvellous 1888 building, the Marqués de Comillas' summer palace, Modernista architect
Joan Martorell truly managed to out-Gothic
real Gothic. The interior can only be seen
on 30-minute guided tours (in Spanish),
run five to eight times a day: you'll see the
grand central hall with sweeping carved-
stone staircases; a reception/billiard room
featuring an ornate wood-carved fireplace
with dragons by the young Gaudí; beautiful
stained-glass windows; and vibrant original
murals detailing the marquis' story.

Capricho de Gaudí
Architecture

(☎942 72 03 65; www.elcaprichodegaudi.
com; Barrio de Sobrellano; adult/child €5/2.50;
⊙10.30am-8pm Mar-Jun & Oct, to 9pm Jul-Sep,
to 5.30pm Nov-Feb) Antoni Gaudí left few
reminders of his genius beyond Catalonia,
but of them the 1885 Capricho is easily the
most flamboyant. This brick building, one of
Gaudí's earliest works and originally a summer playpad for the Marqués de Comillas'
sister-in-law's brother, is striped all over the
outside with ceramic bands of alternating
sunflowers and green leaves. The elegant
interior is comparatively restrained, with
quirky touches including *artesonado*
ceilings (interlaced beams with decorative
insertions), stained-glass windows and slim
spiral staircases.

Playa Oyambre
Beach

(℗) The 2km-long, soft-blonde Playa
Oyambre, 5km west of Comillas, is a sandy
dream protected by the Parque Natural
Oyambre. It has frequently surfable waves,
a couple of campgrounds and a dash of
intriguing history as the emergency landing
spot of the first ever USA–Spain flight
(1929). Waves and wind can be strong:
swim only when the green flags fly.

From left: Garita de Herbeira (p247); Scorched rice pudding at Casa Gerardo; Cudillero

RAMON ESPELT PHOTOGRAPHY/SHUTTERSTOCK ©

MARGARET STEPHEN/LONELY PLANET ©

⊗ EATING

Restaurante Gurea
Basque €€

(☑942 72 24 46; Calle Ignacio Fernández de Castro 11; mains €9-17; ⊙1.15-4pm Tue, 1.15-4pm & 8.15-11pm Thu-Mon) A friendly, elegant restaurant and social bar, hidden a few blocks east of the town centre, Gurea dishes up Basque-Cantabrian fare with good meat, seafood and some vegetable dishes, and can throw together excellent salads. There's a lunchtime *menú* for €16.

ⓘ GETTING THERE & AWAY

Autobuses La Cantábrica (p242) runs three to four daily buses between Comillas and Santander (€4, one hour), via Santillana del Mar. The main stop is on Calle del Marqués de Comillas, just west of the town centre.

Asturias

Gijón

Gijón has emerged like a phoenix from its industrial roots, having given itself a thorough face-lift with pedestrianised streets,

parks, seafront walks, cultural attractions and lively eating, drinking and shopping scenes. It's a surprisingly engaging city, and a party and beach hot spot, too, with endless summer entertainment. Though it's no quaint Asturian fishing port, Gijón sure knows how to live.

⊗ EATING

La Galana
Asturian €€

(☑985 17 24 29; www.restauranteasturianola galana.es; Plaza Mayor 10; mains & raciones €8-26; ⊙noon-4pm & 7pm-midnight; 🛜🍴) The front bar is a boisterous *sidrería* (cider bar) for snacking on tapas (€6 to €9) or *raciones*, accompanied by free-flowing cider. For sit-down dining, head to the spacious back room with mural-covered ceilings. The food in both parts is wide-ranging and very good, with fish – like wild sea bass, or *pixín* (monkfish) in barnacle sauce – an especially strong suit.

Casa Gerardo
Asturian €€€

(☑985 88 77 97; www.restaurantecasagerardo. es; Carretera AS19, Km 9, Prendes; mains €20-36, set menus €77-132; ⊙1-3.45pm Tue-Sun,

9-10.45pm Fri & Sat; P) About 12km west of Gijón, this stone-fronted modern-rustic house has been preparing top-quality local dishes since 1882. Five generations of the Morán family have refined their art to the point of snagging a Michelin star. The *fabada*, fish and oysters, are famously delectable. To best sample the Morán blend of tradition and innovation, splash out on a set menu.

ℹ INFORMATION

Gijón Turismo (☑985 34 17 71; www.gijon. info; Espigón Central de Fomento; ☺10am-8pm May-Jul & Sep-Oct, to 9pm Aug, 10am-2.30pm & 4.30-7.30pm Nov-Apr) The main tourist office on a Puerto Deportivo pier is very helpful.

ℹ GETTING THERE & AWAY

All Renfe and FEVE trains depart from the Estación Sanz Crespo, 1.5km west of the city centre. Destinations include Cudillero (€3.30, 1¾ hours, five to 10 direct FEVE trains daily) and Madrid (€17 to €73, five to eight hours).

Cudillero

Cudillero, 60km northwest of Oviedo, is the most picturesque fishing village on the Asturian coast – and it knows it. The houses, painted in a rainbow of pastels, cascade down to a tiny port on a narrow inlet. Despite its touristy feel, Cudillero is reasonably relaxed and makes an appealing stop, even in mid-August when every room in town is taken. The surrounding coastline is a dramatic sequence of sheer cliffs and fine beaches.

◎ SIGHTS

Playa del Silencio   Beach

(Castañeras) Silencio is one of Spain's most beautiful beaches: a long, silver-sandy cove backed by a natural rock amphitheatre. It isn't particularly good for swimming due to underwater rocks, but it's a stunning spot for a stroll and, weather permitting, some sun-soaking. It's 15km west of Cudillero: take exit 441 off the A8, then head 2.5km west on the N632 to Castañeras, where the beach is signposted. The last 500m is on foot.

Playa del Silencio (p245)

EATING

El Faro Seafood €€
(☑985 59 15 32; Calle del Ríofrío 4; mains €14-30; ⊙noon-4pm & 8pm-midnight Thu-Tue, daily Aug, closed 2nd half Oct) El Faro's stone-and-timber surrounds and colourful artwork help create a welcoming atmosphere for digging into fish of the day, seafood salads, *parrilladas de marisco* (mixed grilled shellfish) or even an Asturian beef tenderloin with goat cheese. It's tucked one street back from the port.

INFORMATION

Oficina de Turismo (☑985 59 13 77; www.turis-mocudillero.com; Puerto del Oeste; ⊙10am-2pm & 4-7.30pm Jul & Aug, 11am-2pm & 4-6pm Jun & Sep, 10am-3pm Mon-Sat Oct-May) By the port.

GETTING THERE & AWAY

The **train station** (Camin de la Estación) is 2km inland from the port: FEVE (☑91 232 03 20; www.renfe.com/viajeros/feve) trains to Gijón (€3.30, 1¾ to two hours) run about hourly until 6pm (fewer on weekends); for Oviedo (€3.30, 1½ to 2½ hours) you usually change at Pravia. Two trains run west to Luarca (€3.60, 1¼ hours) and into Galicia.

Galicia

The wild, rugged coastline for which the Rías Altas are famous begins above Cedeira. No public transport serves the main places of interest, but if you have wheels (and, even better, time for some walks), Galicia's northwestern corner is a spectacular place to explore, with lush forests, vertigo-inducing cliffs, stunning oceanscapes and horses roaming free over the hills.

SIGHTS

Cabo Ortegal Viewpoint
(ℙ) Four kilometres north of the workaday fishing town of Cariño looms the mother of Spanish capes, Cabo Ortegal, where the Atlantic Ocean meets the Bay of Biscay.

LUNAMARINA/SHUTTERSTOCK ©

Great stone shafts drop sheer into the ocean from such a height that the waves crashing on the rocks below seem pitifully benign. **Os Tres Aguillóns**, three jagged rocky islets, provide a home to hundreds of marine birds.

Garita de Herbeira   Viewpoint
(P) From San Andrés de Teixido, the DP2205 winds up and across the Serra da Capelada towards Cariño. Six kilometres from San Andrés is the must-see Garita de Herbeira, a naval lookout built in 1805, 615m above sea level and the best place to be awed by southern Europe's highest ocean cliffs.

⊗ EATING
Chiringuito de San Xiao   Galician €€
(✆621 243651; www.facebook.com/sanxiaodo trevo; Lugar San Xiao do Trebo; raciones €6-18; ⊗noon-11.30pm Tue-Sun Easter-Sep, Fri-Sun mid-Oct–Easter) Fish and meat grilled over open coals, and *caldeiradas* (fish or seafood stews) are very good reasons to stop at this friendly little wood-beamed bar, with a dining room and terrace overlooking the ocean, beside the Cariño–Ortegal road, 1.5km before the cape.

ⓘ GETTING THERE & AWAY
Your own wheels are the only practical way of getting around this area.

🌊🚤 Costa da Morte

Rocky headlands, winding inlets, small fishing towns, plunging cliffs, wide sweeping bays and many a remote, sandy beach – this is the eerily beautiful 'Coast of Death'. One of the most enchanting parts of Galicia, this relatively isolated and unspoilt shore runs from Muros, at the mouth of the Ría de Muros y Noia, round to Caión, just before A Coruña. It's a coast of legends, like the one about villagers who used to put out lamps to lure passing ships on to deadly rocks. This treacherous coast has certainly seen a lot of shipwrecks, and the idyllic landscape can undergo a rapid transformation when ocean mists blow in.

NORADOA/SHUTTERSTOCK ©

LA RIOJA
WINE REGION

In this Chapter

La Rioja Wine Region at a Glance...

La Rioja produces some of the best red wines in the country. Wine goes well with the region's ochre earth and vast blue skies, which seem far more Mediterranean than the Basque greens further north. The bulk of the vineyards line Río Ebro around the town of Haro, but some also extend into neighbouring Navarra and the Basque province of Álava. A few days here can see you mixing it up in lively towns and quiet pilgrim churches, and even hunting for the remains of giant reptiles.

La Rioja Wine Region in Two Days

With just two days, take a tour of the **Bodegas Marqués de Riscal** (p252) and stay for dinner. Also visit **Vivanco** (p253) and take the tour run by **Rioja Trek** (p253). Base yourself in **Laguardia** (p255), the prettiest of La Rioja's small wine towns.

La Rioja Wine Region in Four Days

A couple of extra days allows you to spend a day in **Logroño** (p254), enjoying its excellent eating scene and shopping for your very own animal-skin wine carrier and the best Rioja wines. An extra day could be spent visiting the fine monasteries in **San Millán de Cogolla** (p256).

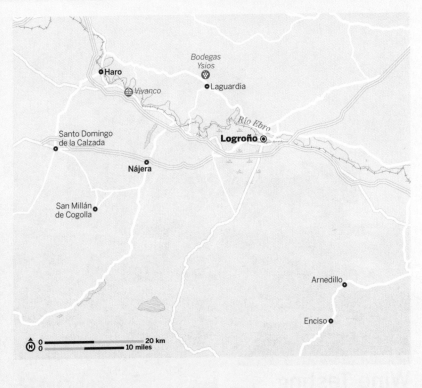

Arriving in La Rioja Wine Region

Most travellers choose to explore this region by car. There are no air links to the regional capital of Logroño, but regular trains connect the city with Madrid, Bilbao and other cities. There are also buses to/from nearby towns. Logroño's old town lies just north of the bus and train stations.

Where to Stay

There are many charming guesthouses and B&Bs scattered throughout La Rioja's wine country, plus a handful of good hotels in Logroño. Besides Logroño, the best range of accommodation is in the wine towns of Haro and charming Laguardia, with some good choices also in Santo Domingo de la Calzada.

Wine Tasting in La Rioja

La Rioja is Spain's most celebrated (and most accessible) wine region, best known for its high-quality reds, charming villages and good mix of wine-centred activities.

Great For...

Don't Miss

The Hotel Marqués de Riscal, a Guggenheim for the Rioja region.

Hotel Marqués de Riscal

When the owner of Elciego's Bodegas Marqués de Riscal decided he wanted to create something special, he didn't hold back. The result is the spectacular Frank Gehry–designed **Hotel Marqués de Riscal** (☑945 18 08 80; www.hotel-marquesderiscal. com; Calle Torrea 1, Elciego; d from €371; P ※ ?). Costing around €85 million, the building is a flamboyant wave of multi-coloured titanium sheets that stand in utter contrast to the village behind. If you're not staying at the hotel, join one of the bodega's wine tours or reserve a table at one of the two superb in-house **restaurants** (☑945 18 08 80; www.restaurantemarquesde riscal.com; Hotel Marqués de Riscal, Calle Torrea 1, Elciego; 14-/21-course menu €110/140; ⊙8-10pm Tue, 1.30-3.30pm & 8-10pm Wed-Sun).

Grapes from the harvest

❶ Need to Know

Base yourself in Laguardia, the prettiest village. On 29 June, Haro stages a wine festival (p257).

✖ Take a Break

Restaurante Amelibia (p255) in Laguardia serves outstanding Spanish cuisine with fine wine-country views.

★ Top Tip

If you want to make your own wine, visit Rioja Trek.

Bodegas Muga

Close to Haro, this **bodega** (🕿941 31 18 25; www.bodegasmuga.com; Barrio de la Estación; 1hr winery tour €15, 2½hr hot-air balloon tour €170; ⊙by reservation Mon-Sat) is particularly receptive and gives daily guided tours (except Sunday) and tastings in Spanish. Although technically you should book in advance in high season, you can often just turn up and join a tour.

Bodegas Ysios

A couple of kilometres north of Laguardia, **Bodegas Ysios** (🕿945 60 06 40; www.bodega sysios.com; Camino de la Hoya; 90min tour & tasting €25; ⊙tours 11am daily) was designed by Santiago Calatrava as a 'temple dedicated to wine'. It features an aluminium wave for a roof and a cedar exterior that blends into the mountainous backdrop. Daily tours of the bodega are an excellent introduction to wine production; book ahead.

Vivanco

Vivanco (Museo de la Cultura del Vino; 🕿941 32 23 23; www.vivancoculturadevino.es; Carretera Nacional, Km 232; museum only adult/child €16.50/free, guided visit with wine tasting €45-97; ⊙10am-6pm Tue-Fri & Sun, 10am-8pm Sat) is a must for wine lovers. Tour the winery before a visit to the excellent, interactive Museum of the Culture of Wine. The treasures on display include Picasso-designed wine jugs and wine-inspired religious artefacts.

Rioja Trek

Based in the small village of Fuenmayor (10 minutes west of Logroño), **Rioja Trek** (🕿941 58 73 54; www.riojatrek.com; Calle Francisco de Quevedo 12) offers three-hour wine 'experiences' where you visit a vineyard and bodega and participate in the process of actually making some wine yourself (and keep the bottle afterwards).

Logroño

Logroño is a stately wine-country service town with a heart of tree-studded squares, narrow streets and hidden corners. There are few monuments here, but perhaps more importantly to some, a great selection of bars serving tapas and *pintxos* (Basque tapas).

◎ SIGHTS

Museo de la Rioja   Museum

(☑941 29 12 59; www.museodelarioja.es; Plaza San Agustín 23; ☺10am-2pm & 4-9pm Tue-Sat, 10am-2pm Sun) **FREE** Housed in a lovely 18th-century baroque building, this superb museum takes you on a wild romp through Riojan history and culture in both Spanish and English. Highlights include mystifying Celtiberian stone carvings from the 5th century BCE, beautiful jewellery and statuary displays from the Roman period and colourful medieval altarpieces, as well as lush portraits and landscape paintings from the 19th century.

**Catedral de Santa
María de la Redonda**   Cathedral

(www.laredonda.org; Calle de Portales 14; ☺8.30am-1pm & 6-8.45pm Mon-Sat, 8.30am-2pm Sun) The Catedral de Santa María de la Redonda sits on the site of a 12th-century oratory, and was built in varying styles between the 15th and 18th centuries. The eye-catching towers (known as the *gemelas* or twins) and splendid altarpiece are fine examples of the Rioja baroque manner. Don't miss the small exquisite painting depicting Christ on the Cross, attributed to Michelangelo. It's behind the main altar and can be illuminated by placing a coin in the box.

🔒 SHOPPING

**Félix Barbero
Botas Rioja**   Arts & Crafts

(www.botasrioja.com; Calle de Sagasta 8; ☺9am-1.30pm & 4-8pm Mon-Sat) Maintaining a dying art, fifth-generation artisan Félix Barbero handcrafts the classic Spanish animal-skin wine carriers, in which farmers carried their daily rations while working in the fields. Wine carriers can be embroidered.

La Luci Delicatessen   Food & Drinks

(☑941 44 18 54; www.facebook.com/lalucideli; Calle de Portales 3; ☺10.30am-2pm & 5.30-9pm Tue-Sun) Browse for wines, cheeses, olive oils, craft beers, vermouth and boxed biscuits in carousel tins at this tantalising little store.

✕ EATING

Bar Torrecilla   Pintxos €

(☑608 344694; Calle Laurel 15; pintxos €2-3.50; ☺1-4pm & 8pm-12.30am Wed-Sun) The best *pintxos* in town? You be the judge. Go for the melt-in-your-mouth foie gras or the mini-burgers, or anything else that takes your fancy, at this modern bar on buzzing Calle Laurel.

Tastavin   Pintxos €

(www.facebook.com/tastavinbardepinchos; Calle San Juan 25; pintxos €2.50-4; ☺8-11pm Tue, 1-4pm & 8-11pm Wed-Sun; 🛜) On *pintxo*-bar-lined San Juan, stylish Tastavin whips up some of the tastiest morsels in town, including smoked trout and lemon cream cornets, fried artichokes, tuna tataki and braised oxtail. The wines are outstanding.

La Cocina de Ramón   Spanish €€€

(☑941 28 98 08; www.lacocinaderamon.es; Calle de Portales 30; mains €18-27; ☺1.30-4pm & 8.30-11pm Mon, Tue & Thu-Sat, 1.30-4pm Wed) It looks unassuming from the outside, but Ramón's high-quality, locally grown produce and tried-and-tested family recipes, such as chargrilled lamb cutlets or beef tenderloin cooked with wines from La Rioja, have earned him a lot of fans. The fine cooking is matched by the white tablecloths and top service; Ramón likes to come and explain the dishes to guests.

🛈 INFORMATION

Tourist Office (☑941 29 12 60; www.larioja turismo.com; Calle de Portales 50; ☺9am-2pm & 5-8pm Mon-Fri, from 10am Sat & Sun Jul-Sep, shorter hours Oct-Jun) At the historic centre's western edge; can provide lots of information on both the city and La Rioja in general.

ℹ GETTING THERE & AWAY

Buses go from the bus station to Bilbao (€10 to €15, 1¾ hours) and Haro (€5, 40 minutes). By train, Logroño is regularly connected to Bilbao (from €9, 2½ hours) and Madrid (from €41, 3½ hours).

Laguardia

The medieval fortress town of Laguardia, or the 'Guard of Navarra' as it was once appropriately known, sits proudly on its rocky hilltop. The walled old quarter, which makes up most of the town, is virtually traffic-free and is a joy to wander around. Laguardia is part of La Rioja Alavesa, the Basque Country's wine-producing region. Tours of the town's wineries depart regularly; the tourist office has a list.

◉ SIGHTS

Maybe the most impressive feature of the town is the castle-like **Puerta de San Juan**, one of the most stunning city gates in Spain.

Centro Temático del Vino Villa Lucía   Museum

(🖉945 60 00 32; www.villa-lucia.com; Carretera de Logroño; 90min tour €12; ⊙9am-2pm & 4-8pm Tue-Sat, 9am-2pm Sun) Just outside Laguardia, 700m to the southeast, is this impressive wine museum and shop selling high-quality bottles from small local producers. Museum visits are by guided tour only and finish with a 4D film and wine tasting.

Iglesia de Santa María de los Reyes   Church

(🖉945 60 08 45; Travesía Mayor 1; tours €3; ⊙guided tours by reservation Jun-Sep) The impressive Iglesia de Santa María de los Reyes has a breathtaking late-14th-century Gothic doorway, adorned with beautiful sculptures of the disciples and other motifs. If the church doors are locked, stop by

the tourist office, where you can get a key. Guided tours (English available) must be booked through the tourist office.

Bodegas Palacio   Winery

(🖉945 60 00 57; www.bodegaspalacio.com; San Lazaro 1; 90min tour & tasting from €25; ⊙by appointment) Bodegas Palacio, just 800m south of Laguardia, arranges tours and tastings by appointment. Check the website for details of its wine courses (from €35 for one hour).

✕ EATING

Restaurante Amelibia   Spanish €€

(🖉945 62 12 07; www.restauranteamelibia.com; Barbacana 14; mains €15-22; ⊙1-3.30pm Mon & Wed-Sun, 8.30-10.30pm Fri & Sat; 👶) Gaze out the windows at a view over the scorched plains and distant mountain ridges while dining on sublime traditional cuisine, such as oxtail and wild mushrooms in red wine sauce with seasonal vegetables, or pig's trotters in a sherry reduction. Half-portions are available for kids.

ℹ INFORMATION

Tourist Office (🖉945 60 08 45; www. laguardia-alava.com; Calle Mayor 52; ⊙10am-2pm & 4-7pm Mon-Sat, 10.45am-2pm Sun) On the main road in the heart of town; has a list of local bodegas that can be visited.

ℹ GETTING THERE & AWAY

Buses serve Bilbao (€8, 1½ hours, five daily) via Haro (€3.50, 25 minutes), and Logroño (€3, 20 minutes). Buses stop at the covered shelters on the main road that runs through town.

Santo Domingo de la Calzada

Santo Domingo is small-town Spain at its best. A large number of the inhabitants continue to live in the partially walled old quarter, a labyrinth of medieval streets where the past is alive and the sense of community is strong. Santiago-bound pilgrims have long been a part of the fabric of this town, and that tradition continues to this day.

⊙ SIGHTS

Catedral de Santo Domingo de la Calzada   Cathedral

(☑941 34 00 33; www.catedralsantodomingo. com; Plaza del Santo 4; adult/child €7/2; ⊙10am-8pm Mon-Fri, to 7pm Sat, 10am-noon & 2-8pm Sun Apr-Oct, shorter hours Nov-Mar) The monumental cathedral and its attached museum glitter with the gold that attests to the great wealth the Camino has bestowed on otherwise backwater towns. An audio guide to the cathedral and its treasures is €1. Construction was begun in 1040 by Santo Domingo de la Calzada, who also built a bridge, hospital and pilgrims' hostel; he is buried in the cathedral.

Rooster in a Church?

Santo Domingo de la Calzada's cathedral has an eccentric feature utterly unlike any other in Spain: a live white rooster and hen that forage in a glass-fronted cage opposite the entrance to the crypt (look up!). The rooster and hen have been changed every 15 days since 1350. Their presence celebrates a long-standing legend, the Miracle of the Rooster, which tells of a young man who was unfairly executed only to recover miraculously, while the broiled cock and hen on the plate of his judge suddenly leapt up and chickened off, fully fledged.

JUAN CARLOS MUNOZ/SHUTTERSTOCK ©

✕ EATING

Los Caballeros   Spanish €€€

(☑941 342 789; www.restauranteloscaballeros. com; Calle Mayor 56; mains €18-32; ⊙1-3.30pm & 7.30-10.30pm Tue-Sat, 1-3.30pm Sun) Beside the cathedral in a classy dining room set with exposed brick, wood-beamed ceiling and stained-glass details, Los Caballeros serves suckling pig and lamb, among other classic Navarran fare. Don't miss house speciality cinnamon and vanilla *nuestra tarta del abuelito* ('our grandfather's pudding') for dessert. Advance reservations are a must at busy times.

ⓘ GETTING THERE & AWAY

Frequent buses run to Logroño (€5, one hour, six daily Monday to Saturday, four Sunday) from the bus stop on Plaza San Jerónimo Hermosilla, on the historic centre's southern edge.

San Millán de Cogolla

In a wooded valley 19km southeast of Santo Domingo de la Calzada, the hamlet of San Millán de Cogolla, has a long and fascinating Jewish history that dates back to the 10th century CE. But most people come here to see two remarkable monasteries that helped give birth to the Castilian language. On account of their linguistic heritage and artistic beauty, they have been recognised by Unesco as World Heritage Sites.

⊙ SIGHTS

Monasterio de Suso   Monastery

(☑941 37 30 82; www.monasteriodesanmillan. com/suso; Calle de Suso; €4; ⊙9.30am-1.30pm & 3.30-6.30pm Tue-Sun Apr-Sep, to 5.30pm Oct-Mar) Built above the caves where San Millán once lived, the Monasterio de Suso was consecrated in the 10th century. It's believed that in the 13th century a monk, Gonzalo de Berceo, wrote some of the first Castilian words here. It can only be visited on a 40-minute guided tour. Tickets include a short bus ride up to the monastery from Monasterio de Yuso, whose reception area sells tickets; you can't arrive independently.

Monasterio de Yuso — Monastery

(☑941 37 30 49; www.monasteriodesanmillan.
com/yuso; Calle Convento; adult/child €7/3;
⌚10am-1.30pm & 4-6.30pm Tue-Sun Apr-Sep,
to 5.30pm Oct-Mar, also open Mon Aug) The
6th-century Monasterio de Yuso, sometimes called El Escorial de La Rioja, contains numerous treasures in its museum.
You can only visit as part of a guided tour
(in Spanish only; non-Spanish speakers will
be given an information sheet in English
and French). Tours last 50 minutes and run
every half-hour or so. Maps detailing short
walks in the region are available here.

ⓘ GETTING THERE & AWAY

San Millán de Cogolla is not served by public
transport. It's a 44km drive southwest of
Logroño.

Haro

The capital of La Rioja's wine-producing
region, Haro has a compact old quarter,
leading off Plaza de la Paz, where intriguing
alleyways shelter bars and wine shops.

There are plenty of bodegas in the vicinity of the town, some of which are open to
visitors (almost always with advance reservation). The tourist office keeps a full list.

✪ EATING

El Rincón del Noble — Spanish €€

(☑941 31 29 32; www.elrincondelnoble.net;
Martinez Lacuesta 11; mains €13-20; ⌚1-4pm
Sun-Thu, 1-4pm & 9-11pm Fri & Sat) Simple
but thoughtfully prepared classics at this
easygoing spot include *huevos rotos* (fried
potatoes topped with egg), *espinacas con
garbanzos* (spiced chickpeas with spinach)
and *caparrones* (bean and chorizo stew).
Unsurprisingly, the wine list is superb.

✦ Haro's Wine Fight

Batalla del Vino (Wine Battle; www.
batalladelvino.com; ⌚29 Jun) During the
Batalla del Vino, Haro's otherwise mild-
mannered citizens splash wine all over
each other in the name of San Juan, San
Felices and San Pedro. Plenty of it goes
down the right way, too.

LAKISHA BEECHAM/SHUTTERSTOCK ©

ⓘ INFORMATION

Tourist Office (☑941 30 35 80; www.haroturis
mo.org; Plaza de la Paz 1; ⌚10am-2pm Mon,
10am-2pm & 4-7pm Tue-Sun mid-Jun–Sep, 10am-
2pm Tue-Thu & Sun, 10am-2pm & 4-7pm Fri & Sat
Oct–mid-Jun) Just off the main plaza; provides
useful info on the area's many wineries.

ⓘ GETTING THERE & AWAY

Up to three trains per hour connect Haro with
Logroño (€4.50 to €7.35, 40 minutes).

The **bus station** (Calle Castilla) is 400m
southwest of the historic centre. Services
include Bilbao (€6.65, one hour, up to seven
daily), Laguardia (€7, 25 minutes, five daily) and
Logroño (€5, one hour, up to four per hour).

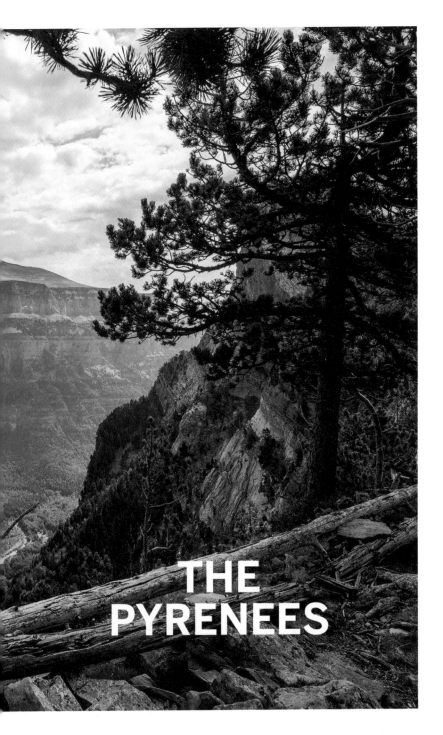

THE
PYRENEES

In this Chapter

The Pyrenees at a Glance...

The crenellated ridges of the Pyrenees fill Spain's northern horizon, offering up magnificent scenery, medieval stone-built villages, several ski resorts and great walking. This dramatic mountain range is awash in greens and often concealed in mists. Each region has its calling card, from the prim Basque pueblos of Navarra to the stunning Romanesque churches of Catalonia. Beyond, where the paved road ends and narrow hiking trails take over, two national parks are the jewel in the Pyrenean crown – Catalonia's Parc Nacional d'Aigüestortes i Estany de Sant Maurici and Aragón's Parque Nacional de Ordesa y Monte Perdido.

The Pyrenees in Three Days

With just three days, focus your attention on the **Catalan Pyrenees** (p266), spending a day on foot exploring the **Parc Nacional d'Aigüestortes i Estany de Sant Maurici** (p262), and another day meandering among the Romanesque churches around **Boí** (p266) and **Taüll** (p267). On your third day, head over to Aragón to spend a night in **Aínsa** (p269), a lovely stone village with fine Pyrenean views.

The Pyrenees in One Week

Add to your three-day itinerary an extra day's hiking in Aragón's **Parque Nacional de Ordesa y Monte Perdido** (p264). Also factor in a night or two in beautifully preserved villages such as **Sos del Rey Católico** (p270), plus many pleasurable hours driving quiet Pyrenean back roads, spilling over into the valleys of Navarra.

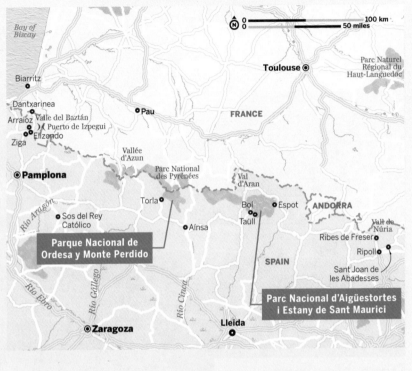

Parque Nacional de Ordesa y Monte Perdido

Parc Nacional d'Aigüestortes i Estany de Sant Maurici

Arriving in the Pyrenees

Almost everyone arrives in the Pyrenees with their own car. The nearest international airports, a day's drive away, are in Zaragoza, Girona and Barcelona. From here, you can reach many of the villages by bus, but you'll miss the best the region has to offer if you don't get behind the wheel yourself.

Where to Stay

The Aragonese Pyrenees has the largest selection of charming accommodation options, especially in Aínsa and Torla. The smaller villages here and elsewhere have few hotels, but instead have a scattering of down-to-earth *hostales* (budget hotels) or *casas rurales* (rural homes). Accommodation is open pretty much year-round, except in ski towns.

Estany Llong

Parc Nacional d'Aigüestortes i Estany de Sant Maurici

There are few more beautiful national parks in Europe: the park's rugged terrain sparkles with hundreds of lakes, countless streams and waterfalls, and a backdrop of pine and fir forests.

Great For...

Don't Miss

Estany Llong, a natural amphitheatre in the heart of the park.

Sculpted by glaciers over two million years, the park is essentially two U-shaped, east–west valleys that begin at an altitude of 1600m and don't stop until they reach the dizzy heights of close to 3km high. Jagged granite shards, transparent mountain waters, forests of pine and fir, and high mountain pastures (carpeted with wildflowers in spring) are a backdrop for natural features with mythic names such as Agujas Perdut (Lost Peaks) and Estany Perdut (Lost Lake). There's even a 600-year-old black pine tree with a birth date that predates Columbus.

You could cross the park in a day – it's a 30km hike between Boí and Espot – but you'll be amply rewarded if you spend your day exploring Llong and Llobreta, the two main valleys in the park's west.

Cascada de Sant Esperit

🛈 Need to Know

You'll need your own vehicle to reach gateway towns. **Taxis** (☑973 69 63 14; www.taxisvalldeboi.com; Plaça del Treio 3, Boí; one-way Boí–Estany de Sant Maurici adult/child €5.25/3.25; ☺9am-7pm) run into the park from Boí.

✗ Take a Break

In Taüll, **Cafe Sedona** (☑973 69 62 54; Les Feixes 2; mains €10-16; ☺1-4pm & 8-11pm; 🛜☑) serves Catalan dishes and tapas.

★ Top Tip

Stay at least one night in Taüll, a gorgeous mountain village.

Estany Llong

Estany Llong, in the heart of the park, captures the essence of the park's appeal, with lammergeiers invariably soaring high above on the thermals and the valley's bowl – at once vast and intimate – feeling like a natural amphitheatre. Climb the moraine off the lake's northeastern tip and watch for the fortress-like outcrops of Agujas Perdut away to the southeast. It's here that you'll find the iconic, 600-year-old **black pine tree**.

Estany Llobreta

On your way between Estany Llong and the valley of Llobreta, watch along the side of the main trail for a celebrated **dwarf pine** growing out of a rock. There's a dramatic **lookout** where the road up from Taüll ends. Llobreta is fed by the **Cascada de Sant**

Esperit (a waterfall) and its shoreline turns autumnal yellow in September.

Day Hikes

Numerous good walks of three to five hours return will take you up into spectacular side valleys from Estany de Sant Maurici or Aigüestortes.

From the eastern end of Estany de Sant Maurici, one path heads south 2.5km up the Monastero valley to Estany de Monastero (2171m), passing the two peaks of Els Encantats on the left. Another goes 3km northwest up by Estany de Ratero to Estany Gran d'Amitges (2350m).

From Planell Gran (1850m), 1km up the Sant Nicolau valley from Aigüestortes, a path climbs 2.5km southeast to Estany de Dellui (2370m). You can descend to Estany Llong (3km); it takes about four hours from Aigüestortes to Estany Llong.

Iglesia de San Salvador, Torla

ALBERTO LOYO/SHUTTERSTOCK©

Parque Nacional de Ordesa y Monte Perdido

This is where the Spanish Pyrenees really take your breath away. Shapely peaks rise to impossible heights. It's best explored on foot, but there are numerous fine vantage points for those on wheels.

Great For...

Don't Miss

The view from the 13th-century Iglesia de San Salvador in Torla.

Your first sighting of Ordesa y Monte Perdido National Park is one that never quite leaves you, evoking as it does the jagged ramparts of some hidden mountain kingdom. Perhaps it's the name – 'Monte Perdido' translates as 'Lost Mountain' – that lends these mountains their cachet. Or perhaps it's because the park's impossibly steep summits and often-impassable mountain passes have always served as a barrier to France and to the rest of Europe, which lies just beyond, preserving until well into the 20th century that sense of Spain as a place apart. Then again, perhaps it's altogether simpler than that – this is one of Europe's most beautiful corners.

Challenging Hikes

The classic hike in this part of the Pyrenees is the **Circo de Soaso**, a difficult but

Autumn hiking

Parque Nacional
❶ de Ordesa y
Monte Perdido

•Torla

❶ Need to Know

Torla, 3km southwest of the park, is the main gateway town.

✕ Take a Break

Restaurante el Duende (📞974 48 60 32; www.restauranteelduende.com; Calle de la Iglesia; mains €15-22, set menus €23-34; ⏲1.30-3.30pm & 8-10.30pm Feb-Dec; 📶) in Torla serves fabulous meals.

★ Top Tip

At Easter and in summer, you can't drive beyond Torla; take the shuttle bus.

infinitely rewarding day walk (seven hours return, 15km) that follows the Valle de Ordesa to Circo de Soaso, a rocky balcony whose centrepiece is the Cola del Caballo (Horsetail) waterfall. Another famous hike on the other side of the park is the **Balcón de Pineta**. This eight-hour-return hike begins close to the village of Bielsa and climbs via a series of steep switchbacks up to the 'Pineta Balcony' for stunning glacier and mountain views.

Pretty Drives

Numerous roads circle and dip into the park, so get a set of wheels and get ready to explore. Begin at ridge-top Aínsa, one of northern Spain's most beautiful stone villages, and drive north to Escalona where

the road branches. First take the northern branch (turn right at the fork) for the drive up to Bielsa, from where a 12km paved road runs up the Valle de Pineta in the park's northeastern corner with stunning views all the way.

Return to Escalona, then follow the HU631 that runs, bucks and weaves west over the mountains to Sarvisé, crossing the park's southern tip in the process and passing through the dramatic, sinuous road through the Bellos Valley. If you're here from July to mid-September, or during Easter week, a one-way system operates on part of the Escalona–Sarvisé road. Continue on to Torla, then north to the Pradera de Ordesa, the starting point of so many trails and a pretty spot in the shadow of high mountains in its own right; in summer and at Easter, private vehicles cannot drive this road, so take the shuttle bus.

The Catalan Pyrenees

Catalonia's Pyrenees are more than an all-season adventure playground. Certainly, the Val d'Aran draws skiers and snowboarders in winter, with resorts ranging from red-carpet to family-friendly. Summer and autumn lure hikers to the jewel-like lakes and valleys of the Parc Nacional d'Aigüestortes i Estany de Sant Maurici and the climbing terrain of the Serra del Cadí.

But there is also Catalan heritage to be discovered amid the breathtaking scenery. Centuries-old monasteries slumber in these mountains, meaning treks in the Pyrenees are as likely to pass by ruined Romanesque churches as offer a valley panorama. Taste buds yearning for more than hiking fodder will find satisfaction in the rich gastronomy of Garrotxa's volcanic zone. Beyond the big-ticket sights and major resorts, Catalonia's Pyrenees conceal a raw beauty that awaits discovery

Boí

The delightful valley location of petite Boí, 3km northwest of Taüll, draws hikers and winter-sports lovers, while its church bell tower is one of the jewels of the Vall de Boí's Catalan Romanesque architecture.

◉ SIGHTS

Sant Joan de Boí   Church
(www.centreromanic.com; Plaça del Treio; €2; ⊙10am-2pm & 4-7pm Sep-Jun, to 8pm Jul & Aug) Boí's 11th-century church gives the village an air of romance with its angular five-storey stone bell tower, which was restored after a major 13th-century fire and can now be climbed (all 75 steps of it). The paintings that brighten the interior are copies of Romanesque originals, preserved in Barcelona's Museu Nacional d'Art de Catalunya.

Santa Eulàlia d'Erill la Vall   Church
(Erill la Vall; €2; ⊙10am-2pm & 4-7pm Sep-Jun, to 8pm Jul & Aug) The slender six-storey, 12th-century tower of Santa Eulàlia d'Erill

Paintings, Sant Joan de Boí

la Vall, a 2.5km walk or drive west of Boí, once used for communications and valley surveillance, is thought to be the most elegant in the area. The church interior is decorated by copies of seven Romanesque poplar-wood sculptures depicting the Descent from the Cross; the originals are split between Barcelona's Museu Nacional d'Art de Catalunya and Vic's Museu Episcopal.

❶ INFORMATION

Casa del Parc de Boí (📞973 69 61 89; Carrer de les Graieres 2; 🕙9am-2pm & 3.30-5.45pm, closed Sun afternoon Sep-Jun) Pick up trekking and winter-sports information.

❶ GETTING THERE & AWAY

ALSA (www.alsa) buses from Barcelona (€33, four to five hours, four to six daily) and Lleida (€18, two to 2¼ hours, six to 10 daily) to Vielha stop year-round at El Pont de Suert, 19km southwest of Boí. From here, there may be irregular services to Boí.

From late June to September, a twice-daily park bus connects Boí with Espot (€12.25, 2½ hours) via Erill la Vall and Vielha.

Taüll

Three kilometres uphill from Boí, Taüll is by far the most picturesque place to stay on the western side of the Parc Nacional d'Aigüestortes i Estany de Sant Maurici.

◎ SIGHTS

Sant Climent de Taüll   Church
(www.centreromanic.com; €5; 🕙10am-2pm & 4-7pm Sep-Jun, to 8pm Jul & Aug) On Taüll's fringes, this 12th-century Romanesque church is a gem not only for its elegant, simple lines and slender six-storey bell tower (which you can climb), but also for the art that once graced its interior. The central apse contains a copy of a famous 1123 mural that now resides in Barcelona's Museu Nacional d'Art de Catalunya; at its centre is a Pantocrator, whose rich

Skiing in the Catalan Pyrenees

Baqueira-Beret-Bonaigua Ski Resort
(www.baqueira.es; day pass adult/child €55/36; 🕙late Nov-early Apr) Pound the pistes at Catalonia's sophisticated top winter-sports resort, beloved of Spanish royals, European celebrities and loyal skiers. Its quality lift system gives access to pistes totalling 156km (larger than any other Spanish resort), amid fine scenery at between 1500m and 2510m.

La Molina and Masella Ski Resorts
(www.lamolina.cat; day pass adult/child €48/38; 🕙mid-Nov-Apr) These two ski resorts lie either side of Tosa d'Alp (2537m), 15km south of Puigcerdà. They're connected by the Alp 2500 lift, and have a combined total of 141km of runs for all grades, at altitudes of 1600m to over 2500m. La Molina has true pedigree as Spain's oldest ski resort, its first lifts dating to 1943.

La Molina ski lift
IAKOV FILIMONOV/SHUTTERSTOCK©

Mozarabic-influenced colours and expressive but superhuman features have become an emblem of Catalan Romanesque art.

Santa Maria de Taüll   Church
(www.centreromanic.com; 🕙10am-7pm Sep-Jun, to 8pm Jul & Aug) FREE Up in Taüll's old centre, at the northwestern end of town, the 12th-century Romanesque Santa Maria church is crowned by a five-storey tower. As with many churches in the Vall de Boí, its original artwork has been whisked away to Barcelona.

 Monestir de Santa María

Consecrated in CE 888, Ripoll's **Monestir de Santa Maria** (www.monestirderipoll.cat; Plaça de l'Abat Oliba; adult/child €6.80/5; ⏱10am-2pm & 4-7pm Apr-Sep, 10am-1.30pm & 3.30-6pm Mon-Sat, 10am-2pm Sun Oct-Mar) was Catalonia's spiritual and cultural heart from the mid-10th to mid-11th century. The five-naved **basilica** was adorned in about 1100 with a stone portal that ranks among Spain's most splendid Romanesque art; its well-restored interior contains admirable floor mosaics, a multilanguage display on the Bibles of Ripoll (rare illustrated manuscripts created between 1008 and 1020), plus the **tomb of Guifré el Pilós**, who founded the monastery.

JOAN_BAUTISTA/SHUTTERSTOCK©

⊗ EATING

There is a handful of restaurants in the village, though some close their doors outside tourist season.

❶ GETTING THERE & AWAY

Year-round **ALSA** (www.alsa.com) buses from Barcelona (€31, four to five hours, two to six daily) and Lleida (€11, two to 2¼ hours, six to

> *The beautiful hilltop village of Aínsa is one of Aragón's gems*

10 daily) stop at El Pont de Suert, from where irregular local buses reach Taüll.

Espot

Scenic little Espot is the main eastern gateway for the Parc Nacional d'Aigüestortes i Estany de Sant Maurici; the park begins 4km west of town. Espot makes an excellent, well-equipped base, with plenty of hotels, restaurants and charming stone buildings, while its mountain views will have you keen to lace up your hiking boots.

⊗ EATING

Restaurant Juquim   Catalan €€ (☎973 62 40 09; Plaça Sant Martí 1; mains €10-19; ⏱1-4pm & 7.30-10.30pm; ✐) Spread over two levels, this popular place on Espot's main street focuses on filling country fare like grilled wild-boar leg, lamb ribs with fried potatoes and vegetarian-friendly mushroom cannelloni. Eat in the atmospheric stone-walled dining room downstairs or on the front terrace on sunny days.

❶ INFORMATION

Casa del Parc d'Espot (☎973 62 40 36; www.gencat.cat/parcs/aiguestortes; Carrer de Sant Maurici 5; ⏱9am-2pm & 3.30-5.45pm, closed Sun afternoon Sep-Jun) Maps, hiking tips, transport advice, weather forecasts and more from Espot's national park office.

❶ GETTING THERE & AWAY

ALSA buses from Barcelona (€39, five hours, daily) and Lleida (€13, 2½ hours, one to two daily) to Esterri d'Àneu stop at the Espot turn-off on the C13. From there, it's a 7km uphill walk west to Espot along the LV5004.

Val d'Aran

Catalonia's northernmost region, famous for its plunging valleys and snowy peaks, is an adventure playground for skiers and snowboarders. Baqueira-Beret's pistes lure the winter-sports jet-set. Meanwhile, charming villages like Salardú enchant hikers with views of cloud-scraping mountains. From Aran's pretty side valleys, walkers can go over the mountains in any direction, notably southward to the Parc Nacional d'Aigüestortes i Estany de Sant Maurici.

Thanks in part to its geography, Aran's native language is not Catalan but Aranese (Aranés), which is a dialect of Occitan or the *langue d'oc*, the old Romance language of southern France.

The Aragonese Pyrenees

The Aragonese Pyrenees are well over the 3000m-high mark and among the most dramatic peaks of the range. The villages here are some of the prettiest in this corner of the country.

Aínsa

The beautiful hilltop village of Aínsa, which stands above the small modern town of the same name, is one of Aragón's gems, a medieval masterpiece hewn from uneven stone. From its perch, you'll have commanding panoramic views of the mountains, particularly the great rock bastion of La Peña Montañesa.

◎ SIGHTS

Castillo   Castle

FREE The castle precinct off Plaza Mayor mostly dates from the 16th and 17th centuries; there are good views from the walls. The two surviving towers house moderately interesting museums: the **Eco Museo** (✆974 50 05 97; www.quebrantahuesos.org; €4; ⊘10.30am-2.30pm & 3.30-8pm Jul-Sep, 11am-7pm Oct-Jun; 🚸) 🍃 on Pyrenean birds of prey and other fauna, and the **Espacio del Geoparque de Sobrarbe** (www.geoparque pirineos.com; ⊘9.30am-2pm & 4.30-7pm Wed-Sun Jul-Aug, hours vary Sep-Jun) **FREE** on the region's intriguing geology.

Plaza Mayor   Square

Old Aínsa's broad, cobbled main plaza, lined by handsome stone arcades and

 Sant Joan de Les Abadesses

Who gallops through the hills around Sant Joan de les Abadesses on stormy nights, on a horse engulfed in flames and accompanied by ravenous black dogs? If you believe the legends, it's the cursed Count Arnau, whose association with the **Monestir de Sant Joan de les Abadesses** (www.monestirsantjoanabadess es.cat; Plaça de l'Abadia; adult/child €3/free; ⊘10am-7pm Jul & Aug, 10am-2pm & 4-7pm May, Jun & Sep, 10am-2pm & 4-6pm Mar, Apr & Oct, 10am-2pm Mon-Fri, 10am-2pm & 4-6pm Sat & Sun Nov-Feb) has bequeathed it a heritage of brooding fairytales alongside its centuries of spiritual activity. The monastery, founded in CE 887 by Guifré el Pilós, is notable for both its architectural treasures and the legend.

CLAUDIO GIOVANNI COLOMBO/SHUTTERSTOCK ©

houses, is one of Spain's loveliest. It was created as a market place and fairground back in the 12th and 13th centuries and the architecture has changed little since then – even if the buzz today comes not from market stalls but from the tables and sunshades of numerous restaurants.

✖ EATING

Bodegón de Mallacán   Aragonese €€

(✆974 50 09 77; Plaza Mayor 6; mains €17-21, set menus €22; ⊘noon-4pm & 7-11pm) Meat-eaters won't want to wave *adiós* to Aragón without tasting *ternasco*, the slow-roasted local lamb, and this is a fine place to try it. Duck,

From left: Sos del Rey Católico; Aínsa village (p269); Val d'Aran (p268)

boar, beef, partridge, frogs' legs and venison pâté are other classics you can enjoy here.

Restaurante
Callizo
Contemporary Spanish €€€
(☑974 50 03 85; www.restaurantecallizo.es; Plaza Mayor; set menus €60-80; ☺1-2.30pm & 8.45-9.45pm Wed-Sun Apr-Oct) Callizo succeeds in marrying Aragonese tradition with modern gastronomic theatre and the result is not just a meal but a true eating experience. Dishes include Río Cinca trout, rack of lamb and veal tournedos, all in imaginative preparations – and with lovely views wherever you sit. It's essential to reserve (possible on the website) and to arrive on time!

ⓘ INFORMATION

Municipal Tourist Office (☑974 50 07 67; www.villadeainsa.com; Avenida Ordesa 5; ☺10am-2pm & 4-7.30pm, closed Sun afternoon Sep-Jun) In the new town down the hill.

Oficina Comarcal de Turismo (District Tourist Office; ☑974 50 05 12; www.turismosobrarbe.com; Torre Nordeste, Plaza del Castillo 1; ☺9.30am-2pm & 4-7pm) Inside the Castillo.

ⓘ GETTING THERE & AWAY

There are one or two daily buses to/from Barbastro (€5.85, one hour). For Barcelona, change at Barbastro.

Sos del Rey Católico

If King Ferdinand II of Aragón were reincarnated in the 21st century, he'd probably still recognise his modest birthplace in Sos del Rey Católico. Take away the petrol station and the smattering of parked Peugeots and Fiats, and little has changed in this small, tightly packed hilltop village since 1452, when the future king of a united Spain was born in the Sada palace. Royalty aside, Sos is a fine place to soak up the tranquil essence of Aragonese village life.

◉ SIGHTS

Casa Palacio
de Sada
Historic Building
(Plaza de la Hispanidad; adult/child €2.90/1.90; ☺10am-1pm & 4-7pm Mon-Fri, 10am-2pm & 4-7pm Sat & Sun, closed Mon Sep-Jun) Fernando II of Aragón was born in this building in

SERGI BOUDADER CATOT/SHUTTERSTOCK ©

1452. It's an impressive mansion – more so now than back then, following a major expansion around 1600 and a 20th-century restoration. The rooms contain Spanish-language information panels on Fernando's highly eventful and historically significant life, plus a model of Sos village in wood and a chapel where an audiovisual on Sos' history is shown.

Iglesia de San Esteban Church
(Calle Salud; €1; ⊙10am-1pm & 4-6pm Mon-Sat, 10am-12.30pm Sun) This Romanesque-Gothic church, with a weathered Romanesque portal, has a deliciously gloomy crypt decorated with medieval frescos.

🍴 EATING

La Cocina del Principal Aragonese €€€
(⊡948 88 83 48; www.lacocinadelprincipal. es; Calle Fernando el Católico 13; mains €19-26, set menu €28; ⊙1.30-3.30pm & 8.30-10.30pm

Tue-Sat Mar-Nov, by reservation Dec-Feb) This place wins plaudits for its roast *ternasco* (suckling lamb), barbecued beef tenderloin and *pochas viudas*, a local bean-and-veggie stew. It's set down steps that seem to lead to a basement cellar but reveal a stone-walled dining room with a panoramic terrace.

ℹ️ INFORMATION

Tourist Office (⊡948 88 85 24; www.oficina-turismosdelreycatolico.com; Plaza Hispanidad; tours adult/child €4.40/1.90, incl Palacio de Sada €6.40/2.90; ⊙10am-1pm & 4-7pm Mon-Fri, 10am-2pm & 4-7pm Sat & Sun, closed Mon Sep-Jun) Housed in the Palacio de Sada.

ℹ️ GETTING THERE & AWAY

Autobuses Cinco Villas (⊡976 33 33 71; www.autobusescincovillas.com) runs a bus from Sos to Zaragoza (€13, 2¾ hours) at 7am Monday to Friday, returning at 5pm.

Capilla Real, Granada (p133)

In Focus

Sculptural reconstruction of *Homo antecessor* by Elizabeth Daynès

History

Spain's story is one of Europe's grand epics. It is a story shaped by ancient and not-so-ancient civilisations sweeping down through the Iberian Peninsula, and by the great ideological battles between Muslims and Christians of the Middle Ages. The 20th century was a match for anything that went before with civil war, dictatorship and a stunning return to democracy.

c 1.2 million BCE
Europe's earliest-known humans leave their fossilised remains in the Sima del Elefante at Atapuerca, near the northern city of Burgos.

c 15,000–10,000 BCE
Palaeolithic hunters paint sophisticated animal images in caves at Altamira and other sites along Spain's northern coastal strip.

218 BCE
Roman legions arrive in Spain, initiating the 600-year Roman occupation of the Iberian Peninsula.

Universidad Civil (p198), Salamanca

Ancient Civilisations

From their base on what is now the southern coast of Lebanon, the seafaring Phoenicians were the first to rule the Mediterranean: in the 8th century BCE, they established the port of Gadir, the site of modern Cádiz in southwestern Andalucía.

In the 7th century BCE, Greek traders arrived along the Mediterranean coast and brought with them several things now considered quintessentially Spanish – the olive tree, the grapevine and the donkey – along with writing, coins, the potter's wheel and poultry. But the Romans, who ruled Hispania (as Roman Iberia was known) for 600 years until the 5th century CE, left a far more lasting impression. By 50 CE, most of Hispania had adopted the Roman way of life. Rome gave the country a road system, aqueducts, temples, theatres, amphitheatres and bathhouses, but it began the process of deforestation as it culled the extensive forests that in their time covered half the *meseta* (plateau). Even more so than these, Rome's cultural impact was profound. It brought Christianity to Spain, planted olive trees on a massive scale, introduced olive oil production and may even have invented

711 CE	718	1218
Muslims invade Iberia from North Africa and become a major force on the peninsula for nearly eight centuries.	Christian noble Pelayo establishes the Kingdom of Asturias. With his victory in the Battle of Covadonga, the Reconquista begins.	The University of Salamanca is founded by Alfonso IX, King of León, making it Spain's oldest and most prestigious university.

Rainwater tanks, Real Alcázar (p170), Seville

jamón (cured ham). The basis of most of the languages still spoken here – Castilian, Catalan, Galician and Portuguese – are versions of the vernacular Latin spoken by Roman legionaries and colonists, filtered through 2000 years of linguistic mutation. The Roman era also saw the arrival of Jewish people in Spain, who were to play a big part in Spanish life for over 1000 years.

Islamic Spain

In 711 CE, Tariq ibn Ziyad, the Muslim governor of Tangier, landed at Gibraltar with around 10,000 men, mostly Berbers (indigenous North Africans). Within a few years, the Muslims (often referred to as Moors) had conquered the whole Iberian Peninsula, except small areas in the Asturian mountains in the north. Their advance into Europe was only checked by the Franks at the Battle of Poitiers in 732.

The name given to Muslim territory on the peninsula was Al-Andalus. Political power and cultural developments centred initially on Córdoba (756–1031), then Seville (c 1040–1248) and lastly Granada (1248–1492).

Muslim rule left an indelible imprint upon the country. Architectural monuments such as the Alhambra in Granada and the Mezquita in Córdoba are the stars of the Moorish legacy, but thousands of other buildings large and small are Moorish in origin. The tangled, narrow street plans of many a Spanish town and village, especially in the south, date back to Moorish times, and the Muslims also developed the Hispano-Roman agricultural base by improving irrigation and introducing new fruits and crops, many of which are still widely grown today. The Spanish language contains many common words of Arabic origin, including the names of some of those new crops – *naranja* (orange), *azúcar* (sugar) and *arroz* (rice). Flamenco, though brought to its modern form by Roma people in post-Moorish times, has clear Moorish roots. It was also through Al-Andalus that much of the learning of ancient Greece and Rome – picked up by the Arabs in the eastern Mediterranean – was transmitted to Christian Europe, where it would exert a profound influence on the Renaissance.

1469	April 1492	October 1492
Isabel, heir to Castilla, marries Fernando, heir to Aragón, uniting Spain's two most powerful Christian states.	Isabel and Fernando expel Jews who refuse Christian baptism. Some 200,000 leave.	Christopher Columbus, funded by Isabel and Fernando, lands in the Bahamas, opening the Americas to colonisation.

The Reconquista

The Christian Reconquest of Iberia began in about 722 at Covadonga, Asturias, and ended with the fall of Granada in 1492. It was a stuttering affair, conducted by Christian kingdoms that were as often at war with each other as with the Muslims.

An essential ingredient in the Reconquista was the cult of Santiago (St James), one of the 12 apostles. In 813, the saint's supposed tomb was discovered in Galicia. The city of Santiago de Compostela grew here, to become the third most popular medieval Christian pilgrimage goal after Rome and Jerusalem. Santiago became the inspiration and special protector of soldiers in the Reconquista, earning the sobriquet Matamoros (Moor-slayer). By 757, Christians occupied nearly a quarter of the Iberian Peninsula, although progress thereafter was slow.

The Spanish Inquisition

An ecclesiastical tribunal set up by Fernando and Isabel in 1478, the Spanish Inquisition in Al-Andalus focused first on *conversos* (Jews converted to Christianity), accusing many of continuing to practise Judaism in secret. In April 1492, Isabel and Fernando expelled all Jews who refused Christian baptism. Up to 100,000 converted, but some 200,000 (the first Sephardic Jews) fled into exile. The Inquisitors also carried out forced mass baptisms of Muslims, burnt Islamic books and banned the Arabic language. In 1500, Muslims were ordered to convert to Christianity or leave. Those who converted (*moriscos*) were later expelled between 1609 and 1614.

The year 1212, when the combined Christian armies routed a large Muslim force at Las Navas de Tolosa in Andalucía, marked the beginning of the end for Islamic Al-Andalus. The royal wedding of Isabel (of Castilla) and Fernando (of Aragón) in 1469 united two of the most powerful Christian kingdoms, enabling the armies of the Reconquista to make a final push. On 2 January 1492, Isabel and Fernando entered Granada. The surrender terms were fairly generous to Boabdil, the last emir, who was given the Alpujarras valleys south of Granada and 30,000 gold coins. The remaining Muslims were promised respect for their religion, culture and property, but this promise was quickly discarded.

The Golden Age of Empire

Isabel and Fernando were never going to be content with Spain alone. In April 1492, Los Reyes Católicos (the Catholic Monarchs) granted the Genoese sailor Christopher Columbus (Cristóbal Colón to Spaniards) funds for his long-desired voyage across the Atlantic in search of a new trade route to the Orient. Columbus set off from the Andalucian port of Palos de la Frontera on 3 August 1492, with three small ships and 120 men.

After a near mutiny as the crew despaired of sighting land, they finally arrived on the island of Guanahaní, in the Bahamas, and went on to find Cuba and Hispaniola. Columbus

1512
After Isabel's death in 1504, Fernando annexes Navarra, uniting Spain for the first time since Roman days.

1521
Hernán Cortés, from Medellín, Extremadura, conquers the Aztec empire in present-day Mexico and Guatemala.

1556–98
Reign of Felipe II, the zenith of Spanish power. Enormous colonial wealth is used for grand architectural projects.

Marxist militia, Barcelona, 1936

★ **Civil War Reads**

For Whom the Bell Tolls by Ernest Hemingway

Homage to Catalonia by George Orwell

Blood of Spain by Ronald Fraser

The Spanish Civil War by Hugh Thomas

returned to a hero's reception from the Catholic Monarchs in Barcelona, eight months after his departure.

Brilliant but ruthless conquistadors followed Columbus' trail, seizing vast tracts of the American mainland for Spain. By 1600, Spain controlled Florida, all the biggest Caribbean islands, nearly all of present-day Mexico and Central America, and a large strip of South America. The new colonies sent huge cargoes of silver, gold and other riches back to Spain. Seville enjoyed a monopoly on this trade and grew into one of Europe's richest cities.

Two Spains

Spain was united for the first time in almost eight centuries after Fernando annexed Navarra in 1512, and in 1519 Carlos I (Fernando's grandson) succeeded to the Habsburg lands in Austria and was elected Holy Roman Emperor (as Charles V). He ruled all of Spain, the Low Countries, Austria, several Italian states, parts of France and Germany, and the expanding Spanish colonies in the Americas.

But the storm clouds were brewing. Colonial riches lined the pockets of a series of backward-looking monarchs, a wealthy, highly conservative Church, and idle nobility. Although some of this wealth was used to foster the Golden Age of art, little was done to improve the lot of ordinary Spaniards and food shortages were rife. Spain's overseas possessions were ebbing away, but problems at home were even more pressing. In 1812, a national Cortes (parliament) meeting at Cádiz drew up a new liberal constitution for Spain, prompting a backlash from conservatives (the Church, the nobility and others who preferred the earlier status quo) and liberals (who wanted vaguely democratic reforms). Over the next century, Spain alternated between federal republic and monarchy, a liberal–conservative schism that saw the country lurch from one crisis to the next. By the 1930s, Spain was teetering on the brink of war.

c 1600–60	1809–24	1936
Spain enjoys a cultural Golden Age with Cervantes, Velázquez, Zurbarán and El Greco scaling new heights of excellence.	Most of Spain's American colonies win independence as Spain is beset by problems at home.	The left-wing National Front wins elections. Right-wing 'Nationalist' rebels led by General Francisco Franco begin the Spanish Civil War.

The Spanish Civil War

On 17 July 1936, the Spanish army garrison in Melilla, North Africa, rose up against the left-wing government, followed the next day by garrisons on the mainland. The leaders of the plot were five generals, among them Francisco Franco, who on 19 July flew from the Canary Islands to Morocco to take charge of his legionnaires. The civil war had begun.

Wherever the blame lies, the civil war split communities, families and friends, killed an estimated 350,000 Spaniards (some historians put the number as high as 500,000) and caused untold damage and misery. Both sides (Franco's Nationalists and the left-wing Republicans) committed atrocious massacres and reprisals, and employed death squads to eliminate opponents. On 26 April 1937, German planes bombed the Basque town of Gernika (Guernica), causing terrible casualties. The USSR withdrew their support from the war in September 1938, and in January 1939 the Nationalists took Barcelona unopposed. The Republican government and hundreds of thousands of supporters fled to France and, on 28 March 1939, Franco's forces entered Madrid.

Franco's Spain

Francisco Franco would go on to rule Spain with an iron fist for almost four decades until his death in 1975. An estimated 100,000 people were killed or died in prison after the war. The hundreds of thousands imprisoned included many intellectuals and teachers; others fled abroad, depriving Spain of a generation of scientists, artists, writers, educators and more. The army provided many government ministers and enjoyed a most generous budget. Catholic supremacy was fully restored, with secondary schools entrusted to the Jesuits, divorce made illegal and church weddings compulsory.

During WWII Franco flirted with Hitler (although Spain watched the war from the side-lines), but Spain was desperately poor to the extent that the 1940s are known as *los años de hambre* (years of hunger). Despite small-scale rebel activity, ongoing repression and international isolation (Spain was not admitted to the UN until 1955), an economic boom began in 1959 and would last through much of the 1960s. The recovery was funded in part by US aid and remittances from more than a million Spaniards working abroad, but above all by tourism, which was developed initially along Andalucía's Costa del Sol and Catalonia's Costa Brava. By 1965, the number of tourists arriving in Spain was 14 million a year.

But with the jails still full of political prisoners and Spain's restive regions straining under Franco's brutal policies, labour unrest grew and discontent began to rumble in the universities and even in the army and the Church. The Basque nationalist terrorist group Euskadi Ta Askatasuna (ETA; Basque Homeland and Freedom) also appeared in 1959. In the midst of it all, Franco chose as his successor Prince Juan Carlos. In 1969 Juan Carlos I swore loyalty to Franco and the Movimiento Nacional, Spain's fascist and only legal political party. Franco died on 20 November 1975.

1936–39	**1939–50**	**1955–65**
Nationalist rebels supported by Nazi Germany and Fascist Italy, defeat USSR-supported Republicans.	Franco establishes a right-wing dictatorship, imprisoning hundreds of thousands.	Spain is admitted to the UN after agreeing to host US bases. The economy is boosted by US aid and mass tourism.

La Movida

After the long, dark years of dictatorship and conservative Catholicism, Spaniards, especially those in Madrid, emerged onto the streets with all the zeal of ex-convent schoolgirls. Nothing was taboo in a phenomenon known as 'la movida' (the scene) or 'la movida madrileña' (the Madrid scene) as young madrileños discovered the 1960s, '70s and early '80s all at once. Drinking, drugs and sex suddenly were OK. All-night partying was the norm, drug taking in public was not a criminal offence (that changed in Madrid in 1992) and Madrid, in particular, howled. All across Madrid and other major cities, summer terraces roared to the chattering, drinking, carousing crowds and young people from all over Europe (not to mention cultural icons such as Andy Warhol) flocked here to take part in the revelry.

La movida was also accompanied by an explosion of creativity among the country's musicians, designers and film-makers keen to shake off the shackles of the repressive Franco years. The most famous of these was film director Pedro Almodóvar, whose riotously colourful films captured the spirit of la movida, featuring larger-than-life characters who pushed the limits of sex and drugs.

Spain's Democratic Transition

Juan Carlos I, aged 37, took the throne two days after Franco died. The new king's links with the dictator inspired little confidence in a Spain now clamouring for democracy, but Juan Carlos had kept his cards close to his chest and can take most of the credit for the successful transition to democracy that followed.

He appointed Adolfo Suárez, a 43-year-old former Franco apparatchik with film-star looks, as prime minister. To general surprise, Suárez got the Francoist-filled Cortes to approve a new, two-chamber parliamentary system, and in early 1977 political parties, trade unions and strikes were all legalised and the Movimiento Nacional was abolished. After elections in 1977, a centrist government led by Suárez granted a general amnesty for acts committed in the civil war and under the Franco dictatorship. In 1978, the Cortes passed a new constitution making Spain a parliamentary monarchy with no official religion and granting a large measure of devolution to Spain's regions. Despite challenges, such as the brutal campaign by ETA that killed hundreds in the 1980s and an unsuccessful coup attempt by renegade Civil Guards in 1981, Spain's democratic, semifederal constitution and multiparty system have proved at once robust and durable.

Spain Grows Up

The 1980s saw Spain pass a succession of milestones along the road to becoming a mature European democracy. That they took these steps so quickly and so successfully after four decades of fascism is one of modern Europe's most remarkable stories.

1975
Franco dies and is succeeded by King Juan Carlos I, who soon demonstrates his desire for change.

1978
A new constitution, approved by referendum, establishes Spain as a parliamentary democracy.

1986
Spain joins the European Community (now the EU) and becomes a member of NATO.

In 1982 the left-of-centre Partido Socialista Obrero Español (PSOE; Spanish Socialist Workers' Party) was elected to power, led by a charismatic young lawyer from Seville, Felipe González. During its 14 years in power, the PSOE brought Spain into mainstream Europe, joining the European Community (now the EU) in 1986. It also oversaw the rise of the Spanish middle class, established a national health system and improved public education, and Spain's women streamed into higher education and jobs, although unemployment was still the highest in Europe.

But the PSOE finally became mired in scandal and in the 1996 elections, the centre-right Partido Popular (PP; People's Party), led by José María Aznar, swept the PSOE from power. Upon coming to power, José María Aznar promised to make politics dull, and he did, but he also presided over eight years of solid economic progress. Spain's economy grew annually by an average of 3.4% and unemployment fell from 23% (1996) to 8% (2006). Not surprisingly, the PP won the 2000 election as well, with an absolute parliamentary majority. Aznar's popularity began to wane thanks to his strong support for the US-led invasion of Iraq in 2003 (which was deeply unpopular in Spain) and his decision to send Spanish troops to the conflict.

Troubled Times

On 11 March 2004, Madrid was rocked by 10 bombs on four rush-hour commuter trains heading into the capital's Atocha station. When the dust cleared, 191 people had died and 1755 were wounded. In a stunning reversal of prepoll predictions, the PP, who insisted that ETA was responsible despite overwhelming evidence to the contrary, was defeated by the PSOE in elections three days after the attack.

The new Socialist government of José Luis Rodríguez Zapatero introduced a raft of liberalising social reforms. Gay marriage was legalised, Spain's arcane divorce laws were overhauled and almost a million illegal immigrants were granted residence. Although Spain's powerful Catholic Church cried foul, the changes played well with most Spaniards. Spain's economy was booming, the envy of Europe. And then it all fell apart.

Spain's economy went into free fall in late 2008. Zapatero's government waited painfully long to recognise that a crisis was looming and was replaced in November 2011 with a right-of-centre one led by Mariano Rajoy. A deep austerity program followed, cutting into the generous welfare state on which Spaniards had come to depend. Spanish banks were bailed out by the EU to the tune of €100 billion. The conservative government also turned back the liberalising reforms of the socialists, introducing some of Europe's strictest anti-abortion laws and restoring the role of the Catholic Church in education.

In 2015 and 2016, a groundswell of popular anger roiled Spanish politics, with two new anti-corruption parties – the radical, anti-austerity Unidas Podemos ('United We Can') and the centrist, pro-business Ciudadanos (Citizens) – winning seats in general elections. The PP eventually formed a minority government, but it only lasted until June 2018 when

1992	**11 March 2004**	**July 2010**
Barcelona holds the Olympic Games, putting Spain in the international spotlight and highlighting the country's progress since 1975.	A terrorist bombing kills 191 people on 10 Madrid commuter trains.	Spain's national football team wins the World Cup for the first time, two years after its maiden European Championship trophy.

Coronavirus in Spain

For all the tumult that has buffeted Spain in recent years, the coronavirus, or COVID-19, took the hardship to a whole new level. At a time when the Spanish economy was improving steadily, in February 2020 the COVID-19 virus began to sweep through the country, with Madrid hardest hit. By early May, there were over 218,000 confirmed cases, with more than 25,000 deaths, the third highest in the world after the US and Italy. Numbers fell and Spaniards were able to enjoy a relatively normal summer. But a second wave followed. By early November, Spain had recorded nearly 1.2 million cases with almost 36,000 deaths, and many Spanish regions were heading back into lockdown.

it was unseated by a parliamentary vote of no confidence following a long-running corruption case.

The next two years under prime minister Pedro Sánchez of the PSOE saw increased fragmentation, with two new national elections being held in 2019. As 2020 began, the far-right Vox party had surged to hold 52 seats in the Congress of Deputies, while Pedro Sánchez's PSOE presided over a fragile coalition government with left-leaning Unidas Podemos.

The Catalan Question

In 2015, an alliance of pro-independence parties, led by Carles Puigdemont, came to power in Catalonia promising to hold a referendum on independence. Despite uncompromising opposition to such a referendum from the PP government in Madrid, and a judgement by Spain's constitutional court that it would be illegal, the referendum was held on 1 October 2017. Madrid sent in national police to try to prevent voting at some polling stations, resulting in violent scenes. According to the Catalan government, 43% of the Catalonia electorate voted in the referendum, and 90% of those voted for independence.

In reaction to the referendum, a wave of support for Spanish national unity swept through much of Spain. Huge demonstrations, both for and against independence, took place in Barcelona (by most estimates slightly more than half the population of Catalonia opposes independence). On 27 October, the Catalan parliament went ahead and declared Catalonia independent, prompting the national parliament in Madrid to invoke Article 155 of the Spanish Constitution, suspending Catalonia's regional autonomy and the Catalan parliament with it.

New Catalan elections in December 2017 saw separatist parties win a narrow majority in the regional parliament, though the Spanish government continued its period of direct rule over Catalonia for another seven months, finally restoring regional autonomy in June 2018.

In October 2019, Spain's Supreme Court unanimously convicted nine former Catalan government officials – including former vice president Oriol Junqueras – of sedition and misappropriation of public funds for their role in the 2017 independence referendum. Sentences ranged from nine to 13 years, provoking massive protests in Barcelona.

June 2014	21 December 2017	2018
After a series of scandals, King Juan Carlos I, who had reigned since 1975, abdicates and his son begins his reign as Felipe VI.	Pro-independence parties win a narrow majority in Catalonia's regional elections.	The Partido Popular loses a parliamentary no-confidence vote. The PSOE forms a minority government, headed by Pedro Sánchez.

Flamenco dancers in Seville

Flamenco

Flamenco's passion is clear to anyone who has heard its melancholic strains in the background of a crowded Spanish bar or during a rivetting live performance. If you're lucky, you'll experience that single uplifting moment when flamenco's raw passion suddenly transports you to another place (known as duende*), where joy and sorrow threaten to overwhelm.*

The Birth of Flamenco

Flamenco's origins have been lost to time, but most musical historians agree that it probably dates back to a fusion of songs brought to Spain by the Roma people, with music and verses from North Africa crossing into medieval Muslim Andalucía.

Flamenco as we now know it first took recognisable form in the 18th and early 19th centuries among Roma people in the lower Guadalquivir valley in western Andalucía. The Seville, Jerez de la Frontera and Cádiz axis is still considered flamenco's heartland and it's here, purists say, that you'll encounter the most authentic flamenco experience.

★ **Flamenco Festivals**

Festival de Jerez (p158), Jerez de la Frontera

Suma Flamenca (June), Madrid

Festival de la Guitarra de Córdoba (p190), Córdoba

Bienal de Flamenco (p176), Seville

Flamenco Legends

The great flamenco singers of the 19th and early 20th centuries were Silverio Franconetti and La Niña de los Peines, from Seville, and Antonio Chacón and Manuel Torre, from Jerez de la Frontera. Torre's singing, legend has it, could drive people to rip their shirts open and upturn tables. The dynamic dancing and wild lifestyle of Carmen Amaya (1913–63), from Barcelona, made her the Roma dance legend of all time. Her long-time partner Sabicas was the father of the modern solo flamenco guitar, inventing a host of now-indispensable techniques.

After a trough in the mid-20th century, when it seemed that the *tablaos* (touristy flamenco shows emphasising the sexy and the jolly) were in danger of taking over, *flamenco puro* got a new lease of life in the 1970s through singers such as Terremoto, La Paquera, Enrique Morente, Chano Lobato and, above all, El Camarón de la Isla (1950–92; whose real name was José Monge Cruz) from San Fernando near Cádiz.

Some say that Madrid-born Diego El Cigala (b 1968) is El Camarón's successor. This powerful singer launched onto the big stage with the extraordinary *Lágrimas negras* (2003), a wonderful collaboration with Cuban virtuoso Bebo Valdés that mixes flamenco with Cuban influences, and its follow-up, *Dos Lagrimas* (2008). Other fine Diego El Cigala albums include *Picasso en mis Ojos* (2005), *Cigala&Tango* (2010), *Romance de la Luna Tucumana* (2013) and *Indestructible* (2016).

Another singer whose fame endures is Enrique Morente (1942–2010), referred to by one Madrid paper as 'the last bohemian'. While careful not to alienate flamenco purists, Morente, through his numerous collaborations across genres, helped lay the foundations for *nuevo flamenco* and fusion. His untimely death in 2010 was mourned by a generation of flamenco aficionados.

Paco de Lucía (1947–2014), from Algeciras, was the doyen of flamenco guitarists. By the time he was 14, his teachers admitted that they had nothing left to teach him and, for many in the flamenco world, he is the personification of *duende,* that indefinable capacity to transmit the power

Flamenco Playlist

- Camarón de la Isla, *La leyenda del tiempo* (1979)

- Pata Negra, *Blues de la frontera* (1987)

- Paco de Lucía, *Antología* (1995)

- Chambao, *Flamenco chill* (2002)

- Diego El Cigala & Bebo Valdés, *Lágrimas negras* (2003)

- Paco de Lucía, *Cositas buenas* (2004)

- Enrique Morente, *Sueña la Alhambra* (2005)

- Diego El Cigala, *Indestructible* (2016)

- Rosalía, *Los Angeles* (2017)

and passion of flamenco. In 1968 he began flamenco's most exciting partnership with his friend El Camarón de la Isla; together they recorded nine classic albums. De Lucía would go on to transform the flamenco guitar into an instrument of solo expression with new techniques, scales, melodies and harmonies that have gone far beyond traditional limits.

Other guitar maestros include Tomatito (b 1958), who also accompanied El Camarón de la Isla, and members of the Montoya family (some of whom are better known by the sobriquet of Los Habichuela), especially Juan (b 1933) and Pepe (b 1944).

Carmen Linares is said to have flamenco's most enduring voice, while Joaquín Cortés is a dance star fusing flamenco with jazz and ballet.

Seeing Flamenco

The intensity and spontaneity of flamenco have never translated well onto recordings. Instead, to ignite the goosebumps and inspire the powerful emotional spirit, 'duende', you have to be there, stamping your feet and passionately yelling 'ióle!'. Flamenco is easiest to catch in Seville, Jerez de la Frontera, Granada and Madrid.

Flamenco Essentials

A flamenco singer is known as a *cantaor* (male) or *cantaora* (female); a dancer is a *bailaor* or *bailaora*. Most of the songs and dances are performed to a blood-rush of guitar from the *tocaor* or *tocaora* (male or female flamenco guitarist). Percussion is provided by tapping feet, clapping hands, the *cajón* (a box beaten with the hands) and sometimes castanets.

Flamenco *coplas* (songs) come in many types, from the anguished *soleá* or the intensely despairing *siguiriya* to the livelier *alegría* or the upbeat *bulería*. The first flamenco was *cante jondo* (deep song), an anguished instrument of expression for a group on the margins of society. *Jondura* (depth) is still the essence of pure flamenco.

The traditional flamenco costumes – shawl, fan and long, frilly *bata de cola* (tail gown) for women, and flat Cordoban hats and tight black trousers for men – date from Andalucian fashions in the late 19th century.

Seeing flamenco can be expensive – at the *tablaos* (restaurants where flamenco is performed) expect to pay €25 to €35 just to see the show. The admission price usually includes your first drink, but you pay extra for meals (up to €50 per person) that aren't always worth the money. For that reason, we often suggest you eat elsewhere and simply pay for the show (after having bought tickets in advance), albeit on the understanding that you won't have a front-row seat. The other important thing to remember is that most of these shows are geared towards tourists. That's not to say that the quality isn't often top-notch – on the contrary, often it's magnificent, spine-tingling stuff – it's just that they sometimes lack the genuine, raw emotion of real flamenco.

The best places for live performances are *peñas* (clubs where flamenco fans band together). The atmosphere in such places is authentic and at times very intimate, proof that flamenco feeds off an audience that knows its flamenco. Most Andalucian towns have dozens of *peñas,* and many tourist offices – especially those in Seville, Jerez de la Frontera and Cádiz – have lists of those that are open to visitors.

Festivals are another place to see fabulous live flamenco.

The Surrender of Breda, Velázquez

Master Painters

Spain has an artistic legacy that rivals anything found elsewhere in Europe. In centuries past, this impressive portfolio owed much to the patronage of Spanish kings who lavished money upon the great painters of the day. In the 20th century, it was the relentless creativity of artists such as Pablo Picasso, Salvador Dalí and Joan Miró who became the true masters.

The Golden Century

The star of the 17th-century art scene, which became known as Spain's artistic Golden Age, was the genius court painter, Diego Rodríguez de Silva Velázquez (1599–1660). Born in Seville, Velázquez later moved to Madrid as court painter and composed scenes (landscapes, royal portraits, religious subjects, snapshots of everyday life) that owe their vitality not only to his photographic eye for light, contrast and the details of royal finery, but also to a compulsive interest in the humanity of his subjects so that they seem to breathe on the canvas. His masterpieces include *Las meninas* (Maids of Honour) and *La rendición de Breda* (Surrender of Breda), both in Madrid's Museo del Prado (p38).

Francisco de Zurbarán (1598–1664), a friend and contemporary of Velázquez, ended his life in poverty in Madrid and it was only after his death that he received the acclaim that his

Saturn Devouring His Son, Goya

masterpieces deserved. He is best remembered for the startling clarity and light in his portraits of monks, a series of which hangs in Madrid's Real Academia de Bellas Artes de San Fernando, with other works in the Museo del Prado.

Other masters of the era whose works hang in the Museo del Prado include José (Jusepe) de Ribera (1591–1652), who was influenced by Caravaggio and produced fine chiaroscuro works, and Bartolomé Esteban Murillo (1618–82).

Goya & the 19th Century

Francisco José de Goya y Lucientes (1746–1828) began his career as a cartoonist in the Real Fábrica de Tapices (Royal Tapestry Workshop) in Madrid. Illness in 1792 left him deaf; many critics speculate that his condition was largely responsible for his wild, often merciless style that would become increasingly unshackled from convention. By 1799, Goya was appointed Carlos IV's court painter.

In the last years of the 18th century, Goya painted enigmatic masterpieces, such as *La maja vestida* (The Young Lady Dressed) and *La maja desnuda* (The Young Lady Undressed), identical portraits but for the lack of clothes in the latter. The Inquisition was not amused by the artworks, which it covered up. Nowadays all is bared in Madrid's Museo del Prado.

The arrival of the French and the war in 1808 had a profound impact on Goya. Unforgiving portrayals of the brutality of war are *El dos de mayo* (The Second of May) and, more dramatically, *El tres de mayo* (The Third of May). The latter depicts the execution of Madrid rebels by French troops.

Goya saved his most confronting paintings for the end. After he retired to the Quinta del Sordo (Deaf Man's House) in Madrid, he created his nightmarish *Pinturas negras* (Black Paintings), which now hang in the Museo del Prado. *The Saturno devorando a su hijo* (Saturn Devouring His Son) captures the essence of Goya's genius, and *La romería de San Isidro* (The Pilgrimage to San Isidro) and *El akelarre* (*El gran cabrón*; The Great He-Goat) are profoundly unsettling.

Other places, both in Madrid, to see Goya's works include the Real Academia de Bellas Artes de San Fernando (p48) and the Ermita de San Antonio de la Florida (p44); the latter has fabulous ceiling frescoes painted by Goya.

Picasso, Dalí & Miró

Pablo Ruíz Picasso (1881–1973) underwent repeated creative revolutions as he passed from one creative phase to another. From his gloomy Blue Period, through the brighter Pink Period and on to cubism – in which he was accompanied by Madrid's Juan Gris

Centro de Arte Reina Sofía (p49), Madrid

CHRISTIAN MUELLER/SHUTTERSTOCK©

★ Best Galleries

Museo del Prado (p38; Madrid) One of the world's best galleries.

Centro de Arte Reina Sofía (p49; Madrid) Picasso's *Guernica*, Dalí and Miró.

Museu Picasso (p91; Barcelona) Collection from Picasso's early years.

Teatre-Museu Dalí (p112; Figueres) As weird and wonderful as the man himself.

(1887–1927) – Picasso was nothing if not surprising. Cubism, his best-known form, was inspired by the artist's fascination with primitivism, primarily African masks and early Iberian sculpture. This highly complex form reached its high point in *Guernica,* which hangs in Madrid's Centro de Arte Reina Sofía (p49). A good selection of his early work can be viewed in Barcelona's Museu Picasso (p91).

Separated from Picasso by barely a generation, two other artists reinforced the Spanish contingent in the vanguard of 20th-century art: Dalí and Miró. Although he started off dabbling in cubism, Salvador Dalí (1904–89) became more readily identified with the surrealists. This complex character's 'hand-painted dream photographs', as he called them, are virtuoso executions brimming with fine detail and nightmare images dragged up from a feverish and Freud-fed imagination. The single best display of his work can be seen at the Teatre-Museu Dalí (p113) in Figueres, but you'll also find important works in the Museu de Cadaqués in Cadaqués, the Casa Museu Dalí (p115) in Port Lligat, and Madrid's Centro de Arte Reina Sofía.

Barcelona-born Joan Miró (1893–1983) developed a joyous and almost childlike style. His later period is his best known, characterised by the simple use of bright colours and forms in combinations of symbols that represented women, birds and stars. The Fundació Joan Miró (p93) in Barcelona and the Fundació Pilar i Joan Miró in Palma de Mallorca are the pick of the places to see his work, with some further examples in Madrid's Centro de Arte Reina Sofía.

Metropol Parasol (p173), Seville

DAVID IGNOTY/SHUTTERSTOCK ©

Architecture

Spain's architectural landscapes are some of the richest of their kind in Europe. The country's architecture tells a beguiling story that takes in the cinematic sweep of its history, from glorious Moorish creations in Andalucía and soaring cathedrals and temples, to the singular imagination of Gaudí and contemporary creativity.

The Islamic Era

In 784, with Córdoba well established as the new capital of the western end of the Umayyad Empire, Syrian architects set to work on the grand Mezquita, conjuring up their homeland with details that echo the Umayyad Mosque in Damascus, such as delicate horseshoe arches and exquisite decorative tiles with floral motifs. But the building's most distinctive feature – more than 500 columns that crowd the interior of the mosque – was repurposed from Roman and Visigothic ruins.

In the centuries that followed, Moorish architecture incorporated trends from all over the Islamic empire. The technique of intricately carved stucco detailing was developed in 9th-century Iraq, while *muqarnas* (honeycomb) vaulting arrived via Egypt in the 10th century. Square minarets, such as the Giralda in Seville (now a church tower), came with

Spanish Architecture: the Basics

Roman (210 BCE–409 CE) Bridges, waterworks, walls and whole cities that inspired later traditions.

Visigothic (409–711) Sturdy stone churches with simple decoration and horseshoe arches.

Moorish (711–1492) Horseshoe arches, square minarets and intricate geometric design.

Mudéjar (1100–1700) Post-Reconquista work by Muslims adapting the Moorish tradition of decoration to more common materials.

Romanesque (1100–1300) Spare decoration and proportions based on Byzantine churches.

Gothic (1200–1600) Flying buttresses enable ceilings to soar and arches become pointy to match.

Plateresque (1400–1600) A dazzling ornate style of relief carving on facades.

Churrigueresque (1650–1750) Spain's special twist on baroque with spiral columns and gold-leaf everything.

Modernisme (1888–1911) The Spanish version of art nouveau took a brilliant turn in Barcelona.

Contemporary (1975–present) Previously unimaginable directions since the death of Franco.

the Almohad invasion from Morocco in the 12th century.

Perhaps the most magnificent creation is the core of Granada's Alhambra, the Palacios Nazaríes (Nasrid Palaces; p126). From the 13th to the 15th century, architects reached new heights of elegance, creating a study in balance between inside and outside, light and shade, spareness and intricate decoration. Eschewing innovation, the Alhambra refined well-tried forms, as if in an attempt to freeze time and halt the collapse of Moorish power, which, at the time, was steadily eroding across the peninsula.

Andalucía's Formal Gardens

Paradise, according to Islamic tradition, is a garden. It's an idea that architects took to heart in Al-Andalus, surrounding some of Andalucía's loveliest buildings with abundant greenery, colour, fragrances and the tinkle of water.

o   Alhambra (p126; Granada) Landscaping of near-perfect sophistication.

o   Alcázar gardens (p171; Seville) A classic Islamic palace pleasure garden.

o   Gardens of the Alcázar de los Reyes Cristianos (p189; Córdoba) Lush terrace with abundant water.

o   Parque de María Luisa (p177; Seville) Sprawling greenery in the heart of Seville.

o   Palacio de Viana (p189; Córdoba) Formal gardens with an emphasis osymmetry.

Romanesque & Gothic

As the tide turned against the Muslims, the Romanesque style was sweeping medieval Europe, taking root in Spain in part because it was the aesthetic opposite of Islamic fashions. These buildings were spare, angular and heavy, inspired by the proportions of classical structures.

Romanesque structures had perfectly semicircular arches. In churches, this was expressed in a semi-cylindrical apse, a shape previously found in Byzantine churches. The round arch also graced doorways, windows, cloisters and naves. Entrances supported stacks of concentric arches – the more eye-catching because they were often the only really decorative detail. The pilgrimage cathedral of Santiago de Compostela (p240) is arguably Spain's greatest Romanesque building; a great, lesser-known example is the Sant Climent de Taüll (p267), one of many fine examples in the Catalan Pyrenees.

Later, during the 12th century, Spanish architects began to modify these semicircles, edging towards the Gothic style, as they added pointed arches and ribbed vaults. The trend elsewhere in Europe towards towering cathedrals made possible by the newfangled flying buttresses caught on in Spain by the 13th century. Some changes were subtle, such as placing choir stalls in the centre of the nave, but one was unmissable: the towering, decorative *retablo* (altarpiece) that graced the new churches.

The Gothic fascination lasted into the 16th century, when there was a revival of pure Gothic, perhaps best exemplified in the new cathedral in Salamanca (p196).

Renaissance & Plateresque

Arising from the pan-European Renaissance, the uniquely Spanish vision of plateresque drew partly on Italian styles and was also an outgrowth of the Isabelline Gothic look. It is so named because facade decoration was so ornate that it looked as though it had been wrought by *plateros* (silversmiths). To visit Salamanca, where the Spanish Renaissance first took root, is to receive a concentrated dose of the most splendid work in the genre.

A more purist Renaissance style, reflecting classical proportions and styles already established in Italy and France, prevailed in Andalucía, as seen in the Palacio de Carlos V in Granada's Alhambra.

Modernisme & Art Deco

At the end of the 19th century, Barcelona's prosperity unleashed one of the most imaginative periods in Spanish architecture. The architects at work here, who drew on prevailing art nouveau trends as well as earlier Spanish styles, came to be called the Modernistas. Chief among them, Antoni Gaudí sprinkled Barcelona with jewels of his singular imagination.

While Barcelona went all wavy, Madrid embraced the rigid glamour of art deco. This global style arrived in Spain just as Madrid's Gran Vía was laid out in the 1920s. One of the more overwhelming caprices from that era is the Palacio de Comunicaciones on Plaza de la Cibeles.

Antoni Gaudí

Born in Reus and initially trained in metalwork, Antoni Gaudí i Cornet (1852–1926) personifies, and largely transcends, the Modernisme movement that brought a thunderclap of innovative greatness to turn-of-the-century Barcelona.

He devoted much of the latter part of his life to what remains Barcelona's call sign: the unfinished Sagrada Família (p72). His inspiration in the first instance was Gothic, but he also sought to emulate the harmony he observed in nature, eschewing the straight line and favouring curvaceous forms. Gaudí used complex string models weighted with plumb lines to make his calculations; you can see examples in the cathedral's Museu Gaudí.

The architect's work is an earthy appeal to sinewy movement, but often with a dreamlike or surreal quality. The private apartment house Casa Batlló (p80) is a fine example. Not only are straight lines eliminated, but the lines between real and unreal, sober and dream-drunk, good sense and play are all blurred.

He seems to have particularly enjoyed himself with rooftops, especially at La Pedrera (p80) and Palau Güell (p90).

Casa Battló

GUY VANDERELST/GETTY IMAGES ©

★ **Gaudí**

La Sagrada Família (p72) A symphony of religious devotion.

La Pedrera (p80) Dubbed 'the Quarry' because of its flowing facade.

Casa Batlló (p80) A fairy-tale dragon.

Park Güell (p92) A park full of Modernista twists.

Contemporary Innovation

Post-Franco, Spain has made up for lost time and, particularly since the 1990s, the unifying theme appears to be that anything goes.

Catalan Enric Miralles had a short career, dying of a brain tumour in 2000 at the age of 45, but his Mercat de Santa Caterina (p91) in Barcelona shows brilliant colour and inventive use of arches.

In 1996, Rafael Moneo won the Pritzker Prize, the greatest international honour for living architects, largely for his long-term contributions to Madrid's cityscape, such as the revamping of the Atocha railway station. His Kursaal Palace in San Sebastián is staunchly functional, but shining, like two giant stones swept up from the sea.

In the years since, Spain has become something of a Pritzker playground. Norman Foster designed the eye-catching metro system in Bilbao and Spain's tallest building the 250m Torre Caja Madrid. But it was Frank Gehry's 1998 Museo Guggenheim (p208) in the Bilbao that really sparked the quirky-building fever. Now the list of contemporary landmarks includes Jean Nouvel's spangly, gherkin-shaped Torre Agbar, in Barcelona; Richard Rogers' dreamy, wavy Terminal 4 at Madrid's Barajas airport, for which he won the prestigious Stirling Prize in October 2006; Oscar Niemeyer's flying-saucerish Centro Cultural Internacional Avilés in Asturias; and Jürgen Mayer's Metropol Parasol (p173) in Seville.

Octopus *pintxo*

The Spanish Kitchen

For Spaniards, eating is one of life's more pleasurable obsessions. In this chapter, we'll help you make the most of this fabulous culinary culture, whether it's demystifying the art of ordering tapas or taking you on a journey through the regional specialities of Spanish food.

Regional Specialities

Basque Country & Catalonia

Seafood and steaks are the pillars upon which Basque cuisine was traditionally built. San Sebastián, in particular, showcases the region's diversity of culinary experiences and it was from the kitchens of San Sebastián that *nueva cocina vasca* (Basque nouvelle cuisine) emerged, announcing Spain's arrival as a culinary superpower.

Catalonia blends traditional Catalan flavours and expansive geographical diversity with an openness to influences from the rest of Europe. All manner of seafood, paella, rice and pasta dishes, as well as Pyrenean game dishes, are regulars on Catalan menus. Sauces are more prevalent here than elsewhere in Spain.

Menu Decoder

a la parilla grilled

asado roasted or baked

bebidas drinks

carne meat

carta menu

casera home-made

ensalada salad

entrada entree or starter

entremeses hors d'oeuvres

frito fried

menú usually refers to a set menu

menú de degustación tasting menu

pescado fish

plato combinado main-and-three-veg dish

postre dessert

raciones large-/full-plate size servings of tapas

sopa soup

Inland Spain

The best *jamón ibérico* (cured ham) comes from Extremadura, Salamanca and Teruel, while *cordero asado lechal* (roast spring lamb) and *cochinillo asado* (roast suckling pig) are winter mainstays. King of the hearty stews, especially in Madrid, is *cocido*, a hotpot or stew with a noodle broth, carrots, cabbage, chickpeas, chicken, *morcilla* (blood sausage), beef and lard.

Galicia & the Northwest

Galicia is known for its bewildering array of seafood and the star is *pulpo á feira* or *pulpo gallego* (spicy boiled octopus with oil, paprika and garlic).

In the high mountains of Asturias and Cantabria, the cuisine is as driven by mountain pasture as it is by the daily comings and goings of fishing fleets. Cheeses are particularly sought after, with special fame reserved for the *queso de Cabrales* (untreated cow's-milk cheese). *Asturianos* (Asturians) are also passionate about their *fabada asturiana* (a stew made with pork, blood sausage and white beans) and *sidra* (cider) straight from the barrel.

Andalucía

Seafood is a consistent presence the length of the Andalucian coast. Andalucians are famous above all for their *pescaito frito* (fried fish). A particular speciality of Cádiz, fried fish Andalucían-style means that just about anything that emerges from the sea is rolled in chickpea-and-wheat flour, shaken to remove the surplus, then deep-fried ever so briefly in olive oil, just long enough to form a light, golden crust that seals the essential goodness of the fish or seafood within.

In a region where summers can be fierce, there's no better way to keep cool than with a *gazpacho andaluz* (Andalucian gazpacho), a cold soup with many manifestations. The base is almost always tomato, cucumber, vinegar and olive oil.

Cheap Treats

Tapas or pintxos Possibly the world's most ingenious form of snacking. Madrid's La Latina and Chamberí *barrios* (districts), Zaragoza's El Tubo and most Andalucian cities offer rich pickings, but a *pintxo* (Basque tapas) crawl in San Sebastián's Parte Vieja is one of life's most memorable gastronomic experiences.

Tortilla de patatas Great for vegetarians and carnivores alike, the Spanish egg-and-potato omelette is especially good when the egg's runny. It's served as an in-between-meals snack, although it can be a meal in itself.

Chocolate con churros These deep-fried doughnut strips dipped in thick hot chocolate are a Spanish favourite for breakfast, afternoon tea or at dawn on your way home from a night out. Madrid's Chocolatería de San Ginés (p63) is the most famous purveyor.

Bocadillos Rolls filled with *jamón* (ham) or other cured meats, cheese or (in Madrid) deep-fried calamari.

Pa amb tomàquet Bread rubbed with tomato, olive oil and garlic – a staple in Catalonia and elsewhere.

Dare to Try

Oreja Pig's ear, cooked on the grill. It's a little like eating gristly bacon.

Callos Tripe cooked in a sauce of tomato, paprika, garlic and herbs. It's a speciality in Madrid.

Rabo de toro Bull's tail, or oxtail stew. It's a particular delicacy during bullfighting season in Madrid and Andalucía, when the tail comes straight from the bullring...

Percebes Goose barnacles from Galicia. The first person to try them sure was one adventurous individual, but we're glad they did.

Garrotxa Formidable Catalan cheese that almost lives up to its name.

Morcilla Blood sausage. It's blended with rice in Burgos, with onion in Asturias.

Criadillas Bull's testicles. Eaten in Andalucía.

Botillo Spanish version of haggis from Castilla y León's Bierzo region.

Pestorejo Fleshy part of a pig's neck; much loved in Mérida.

Paella & Other Rice Dishes

Rice dishes are traditional in Catalonia, Valencia and Andalucía, so that's where they're best eaten. Check out the clientele first. No locals? Walk on by.

Restaurants should take around 20 minutes or more to prepare a rice dish – beware if they don't – so expect to wait. Rice dishes are usually for a minimum of two people.

Paella has all the liquid evaporated: *meloso* rices are wet and *caldoso* rices come with liquid. Traditional Valencian rice can have almost any ingredients, varying by region and season. The base always includes short-grain rice, garlic, olive oil and saffron. The best rice is *bomba,* which opens accordion-like when cooked, allowing for maximum absorption while remaining firm. Paella should be cooked in a large shallow pan to enable maximum contact with flavour. And for the final touch of authenticity, the grains on the bottom (and only those) should have a crunchy, savoury crust known as the *socarrat.*

Jamón

There's no more iconic presence on the Spanish table than cured ham from the high plateau, and the sight of *jamónes* hanging from the ceiling is one of Spain's most enduring images. Spanish *jamón* is, unlike Italian prosciutto, a bold, deep red and well marbled with buttery fat. At its best, it smells like meat, the forest and the field.

Like wines and olive oil, Spanish *jamón* is subject to a strict series of classifications. *Jamón serrano* refers to *jamón* made from white-coated pigs introduced to Spain in the 1950s. Once salted and semidried by the cold, dry winds of the Spanish sierra, most now go through a similar process of curing and drying in a climate-controlled shed for around a year.

Jamón ibérico – more expensive and generally regarded as the elite of Spanish hams – comes from a black-coated pig indigenous to the Iberian Peninsula and a descendant of

Paella

★ **Cooking Classes**

Annie B's Spanish Kitchen (p160), Vejer de la Frontera

Mimo San Sebastián (p226), San Sebastián

Cooking Point (p50), Madrid

Barcelona Cooking (p94), Barcelona

the wild boar. Gastronomically, its star appeal is its ability to infiltrate fat into the muscle tissue, thus producing an especially well-marbled meat. If the pig gains at least 50% of its body weight during the acorn-eating season, it can be classified as *jamón ibérico de bellota*, the most sought-after designation for *jamón*.

The best-quality *jamón* is most commonly eaten as a starter or a *ración* (large tapa) – on menus it's usually called a *tabla de jamón ibérico* (or *ibérico de bellota*). Cutting it is an art form; it should be sliced so wafer-thin as to be almost transparent. Spaniards almost always eat it with bread.

Tapas

In the Basque Country, and many bars in Madrid, Barcelona and elsewhere, ordering tapas couldn't be easier. With tapas varieties lined up along the bar, you either take a small plate and help yourself or point to the morsel you want. If you do this, it's customary to keep track of what you eat (by holding on to the toothpicks, for example) and then tell the bar staff how many you've had when it's time to pay. Otherwise, many places have a list of tapas, either on a menu or posted up behind the bar. If you can't choose, ask for '*la especialidad de la casa*' (the house speciality) and it's hard to go wrong.

Another way of eating tapas is to order *raciones* (literally 'rations'; large tapas servings) or *media raciones* (half-rations; smaller tapas servings). Remember, however, that after a couple of *raciones* you're likely to be full. In some bars, especially in Granada, you'll also get a small (free) tapa when you buy a drink.

Spanish Wines

La Rioja, in the north, is Spain's best-known wine-producing region. The principal grape of Rioja is the tempranillo, widely believed to be a mutant form of the pinot noir. Its wine is smooth and fruity, seldom as dry as its French counterpart. Look for the 'DOC Rioja' classification on the label and you'll find a good wine.

Not far behind are the wine-producing regions of Ribera del Duero in Castilla y León, Navarra and the Somontano wines of Aragón. For white wines, the Ribeiro wines of Galicia are well regarded. Also from the area is one of Spain's most charming whites – *albariño*.

The Penedès region in Catalonia produces whites and sparkling wine such as *cava*, the traditional champagne-like toasting drink of choice for Spaniards at Christmas.

The best wines are often marked with the designation '*crianza*' (aged for one year in oak barrels), '*reserva*' (aged for two years, at least one of which is in oak barrels) and '*gran reserva*' (two years in oak and three in the bottle).

Eating Out

If we could distill the essence of how to make food a highlight of your trip into a few simple rules, they would be these: always ask for the local speciality; never be shy about looking around to see what others have ordered before choosing; always ask the waiter for their recommendations; and, wherever possible, make your meal a centrepiece of your day.

Menú del Día

One great way to cap prices at lunchtime on weekdays is to order the *menú del día*, a full three-course set menu, water, bread and wine. These meals are priced from around €10, although €12 and up is increasingly the norm. You'll be given a menu with a choice of five or six starters, the same number of mains and a handful of desserts – you choose one from each category; it's possible to order two starters, but not two mains.

Street in Barri Gòtic (p82), Barcelona

THEHAGUE/GETTY IMAGES©

Survival Guide

Directory A–Z

Accessible Travel

Spain is not overly accommodating for travellers with disabilities, but things are slowly changing. For example, disabled access to some museums, official buildings and hotels represents a change in local thinking. In major cities, more is slowly being done to facilitate disabled access to public transport and taxis; in some cities, wheelchair-adapted taxis are called 'Eurotaxis'. Newly constructed hotels in most areas of Spain are required to have wheelchair-adapted rooms. With older places, you need to be a little wary of hotels that advertise themselves as being disabled-friendly, as this can mean as little as wide doors to rooms and bathrooms, or other token efforts.

Some tourist offices – notably those in Madrid and Barcelona – offer guided tours of the city for travellers with disabilities.

Inout Hostel (☏93 280 09 85; www.inouthostel.com; Major del Rectoret 2; dm €22-33; @🅟❄🅿; 🇷FGC Baixador de Vallvidrera) 🐾 Worthy of a special mention is Barcelona's Inout Hostel, which is completely accessible

for those with disabilities, and nearly all the staff who work there have disabilities of one kind or another. The facilities and service are first class.

Museo Tiflológico (Museum for the Blind; ☏91 589 42 19; http://museo.once.es; Calle de la Coruña 18; ⏱10am-3pm & 4-7pm Tue-Fri, 10am-2pm Sat, closed 2nd part of Aug; 🇲Estrecho) **FREE** This Madrid attraction is specifically for people who are visually impaired. Run by the Organización Nacional de Ciegos Españoles (National Organisation for the Blind, ONCE), its exhibits (all of which may be touched) include paintings, sculptures and tapestries, as well as more than 40 scale models of world monuments, including Madrid's Palacio Real and Cibeles fountain, as well as La Alhambra in Granada and the aqueduct in Segovia. It also provides leaflets in Braille and audio guides to the museum.

Organisations

Accessible Spain Travel (www. accessiblespaintravel.com; Pujades 152, 3-1, Barcelona) Organises accessible tours, transport and accommodation throughout Spain for travellers with limited mobility.

Barcelona Turisme Accesible (www.barcelona-access.cat) Website devoted to making Barcelona accessible for visitors with a disability. Offers information on barrier-free hotels, museums and beaches adapted to disabled visitors, wheelchair-accessible and sign language tours, and more.

COCEMFE (www.cocemfe.es) Spanish NGO offering a wide range of services and support

to people with physical disabilities, from accessible tourism to education, training, employment and legal assistance.

Madrid Accesible (Accessible Madrid; www.esmadrid.com/madrid-accesible) Your first stop for information on accessibility for travellers in Madrid should be this tourism-focused website, where you can download a PDF of the excellent *Guía Madrid Accesible* in English or Spanish. It has an exhaustive list of the city's attractions and transport and a detailed assessment of their accessibility, as well as a list of accessible restaurants. Most tourist offices in Madrid have a *mapa turístico accesible* in Spanish, English and French.

ONCE (Organización Nacional de Ciegos Españoles; Map p299; ☏91 577 37 56, 91 532 50 00; www.once.es; Calle de Prim 3; 🇲Chueca, Colón) The Spanish association for those who are blind. You may be able to get hold of guides in Braille to Madrid, although they're not published every year.

Society for Accessible Travel & Hospitality (www.sath.org) A good resource, which gives advice on how to travel with a wheelchair, kidney disease, sight impairment or deafness.

Accommodation

Spain's accommodation is generally of a high standard, and prices are reasonable, especially outside big cities.

Hotels Everything from boutique to family-run with a wide range of rates.

Hostales Small, simpler yet comfortable hotel-style places, often with private bathrooms.

Casas Rurales Rural homes generally with rustic, simple rooms that can be reserved individually or as a block.

Paradors These state-run hotels often inhabit stunning historic buildings and can be surprisingly well priced, especially off-season.

Hostels Quality varies, but these budget spots are great places to meet other travellers.

Campsites Located across the country, amid lovely natural settings.

Seasons

What constitutes low or high season depends on where and when you're looking. Most of the year is high season in Barcelona and Madrid, especially during trade fairs that you're unlikely to know about. August can be dead in the cities, but high season along the coast. Winter is peak season in the ski resorts of the Pyrenees and low season along the coast

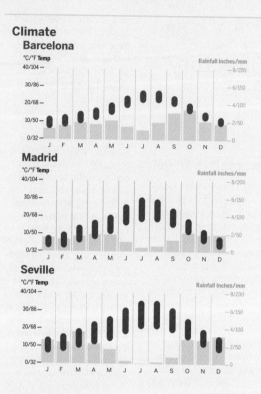

Book Your Stay Online

For more accommodation reviews by Lonely Planet authors, check out http://hotels.lonelyplanet.com/Spain. You'll find independent reviews, as well as recommendations on the best places to stay. Best of all, you can book online.

(indeed, many coastal towns largely shut down between November and Easter).

Weekends are high season for boutique hotels and *casas rurales*, but low season for business hotels (which often offer generous specials) in Madrid and Barcelona.

Reservations

Reserving a room is always recommended in the high season. Finding a place to stay along the coast in July and August without booking ahead can be difficult and many places require a minimum stay of at least two nights during high season.

Always check out hotel websites for discounts.

Although there's usually no need to book ahead for a room in the low or shoulder seasons (Barcelona is an exception), booking ahead is usually a good idea. Most places will ask for a credit-card number or will hold the room for you until 6pm unless you have provided credit card details as security or you have let them know that you'll be arriving later.

Online booking services like Airbnb (www.airbnb.com) offer a range of accommodation types.

Customs Regulations

Duty-free allowances for travellers entering Spain from outside the EU include 2L of wine (or 1L of wine and 1L of spirits), and 200 cigarettes, 50 cigars or 250g of tobacco.

There are no restrictions on the import of duty-paid items into Spain from other EU countries for personal use. You *can* buy VAT-free articles at airport shops when travelling between EU countries.

Electricity

Use two-pin continental plugs typical throughout mainland Europe.

220V/50Hz

230V/50Hz

Food

The following price ranges, used throughout this guide, refer to a standard main dish:

€ less than €12
€€ €12–20
€€€ more than €20

LGBTQ+ Travellers

Spain has become perhaps the most gay-friendly country in southern Europe. Homosexuality is legal, and same-sex marriages were legalised in 2005 – the latter move was extremely popular but met with opposition from the country's powerful Catholic Church.

Lesbians and gay men generally keep a fairly low profile in rural areas, but are quite open in the cities.

Madrid, Barcelona, Sitges, Torremolinos and Ibiza have particularly lively scenes. Sitges is a major destination on the international gay-party circuit; gay people take a leading role in the wild **Carnaval** (www.visitsitges.com; ☉Feb/Mar) there. There are also gay parades, marches and events in several cities on and around the last Saturday in June, including Madrid's **Día del Orgullo LGTBI** (http://orgullolgtb.org; ☉Jun) and Seville's **Orgullo de Andalucía** (www.orgullo lgtbiandalucia.es).

Madrid also hosts the annual **Les Gai Cine Mad** (☎91 593 05 40; www.lesgai cinemad.com; ☉late Oct/early Nov) festival, a celebration of lesbian, gay and transsexual films.

Useful Resources

In addition to the following resources, Barcelona's tourist board publishes *Barcelona: The Official Gay and Lesbian Tourist Guide* biannually, while Madrid's tourist office has useful information on its website (www.esmadrid.com).

Chueca (www.chueca.com) Useful gay portal with extensive links.

GayBarcelona (www.gaybarce lona.com) News and views and an extensive listings section covering bars, saunas, shops and more in Barcelona and Sitges.

Gay Iberia (www.gayiberia. com) Gay guides to Barcelona, Madrid, Sitges and 19 other Spanish cities.

Gay Madrid 4 U (www.gaymadrid4u.com) A good overview of Madrid's gay bars and nightclubs.

Patroc (www.patroc.com) Gay guides to Barcelona, Bilbao, Madrid, Sevilla, Sitges, Torremolinos and Valencia.

NightTours.com (www.nighttours.com) A reasonably good guide to gay nightlife and other attractions in Madrid, Barcelona and 18 other Spanish locations.

Shangay (www.shangay.com) For news, upcoming events, reviews and contacts. It also publishes *Shanguide*, a Madrid-centric biweekly magazine jammed with listings (including saunas and hard-core clubs) and contact ads. Its companion publication *Shangay Express* is better for articles with a handful of listings and ads. They're available in gay bookshops, and gay and gay-friendly bars.

Health

Spain has an excellent healthcare system.

Availability & Cost of Health Care

If you need an ambulance, call 061 or the general emergency number 112. For emergency treatment, go straight to the *urgencias* (casualty/ER) section of the nearest hospital.

Farmacias offer valuable advice and sell over-the-counter medication. In Spain, a system of *farmacias de guardia* (duty pharmacies) operates so that each district has one open all the time. When a pharmacy is closed, it posts the name of the nearest open one on the door.

Medical costs are lower in Spain than in many other European countries, but can still mount quickly if you are uninsured. Costs if you attend casualty/ER range from nothing (in some regions) to around €80.

Tap Water

Tap water is generally safe to drink in Spain. If you are ever in doubt, ask, *¿Es potable el agua (del grifo)?* (Is the (tap) water drinkable?). Do not drink water from rivers or lakes, as it may contain bacteria or viruses that can cause diarrhoea or vomiting.

Insurance

A travel-insurance policy to cover theft, loss, medical problems and cancellation or delays to your travel arrangements is a good idea. Paying for your ticket with a credit card can often provide limited travel-accident insurance.

Worldwide travel insurance is available at www.lonelyplanet.com/travel-insurance. You can buy, extend and claim online anytime – even if you're already on the road.

Internet Access

Wi-fi is almost universally available at hotels, as well as in some cafes, restaurants and airports; usually (but not always) it's free. Connection speed often varies from room to room in hotels (and coverage is sometimes restricted to the hotel lobby), so if you need a good connection, always ask when you check in or make your reservation. Some tourist offices can provide a list of wi-fi hot spots in their area.

A convenient and more universally reliable alternative to wi-fi – especially if you're travelling outside the cities – is to purchase a Spanish SIM card for your phone. Many local prepaid plans include generous data allowances at surprisingly low rates.

Money

The most convenient way to bring your money is in the form of a debit or credit card, with some extra cash in case of an emergency.

Many credit and debit cards can be used for withdrawing money from *cajeros automáticos* (ATMs) that display the relevant symbols such as Visa, MasterCard, Cirrus etc. Some Spanish banks such as Unicaja and Liberbank may offer ATM cash withdrawals free of charge, while others charge rather exorbitant fees (€5 to €7 per transaction); it pays to shop around. Note that your home bank may also impose a fee over and above whatever the Spanish bank charges.

Cash

Most banks will exchange major foreign currencies and offer better rates than exchange offices at the airport. Ask about commissions – these can vary from bank to bank – and take your passport.

Credit & Debit Cards

These can be used to pay for most purchases. You'll often be asked to show your passport or some other form of identification. Among the most widely accepted are Visa, Master-Card, American Express (Amex), Cirrus, Maestro, Plus and JCB. Diners Club is less widely accepted. If your card is lost, stolen or swallowed by an ATM, you can call the card issuer's free-call telephone number to have an immediate stop put on its use.

Moneychangers

You can exchange both cash and travellers cheques at *cambio* (exchange) offices. Generally they offer longer opening hours and quicker service than banks, but worse exchange rates and higher commissions.

Practicalities

Newspapers The three main newspapers are the centre-left *El País* (www.elpais.com), centre-right *El Mundo* (www.elmundo.es) and right-wing *ABC* (www.abc.es); the widely available *International New York Times* includes an eight-page supplement of articles from *El País* translated into English, or check out www.elpais.com/elpais/inenglish.html.

Radio Radio Nacional de España (RNE) has Radio 1, with general interest and current-affairs programs; Radio 5, with sport and entertainment; and Radio 3 (Radio d'Espop). Stations covering current affairs include the left-leaning Cadena Ser, or the right-wing COPE. The most popular commercial pop and rock stations are 40 Principales, Kiss FM, Cadena 100 and Onda Cero.

Smoking Banned in all enclosed public spaces.

TV Spain has the state-run Televisión Española (TVE1 and La 2) as well as independent commercial stations (Antena 3, Tele 5, Cuatro and La Sexta). Regional governments run local stations, such as Madrid's Telemadrid, Catalonia's TV-3 and Canal 33 (both in Catalan), Galicia's TVG, the Basque Country's ETB-1 and ETB-2, Valencia's Canal 9 and Andalucía's Canal Sur.

Weights & Measures The metric system is used.

Taxes & Refunds

- In Spain, value-added tax (VAT) is known as IVA (ee-ba; *impuesto sobre el valor añadido*).

- Hotel rooms and restaurant meals attract an additional 10% (usually included in the quoted price but always ask); most other items have 21% added.

- Visitors are entitled to a refund of the 21% IVA on purchases costing more than €90.15 from any shop, if they are taking them out of the EU within three months. As of 2019, Spain has instituted a new electronic tax refund system known as DIVA. Ask the shop for an official DIVA refund form showing the price and IVA paid for each item, and identifying the vendor and purchaser. Upon arrival at your departure airport, get your refund forms electronically stamped by scanning them at a DIVA kiosk, or have them manually stamped by a customs agent. You can then present the stamped forms at tax free kiosks in the boarding area to get your refund.

Tipping

Tipping is almost always optional.

Bars It's rare to leave a tip in bars (even when the

bartender gives you your change on a small dish).

Restaurants Many Spaniards leave small change, others up to 5%, which is considered generous.

Taxis Optional, but locals sometimes round up to the nearest euro.

Opening Hours

Banks 8.30am to 2pm Monday to Friday; some also open 4pm to 7pm Thursday and 9am to 1pm Saturday

Central post offices 8.30am to 9.30pm Monday to Friday, 8.30am to 2pm Saturday; most other branches 8.30am to 2.30pm Monday to Friday, 9.30am to 1pm Saturday

Nightclubs Midnight or 1am to 5am or 6am Friday and Saturday

Restaurants Lunch 1pm to 4pm; dinner 8.30pm to 11pm or midnight

Shops 10am to 2pm and 4.30pm to 7.30pm or 5pm to 8pm Monday to Friday or Saturday; big supermarkets and department stores generally open 10am to 10pm Monday to Saturday

Public Holidays

The two main periods when Spaniards go on holiday are Semana Santa (the week leading up to Easter Sunday) and July and August. At these times accommo-

dation in resorts can be scarce and transport heavily booked, but other places are often half-empty.

There are at least 14 official holidays a year – some observed nationwide, some locally. When a holiday falls close to a weekend, Spaniards like to make a *puente* (bridge), meaning they take the intervening day off too. Occasionally when two holidays fall within the same week, they make an *acueducto* (aqueduct)! Here are the national holidays:

Año Nuevo (New Year's Day) 1 January

Viernes Santo (Good Friday) March/April

Fiesta del Trabajo (Labour Day) 1 May

La Asunción (Feast of the Assumption) 15 August

Fiesta Nacional de España (National Day) 12 October

La Inmaculada Concepción (Feast of the Immaculate Conception) 8 December

Navidad (Christmas) 25 December

Regional governments set five holidays and local councils two more. Common dates include the following:

Epifanía (Epiphany) or **Día de los Reyes Magos** (Three Kings' Day) 6 January

Jueves Santo (Maundy Thursday) March/April; not observed in Catalonia and Valencia.

Corpus Christi June; the Thursday after the eighth Sunday after Easter Sunday.

Día de Santiago Apóstol (Feast of St James the Apostle) 25 July

Día de Todos los Santos (All Saints' Day) 1 November

Día de la Constitución (Constitution Day) 6 December

Safe Travel

Most visitors to Spain never feel remotely threatened, but enough have unpleasant experiences to warrant some care. The main thing to be wary of is petty theft.

o In cities, especially Madrid and Barcelona, stick to areas with plenty of people around and avoid deserted streets.

o Keep valuables concealed or locked away in your hotel room.

o Try not to look like a tourist (eg don't consult maps in crowded tourist areas).

o Be wary of pickpockets in areas heavily frequented by tourists, such as the Madrid metro or Seville's crowded streets and squares during Semana Santa parades.

Scams

There must be 50 ways to lose your wallet. As a rule, talented petty thieves work in groups and capitalise on distraction. Tricks usually involve a team of two or more (sometimes one of them an attractive woman to distract male victims). While one attracts your attention, the other empties your pockets. More imaginative strikes include someone dropping a milk mixture onto the victim from a balcony. Immediately a concerned citizen comes up to help you brush off what you assume to be pigeon poo, and thus suitably occupied, you don't notice the contents of your pockets slipping away.

Beware: not all thieves look like thieves. Watch out for an old classic: the women offering flowers for good luck. We don't know how they do it, but if you get too involved in a friendly chat, your pockets sometimes wind up empty.

On some highways, especially the AP7 from the French border to Barcelona, bands of thieves occasionally operate. Beware of men trying to distract you in rest areas, and don't stop along the highway if people driving alongside indicate you have a problem with the car. While one inspects the rear of the car with you, his pals will empty your vehicle. Another scam has them puncturing tyres of cars stopped in rest areas, then following and 'helping' the victim when they stop to change the wheel. Hire cars with the company's stickers and those with foreign plates are especially targeted. When you do call in at highway rest stops, try to park close to the buildings and leave nothing of value in view. If you do stop to change a tyre and find yourself getting unsolicited aid, make sure doors are all locked and don't allow yourself to be distracted.

Even parking your car can be fraught. In some towns, fairly dodgy self-appointed parking attendants operate

Government Travel Advice

The following government websites offer travel advisory services and information for travellers:

o **Australian Department of Foreign Affairs and Trade** (www.smartraveller.gov.au)

o **Global Affairs Canada** (www.travel.gc.ca)

o **Japanese Ministry of Foreign Affairs** (www.anzen.mofa.go.jp)

o **New Zealand Ministry of Foreign Affairs and Trade** (www.safetravel.govt.nz)

o **UK Foreign & Commonwealth Office** (www.gov.uk/foreign-travel-advice)

o **US Department of State** (www.travel.state.gov)

in central areas where you may want to park. They will direct you frantically to a spot. If possible, ignore them and find your own. If unavoidable, you may well want to pay them some token not to scratch or otherwise damage your vehicle after you've walked away. You definitely don't want to leave anything visible in the car (or open the boot – trunk – if you intend to leave luggage or anything else in it) under these circumstances.

Theft

Theft is mostly a risk in tourist resorts, big cities and when you first arrive in a new destination and may be off your guard. You are at your most vulnerable when dragging around luggage to or from your hotel. Barcelona, Madrid and Seville have the worst reputations for theft and, on very rare occasions, muggings.

Anything left lying on the beach can disappear in a flash when your back is turned. At night, avoid dingy, empty city alleys and backstreets, or anywhere that just doesn't feel 100% safe.

Report thefts to the national police – visit www.policia.es for a full list of *comisarías* (police stations) around the country; click 'Comisaría Virtual', then 'Dependencias'. You are unlikely to recover your goods, but you need to make a formal *denuncia* for insurance purposes. To avoid endless queues at the *comisaría*, you can make the report by phone (902 102 112) in various languages or online at www.policia.es (click on 'Denuncias por internet'); instructions are in Spanish, English, French and German. The following day you go to the station of your choice to pick up and sign the report, without queuing.

Telephone

Mobile Phones

Prepaid Spanish SIM cards can be used in any unlocked European or Australian phone, and in most newer phones brought from elsewhere (Spain uses GSM 900/1800, which is compatible with the rest of Europe and Australia but not with the North American or Japanese systems, so you'll need a tri- or quad-band phone if travelling from these latter regions).

The leading Spanish mobile-phone companies (MoviStar, Orange, Vodafone and Yoigo) all offer *prepagado* (prepaid) accounts for mobiles. A SIM card costs from €10, and promotional packages including start-up amounts of calls, texts and data are widely available. You can top up your account as needed at phone company shops or outlets such as *estancos* (tobacconists) and newspaper kiosks. Smaller providers such as Pepephone (www.pepephone.com) are another option.

If you're from the EU, there is EU-wide roaming so that call and data plans for mobile phones from any EU country should be valid in Spain without any extra roaming charges. If you're from elsewhere and want to use your home country phone plan in Spain, check with your mobile provider

for information on roaming charges. Wi-fi is common.

Useful Numbers

There are no area codes in Spain.

Spain's country code	☎34
International access code	☎00
International directory inquiries	☎11825
National directory inquiries	☎11818
Emergencies	☎112

Time

Spain is in the same zone as most of Western Europe (GMT/UTC plus one hour during winter and GMT/UTC plus two hours during the daylight-saving period).

Daylight saving runs from the last Sunday in March to the last Sunday in October.

Toilets

Public toilets are rare to nonexistent in Spain, and it's not really the done thing to go into a bar or cafe solely to use the toilet; ordering a quick coffee is a small price to pay for relieving the problem. Otherwise you can usually get away with it in larger, crowded places, where they can't really keep track of who's coming and going. Another option in some larger cities is to visit

the department stores of El Corte Inglés.

Tourist Information

All cities and many smaller towns have an *oficina de turismo* or *oficina de información turística*. In the country's provincial capitals you will sometimes find more than one tourist office – one specialising in information on the city alone, the other carrying mostly provincial or regional information. National and natural parks also often have their own visitor centres offering useful information.

Turespaña (www.spain.info) is the country's national tourism body, and it operates branches around the world. Check the website for office locations.

Visas

Spain is one of 26 member countries of the Schengen Convention, under which 22 EU countries (all but Bulgaria, Cyprus, Ireland and Romania) plus Iceland, Norway, Liechtenstein and Switzerland have abolished checks at common borders.

The visa situation for entering Spain is as follows:

Citizens or residents of EU & Schengen countries No visa required.

Citizens or residents of Australia, Canada, Israel, Japan, New Zealand & the USA No visa required for tourist visits of up to 90 days out of every 180 days.

Other countries Check with a Spanish embassy or consulate.

To work or study in Spain A special visa may be required – contact a Spanish embassy or consulate before travel.

Transport

Getting There & Away

Spain is one of Europe's top holiday destinations and is well linked to other European countries by air, rail and road. Regular car ferries and hydrofoils run to and from Morocco, and there are ferry links to the UK, Italy, the Canary Islands and Algeria.

Flights, cars and tours can be booked online at www.lonelyplanet.com/bookings.

Entering Spain

Immigration and customs checks (which usually only take place if you're arriving from outside the EU) normally involve a minimum of fuss, although there are exceptions.

Your vehicle could be searched on arrival from Andorra. The tiny principality of Andorra is not in the European Union (EU), so border controls remain in place. Spanish customs look out for contraband duty-free products destined for illegal resale in Spain. Similarly, travellers arriving from Morocco or the Spanish North African enclaves of Ceuta and Melilla may be searched for controlled substances. Expect long delays at these borders, especially in summer.

Air

There are direct flights to Spain from most European countries, as well as from North America, South America, Africa, the Middle East and Asia. Those coming from Australasia will usually have to make at least one change of flight.

High season for flights in Spain generally means Christmas, New Year, Easter and roughly June to September. The applicability of seasonal fares varies depending on the specific destination. You may find reasonably priced flights to Madrid from elsewhere in Europe in August, for example, because it is stinking hot and everyone else has fled to the mountains or the sea. As a general rule, November to March (aside from Christmas and New Year) is when airfares to Spain are likely to be at their lowest, and the intervening months can be considered shoulder periods.

Departure Tax

Departure tax is included in the price of a ticket.

Airports & Airlines

All of Spain's airports share the user-friendly website and flight information telephone number of **Aena** (☑91 321 10 00; www.aena.es), the national airports authority. To find more information on each airport, choose 'English' and click 'Airports'. Each airport's page has practical information, including parking and public transport, and a full list of (and links to) airlines using that airport. It also has current flight information.

Spain's national carrier is **Iberia** (www.iberia.com), with an extensive international network of flights and a good safety record.

Madrid's **Adolfo Suárez Madrid-Barajas Airport** (Map p307; ☑902 404704; www.aena.es; Ⓜ Aeropuerto T1, T2 & T3, Aeropuerto T4) was Spain's busiest (and Europe's sixth-busiest) airport in 2019, followed closely by Barcelona's **El Prat Airport** (☑91 321 10 00; www.aena.es; 🔊) – second-busiest in Spain, seventh in Europe. Other major airports include Málaga, Palma de Mallorca, Alicante, Girona, Valencia, Seville, Vigo and Bilbao.

Land

Spain shares land borders with France, Portugal and Andorra.

Apart from shorter cross-border services, **Eurolines** (www.eurolines.com) is the main operator of international bus services to Spain from most of Western Europe and Morocco.

In addition to the rail services connecting Spain with France and Portugal, there are direct trains between Zürich and Barcelona (via Bern, Geneva, Perpignan and Girona), and between Milan and Barcelona (via Turin, Perpignan and Girona). For these and other services, visit the 'International' section of the website of **Renfe** (www.renfe.com), the Spanish national railway company.

Andorra

Regular buses (including winter ski buses) connect Andorra with Barcelona and other destinations in Spain (including Madrid) and France. **Directbus** (www.andorradirectbus.es) offers the most frequent service between Andorra and Barcelona's Estació d'Autobusos de Sants (€30.50, three hours) or El Prat Airport (€34, 3½ to 3¾ hours).

France

Bus

FlixBus/Eurolines (www.flixbus.com) heads to Spain from Paris and more than 20 other French cities and towns. It connects with Madrid (from €45, 15½ to 17¾ hours), Barcelona (from €35, 13¾ to 15¾ hours) and many other destinations. There's at least one departure per day for main destinations.

Train

The principal rail crossings into Spain pierce the Franco-Spanish frontier along the Mediterranean coast and via the Basque Country. Another minor rail route runs inland across the Pyrenees from Latour-de-Carol to Barcelona.

In addition to the options listed below, two or three TGVs (high-speed trains) leave from Paris-Montparnasse for Irún, where you change to a normal train for the Basque Country and on towards Madrid. Up to three TGVs also put you on track to Barcelona (leaving from Paris Gare de Lyon), with a change of train at Montpellier or Narbonne. For more information on French rail services, check out the **OuiSNCF** (https://en.oui.sncf/en) website.

There are plans for a high-speed rail link between Madrid and Paris. In the meantime, two direct high-speed trains (advance-purchase promo fares from €34, standard second-class fares from €89, 6¾ hours) run daily via Valence, Nîmes, Montpellier, Beziers, Narbonne, Perpignan, Figueres and Girona.

Portugal

Bus

Avanza (☏91 272 28 32; www.avanzabus.com) runs daily buses between Lisbon and Madrid (€42 to €47, seven hours, two to three daily).

Other bus services run north via Porto to Tui, Santiago de Compostela and A Coruña in Galicia, while local buses cross the border from towns such as Huelva in Andalucía, Badajoz in Extremadura and Ourense in Galicia.

Climate Change & Travel

Every form of transport that relies on carbon-based fuel generates CO_2, the main cause of human-induced climate change. Modern travel is dependent on aeroplanes, which might use less fuel per kilometre per person than most cars but travel much greater distances. The altitude at which aircraft emit gases (including CO_2) and particles also contributes to their climate-change impact. Many websites offer 'carbon calculators' that allow people to estimate the carbon emissions generated by their journey and, for those who wish to do so, to offset the impact of the greenhouse gases emitted with contributions to portfolios of climate-friendly initiatives throughout the world. Lonely Planet offsets the carbon footprint of all staff and author travel.

Train

From Portugal, the main line runs from Lisbon across Extremadura to Madrid.
Lisbon to Irún-Hendaye (chair/sleeper class from €43/77, 13¼ hours, one daily)
Lisbon to Madrid (chair/sleeper class from €38/69, 10 hours, one daily)
Porto to Vigo (€15, 2½ hours, two daily)

Sea

A useful website for comparing routes and finding links to the relevant ferry companies is www.ferrylines.com.

Algeria

Algérie Ferries (www.algerie ferries.dz) Operates year-round services from Alicante to Oran (one to three weekly) as well as summer services from Alicante to Algiers and Barcelona to Oran.
Trasmediterránea (☑902 454 645; www.trasmediterranea.es) Runs year-round ferries from Almería to the Algerian ports of Ghazaouet and Oran (at least once weekly).
Baleària (☑865 608 423; www.balearia.com) Operates a ferry service at least once weekly from Valencia to Mostaganem.

Italy

Most Italian routes are operated by **Grimaldi Lines** (www.grimaldi-lines.com) or **Grandi Navi Veloci** (www.gnv.it).

Civitavecchia (near Rome) to Barcelona 20 hours, six weekly.
Genoa to Barcelona 19 hours, two to three weekly.

Rail Passes

Interrail Passes

Interrail (www.interrailnet.eu) passes are available to people who have lived in Europe for six months or more. They can be bought at most major stations, student travel outlets and online.

Youth passes are for people aged 12 to 25 and adult passes are for those 26 and over. Children aged 11 and under travel for free if travelling on a family pass.
Global Pass Encompasses 30 countries and comes in seven versions, ranging from five days' travel in 15 days to a full month's travel. Check out the website for details.
One-Country Pass Can be used for three, four, six or eight days within one month in Spain. For the eight-day pass you pay €339/255/192 for adult 1st/2nd class/youth 2nd class.

Eurail Passes

Eurail (www.eurail.com) passes are for those who've lived in Europe for less than six months. They are supposed to be bought outside Europe, either online or from leading travel agencies.

Be sure you will be covering a lot of ground to make your Eurail pass worthwhile. To be certain, check the **Renfe** (www.renfe.com) website for sample prices in euros.

For most of the following passes, children aged between four and 11 pay half-price for the 1st-class passes, while those aged under 26 can get a cheaper 2nd-class pass. The Eurail website has a full list of prices, including special family rates and other discounts.
Eurail Global Passes Good for travel in 28 European countries; forget it if you intend to travel mainly in Spain. There are nine different passes, from five days within one month to three months' continuous travel.
Eurail Select Pass Provides between five and 10 days of unlimited travel within a two-month period in two to four bordering countries (eg Spain, France, Italy and Switzerland).
Spain Pass With the one-country Spain Pass, you can choose from three to eight days' train travel in a one-month period for any of these passes. The eight-day Spain Pass costs €325/261/213 for adult 1st class/adult 2nd class/youth 2nd class.

Porto Torres (Sardinia) to Barcelona 12 hours, at least two weekly.

Savona (near Genoa) to Barcelona 20 hours, weekly in summer.

Morocco

Ferries run to Morocco from mainland Spain. Most services are run by the Spanish national ferry company, **Trasmediterránea** (📞902 454 645; www.trasmediterranea.es). You can take vehicles on most routes. Other companies that connect Spain with Morocco include:

Baleària (www.balearia.com)

FRS Iberia (www.frs.es)

Grandi Navi Veloci (www.gnv.it)

Grimaldi Lines (www.grimaldi-lines.com)

Naviera Armas (www.navieraarmas.com)

UK & Ireland

Brittany Ferries (📞in the UK 0330 159 7000; www.brittany-ferries.co.uk) runs the following services:

Plymouth to Santander 19 hours, weekly. Mid-March to October only.

Portsmouth to Bilbao 24 to 32 hours, two weekly.

Portsmouth to Santander 24 to 32 hours, three weekly.

Rosslare to Bilbao 27 to 31½ hours, two weekly.

Getting Around

Spain's network of train and bus services is one of the best in Europe and there aren't many places that can't be reached using one or the other. The tentacles of Spain's high-speed train network are expanding rapidly, while domestic air services are plentiful over longer distances and on routes that are more complicated by land.

Air

Spain has an extensive network of internal flights. These are operated by both Spanish airlines and a handful of low-cost international airlines. Carriers include:

Air Europa (www.aireuropa.com) Madrid to A Coruña, Alicante, Barcelona, Bilbao, Málaga, Oviedo, Seville, Vigo, the Canaries and the Balearics, as well as other routes between Spanish cities.

Iberia (www.iberia.com) Spain's national airline, together with its subsidiaries Iberia Express and Iberia Regional-Air Nostrum, has an extensive domestic network.

Ryanair (www.ryanair.com) Some domestic Spanish routes.

Volotea (www.volotea.com) Budget airline that flies domestically and internationally. Domestic routes take in Alicante, Bilbao, Málaga, Murcia, Oviedo, Santander, Seville, Tenerife, Valencia, Zaragoza and the Balearics (but not Madrid or Barcelona).

Vueling (www.vueling.com) Spanish low-cost company with lots of domestic flights within Spain, especially from Barcelona.

Boat

Ferries and hydrofoils link the mainland (La Península) – or more specifically, Barcelona, Valencia, Denia and Gandia – with Palma de Mallorca, Menorca, Ibiza and/or Formentera. There are also services from various Andalucian ports to Gran Canaria and Tenerife in the Canary Islands, and to Spain's North African enclaves of Ceuta and Melilla.

Baleària (www.balearia.com) Runs multiple routes between the mainland and the Balearic Islands. On overnight services, you can opt for seating or sleeping accommodation in a cabin.

Trasmediterránea (📞902 454 645; www.trasmediterranea.es) The main national ferry company runs a combination of slower car ferries and modern, high-speed, passenger-only fast ferries and hydrofoils.

Bus

There are few places in Spain where buses don't go. Numerous companies provide bus links, from local routes between villages to fast intercity connections. It is often cheaper to travel by bus than by train, particularly on long-haul runs, but also less comfortable.

Local services can get you just about anywhere, but most buses connecting villages and provincial towns are not geared to tourist needs. Frequent weekday services reduce to a trickle, if they operate at all, on Saturday and Sunday. Often just one bus runs daily between smaller places during the week, and none operate on Sunday. It's usually unnecessary to make reservations; just arrive early enough to get a seat.

On many regular runs – say, from Madrid to Toledo – the ticket you buy is for the next bus due to leave and *cannot* be used on a later bus. Advance purchase in such cases is generally not possible. For longer trips (such as Madrid to Seville or to the coast), and certainly in peak holiday season, you can (and should) buy your ticket in advance. On some routes you have the choice between express and stopping-all-stations services.

In most larger towns and cities, buses leave from a single *estación de autobuses* (bus station). In smaller places, buses tend to operate from a set street or plaza, often unmarked. Locals will know where to go and where to buy tickets.

Bus travel within Spain is not overly costly, but there's a vast range of prices. The trip from Madrid to Barcelona starts from around €22 one way but can cost more than double that. Tickets from Barcelona to Seville – one of Spain's longest domestic journeys (15 to 17 hours) – can cost as much as €91 one way.

People under 26 should inquire about discounts on long-distance trips.

Among the hundreds of bus companies operating in Spain, the following have the largest range of services:

ALSA (☑902 422242; www.alsa.es) The biggest player, this company has routes all over the country in association with various other companies. Check online for discounts for advance ticket purchases.

Avanza (☑91 272 28 32; www.avanzabus.com) Operates buses from Madrid to Extremadura, western Castilla y León and Valencia via eastern Castilla-La Mancha (eg Cuenca), often in association with other companies.

Socibus (☑902 229292; www.socibus.es) Operates services between Madrid, western Andalucía and the Basque Country.

Car & Motorcycle

Automobile Association

The **Real Automóvil Club de España** (RACE; ☑902 404545; www.race.es) is the national automobile club. They may well come to assist you in case of breakdown, but in any event you should obtain an emergency telephone number for Spain from your own insurer or car-hire company.

Driving Licences

All EU member states' driving licences are fully recognised throughout Europe. Those with a non-EU licence are technically required to obtain a 12-month International Driving Permit (IDP) to accompany their national licence, which your national automobile association can issue. In practice, however, car-hire companies and police rarely ask for one. If you have held residency in Spain for one year or more, you should apply for a Spanish driving licence or check whether your home licence entitles you to a Spanish licence under reciprocal agreements between countries.

Fuel

○ *Gasolina* (petrol) is pricey in Spain, but generally slightly cheaper than in its major European neighbours (including France, Germany, Italy and the UK); *gasóleo* is diesel fuel.

○ Petrol is about 10% cheaper in Gibraltar than in Spain and 15% cheaper in Andorra.

○ You can pay with major credit cards at most service stations.

Hire

To rent a car in Spain, you have to have a licence, be aged 21 or over and, for the major companies at least, have a credit card; note that some car-hire companies don't accept debit cards. Smaller firms in areas where car hire is particularly common sometimes waive this last requirement. Those with a non-EU licence should officially also carry an IDP, though you will find that national licences from countries such as Australia, Canada, New Zealand and the US are usually accepted without question.

Rates vary by season. In winter you can find deals as low as €5 per day, while summer rates are significantly higher. You'll almost always save money by booking ahead. With some of the low-cost companies, beware of 'extras' that aren't quoted in initial prices.

Avis (☏902 180854; www.avis.es)

Enterprise Rent-a-Car (☏902 100101; www.enterprise.es)

Europcar (☏91 150 50 00; www.europcar.es)

Firefly (☏91 305 43 29; www.fireflycarrental.com)

Hertz (☏91 749 90 69; www.hertz.es)

Pepecar (☏902 996666; www.pepecar.com)

Sixt (☏871 18 01 92; www.sixt.es)

Other possibilities:

Auto Europe (www.autoeurope.com) US-based clearing house for deals with major car-rental agencies.

BlaBlaCar (www.blablacar.com) Car-sharing site that can be really useful for outlying towns, and if your Spanish is up to it, you get to meet people too.

Holiday Autos (☏902 848304; www.holidayautos.com) A clearing house for major international companies.

Ideamerge (www.ideamerge.com) Car-leasing plans, motorhome hire and much more.

Insurance

Third-party motor insurance is a minimum requirement in Spain and throughout Europe. Ask your insurer for a European Accident Statement form, which can simplify matters in the event of an accident. A European breakdown-assistance policy such as those provided by AA (www.theaa.com) or RAC (www.rac.co.uk) is a good investment.

Car-hire companies also provide this minimum insurance, but be careful to understand what your liabilities and excess are, and what waivers you are entitled to in case of accident or damage to the hire vehicle.

Road Rules

Blood-alcohol limit The limit is 0.05%. Breath tests are common, and if found to be over the limit, you can be judged, condemned, fined and deprived of your licence within 24 hours. Fines range up to around €600 for serious offences. Nonresident foreigners may be required to pay up on the spot (at 30% off the full fine). Pleading linguistic ignorance will not help – the police officer will produce a list of infringements and fines in as many languages as you like.

Legal driving age Minimum age is 18 years for cars, 16 years for motorcycles and scooters. A licence is required.

Mobile phones Use of handheld mobile phones and similar devices while driving is strictly prohibited and punishable by a €200 fine.

Motorcyclists Must use headlights at all times and wear a helmet if riding a bike of 125cc or more.

Overtaking Spanish truck drivers often take the courtesy to turn on their right indicator to show that the way ahead of them is clear for overtaking (and the left one if it is not and you are attempting this manoeuvre). Make sure, however, that they're not just turning right!

Roundabouts (traffic circles) Vehicles already in the circle have right of way.

Side of the road Drive on the right.

Speed limits In built-up areas, 50km/h (and in some cases, such as inner-city Barcelona, 30km/h), 100km/h on major roads and up to 120km/h on *autovías* and *autopistas* (toll-free and tolled dual-lane highways, respectively). Cars towing caravans are restricted to a maximum speed of 80km/h.

Train

Renfe (☏91 232 03 20; www.renfe.com) is the excellent national train system that runs most of the services in Spain. A handful of small private railway lines also operate.

Spain has several types of trains and *largo recorrido* or *Grandes Líneas* (long-distance trains), in particular, have a variety of names.

Alaris, Altaria, Alvia, Arco & Avant Long-distance, intermediate-speed services.

Cercanías (*rodalies* in Catalonia) For short hops and services to outlying suburbs and satellite towns in Madrid, Barcelona and 11 other cities.

Euromed Similar to the Tren de Alta Velocidad Española (AVE) trains, they connect Barcelona with Valencia and Alicante.

FEVE (Ferrocarriles de Vía Estrecha) Narrow-gauge network along Spain's north coast between Bilbao and Ferrol (Galicia), with a branch down to León.

Regionales Trains operating within one region, usually stopping all stations.

Talgo & intercity Slower long-distance trains.

Tren de Alta Velocidad Española (AVE) High-speed trains that link Madrid with Albacete, Alicante, Barcelona, Córdoba, Cuenca, Granada, Huesca, León, Lleida, Málaga, Palencia, Seville, Valencia, Valladolid and Zaragoza. There are also Barcelona–Seville, Barcelona–Granada, Barcelona–Málaga and Valencia–Seville services. Additional AVE routes currently under construction include Madrid–Bilbao and Madrid–Badajoz.

Trenhotel Overnight trains with sleeper berths.

Classes & Costs

All long-distance trains have 1st and 2nd classes, known as *preferente* and *turista,* respectively. First class is 20% to 40% more expensive.

Fares vary enormously depending on the service (faster trains cost considerably more) and, in the case of some high-speed services such as the AVE, on the time and day of travel. Tickets for AVE trains are by far the most expensive.

A one-way trip in 2nd class from Madrid to Barcelona (a route on which only AVE trains run) could cost as much as €108 (it could work out significantly cheaper if you book well in advance).

Children aged between four and 12 years are entitled to a 40% discount; those aged under four travel for free (except on high-speed trains, for which they pay the same as those aged four to 12). Buying a return ticket often gives you a 10% to 20% discount on the return trip. Students and people up to 25 years of age with a Euro<26 Card (Carnet Joven in Spain) are entitled to 20% to 25% off most ticket prices.

If you're travelling as a family, ask for a group of four seats with a table when making your reservation.

On overnight trips within Spain on *trenhoteles,* it's worth paying extra for a *litera* (couchette; a sleeping berth in a six- or four-bed compartment) or, if available, single or double cabins in *preferente* or *gran clase* class. The cost depends on the class of accommodation, type of train and length of journey. The lines covered are Madrid–A

Cheaper Train Tickets

Train travel can be expensive in Spain but there is one trick worth knowing. Return tickets cost considerably less than two one-way tickets. If you're certain that you'll be returning on the same route sometime over the coming months (three months is usually the limit), buy a return ticket and you can later change the return date, which works out a lot cheaper than buying two one-way tickets.

Coruña, Barcelona–Granada, Barcelona–A Coruña–Vigo and Madrid–Lisbon, as well as international services to France.

Reservations

Reservations are recommended for long-distance trips; you can make them in train stations, Renfe offices and travel agencies, as well as online. In a growing number of stations, you can pick up pre-booked tickets from machines scattered about the station concourse.

Language

Spanish pronunciation is not difficult as most of its sounds are also found in English. You can read our pronunciation guides below as if they were English and you'll be understood just fine. And if you pronounce 'th' in our guides with a lisp and 'kh' as a throaty sound, you'll even sound like a real Spanish person.

To enhance your trip with a phrase-book, visit **lonelyplanet.com**.

Basics

Hello.
Hola. ⸱ *o·la*

How are you?
¿Qué tal? ⸱ *ke tal*

I'm fine, thanks.
Bien, gracias. ⸱ byen *gra·*thyas

Excuse me. (to get attention)
Disculpe. ⸱ dees·*kool·*pe

Yes./No.
Sí./No. ⸱ see/no

Thank you.
Gracias. ⸱ *gra·*thyas

You're welcome./That's fine.
De nada. ⸱ de *na·*da

Goodbye. /See you later.
Adiós./Hasta luego. ⸱ a·*dyos/as·*ta *lwe·*go

Do you speak English?
¿Habla inglés? ⸱ a·bla een·*gles*

I don't understand.
No entiendo. ⸱ no en·*tyen·*do

How much is this?
¿Cuánto cuesta? ⸱ *kwan·*to *kwes·*ta

Can you reduce the price a little?
¿Podría bajar un ⸱ po·*dree·*a ba·*khar* oon
poco el precio? ⸱ po·ko el *pre·*thyo

Accommodation

I'd like to make a booking.
Quisiera reservar ⸱ kee·*sye·*ra re·ser·var
una habitación. ⸱ *oo·*na a·bee·ta·*thyon*

How much is it per night?
¿Cuánto cuesta ⸱ *kwan·*to *kwes·*ta
por noche? ⸱ por *no·*che

Eating & Drinking

I'd like ..., please.
Quisiera ..., por favor. ⸱ kee·*sye·*ra ... por fa·*vor*

That was delicious!
¡Estaba buenísimo! ⸱ es·*ta·*ba bwe·*nee·*see·mo

Bring the bill/check, please.
La cuenta, por favor. ⸱ la *kwen·*ta por fa·*vor*

I'm allergic to ...
Soy alérgico/a al ... (m/f) ⸱ soy a·*ler·*khee·ko/a al ...

I don't eat ...
No como ... ⸱ no *ko·*mo ...

chicken	pollo	*po·*lyo
fish	pescado	pes·*ka·*do
meat	carne	*kar·*ne

Emergencies

I'm ill.
Estoy enfermo/a. (m/f) ⸱ es·*toy* en·*fer·*mo/a

Help!
¡Socorro! ⸱ so·*ko·*ro

Call a doctor!
¡Llame a un médico! ⸱ *lya·*me a oon *me·*dee·ko

Call the police!
¡Llame a la policía! ⸱ *lya·*me a la po·lee·*thee·*a

Directions

I'm looking for (a/an/the) ...
Estoy buscando ... ⸱ es·*toy* boos·*kan·*do ...

ATM
un cajero ⸱ oon ka·*khe·*ro
automático ⸱ ow·to·*ma·*tee·ko

bank
el banco ⸱ el *ban·*ko

... embassy
la embajada de ... ⸱ la em·ba·*kha·*da de ...

market
el mercado ⸱ el mer·*ka·*do

museum
el museo ⸱ el moo·*se·*o

restaurant
un restaurante ⸱ oon res·tow·*ran·*te

toilet
los servicios ⸱ los ser·*vee·*thyos

tourist office
la oficina de ⸱ la o·fee·*thee·*na de
turismo ⸱ too·*rees·*mo

Behind the Scenes

Acknowledgments

Climate map data adapted from Peel MC, Finlayson BL & McMahon TA (2007) 'Updated World Map of the Köppen-Geiger Climate Classification', *Hydrology and Earth System Sciences*, 11, 1633–44.

Illustrations pp 40-1, 74-5, 128-9 and 168-9 Javier Zarracina

Cover photograph: Vineyards in autumn, La Rioja district, Olimpio Fantuz/4Corners Images ©

This Book

This 3rd edition of Lonely Planet's *Best of Spain* guidebook was researched and written by Anthony Ham, Gregor Clark, Duncan Garwood, Catherine Le Nevez, Isabella Noble, John Noble and Regis St Louis. The previous edition was written by Anthony Ham, Gregor Clark, Sally Davies, Duncan Garwood, Catherine Le Nevez, Isabella Noble, John Noble, Brendan Sainsbury, Regis St Louis and Andy Symington. This guidebook was produced by the following:

Senior Product Editor Sandie Kestell

Regional Senior Cartographer Anthony Phelan

Product Editor Bruce Evans

Book Designer Michael Weldon

Assisting Editors Will Allen, James Bainbridge, Melanie Dankel, Carly Hall, Victoria Harrison, Rosie Nicholson, Christopher Pitts

Assisting Cartographers Hunor Csutoros, Valentina Kremenchutskaya

Cover Researcher Naomi Parker

Thanks to Gordon Dow, Amy Lynch, Darren O'Connell, Kirsten Rawlings

Send Us Your Feedback

We love to hear from travellers – your comments keep us on our toes and help make our books better. Our well-travelled team reads every word on what you loved or loathed about this book. Although we cannot reply individually to postal submissions, we always guarantee that your feedback goes straight to the appropriate authors, in time for the next edition. Each person who sends us information is thanked in the next edition, the most useful submissions are rewarded with a selection of digital PDF chapters.

Visit lonelyplanet.com/contact to submit your updates and suggestions or to ask for help. Our award-winning website also features inspirational travel stories, news and discussions.

Note: We may edit, reproduce and incorporate your comments in Lonely Planet products such as guidebooks, websites and digital products, so let us know if you don't want your comments reproduced or your name acknowledged. For a copy of our privacy policy visit lonelyplanet.com/privacy.

Index

Symbols & Map Key

Look for these symbols to quickly identify listings:

- Sights
- Activities
- Courses
- Tours
- Festivals & Events
- Eating
- Drinking
- Entertainment
- Shopping
- Information & Transport

These symbols and abbreviations give vital information for each listing:

- Sustainable or green recommendation
- FREE No payment required

- Telephone number
- Opening hours
- P Parking
- Nonsmoking
- Air-conditioning
- @ Internet access
- Wi-fi access
- Swimming pool
- Bus
- Ferry
- Tram
- Train
- English-language menu
- Vegetarian selection
- Family-friendly

Find your best experiences with these Great For... icons.

- Art & Culture
- Beaches
- Budget
- Cafe/Coffee
- Cycling
- Detour
- Drinking
- Entertainment
- Events
- Family Travel
- Food & Drink
- History
- Local Life
- Nature & Wildlife
- Photo Op
- Scenery
- Shopping
- Short Trip
- Sport
- Walking
- Winter Travel

Sights

- Beach
- Bird Sanctuary
- Buddhist
- Castle/Palace
- Christian
- Confucian
- Hindu
- Islamic
- Jain
- Jewish
- Monument
- Museum/Gallery/Historic Building
- Ruin
- Shinto
- Sikh
- Taoist
- Winery/Vineyard
- Zoo/Wildlife Sanctuary
- Other Sight

Points of Interest

- Bodysurfing
- Camping
- Cafe
- Canoeing/Kayaking
- Course/Tour
- Diving
- Drinking & Nightlife
- Eating
- Entertainment
- Sento Hot Baths/Onsen
- Shopping
- Skiing
- Sleeping
- Snorkelling
- Surfing
- Swimming/Pool
- Walking
- Windsurfing
- Other Activity

Information

- Bank
- Embassy/Consulate
- Hospital/Medical
- @ Internet
- Police
- Post Office
- Telephone
- Toilet
- Tourist Information
- Other Information

Geographic

- Beach
- Gate
- Hut/Shelter
- Lighthouse
- Lookout
- Mountain/Volcano
- Oasis
- Park
- Pass
- Picnic Area
- Waterfall

Transport

- Airport
- BART station
- Border crossing
- Boston T station
- Bus
- Cable car/Funicular
- Cycling
- Ferry
- Metro/MRT station
- Monorail
- P Parking
- Petrol station
- Subway/S-Bahn/Skytrain station
- Taxi
- Train station/Railway
- Tram
- Underground/U-Bahn station
- Other Transport

Catherine Le Nevez

Catherine's wanderlust kicked in when she roadtripped across Europe from her Parisian base aged four, and she's been hitting the road at every opportunity since, travelling to some 60 countries and completing her Doctorate of Creative Arts in Writing, Masters in Professional Writing, and post-grad qualifications in Editing and Publishing along the way. Over the past decade-and-a-half she's written scores of Lonely Planet guides and articles covering Paris, France, Europe and far beyond. Her work has also appeared in numerous online and print publications. Topping Catherine's list of travel tips is to travel without any expectations.

Isabella Noble

English-Australian on paper but Spanish at heart, travel journalist Isabella has been wandering the globe since her first round-the-world trip as a one-year-old. Having grown up in an Andalucian village, she is a Spain specialist, and has written many Lonely Planet guides to Spain (including Barcelona, Andalucía, the Balearic Islands, northern Spain and the Canary Islands) and is a Telegraph Travel Spain expert. Find Isabella on Twitter and Instagram (@isabellamnoble).

John Noble

John has been travelling for Lonely Planet since the 1980s. The number of Lonely Planet titles he's written is well into three figures, on numerous countries scattered across the globe. He's still as excited as ever about heading out to unfamiliar destinations, especially off-the-beaten-track ones. Above all, he loves mountains, from the Pyrenees to the Himalaya. See his pics on Instagram: @johnnoble11.

Regis St Louis

Regis grew up in a small town in the American Midwest—the kind of place that fuels big dreams of travel—and he developed an early fascination with foreign dialects and world cultures. He spent his formative years learning Russian and a handful of Romance languages, which served him well on journeys across much of the globe. Regis has contributed to more than 50 Lonely Planet titles, covering destinations across six continents. His travels have taken him from the mountains of Kamchatka to remote island villages in Melanesia, and to many grand urban landscapes. When not on the road, he lives in New Orleans.

Our Story

A beat-up old car, a few dollars in the pocket and a sense of adventure. In 1972 that's all Tony and Maureen Wheeler needed for the trip of a lifetime – across Europe and Asia overland to Australia. It took several months, and at the end – broke but inspired – they sat at their kitchen table writing and stapling together their first travel guide, *Across Asia on the Cheap*. Within a week they'd sold 1500 copies. Lonely Planet was born. Today, Lonely Planet has offices in Tennessee, Dublin, Beijing and Delhi, with a network of over 2000 contributors in every corner of the globe. We share Tony's belief that 'a great guidebook should do three things: inform, educate and amuse'.

Our Writers

Anthony Ham

In 2001, after years of wandering the world, Anthony finally found his spiritual home when he fell irretrievably in love with Madrid on his first visit to the city. Less than a year later, he arrived there on a one-way ticket, with not a word of Spanish and not knowing a single person in the city. When he finally left Madrid 10 years later, Anthony spoke Spanish with a Madrid accent, was married to a local and Madrid had become his second home. Now back in Australia, Anthony continues to travel the world in search of stories as a freelance writer and photographer who specialises in Spain, East and Southern Africa, the Arctic and the Middle East.

Gregor Clark

Gregor Clark is a US-based writer whose love of foreign languages and curiosity about what's around the next bend have taken him to dozens of countries on five continents. Since 2000, Gregor has regularly contributed to Lonely Planet guides, with a focus on Europe and the Americas. Gregor was born in New York City. He has lived in California, France, Spain and Italy prior to settling with his wife and two daughters in his current home state of Vermont.

Duncan Garwood

From facing fast bowlers in Barbados to side-stepping hungry pigs in Goa, Duncan's travels have thrown up many unique experiences. These days he largely dedicates himself to Spain and Italy, his adopted homeland where he's been living since 1997. He's worked on around 50 Lonely Planet titles, including guidebooks to Spain, Andalucía, Italy, Rome, Sardinia, Sicily and Portugal, and has contributed to books on world food and epic drives. He's also written on Italy for newspapers, websites and magazines.

More Writers

STAY IN TOUCH LONELYPLANET.COM/CONTACT

IRELAND Digital Depot, Roe Lane (off Thomas St), Digital Hub, Dublin 8, D08 TCV4, Ireland

USA 230 Franklin Road, Building 2B, Franklin, TN 37064
☎ 615 988 9713

  twitter.com/ lonelyplanet

 facebook.com/ lonelyplanet

 instagram.com/ lonelyplanet

youtube.com/ lonelyplanet

lonelyplanet.com/ newsletter